Urban Housing
Segregation of Minorities
in Western Europe and
the United States

Urban Housing
Segregation of Minorities
in Western Europe and
the United States

Elizabeth D. Huttman, editor

Wim Blauw and Juliet Saltman,

coeditors

Duke University Press

Durham and London   1991

© 1991 Duke University Press
All rights reserved
Printed in the United States of America
on acid-free paper ∞
Library of Congress Cataloging-in-Publication Data
appear on the last page of this book.

To Terry Jones
For his efforts in the civil rights struggle

Contents

II

Policies and Programs Related to Housing Segregation in Western Europe

III

Housing Segregation in the United States: An Overview

IV

Policies and Programs Related to Housing Segregation in the United States

Preface

A dynamic aspect of life in urban areas of Western Europe today is the existence of large immigrant populations, often concentrated in specific areas of the cities. Most American urbanologists fail to understand the situations of these people and the effect their presence has on city life in West Germany, France, Britain, Sweden, the Netherlands, and Switzerland. As Europe grows entrenched economically and changes in employment activities, the presence of these immigrants and their use of social services and social housing is frequently challenged in elections. As less social housing is built, the immigrants' competition for housing—as it does for jobs—becomes greater. For example, in West Germany, and across Western Europe, Eastern Europeans poured in at the rate of several thousand a day in 1989 and early 1990. As immigrants are made scapegoats for these changes, racism directed toward them increases. For a variety of reasons, housing segregation for Turks, Yugoslavs, Algerians, Surinamese, West Indians, South Asians, and other Third World groups increases. This book will provide the dimensions of such problems in different countries and also make comparisons with the United States.

In the following theoretical introduction by Juliet Saltman, the framework for studying housing segregation is given, including a definition, a description of segregation measurements, and a variety of explanations—sociological, economic, intergroup, social-psychological, and institutional—of why segregation exists. This is followed by a discussion of the negative consequences of segregation, and, finally, an examination of policy to alleviate segregation at the national and local levels. After this theoretical framework, the book moves, in the next section, to a description of housing segregation in six northern European countries (West Germany, Great Britain, France, Sweden, the Netherlands, and Switzerland). The final section compares housing segregation for two American groups, blacks and Hispanics. Because the European situation, and not the American, is of primary concern herein, the information on America illustrates the situation through three reports, one by Leonard Gordon and Albert J. Mayer on the housing segregation and housing conditions of Hispanics in the Southwest, especially in Phoenix; one by Clyde D. McDaniel, Jr., on black households in the South, with special reference to Houston; and one by Barry J. Johnston on black households in the Midwest, especially in Gary, Indiana. The chapters on the six European countries discuss many aspects of the ethnic minorities' housing situation; some general information on the minorities in the different countries; their initial location in terms of segregation and concentration; and changes over time, for example, a move to a different area (suburban and periphery city areas) or a different housing sector (social housing). The minorities' housing condition is also covered. To explore the factors contributing to housing segregation and housing condition, attention is given to government policies and discrimination practices. In contemporary Europe, the immigrant concentration is political dynamite in local and national elections, for example, in Berlin and Frankfurt, France and Switzerland. Yet the fact that some degree of housing segregation exists in postwar European cities is a situation not fully understood by American urbanologists. Minority housing concentrations, whether of Turks in West Berlin, South Indians in Birmingham, Algerians in Paris, Yugoslavs in the Stockholm area, or Surinamese in the cities of the Netherlands such as Amsterdam create new territorialism that shapes a number of developments in these cities, including decisions on urban renewal and rehabilitation and placement of social housing. To a much greater degree than in the United States, government policies have helped create such housing concentration, have determined the type, location, and condition of housing in which minorities live, and have been responsible for dispersal of minorities and their admission into—or dispersal in—some social housing and in fact their location in suburban areas. In theory, government, such as that of West Berlin, has also tried to control their degree of overcrowding in social housing through laws and has also upgraded their housing units, such as those in Kreuzberg, West Berlin.

The dynamics of the ever-changing urban phenomena in these Western European cities need to be better comprehended by American scholars. Herein, leading housing experts from the six countries, cognizant of current developments, have contributed timely discussions on the situation. To date, descriptions of the developments in these six countries have yet to be brought together, but have been scattered throughout reports and in a variety of journals, with only a few exceptions (Deakin 1972; Peach 1975). The lack of an extensive literature is because large-scale immigration from non-neighboring countries did not occur till the 1950s and 1960s; immigration of guest workers was felt to be temporary. By the 1980s, however, a historically homogeneous country such as Sweden was calling itself "multi-cultural" (Swedish Institute 1987), and research on the subject had become more abundant in each country.

The information is brought together herein so comparisons can be made among degrees of segregation, types of housing clustering, housing conditions of immigrants, and government policies. In addition, comparisons with the situation in America are facilitated by the three chapters on segregation of blacks and Hispanics in American housing. Throughout, we provide further opportunities for comparison of government policy as it affects the concentration of minorities in social housing in several European cities, including government policy affecting the reputation and physical condition of the social housing and dispersal policies in Rotterdam and West Berlin. The discussion of U.S. practices also includes chapters on the segregation of American public housing and American desegregation and resegregation of the suburbs, as well as integration maintenance and other fair housing efforts.

References

Deakin, Nicholas. 1972. *Immigrants in Europe.* International Comparisons in Social Policy, no. 2. London: Fabian Society.
Peach, Ceri. 1975. *Urban Social Segregation.* London: Longmans.
Swedish Institute. 1987. *Immigrants in Sweden.* Stockholm: Swedish Institute.

Urban Housing Segregation of Minorities in Western Europe and the United States

1. Theoretical Orientation:
Residential Segregation

The subject of residential segregation has been examined intensely by social science scholars over the past forty years. Six major questions have been raised: What is housing segregation? How is it measured? Where does it occur? Why does it exist? What are its consequences? and what can be done about it? Each of these questions will be considered in this introduction to the writings herein about European and American segregation.

What Is Housing Segregation?

Housing segregation is the spatial separation of different population groups within a given geographical area. The groups are either minority or dominant groups in the region and live in different areas of that region. As minority or dominant groups, they may be further differentiated by socioeconomic level, occupation, family composition, and subculture. Many years ago, Robert Park related the concept of spatial separation to social status and social distance: "It is because geography, occupation, and all the other factors which determine the distribution of population determine so irresistibly and fatally the place, the group, and the associates with whom each one of us is bound to live that spatial relations come to have . . . the importance which they do. . . . It is because physical distances so frequently are . . . the indexes of social distances, that statistics have any significance whatever for sociology" (Park, in Burgess 1926).

How Is Segregation Measured?

Numerous indexes of residential segregation have been developed over the years. The earliest segregation indexes, developed by Jahn, Schmidt, and Schrag (1947), Williams (1948), Cowgill and Cowgill (1951), and Bell (1954), were followed by the better known index of

1

Duncan and Duncan (1955) and the most widely used index of the Taeubers (1965). These and other measures of segregation have been analyzed thoroughly elsewhere (see, for example, Taeuber 1965:195–245 and Farley 1987:235). Here we only selectively review and compare nonstatistically the two principal measures used in this book—those of the Duncans and the Taeubers.

Both of these measures use census data to calculate an index of dissimilarity (D). This index compares the residential location of pairs of groups (e.g., minority versus majority) according to their proportion of the total community population. It then gives a measure of the net percentage of one population that would have to relocate in order to produce an equally distributed (nonsegregated) population. The higher the index, the greater the degree of segregation.

The Duncans' segregation index measures dissimilarity by using census tract data of a city. They examined the residential distribution of eight different occupational groups in the Chicago metropolitan area (1955). They found that as the group differences in occupational prestige increased, a corresponding increase occurred in the index of dissimilarity. Computations of the proportions of each group were made for each census tract, producing the dissimilarity index. This is one-half the sum of the absolute values of the differences between the respective distributions, taken area by area. When the index is computed between one group and all other groups combined, it is referred to as an *index of segregation*. An additional index of centralization measures relative concentration of residences toward the center of the city. Correlations of the different levels of segregation among the groups can then be computed by the Spearman rank formula.

The Taeubers' index of segregation is based on block data, rather than census tracts. As they explain the rationale for their index: "Suppose that whether a person was Negro or white made no difference in his choice of residence, and that his race was not related to any other factors affecting residential location (i.e., income level). Then no neighborhood would be all-Negro- or all-white, but rather each race would be represented in each neighborhood in approximately the same proportion as in the city as a whole" (Taeuber 1965:29).

Here, the value of the segregation index would be zero, indicating no residential segregation. But if there were no residential mixing of whites and blacks, then the segregation index would have a value of 100, indicating total segregation. The higher the index value, the higher the degree of residential segregation; the lower the value, the greater the degree of residential integration. The actual number tells us what percentage of a city's black population would have to move in order to have no segregation. Their formula for computing the index is based on the proportion of nonwhite households in a given block in relation to the proportion of nonwhites in the city as a whole. The Taeubers found that segregation indexes calculated from block data are somewhat higher than indexes computed from census tract data, but there is a high correlation between the two sets of indexes (Taeuber 1965:229). The latest computations of Taeuber's D show persisting although slightly diminishing segregation in the United States, with mean indexes for 109 cities of 85 in 1940 to 82 in 1970 and 76 in 1988 (Taeuber 1988:38).

Where Does Segregation Occur?

Because social stratification and minority-majority populations occur in all human societies, it follows that spatial segregation of living quarters occurs everywhere. We know of no society that does not have housing segregation based on social status differences. This holds true regardless of whether the group comparisons are of whites or blacks, minority or majority, central cities or suburban rings, or European, American, or Third World countries (Schwab 1982:394). What differs from society to society, however, is the extent of segregation, the pattern of segregation, and the specific basis for it. That basis is rooted in the particular history of each society.

The concentration or dispersion of different groups in geographical space is found in its most extreme form when groups live in particular regions separated by water barriers. Somewhat less extreme would be regional concentration in continuous land areas. Ethnic regionalism is found in a number of societies such as in Yugoslavia, where 71 percent of the Serbs live in Serbia, 79 percent of Croats live in Croatia, and 94 percent of Slovenes live in Slovenia (Burkey 1978:39). Likewise, of the twenty-two cantons or regions in Switzerland, fifteen are predominantly German, one is overwhelmingly Italian, three are primarily French, and three are a mixture of German and French. Likewise, the Basques cluster in northern Spain and southern France; the Bretons are in Brittany, France; the Scots, English, Welsh, and Cornish are concentrated in their particular areas of Great Britain; most French-Canadians live in Quebec; and the Lapps live primarily in the northern part of Scandinavia. Blacks in South Africa, although a numerical majority, are concentrated in designated areas within each community. Such minority concentration is typical elsewhere.

In the United States, ethnic and racial minorities are also clustered, with Hispanics living mostly in the southwest, Irish in the East, Asians on the West Coast, Indians on reservations, primarily in the West, and Scandinavians and Germans in the Midwest. Blacks and other minorities are concentrated in areas within U.S. cities and metropolitan regions. Inner-city minority concentration also occurs in some Northern European cities such as Amsterdam, West Berlin, and Hamburg. But in others, such as Stockholm and increasingly Paris, the concentration is in outer fringe areas. In most Northern European cities more recently immigrated minorities cluster in inner central areas and outer areas and suburban public housing.

Why Does Segregation Exist?

Answers to this question are numerous and provide some theoretical framework for this book. Social scientists have long studied the phenomenon of human segregation and have developed various explanations for it. Five general theoretical approaches have emerged: ecological, economic, intergroup, social-psychological, and institutional theories. None of them alone explains segregation fully. Some of the theories have been shown to be more valid than others when tested; it is probable that several theoretical approaches combined offer the best explanation of why segregation exists.

Ecological perspectives suggest that the operation of multiple impersonal forces results in the segregation of groups in various sections of a city. According to this view, if a large concentration of people is heterogeneous in their socioeconomic status, race, ethnicity, or culture, it is inevitable that they will sort themselves out on the basis of types of housing and their location in relation to the center of the city. Spatial differentiation is thus a manifestation of social stratification.

Segregation, according to ecologists, is the clustering of like units in spatial areas; it may be voluntary or involuntary, and it may refer to populations or types of land use. Ecological theories also use the concept of ecological processes, including those of invasion and succession. Here, the invasion process involves the introduction of a new population group or land use to an area; succession refers to the result of that process, that is, the area's total change in population type or land use (Bailey 1966; Hawley 1981; Hoyt 1939; McKenzie 1926; Schwab 1982; Shevky and Bell 1955).

Stages in the life-cycle of neighborhood change, as developed by American urban ecologists, suggest an inevitable transition from white to black once the process of racial succession has begun (Aldrich and Reiss 1976; Little, Nourse, and Phares 1975; Molotch 1972; Varady 1979; Wilson 1983; Yancy and Erickson 1979). This has, in fact, been the prevailing view in urban analyses for more than forty years. Only in the early 1980s did another view emerge that questioned this orthodoxy (Galster 1987; Helper, in Goering 1986, 1979; Lee 1985; Saltman 1989, 1986, 1984). This more recent view suggests that the process of neighborhood racial succession is not inevitable, and neighborhoods may become racially integrated and stabilized if sufficient resources and institutional networks are mobilized early enough for collective action.

Economic theories of residential segregation are linked to income levels. They suggest, for example, that the major reason for housing segregation in the United States is that most blacks cannot afford to live in many of the neighborhoods where whites live. But through the use of a statistical measurement, *indirect standardization,* scholars can determine the validity of this explanation by computing an expected segregation index based on income differences alone, and then comparing this with the actual segregation index for any city. Using this analysis, repeated studies of economic factors indicate their weakness as an explanation of segregation (Farley 1982; Hermalin and Farley 1973; Taeuber and Taeuber 1965). Only a small portion, perhaps one-fourth, of housing segregation can be accounted for by income differences alone.

Intergroup theories of segregation relate to minority-majority relations and migration patterns. Liebersen (1980:329) has suggested that "migration is the basic factor underlying all racial contacts and subsequent relations." Whether the migration was voluntary or involuntary is a critical factor in those subsequent relations, as is which group initially had the greater power (Schermerhorn 1970; Blalock 1982).

The sociological concept of *minority* has nothing to do with numbers. Rather, it relates to power differentials. Numerically, blacks in South Africa are an overwhelming majority; sociologically, they are a minority. In terms of domination, clearly what matters is the power rather than the numbers. The differential treatment of minorities results in their physical separation and segregation in any society; these vary in degrees that range along a continuum from total segregation to pluralism and on to assimilation. "Internal Colonialism" is the model that has been used to describe the dependency relationship between majority and minority, similar to that of colonizer and native (Banton 1967; Blauner 1972; Kinloch 1979). The process is fluid and subject to changing societal conditions and norms.

Social-psychological explanations of residential segregation focus on human preferences and locational choices. One position, for example, is that blacks in the United States prefer living in all-black neighborhoods, a preference that accounts for their segregation (Coleman 1979; Wolf 1981). Research data, however, do not support this view of voluntary segregation as applied to blacks (Darden, in Tobin 1987; Farley et al. 1979, 1978; Frey 1984). In order for true choice to occur, constraints must be absent, which is not the situation of blacks in American society. Thus, voluntary segregation is not possible until involuntary segregation has been eliminated. "Were it not for racial constraints, the black pattern of neighborhood selection would follow very closely the life cycle pattern found among whites" (Darden, in Tobin 1987:29).

Another explanation of past and existing segregation in the United States refers to white preferences. According to this view, whites prefer all-white neighborhoods and behave in ways that exclude blacks from their neighborhoods. Studies of Downs (1973), Pettigrew (1975), and Schuman, Steeh, and Babo (1985) reveal that whites perceive blacks as holding different and undesirable values. Other research by Leven et al. (1976), Taub, Taylor, and Dunham (1984), and O'Brien and Lange (1986) indicates that whites frequently associate racial integration with neighborhood decline and rising crime. Farley et al.'s research (1979, 1978) shows that most whites prefer neighborhoods with few black residents, whereas blacks prefer neighborhoods with more equal mixing.

These explanations of residential segregation in the United States, some of which are supported by research data, do not indicate *why* white neighborhood preferences are so strongly exclusionary of blacks. For this understanding, we must turn to the fifth and final theoretical approach to segregation—the institutional view—which is strongly linked to historical factors that have fostered racial discrimination in housing.

Institutional explanations of segregation focus on the involuntary aspects of residential location and distribution. According to this view, involuntary segregation occurs because of institutional racism in the entire housing delivery system, including real estate practitioners, appraisers, bankers, insurance companies, builders, and individual owners and landlords. Moreover, such racism has in the past been sanctioned by law and mandate. Although later laws made racial discrimination in housing illegal, those earlier sanctioned norms were by then firmly established and entrenched, and the weakly enforced new laws did little to change discriminatory custom.

The substantial research on residential segregation indicates four general factors that have generated and maintained residential segregation in the United States: (1) government policies related to urban renewal, public housing, and suburban development; (2) the inadequate supply of low and moderate income housing dispersed throughout the metropolitan area; (3) suburban zoning regulations; and (4) racial discrimination in the housing industry. Segregation in housing in the United States has had a long history and is the result of past discriminatory practices in which the private housing industry and federal, state, and local governments have been active participants (Rabin, in Tobin 1987; Saltman 1989, 1979; Wienk et al. 1979; Taeuber 1988).

These discriminatory practices have been traced from 1866—when the first open housing law was passed—to 1968, when the constitutionality of that earlier law was reaffirmed by the Supreme Court soon after Congress passed its first federal open housing legislation, Title 8 of the 1968 Civil Rights Act. During the 102 years it took to legally reaffirm the basic human right to shelter, three racist textbooks for the national real estate industry were published by 1923 and reconfirmed as late as 1950. Federal Housing Administration (FHA) manuals from 1935 to 1940 insisted on discriminatory practices in instructions to builders of new housing developments. Federal banking agencies urged similar practices, and approved racially restrictive covenants in deeds during a 16-year period when more than eleven million new homes were built. State courts upheld discriminatory ordinances passed by local and state governments during these 102 years, making the legacy of discrimination complete. It is not surprising that the latest studies of racial segregation in housing in the United States show continuing high levels.

Although other minority groups in the United States, for example, Native Americans and Mexican Americans, also suffer from housing segregation, blacks show the highest levels: "No ethnic or nationality group currently exhibits levels of segregation as high as those for blacks . . . the segregation of these groups declined rapidly over time, while those for blacks have remained at exceptionally high levels" (Kain 1987). Settlement patterns of blacks have frequently been compared with those of other migrants to northern U.S. urban areas. Foreign migrants, too, settled earlier around the central cores of cities, readily accessible to places of employment, transportation, and transient and moderate-cost housing. But as soon as they reached some occupational and economic stability, foreign settlers moved away from central city cores as quickly as possible.

Blacks migrating northward from the South inherited the blight left them by earlier city migrants, and also settled in and around the central cores of U.S. cities. But here the parallel ends. Blacks were not able to leave the blighted areas as readily as the earlier migrants and still remain largely confined there for four reasons. First, blacks arrived in northern urban centers as occupational skills and training began to be necessary for economic opportunity and advancement. Second, blacks had to contend with the past history of slavery as an institution. This resulted in a slave psychology of whites and a continuing inferior status for blacks. Third, black visibility precluded any easy absorption. Whereas the accent of earlier migrants could be lost or modified, and cultural patterns could adapt to the dominant culture, blacks could not change the color of their skin. Thus technological, historical, and cultural factors, coupled with a fourth factor of increasing covert and overt discrimination, have forced U.S. blacks to remain primarily in and near the central areas of decay and blight.

These areas of inner-city blight came to be marked for urban renewal and land clearance in the late 1940s, just as blacks migrated toward them in largest numbers. Forced by urban renewal, discrimination, and lower incomes to seek housing in ever-shrinking ghettos marked by increasing density, blacks shifted from one ghetto area to another in the decades between 1950 and 1970. During the same period, whites moved from those centers to more than 13 million new federally financed homes built in suburban areas after World War II—homes to which blacks were denied access (Rabin, in Tobin 1987), forcing them to remain in central cities. This enforced separation was promoted and sanctioned by the federal government (Abrams 1965) and further reinforced by public housing and government mortgage assistance policies.

When the Supreme Court gave its historic 1968 decision on open housing, it linked housing segregation to slavery: "Just as the Black Codes, enacted after the Civil War to restrict the free exercise of those rights, were substitutes for the slave system, so the exclusion of Negroes from white communities became a substitute for the Black Codes. And when racial discrimination herds men into ghettos and makes their ability to buy property turn on the color of their skin, then it too is a relic of slavery" (*Jones v. Mayer,* June 1968).

Explanations of European housing segregation of minorities, who came not as slaves but as postwar workers and ex-colonials, center less on discrimination than on socioeconomic and cultural factors.

What Are the Consequences of Segregation?

We have seen that established norms of American housing discrimination are rooted in history. Discrimination norms in both the United States and Europe are the bases of institutional racism. Such racism operates as an impersonal web of exclusionary practices, even in the absence of personal prejudice. It effectively denies equality to members of minority groups in the major institutions of society: housing, education, justice and law enforcement, and employment. The extent of denial of opportunity in each of these areas has been documented amply (Burkey 1978; Dworkin and Dworkin 1982; Luhman and Gilman 1980; Lieberson 1980; Marden and Meyer 1978; Peach 1975).

Some urban and race relations scholars have claimed that the most serious domestic problem of the United States is the social and physical separation of blacks and whites. In Europe, minority segregation has also led to different and unequal community and school environments with ensuing social costs. In the United States, segregated housing has led to segregated schools, shopping areas, and recreational facilities, spawning a divided society, with the hostility, mistrust, and discord that characterizes such a society. One statement by twenty-eight leading American scholars summarizes what is known about the impact of racial ghettos on American urban society (Leadership 1987). The scholars represent the disciplines of economics, political science, geography, sociology, public policy, demography, urban planning, and history. Their statement is based on findings compiled in areas such as fair housing enforcement, mortgage and finance practices, race and access to employment, public and subsidized housing, and barriers to black and Hispanic economic progress; "The cumulative effect of the work done in these disciplines shows that society pays a steep price for the urban ghetto system" (Orfield 1987).

Among the costs cited are barriers to black economic progress, including diminished wealth because of black underrepresentation among homeowners. Even when income is held constant, buyers in black neighborhoods have less access to capital for mortgages or home improvements. Blacks who buy homes tend to buy relatively less expensive homes in areas where values increase less rapidly. Thus their net worth is reduced because home equity is the most substantial source of wealth for most American families.

An equally significant cost is the fact that denial of home ownership in desirable neighborhoods also denies access to better education and intercultural contacts for children. Because high school and college completion is a major factor in improving employment and income, where children attend school is a major factor in determining school achievement and completion. "The differences among black, white and integrated schools in terms of dropout rates and achievement scores are highly significant" (Leadership 1987:4). Furthermore, different school and community environments decrease the likelihood of dropping out of school and increase the probability of entering college. These, in turn, are related to much lower probabilities of crime and welfare dependency. Thus, the value of housing opportunities plays a major role in determining lifetime earnings, taxable income for the community, and the demand on public financial and social resources.

Completing this circular process is the relationship among housing opportunity, school achievement, and access to employment. Urban economies and work opportunities in the United States have been seriously altered and redistributed. Industrial work has declined and most new industrial investment is located in suburbia. The decline of industrial work has gravely affected people who have minimal education, for whom such jobs offered major sources of employment. With such sources greatly diminished and new sources relocated, they are no longer accessible to inner-city workers who have low educational levels. The situation is not as clear-cut in Europe, where some minorities, for example, those in Paris, are close to suburban industry. Other European minorities, however, are in suburban public housing isolated from city jobs. But in the United States, "considering the location of new industrial jobs, the absence of public transportation links between the central city and suburban jobs, the location of the uneducated and unemployed minorities, and the school dropout rates of 50% among young central city minority males, it is clear that residential segregation has an extremely high present cost that will multiply over time with an increase in the numbers of men unable to marry and support families" (Leadership 1987:4).

This high cost of segregation affects not only the minorities involved, but also the entire metropolitan area, since a "duplicate infrastructure" is developed outside the city, making the very future of American and European cities uncertain. At the core of all of such segregation is the racism that drives it. The tangible costs are borne by the entire society. The intangible ones of despair, loss of hope, and destruction of self-image are borne by the minorities alone. Ultimately, however, the entire society bears these, too, as they are deprived of huge pools of potential talent and valuable human resources.

What Can Be Done About Segregation?

Evidence exists of positive results of some private and public efforts that have been directed toward the eradication or reduction of segregation. Whether these efforts will continue or be duplicated elsewhere depends on the commitment of decision makers in the public sector. Such commitment to integration is based on values and priorities shaped, ironically, by the very society and culture that harbors the persisting segregative forces we have reviewed.

The efforts directed toward eradicating segregation are of three types: national, regional, and local. Elsewhere, I have described some of these "interventionist" strategies in detail (Saltman 1989, 1984, 1980, 1978, 1977). What follows are a few examples of these efforts to show something of what has been done and what could be done elsewhere if the optimum combination of commitment, values, and priorities is present.

National programs to eradicate or reduce segregation in the United States are embedded in fair housing laws, executive orders, and special acts of Congress developed since 1866, when the first law banning racial segregation was made. It took 102 years for this law to be merely reconfirmed by a 1968 Supreme Court decision (*Jones v. Mayer*). Implementation of such laws, thus, has not been a major part of American public policy, a fact that accounts for the continuing widespread segregation in that society (Tobin 1987).

What is needed on the national level is not new laws. An abundance of them exists. What is needed is a renewed national policy committed to undoing racism through implementing and enforcing existing civil rights laws and establishing a national neighborhood integration maintenance policy. Because government was one of the first institutional forces responsible for racial segregation, should government—at all levels—not be the major force responsible for undoing its past effects?

For Northern European countries, we can also ask that government be a major force in decreasing housing segregation, which is occurring in a number of ways in various European countries, many of which have general laws against discrimination. Some have set-asides of a specified number of units for minorities in public housing. Others have dispersal policies, widely debated and often abandoned. Still others have physical rehabilitation of blighted minority areas. Despite these efforts, more extensive laws against discrimination are needed in European countries, along with a growth of national, regional, and local policies and programs to decrease minority concentrations.

Regional approaches to minority desegregation in the United States include extensive ongoing auditing, regional mobility programs, housing supply extension programs, and social impact statements. Auditing is a field-survey technique well analyzed in the literature as a device for ascertaining the extent of minority access to housing, as well as how well the federal fair housing law is working. In the United States, auditing has been widely used since the passage of the 1968 federal fair housing law. Audits were then conducted for ten years by a number of local private advocacy groups across the country, culminating in a government-sponsored U.S. Housing and Urban Development nationwide audit in 1978 (Wienk et al. 1979; Saltman 1979, 1978).

But it is not enough for funded fair housing agencies to do an annual audit to satisfy their funding source requirements. Auditing must be continual, at the very least monthly, for old and new housing opportunities, both sales and rentals, and throughout the metropolitan area. Simply performing the audit is not enough. The preparation for the audit, the training of the auditors and supervisors, the meticulous analysis of the audit results, and the careful dissemination of those results are critical for the success of this important tool in achieving fair housing—equal housing access for minorities. Several highly effective fair housing agencies across the United States (in Chicago, Cincinnati, Toledo, New York, and Palo Alto) have shown the importance of auditing to gain such access. European cities have not generally conducted audits or other measurement verification of minority discrimination; documentation is necessary to achieve recognition of the extent of existing housing segregation in Europe.

Regional mobility programs and incentive payments for integrative moves (i.e., blacks to white areas and whites to integrated ones) are conducted in several U.S. areas, notably in Chicago, Louisville, and Cleveland. In the Cleveland metropolitan area, for example, municipal governments and public school authorities are cooperating in a joint program to achieve and maintain racial integration in neighborhoods and schools. Funded by the Ford Foundation, this innovative program is perhaps the only one in the country that links these two potent institutional forces in an integrative effort. Incentive payments for integrative moves is also an Ohio program, resulting from intense lobbying and negotiation for more than two years between local groups and the state finance agency. In this program, now expanded to other areas of Ohio, 10 percent of a $20 million state mortgage revenue bond program was set aside in 1985 in the Cleveland area for first-time home buyers making integrative moves (Saltman 1989).

Local strategies in the United States include neighborhood integration maintenance programs (see chapter 20), involving affirmative marketing, housing and business quality maintenance, crime prevention, school racial balance, and equity assurance programs. Neighborhood integration maintenance programs have been analyzed intensively elsewhere (Saltman 1989, 1984, 1980, 1977) as a social movement effort stemming from the U.S. Civil Rights movement of the 1950s. In order to preserve diversity, such programs rely on extensive affirmative marketing to both whites and blacks. The emphasis is on encouraging the race least likely to seek housing in an area to do so (whites to integrated areas, blacks to white areas). The effort is linked to the fair housing effort and to federal fair housing laws, which not only sought equal access to housing for all, but also sought "to replace ghettos with truly integrated and balanced living patterns for persons of all races" (*Zuch v. Hussey* 1975). This goal has been confirmed and reinforced by two executive orders from the president of the United States, the Housing and Community Development Act of 1974, and legal decisions (*NAR v. South Suburban Chicago Housing Centers,* 1989). Unfortunately, implementation has not been thorough on either national, regional, or local levels. But the presence of such legislation at least lends legitimacy to those efforts designed to remove or reduce segregation and increase integration.

One example of an American local strategy designed to maintain neighborhood racial integration is the equity assurance program of Oak Park, a suburb of Chicago, Illinois. This program, sponsored by the local government, reimburses residents for up to 80 percent of any losses incurred in the sale of their homes after five years. It thus reduces white flight and aids stability and racial integration.

In Northern and Western European countries, such local, regional, and national efforts to desegregate housing are not common. The emphasis there is primarily on public rental housing, where other means of desegregation or integration maintenance are used. Parts I and II introduce us to the dimensions of housing segregation in Northern and Western Europe. Parts III and IV focus on housing segregation in the United States, offering the reader a basis for comparison.

We can see that segregation exists everywhere, but in different forms and for different historical and structural reasons. We can also see that efforts to reduce minority concentration vary in design and effectiveness from country to country, region to region, and city to city. We hope this chapter provides a framework for understanding the many dimensions of housing segregation presented in this book.

References

Abrams, Charles. 1965. *The City Is the Frontier.* New York: Harper and Row.

Aldrich, H., and J. A. Reiss. 1976. "The Race Competition of Neighborhood Business." *American Journal of Sociology* 81:846–66.

Bailey, M. J. 1966. "Effects of Race and Other Demographic Factors on the Value of Single-Family Homes." *Land Economics* 42:215–20.

Banton, Michael. 1967. *Race Relations.* New York: Basic Books.

Bell, Wendell. 1954. "A Probability Model for the Measurement of Ecological Segregation." *Social Forces* 32:357–64.

Blalock, Herbert. 1982. *Race and Ethnic Relations.* Englewood Cliffs: Prentice-Hall.

Blauner, Robert. 1972. *Racial Oppression in America.* New York: Harper and Row.

Burkey, Richard M. 1978. *Ethnic and Racial Groups.* Menlo Park, Calif.: Cummings.

Coleman, J. 1979. "Destructive Beliefs and Potential Policies in School Desegregation." Pp. 5–12 in *Detroit Metropolitan City-Suburban Relations,* edited by J. W. Smith. Dearborn: Henry Ford Community College.

Cowgill, D. O., and Mary Cowgill. 1951. "An Index of Segregation Based on Block Statistics." *American Sociological Review* 16:825–31.

Darden, Joe D. 1987. "Choosing Neighbors and Neighborhoods." Pp. 95–114 in *Divided Neighborhoods,* edited by G. Tobin. Beverly Hills: Sage.

Downs, Anthony. 1973. *Opening up the Suburbs.* New Haven: Yale University Press.

Duncan, Otis D., and Beverly Duncan. 1955. "A Methodological Analysis of Segregation Indices." *American Sociological Review* 20:210–17.

Dworkin, A., and R. Dworkin. 1982. *The Minority Report.* New York: CBS College Publishing.

Farley, John. 1982. *Majority-Minority Relations.* Englewood Cliffs: Prentice-Hall.

———. 1987. "Segregation in 1980." Pp. 95–114 in *Divided Neighborhoods,* edited by G. Tobin. Beverly Hills: Sage.

Farley, Reynolds, Susanne Bianchi, and Dianne Colasanto. 1979. "Barriers to the Racial Integration of Neighborhoods: The Detroit Case." *Annals of the American Academy of Political and Social Science* 441:97–113.

Farley, Reynolds, Howard Schuman, Susanne Bianchi, Dianne Colasanto, and S. Hatchett. 1978. "Chocolate City, Vanilla Suburbs: Will the Trend Toward Racially Separate Communities Continue?" *Social Science Research* 7:319–44.

Frey, William H. 1984. "Lifecourse Migration of Metropolitan Whites and Blacks and the Structure of Demographic Change in Large Central Cities." *American Sociological Review* 49:803–27.

Galster, George. 1987. "Federal Fair Housing Policy in the 1980s." Working Paper 5. Cambridge: MIT Center for Real Estate Development.

Hawley, Amos. 1981. *Urban Society.* New York: Wiley.

Helper, Rose. 1979. "Social Interaction in Racially Mixed Neighborhoods." *Housing and Society* 6:20–38.

———. 1986. "Success and Resistance Factors in the Maintenance of Racially Mixed Neighborhoods." Pp. 170–94 in *Housing Desegregation and Federal Policy,* edited by J. Goering. Chapel Hill: University of North Carolina Press.

Hermalin, A., and R. Farley. 1973. "The Potential for Residential Integration in Cities and Suburbs." *American Sociological Review* 38:595–610.

Hoyt, Homer. 1939. "The Structure and Growth of Residential Neighborhoods in American Cities." Washington, D.C.: Federal Housing Administration.

Jahn, J. A., C. Schmidt, and C. Schrag. 1947. "The Measurement of Ecological Segregation." *American Sociological Review* 12:293–303.

Kain, John F. 1987. "Housing Market Discrimination and Black Suburbanization in the 1980s." Pp. 68–94 in *Divided Neighborhoods,* edited by G. Tobin. Beverly Hills: Sage.

Kinloch, Graham. 1979. *The Sociology of Minority Group Relations.* Englewood Cliffs: Prentice-Hall.

Leadership Council for Metropolitan Open Communities. 1987. "The Costs of Housing Discrimination and Segregation." Pp. 268–80 in *Divided Neighborhoods,* edited by G. Tobin. Beverly Hills: Sage.

Lee, Barrett. 1985. "Racially Mixed Neighborhoods during the 1970s." *Social Science Quarterly* 66:346–64.

Leven, C., J. Little, H. Nourse, and R. Read. 1976. *Neighborhood Change.* New York: Praeger.

Lieberson, Stanley. 1980. *A Piece of the Pie: Blacks and White Immigrants 1880.* Berkeley: University of California Press.

Little, J., H. Nourse, and D. Phares. 1975. *The Neighborhood Succession Process.* Washington, D.C.: U.S. Government Printing Office.

Luhman, R., and S. Gilman. 1980. *Race and Ethnic Relations.* Belmont, Calif.: Wadsworth.

McKenzie, R. 1926. "The Scope of Human Ecology." Pp. 170–83 in *The Urban Community,* edited by E. W. Burgess. Chicago: University of Chicago Press.

Marden, Charles, and Gladys Meyer. 1978. *Minorities in American Society.* New York: Van Nostrand.

Molotch, H. 1972. *Managed Integration.* Berkeley: University of California Press.

O'Brien, D., and J. Lange. 1986. "Racial Composition and Neighborhood Evaluations." *Journal of Urban Affairs* 8:43–62.

Orfield, Gary. 1987. *The Costs of Housing Discrimination and Segregation.* Chicago: Leadership Council News Release.

Park, Robert. 1926. "The Urban Community as a Spatial Pattern and a Moral Order." Pp. 21–31 in *The Urban Community,* edited by E. W. Burgess. Chicago: University of Chicago Press.

Peach, Ceri, ed. 1975. *Urban Social Segregation.* London: Longmans.

Pettigrew, Thomas, ed. 1975. *Racial Discrimination in the U.S.* New York: Harper and Row.

Rabin, Yale. 1987. "The Implementation of the Federal Mandate for Fair Housing." Pp. 182–227 in *Divided Neighborhoods,* edited by G. Tobin. Beverly Hills: Sage.

Saltman, Juliet. 1977. *Integrated Neighborhoods in Action.* Washington, D.C.: National Neighbors.

———. 1978. *Open Housing: Dynamics of a Social Movement.* New York: Praeger.

———. 1979. "Housing Discrimination: Policy Research, Methods and Results." *Annals of the Academy of Political and Social Science* 441:186–96.

———. 1980. "Action Research on Redlining." *Urban Affairs Papers* 2:20–35.

———. 1984. "Neighborhood Strategies as Social Inventions." *Journal of Voluntary Action Research* 13:37–45.

———. 1986. "Neighborhood Change: Facts, Perceptions, Prospects." *Housing and Society* 13:136–59.

———. 1989. *A Fragile Movement: The Struggle for Neighborhood Stabilization.* Westport: Greenwood.

Schermerhorn, Richard. 1970. *Comparative Ethnic Relations.* New York: Random House.

Schuman, H., C. Steeh, and L. Bobo. 1985. *Racial Attitudes in America.* Cambridge: Harvard University Press.

Schwab, William. 1982. *Urban Sociology.* Reading: Addison-Wesley.

Shevky, E., and W. Bell. 1955. *Social Area Analysis.* Palo Alto: Stanford University Press.

Taeuber, Karl A. 1988. *Residence and Race: 1619 to 2019.* Working Paper 88–19. Madison: University of Wisconsin Center for Demography and Ecology.

Taeuber, Karl, and A. F. Taeuber. 1965. *Negroes in Cities.* Chicago: Aldine.

Taub, R., D. G. Taylor, and J. Dunham. 1984. *Paths of Neighborhood Change.* Chicago: University of Chicago Press.

Tobin, Gary, ed. 1987. *Divided Neighborhoods.* Beverly Hills: Sage.

Varady, D. 1979. *Ethnic Minorities in Urban Areas.* Boston: Nijhoff.

Wienk, R. E., C. E. Reed, J. C. Simonson, and F. C. Eggers. 1979. *Measuring Racial Discrimination in American Housing Markets.* Washington, D.C.: U.S. Department of Housing and Urban Development.

Williams, J. 1948. "Another Commentary on So-called Segregation Indices." *American Sociological Review* 13:298–303.

Wilson, Thomas. 1983. "White Response to Neighborhood Racial Change." *Sociological Focus* 16:305–18.

Wolf, E. P. 1981. *Trial and Error.* Detroit: Wayne State University Press.

Yancey, W., and E. Erickson. 1979. "The Antecedents of Community." *American Sociological Review* 44:253–62.

I

Housing Segregation
in Western Europe

2. Housing Segregation in Western Europe: An Introduction

The dimensions of housing segregation in Western Europe are complex, and the comparisons that follow have several limitations. First, housing segregation in Western European cities is almost nowhere as great for minorities as it is for blacks in American cities. There is little "ghettoization" that makes 80–90 percent of an area's population to be of one minority. Even in some of the most segregated areas—exceptions to the norm—such as Kreuzberg in West Berlin or the Bijlmermeer buildings in the Netherlands, no more than half of the population is of one minority (chapters 3 and 5).

Another limitation concerns the differences between cities and regions on a variety of aspects related to minority housing concentration. Most of the European contributors to this volume are specific in giving data describing the city to which they refer. In Europe, it is the large cities, the industrial cities (Paris and Lyon), and the entry cities (Marseilles and London) that have high proportions of minority housing. Small cities often have a smaller minority concentration, as Linden and Lindberg (chapter 5) and Hwang and Murdock (1983) point out. Even among large cities, major differences can exist in the degree of housing concentration and of the housing conditions of minorities. The uniqueness of West Berlin (through 1989), with its special limited territory, its large share of small housing units, and its population composition that includes many old people, makes it somewhat different from other German cities (chapter 11). The narrowest of city boundaries, not only in West Berlin, but also in U.S. cities such as St. Louis, affect the situation, causing pressures that make the ghetto population spill over to the suburbs (Farley 1987). The historic development of cities can also influence the degree of ethnic concentration, for example, that of the Algerians in Paris. In Britain, one historical factor was the whole colonial relationship, as was the case in France and the Netherlands. Concentrations of ethnics are also created by recruitment practices of companies that hire guest workers, as well as the country-to-country contracts set up by governments. In the case of Bedford in Britain, Sarre (1986) describes how the local brick company recruited workers from the Naples area because Italian prisoners had worked at the company during the war. Sarre adds that if the company had decided to recruit in the West Indies, as did the London Transport, "Bedford would be a rather different place today." He also adds that the company later filled vacancies with the 1950s' labor supply of Indian immigrants.

In the United States, historic development of cities also influenced residential patterns. Midwestern cities, Chicago in particular, re-cruited blacks from the South in World War I and World War II, and early concentrations of blacks were established. Even today, Chicago, Cleveland, and other midwestern cities have among the highest levels of segregation in the United States (Clark 1987). In the South, settle-ment patterns from slavery days influenced patterns in cities of the "Old South" (chapter 14), and the existence of rural black settlements made the early, and to some degree, present, suburban situation dif-ferent, with more black households.

Different cities, for example, Hamburg, Stockholm, and Zurich, have different mixes of minority populations, which can influence the degree of minority concentration. In the United States, the mix today is likely to be Hispanic and black, as in Miami, or Chinese as in San Francisco, with the two groups often overlapping territory. The situ-ation can effect the degree of concentration of one group, just as the size of the group can effect the index of dissimilarity (Farley 1987).

Status of Minorities

The European reports herein are in regard to a variety of minority groups, although not persons from neighboring countries except for the Finns in Sweden and German-origin groups in West Germany. The groups discussed are new, postwar immigrants, and for Britain include those from nonwhite Commonwealth areas. Some, such as Italians, are already assimilated into the general population in some countries, whereas other groups, such as the Moroccans in the Neth-erlands, Turks in West Germany, West Indians in Britain, and recent refugee groups such as the Vietnamese in Sweden, are much less likely to be assimilated. Because of greater cultural differences and body color unlike that of the host country's population, the latter groups may have continual trouble assimilating into the new societies. Other factors that effect their degree of assimilation include time in the host country, language ability, education, and socioeconomic status. Both Friedrichs and Alpheis for West Germany (chapter 6) and Blauw for the Netherlands (chapter 3) rate these variables. For example, many Surinamese came to the Netherlands understanding Dutch, as did those migrating from Indonesia in the early postwar period. Many groups now have second-generation members who went to school in the host country, for example, the West Indians in Britain, the Algerians in France, and the Yugoslavs in Switzerland. This second generation is now moving to adulthood and forming households.

The legal status of these groups varies. Other than in Britain, many immigrants who arrived after the war were "guest workers," contractual employees brought in on a "rotating" basis to fill the growing labor needs in the host countries during the industrial boom. This was the case during the 1960s in Sweden, West Germany, and Switzerland, as well as for Mediterranean groups brought into the Netherlands and for the Moroccans and Algerians in France, although the Algerians had a more permanent status. Workers were usually single men, even the Algerians. They often were hired for a specific job, often for a specific time.

Contracts among countries specified a variety of conditions. In some cases employers provided housing, as mandated in the 1960s in German entry contracts. In other cases workers found housing in inner-city slums, as in Paris, West Berlin, Birmingham, or Amsterdam. As they began bringing their families with them in the 1970s, such inner-city slums became the workers' major habitat. In Sweden, however, earlier than in other countries, immigrants were placed in outer-area social housing. In Paris, workers were not only in inner-area units, run by their countrymen, but also in shanty-towns in peripheral areas such as Nanterre, where ten thousand once lived (Barou 1988). By the 1980s, many had moved out of single accommodations to family apartments in most countries.

In the 1960s the poor housing situation of these guest workers was not of major concern, as the housing was seen as temporary, with the user accepting it in order to save money to send home (the "self-inflicted deprivation" myth, as Böhning [1972] states for West Germany). That immigrants, especially those with families, desired higher standards has been verified by Meuter (1982), Ipsen (1978), and others. As Deakin (1972) notes, "In these countries where immigration has been treated as a purely economic phenomenon, the initial assumption was that only minimum provision of encampment or barrack housing would be necessary. In most of these cases, the assumption has been falsified by events." (One could add, particularly after families arrived.)

The problem was that the governments thought in terms of bringing in manpower to run their factories' machines and got instead persons with normal human needs, persons who eventually arranged for their families to join them. Government policies did not exist to deal with this influx. As Deakin (1972) writes of the countries that brought in temporary guest workers, "having acquired their immigrant population in a fit of absent-mindedness, the respective European governments are now confronted with some of the consequences of the neglect: the bidonvilles [of France] . . . the squalor of immigrant barracks of West Germany and Switzerland." In the 1970s, instead of barracks, one could mention inner-city slum apartment areas such as Kreuzberg in West Berlin, the 15th arrondissement in Paris, or some Bijlmermeer sections in the Netherlands. Although by the late 1980s either modernization or urban renewal demolition had changed such areas, as Hoffmeyer-Zlotnik (1982:114) writes of Kreuzberg areas slated for urban renewal in the 1970s, "as temporary immigrants, guest workers have been treated—depending on their country of origin—as the 'blacks of West Germany.' Hence, they have settled in ethnic colonies in the old and run-down parts of the town near the CBD." He adds that the fact the housing was designated to be torn down meant not only cheap rents, but also landlord neglect (123). The influx of Turkish households, including many illegal workers, first went unnoticed by authorities. By 1973, however, as authorities did become aware, they "saw themselves increasingly confronted with the hitherto unseen problem of providing a large number of apartments for Turkish families living in condemned buildings. Otherwise, urban renewal could not have continued." Meuter (1982) also describes the concentration of foreign worker households in an inner-city area of Cologne undergoing urban renewal and gentrification. Sometimes urban renewal has been done simply to thin out the concentration of minorities; sometimes to improve their housing, as Blanc points out for the 15th arrondissement in Paris. The description of housing locations of these groups in the 1980s includes the movement of some to social housing on the periphery of the cities (chapter 12), often due to such urban renewal.

Yet, even in the 1980s, after more than twenty-five years' residence in the host country, these guest workers may have limited ability to command a social housing unit. Rights for guest arbeiters are still limited, depending on the country, and workers may still be on specific place and even period work or on labor permits and thus in continual fear of breaking some law that leads to their deportation. If they are illegal workers the fear is greater (chapter 10). In addition to guest workers are those termed "ex-colonials," and it is important to keep in mind the variations in status. The ex-colonials include Surinamese and Dutch Antillians in the Netherlands, South Asians and West Indians in Britain, and Algerians in France, as well as those of "German-origin" in Germany, each group possessing more permanent status and more rights than guest workers. However, like guest workers, bans are placed on the arrival of more ex-colonials and persons of German-origin, including strict regulations for ex-colonials on which family members can join them. After the ban on their continued entry, the influx of family members was high for several years for most groups, whether ex-colonials or foreign workers in the Netherlands, West Germany, and elsewhere. The influx has abated for both groups and some guest workers have gone home, for example, the Algerians in France, enticed by government lump sum grants. Some, like guest workers in Switzerland on seasonal permits, have not been asked to return for the following year. However, the relatively high birth rate of immigrants keeps their numbers high.

Another group is comprised of those refugees given political asylum, such as the Vietnamese, Poles, Afghans, Iranians, and, much earlier, Hungarians and Czechoslovakians. In most European countries, they have more rights than guest workers; after twelve years in Switzerland, for example, they can apply for citizenship.

Comparisons with the American situation on housing segregation of minorities would have been more complete if the new American ethnic groups, such as the Vietnamese and Nicaraguarians or Chinese from Hong Kong and Taiwan, had been included in the comparisons, instead of just blacks and Hispanics, or if the comparisons had been made with experiences of early immigrant groups coming to America. However, most housing segregation research in the United States concerns black households, and to a minor degree, Hispanic ones. Blacks, as Saltman points out (chapter 1) continue to have the hardest time integrating into American society because racism is still strong. Thus comparisons between the research findings on black households in the book edited by Tobin (1987) and the book edited by Goering (1986), and the European reports included herein on Southern European immigrants' segregation, may be hindered by the emphasis in U.S. reports on black households. However, for Europe, the situation of

Africans, Asians, West Indians, or even Turks may be similar to that of blacks in the United States.

Comparisons may also be hindered somewhat by the fact that many American researchers on housing segregation are "race relations" specialists, whereas most of the Europeans write as urbanologists and housing experts or geographers interested in spatial relations. The focus in American literature is more on measurements of dissimilarity or effects of race relation laws and other integration efforts, whereas Europeans focus on spatial location, often with maps, housing type and tenure, and housing conditions of the various groups.

Housing Stock

In terms of making comparisons with the U.S. situation, one must be aware of the character of the available housing stock in reading the European chapters herein. With the exception of Switzerland, European countries have a limited number of private rentals (fewer than 10 percent of the total housing stock in Britain, fewer than 16 percent in the Netherlands [Van Weesep 1986a], nearly a fifth in Sweden [Swedish Institute 1987a], and somewhat higher in West Germany and France). Most is old housing built before the war, as in the Netherlands (Van Weesep 1986a), Britain (Harloe 1985), or France. In addition, there are a few luxury units. Many have been or are presently under rent control, although that has been lifted in a number of places, for example in Hamburg and Munich in the 1970s and in West Berlin in the late 1980s (see Arin). Many units are occupied on a long-term basis by elderly residents.

A substantial proportion of available housing is social housing, that is, rent-subsidized housing for lower-income households, although the proportion of privately owned housing has increased considerably in a number of these countries in the last decade (up to 64 percent of stock in Britain; 55 percent in Sweden, 15 percent of which are units owned by tenants [Swedish Institute 1987a]; and slightly less than 44 percent in the Netherlands). Swiss privately owned housing is still scarce; only 34 percent of all Swiss own their own home (Van Vliet 1989).

Social housing is of different types in these countries and is under complex financing systems not covered herein (Van Vliet 1989). In Britain, almost a third of the housing stock (27 percent) is still "council housing." Social housing is built and managed by local authorities but much of the necessary capital, as in other European countries, comes from the national government so both the building construction guidelines as well as other regulations usually follow national guidelines. As in most European countries, there is no means test for occupancy but rather various criteria of housing need, including substandard condition of a person's present unit, whether it is in an urban renewal or rehabilitation area, whether the person is homeless, the length of his or her residence in the community and composition of the household, as well as his or her rent record (Huttman 1969, 1985). These criteria play into a housing allocation system, a system whereby the large supply of social housing is assigned to certain households. Until the 1970s, British council housing was highly desired because of the housing shortage in Britain; with the push toward home ownership in the 1980s, however, fewer stable working-class demanded it and vacancies were created for some minorities (chapter 4).

In Britain, a very small proportion of the housing stock is comprised of nonprofit housing association units, usually renovated units assigned to poor families in inner-city areas.

In the Netherlands, nearly 43 percent of the housing stock in 1986 was social housing. Sixteen percent of this was owned and managed by municipalities, and 84 percent managed by the large housing association sector, a sector primarily dependent on the national government for capital and government-regulated in terms of rent increases, design, and various other matters. The housing association sector is the dominant source of rental housing for the Dutch and is found everywhere. Many housing associations originally were affiliated with religious bodies, unions, or professional groups and differ markedly from their weaker counterparts in Britain. Very little of the Dutch stock is comprised of private rental housing (Huttman and Huttman 1989).

In Sweden, social housing often means local authority housing with heavy national subsidies; public housing companies have 20 percent of the housing stock (half of all rental housing). In addition, some cooperatives (15 percent of the stock) and an increasing number of privately owned units exist. Private rentals are often of high standard, as in the inner-city area of Stockholm (chapter 5), and are highly prized as residences by the middle class, who acquire them through a system of personal contacts. Social housing is on the city's periphery and in Stockholm's adjacent new towns (Huttman 1988; Swedish Institute 1987a).

In West Germany, social housing availability is smaller, the private investor more involved, the subsidy system complex and now greatly curtailed. Each city has its share of social housing projects, and overall 20 percent of the stock in 1984 was considered social-sector housing. Of this, 80 percent was rental units, 62.5 percent of which were owned by nonprofit organizations. Van Vliet (1989:56) reports that this percentage may decrease because as much as 50 percent of the stock of subsidized rental housing existing in 1984 may be lost as "government offers incentives to private investors for accelerated repayment of conditionally favored loans, thus shortening the period during which such rental units are protected from market forces. In addition, the government has ceased to subsidize construction of rental units" (see also Harloe 1985). Now, with the great influx of German-origin and former East Germans to West Germany in 1989 and early 1990, more subsidized housing is being constructed.

In Switzerland, social housing only exists in a few large cities such as Zurich; immigrants do not usually live in it. Other than the "privileged" foreign residents, the majority of immigrants from non-neighboring countries are guest workers on short-term work permits, usually renewable each year. Some refugees, for example, those from Hungary and Czechoslovakia during the 1960s and recently those from more exotic places, also live in Switzerland. Guest workers are often housed, as singles, in employee housing; this is especially true for the construction industry and hotel industry. Others are in the private rental housing which makes up the majority of the Swiss housing stock. Only 34 percent of Swiss households own their own homes. As Arend (chapter 8) points out, these workers are usually in older housing, where they help keep vacancies low. Because the Swiss have also remained in this inner-area housing stock, often of fairly decent quality, rather than moving in large numbers to the suburbs as has been the case in West Germany, there has been no severe segregation. The number of guest workers has decreased, causing less demand from that sector of the population.

France also has social housing—16 percent of the stock in 1981. Barou (1988:18) describes the work of the special government housing efforts for Algerians and also provides statistics on all the social housing stock:

The National Society for Construction for Algerian Workers was founded in 1956 and has as its primary goal the housing of a population whose living conditions were steadily growing more precarious.

This particular effort was part of an overall effort of a very wide scope which aimed to make up for the considerable tardiness of the French government in this domain. In the next fifteen years, nearly six million lodgings had thus been created, mainly due to intervention of the State. Of the six million lodgings, nearly two million were HLM housing [housing with moderate rents], and three million were subsidized housing.

Barou adds that actions for the immigrant population "favored certain specific types of construction: 'homes' for single men which were often no more than huge horizontal and vertical concentrations of individual rooms, and transitional collective housing for families [in the industrial suburbs]." These replaced the poorer inner-city accommodations and the shanty-town of crude self-made units in Nanterre so that site could be used for HLM housing for the French working class, according to Barou. In addition to moving to these special industrial suburban housing estates, some North Africans in the mid-1970s moved to general social housing for all. Admission of new foreign workers had stopped, but families joining heads of their households were allowed in. "Decent housing" was needed if the workers were to get resident permits for incoming family members, so they applied for general subsidized housing. Because HLM, a government housing subsidization group that built rental units all over France, had many vacancies in the poorly constructed units built in the 1960s, they began to provide the North Africans with those units (chapter 7).

By the late 1980s, new social building activities had greatly decreased in most of the other countries. In Sweden, for example, the number of blocks of apartments built in 1986 was fewer than 15,000, far below the 75,000 built in 1970 (Swedish Institute 1987a). In Britain, subsidized housing building is at a low (Murie and Forrest 1988; Huttman 1985) and sale of council housing encouraged, just as privately owned housing is encouraged and subsidized in the Netherlands (Van Weesep 1986a), in France (chapter 7), and in Sweden (Swedish Institute 1987a). In the Netherlands, government support of subsidized housing such as housing associations' rentals continued through the mid-1970s, motivated in part by the need to keep the construction industry from collapsing. According to Van Weesep (1986a), the government is unwilling to maintain this level of intervention.

As the primary justification for reduced construction of social housing, the European governments have used the idea that the housing shortage has ended and that fiscal austerity is necessary in the national budget expenditures. Experts, including the majority of the European writers herein, point out that cheap standard rental units are still scarce as urban renewal lessens inner-city cheap rentals and as conversion to owner-occupancy becomes profitable (Van Weesep 1986a).

In Holland, he reports (p. 66), "starters and mobile households are finding it increasingly hard to acquire a suitable dwelling" and, "the deteriorating housing situation leads to growing dissatisfaction because of frustrated expectations. Some households find a short-term solution in doubling-up, others move into temporary accommodation, or join the growing ranks of the squatters. . . . The decline in well-being due to the scarce housing resources is unevenly distributed, which leads to increasing disparities within society."

Swedish observers also report a shortage of cheaper rental units; for example, the Swedish Institute's 1987a housing report states (p. 2): "For some years, there were plenty of vacant flats but the situation has now changed once more, and in many areas, especially in big cities, there is a housing shortage." The number of homeless in large cities in Britain, even after "hard-to-let" council housing units are opened to them (chapter 12), indicates a housing shortage of cheap units (Murie and Forrest 1988; Baum 1989). Arin (chapter 11) likewise indicates a shortage of cheap units in West Berlin, and a housing situation which combined with increasing rents, is considered a prime cause of the upheaval in the 1989 local election, along with a reaction to the many guest workers and refugees (Smolowe 1989). With the 1989–90 influx of Eastern Europeans into Berlin, the situation has become worse.

In some cities in West Germany cheap substandard rental units have existed in fair numbers but have been decreased in numbers by urban renewal and gentrification (Meuter 1982). The units existed in part because the native German population in places like Hamburg had been moving out of inner-city areas in large numbers in the 1970s (chapter 6; Bonacker 1982). Of course, gentrification brings a small part of this German group back in (Dengschat 1988). In the cases of Amsterdam and Rotterdam, Anderiesen and Reijndorp (1988) note that urban renewal in the 1970s was accomplished with priority to public housing and by giving original inhabitants the right to move back and enjoy substantially lower rents than elsewhere. The same approach was taken in Frankfurt's Bockenheim urban renewal (Vaughn 1985). The Dutch cities and Frankfurt experienced an influx of young people in the 1970s, along with a continued and increased immigrant population (to 30–40 percent of Amsterdam's population), a "stayers" population born and raised in the neighborhood, and, for Amsterdam, a "new urbanites" group. Dutch scholars report stayers as having a changing attitude toward the immigrant group: "It is no longer this group as such that is held responsible for the decline of the neighbor-

hood . . . immigrants . . . Turkish, Moroccan or Surinam *families* . . .
are not seen as the cause of the mess the street sometimes is or the
growth of 'petty crime' " (Anderiesen and Reijnsdorp 1988:5).

In Paris, urban renewal in some areas, Blanc (chapter 7) reports,
meant the removal of the large concentration of North Africans in the
early 1970s, with many moved to social housing in industrial suburbs.
Some also sought areas not renewed in their two districts of concentration, the 15th and 18th arrondissements. Since 1977, home improvement, rather than destruction of buildings in these areas, has been
encouraged, with the low-income population given a chance to stay
by means of a nine-year subsidy for those unable to afford the higher
rents. According to Blanc, many did not take the subsidy, and many
moved.

Explanations

The explanations for housing segregation, as well as housing and immigrant enclave characteristics, are somewhat different for situations
in Northern European countries and those in America. The European
research focus includes historical factors determining housing location,
such as availability of a deteriorated harbor area in Hamburg or a
prewar immigrant enclave in the 9th arrondissement (Faubourg Mont-
martre) of Paris. The focus is more on socioeconomic status explanations than is found in current American studies. Cultural reasons
are also given some significance as explanations in the European literature, whereas most American research focusing on the black population's residential segregation, does not center on cultural reasons.

A European example of emphasis on the cultural aspect of a minority concentration is the situation of Algerians in Paris. Barou reports that a villagelike community developed as members of the early
prewar Algerian immigrant group acquired hotels and cafes where
people from the same villages lived and gathered. Of the 15th arrondissement and other industrial areas in the Paris area where Algerians
worked in the 1930s, he reports (1988:15) that settlements developed
around such places:

The savings of certain individuals, those who had arrived in the early days,
was invested in the purchase of cafe-hotels which soon became the center of
life and lodging for this community. . . . the hotel-owners offered a place for
gatherings of people of the same village. These "tajmaat" dealt with problems
of concern to immigrants of the same village; providing help to the unemployed, settling differences between individuals, collecting money for cele-

brations . . . and the sending of money to the village to help with various projects (the construction of roads, aqueducts, etc.). Territoriality thus became a positive case facilitating the transfer of the village organization.

This focus on the positive aspects of ethnic concentration is less evident in other European studies because signs of ethnic institutions in other European cities are less obvious, possibly because of the mix of ethnic groups or their newness to an area. In the "Old Station" area of Hamburg in the late 1970s, Bonacker (1982) found primarily social clubs catering to the Yugoslavs and Italians in the area, and two shops for the Turks, who dominate street life, especially in the summer. Crane-Engel (1987) reports that half the Kreuzberg, West Berlin, residents were Turkish, but then describes a mixed street population of hippies, artists, elderly widows, alcoholics, and young punks as well as Turks. Anderiesen and Reijnsdorp (1988) describe a mix in old neighborhoods of Amsterdam. In Stockholm, the district with the highest foreign-born population had a mix of ethnic groups (chapter 5). However, in Britain, South Asians crowd into areas in which their particular group is already numerous, and mosques, restaurants, and specialized shops spring up (Oc 1988; chapter 4).

Although American scholarly emphasis on this explanation has waned, cultural enclaves for new immigrants to the United States were often described in the early immigration literature, such as the book by Handlin (1951), and their institutions and services mentioned. For example, Gans (1962) describes the "urban village" atmosphere of one Boston Italian area. In this literature, the positive functions of such areas were described, including giving newcomers a helping hand and finding them housing and jobs. In addition, safety from harassment and violence by native-born, as the Chinese experienced in American cities, was seen as an advantage (chapter 4). In the literature, continued "voluntary" segregation is attributed to positive functions. In several of the chapters herein, authors discuss the pros and cons of dispersal policy and mention the advantages of clustering. Blanc (chapter 7) and Barou (1988) criticize the French government's movement of Algerians to special industrial suburban housing and away from inner-city Algerian communities and the Nanterre shantytown (Barou). Both locations had territorial village divisions, from which people were taken and placed in situations in which they mixed with others in this new suburban housing. Barou states (p. 16):

Housing assignments [in the new suburban social housing] were made without taking into account the ethnic affinities which lay at the heart of the spatial structure of the shanty-town. A forced disharmony between living space and way of life seriously disrupted the behavior of the groups in question. Where the territoriality of the shanty-town had been felt as a rather positive factor of identification, settlement in housing projects and transitional homes was seen as negative, a dissociation. This perception led, especially among youth, to aggressive, deviant behaviour.

This picture of positive attributes of clustering and the negative effects of assimilation (and loss of one's life-style)—causing, Barou feels, social isolation and loss of a positive identity, is not discussed in most contemporary American housing segregation literature; that integration is positive is a given by most writers, except for a few who are minority and organization leaders. European policymakers still debate the continuation of cultural enclaves, albeit ones with improved renovated housing, versus dispersal to new housing estates (chapters 10 and 11). Choice (voluntary segregation) versus constraint (by institutions discriminating) is an ongoing research topic (Sarre 1986).

In the present American housing segregation research, the "choice" focus is in terms of determining the degree of preference blacks have for living in integrated areas. Polls do show the willingness of black households to live in largely white communities (Farley 1987). In several European reports herein, some minor attention is paid to immigrants' willingness to move for higher-quality housing (chapters 6 and 4).

As far as socioeconomic explanations of housing segregation, European researchers are likely to point out that the immigrants' socioeconomic status does not allow them to afford housing comparable to the native population's. Friedrichs and Alpheis cite the worsening situation for immigrants in West Germany, where unemployment increases as the German economy stagnates and the skill needs in the post-industrial age move beyond those held by many immigrants. For Britain, Phillips and Karn also mention increased unemployment and competition for jobs among South Asian and West Indian groups and thus their limited ability to buy housing. Both chapters allude to the problems of the second generation, closer attuned than their parents to the host country's housing norms and desiring such but having trouble in the labor market. In the Netherlands, writers again describe immigrants' low socioeconomic level and the hardships they face in meeting rents. Linden and Lindberg (chapter 5) are optimistic about immigrants to Sweden developing housing quality standards similar to those of native Swedes and consider some groups close to parity. But their data also indicate a high level of housing segmentation, that is, segmentation by housing tenure and housing type. Swedes are much more likely to be in owner-occupied units, in part related to the socio-economic position of the two groups. Even segments of long-term immigrant groups who have higher socioeconomic levels are less likely to own (Kemeny 1987).

Some of the European chapters herein (chapter 10) point out that immigrants often pay more rent than their native household counter-parts for the same type of nonsocial housing (also see Meuter 1982; Ipsen 1978). Arin also notes immigrants in West Berlin paying bribes to stop their removal from overcrowded housing disallowed by resi-dent permit standards. For the Netherlands, Blauw (chapter 3) notes that Surinamese pay a high proportion of their low incomes for rent. Both in the Netherlands (Van Weesep 1986a) and Britain (Oc 1988; Rex and Moore 1967), researchers report that immigrants are forced to buy substandard units. The European authors put varying emphases on these different socioeconomic factors.

In the United States, few reports on housing segregation center on the poor socioeconomic position of minorities in the housing market, or on the fact that they pay high rents. Some reports, however, do cover the fact that blacks who buy in transitional areas often pay more than do whites in comparable all-white areas. Housing segregation researchers, perhaps because they feel that the poor socioeconomic position of blacks is overused as a reason for underrepresentation in quality housing areas, focus on the fact that a proportion of the black community has a high enough socioeconomic position to buy in higher-quality areas, usually suburbs. Thus American researchers take the opposite thrust from their European counterparts. American research-ers, such as Kain (1986; 1987), investigate the degree of underrepre-sentation of black households in the suburbs, comparing the actual number of households there with the predicted number of black house-holds according to the number that could afford such housing in terms of socioeconomic status (income). These researchers, Kain, for ex-ample, then point out that because surveys show that many blacks, especially those in the middle class, prefer integrated communities rather than all-black ones, they are not underrepresented for social-psychological reasons nor economic reasons, but rather for reasons of discrimination. European researchers do not seem to have looked at the socioeconomic situation or social-psychological preferences in this way. They have cited white preferences not to live next to certain minorities, especially Turks and more exotic groups, as possibly being a reason for whites moving out of immigrant enclave areas such as

Hamburg's harbor area, some Dutch social housing, or French social housing. However, it may be that in some areas, Amsterdam, for example, young punks and not immigrants are the group that bothers whites (Anderiesen and Reijnsdorp 1988).

Intergroup relations as an explanation is an aspect of American literature. Black militant writers, for example, have long discussed how the establishment has kept blacks confined to ghettos in the colonial-like existence that Fanan (1966) long ago described for Algeria. European writers, such as Arin on West Berlin, allude to such a situation. In addition, Blanc cites Jean-Marie LePen's political campaign against social housing for immigrants. The rightist party (Republicans) in West Berlin has won votes by denouncing foreigners for taking jobs and housing that should go to Germans (Smolowe 1989). Rex and Moore (1967) reported this competition for housing in Britain, then a scarce good, particularly in Birmingham, and considered South Asians as powerless and unable to be successful against native British with greater power to get good council housing. A number of other European housing researchers, such as Henderson and Karn (1986), quote this argument in describing the allocation of council housing.

Institutional explanations in the following chapters focus primarily on discriminatory practices in the government allocation system in Europe, but in the United States refer more to discriminatory activities of lending institutions, realtors, and even insurance companies, although government practices are also examined. The latter groups are covered in a variety of American research (Wienk et al. 1979; Saltman 1989; Feins and Bratt 1983). Saltman feels that the audit is a way to detect such discriminatory practices. Although interest in researching such activities has been much less in Europe, Phillips and Karn (chapter 4) cite studies of British building societies and realtors, and Linden and Lindberg (chapter 5), rate selective housing allocation by public authorities in Sweden, as Blauw does for housing associations in the Netherlands and Blanc does for French social housing management. Henderson and Karn (1986) also find council housing discrimination.

European researchers are less likely to mention lending institutions and realtor activities in relation to the purchase of a house because these various European immigrants are unlikely to buy, with the exception of South Asians in Britain, who buy large old houses and rent rooms to fellow immigrants, and some immigrants in Dutch cities. Even among natives in these countries, the proportion who buy houses has not been high until recently. In the Netherlands, only 43 percent of the Dutch own an apartment or a house, and only 15 percent or less of the Turks, Surinamese, and other groups, Blauw reports. Only 34 percent of the Swiss own, Arend reports.

As far as private rentals are concerned, in the United States these are the major type of rental and are of more interest. American investigators find the institutional discrimination explanation for why certain minorities are underrepresented in standard-quality rentals is of interest and they produce supportive data through audits which sample landlord reactions to pairs of similar black and white applicants for apartments. Income data on black households' ability to pay, and thus their predicted presence in areas of high-standard rentals versus their actual presence in these areas, is also calculated. Such studies of the Western European situation are for the most part missing. This may be partially explained by the low proportion of private rentals in many countries and even their general substandard quality; if immigrants are to move to better-quality rentals, they must move to social housing, which is normally allocated in a way that does not lend itself to audits. Other data, such as housing authority records on assignments, have been examined by Henderson and Karn (1986) for Britain. Discrimination in placement of West Indians in council housing has been found; authorities are slow to put them in council housing and often place them in unpopular housing, frequently in inner-city areas. As noted previously, such housing allocation has also been studied in other countries, and, again, an overuse of unpopular or poor-standard projects for immigrants is the norm (chapter 12).

The ecological explanations of housing segregation, especially the invasion and succession theories of Burgess (1926), are closer to the interests of European urbanologists. The focus of this volume is urban settlement and territorialism, that is, location of minorities, including by use of maps and district statistics; a discussion of change over time, again using these data sources, is a prominent aspect of these researchers' focus. Another is use of the population data on groups to obtain index of dissimilarity measurements or other such measurements of segregation. In general, all the researchers find these index numbers low compared to those found for black populations in the United States. Even in areas of high concentration, they often find a number of minority groups represented, such as the Hamburg harbor area on which Bonacker (1982) reports. In some areas of Britain, the index may be high for a census ward, and very high for a particular street (chapter 4). For a few parts of Paris, Barou (1988) reports that the index has been high, but that urban renewal may be lowering it (chapter 7). A number of European researchers find that the invasion and succession theory applies only in a limited way. Some examples exist, such as in Paris (Barou 1988), in West Berlin, and other inner-city areas, but the Europeans report that many moves to the suburbs often leapfrog to government-built social housing on the city's periphery (Van Hoorn and Van Ginkel 1986). The increased proportion of immigrants may grow in inner-city areas, as Hamburg's, simply because Germans are moving out at a faster rate than the immigrants, even though many of the latter are also moving out, as Friedrichs and Alpheis (chapter 6) report. In Switzerland, Sweden, and most parts of the Netherlands this theory does not seem to work; in the latter two countries, the dominance of government policies, on both social housing and urban renewal, is a major reason. Unlike in the United States, in most of these countries low-income households are found in suburban peripheral locations where much of the social housing is located.

In the United States, invasion and succession have long been known facts of urban city life. Studies of black movement into the suburbs show that the dominant trend is for the extension of an existing ghetto area over the city line into the suburbs (chapters 20 and 21). However, some leapfrogging to farther out suburbs also occurs (Lake 1986). As suburbs develop a noticeable black population, many resegregate, and a predominating black population is the result.

Policies

A major government policy on housing segregation in Western Europe has been dispersal, a hotly debated issue in some areas. In the United States, as far as policies against discrimination, laws and court decisions are the dominant concern. In this volume, the dispersal approach, which stems from the idea that a concentration of minorities is wrong and that dispersing groups of migrants through social housing stock (or even private rental stock) is best, is described for the Netherlands, France, Britain, Sweden, and Germany's West Berlin. Mik (chapter 10) describes Rotterdam's 5 percent minority quota for each area and its abandonment because of outcries against freedom of choice; Arin (chapter 11) describes the continuing ban on increased minority population in the Berlin Kreuzberg and adjacent areas. Both researchers seriously criticize dispersal policies and approve instead of more recent policies of improving poor housing areas, usually inhabited by minorities as well as natives—that is, a policy to treat all poor in an area equally. Mik also notes, as does Blauw (chapter 3), the obligation of Dutch housing authorities to provide a certain proportion of their units to minorities, especially Surinamese and Antillians. Phillips and Karn (chapter 4) cite dispersal of Birmingham's immigrants and of refugees from Africa. All discuss the fact that these policies do not work, or are administered only half-heartedly by government and housing authorities. Mik and Arin argue for the cultural benefits of clustering of immigrants.

Dispersal of Algerians in Paris from inner-city areas and the Nanterre shanty-town to public housing in the industrial suburbs has already been described. The new housing was primarily for these immigrants; however, Blanc (chapter 7) does report that the National Commission for Immigrants worried about provoking new urban segregation via special housing for immigrants and turned instead to funding public and private housing organizations to encourage them to accept immigrants. Certainly, by making the general social housing available to minorities, especially the unpopular, poorly constructed projects of the 1960s, some dispersement of minorities occurred, although many such projects have a high minority population, as Le Pen complained during his political campaign.

Dispersal policy in Sweden, Linden and Lindberg report (chapter 5), is seen in terms of dispersing refugees to various communities. Government dispersal policy in the United States could be thought of in terms of desegregating public housing, a difficult goal because of the large black population in the projects (chapter 18). Most interest is in desegregation through compliance with court orders, such as the Mt. Laurel, New Jersey, case demanding inclusion of low-cost housing in New Jersey communities and an end to exclusionary zoning (*New York Times*, June 1, 1987, p. 1), or the Yonkers case (1988) demanding that the city provide low-cost housing.

The U.S. government has had little success in trying to disperse incoming Vietnamese and Cuban refugees, as well as other refugee groups. Some of the European researchers herein provide immigrants' mixed but primarily negative reactions to dispersal, such as those in the Netherlands, West Berlin, and Britain. For the latter, Phillips and Karn demonstrate how minorities want some clustering for protection and religious and other institutions, but also want some integration, and some (particularly the second generation) want outer area council housing, with an integrated, primarily British, population, as Henderson and Karn (1986) report.

Dispersal of Italians in all these countries by their own volition is described. Turks experience much less dispersal because of native populations that consider the group's customs, religious orientation, extended family, and other attributes very distant from its own (chapters 6 and 3; Bonacker 1982).

In the United States, dispersal situations, about which the minority population may have mixed feelings, are integration maintenance programs. Efforts, primarily by nonprofit groups, are made to keep suburban communities integrated by steering new black potential home buyers away from suburbs that already have a substantial number of black households (chapters 20 and 21). Emphasis is put on enforcement of laws against housing discrimination, that is, in encouraging integration. Major works such as Tobin's edited work (1987) and Goering's edited book (1986) contain descriptions of enforcement activities. European literature contains little information on enforcement of nondiscrimination laws. With the exception of Britain, there are few laws, except those concerning council housing or housing association units (chapters 3 and 10). Blanc points out how much weaker the laws are in France than in Britain, and Arin describes laws in West Berlin that in reality harass immigrants in their substandard housing, rather than help them.

The purpose herein has been to relate the following theoretical sections to the European situation; to highlight the differences in focus between European and U.S. research; and to emphasize the differences between countries regarding housing markets, housing settlement patterns and areas of ethnic concentration, government policies, and the types and circumstances of minority groups. The following six chapters provide details on the Netherlands, Great Britain, West Germany, Sweden, France, and Switzerland.

References

Anderiesen, Gerard, and Arnold Reijndorp. 1988. "Old and New Urbanites." Paper presented at the International Housing Policy and Urban Innovation Conference. Amsterdam.

Barou, Jacques. 1988. "North African Ethnic Minorities and Urban Changes: An Historical Survey of the Paris Region." Paper presented at the International Housing Policy and Urban Innovation Conference. Amsterdam.

Baum, Julian. 1989. "Youth Homelessness on the Rise in Britain." *Christian Science Monitor* January: 19–25.

Böhning, Roger. 1972. "The Problems of Immigrant Workers in West Germany." Pp. 18–29 in *Immigrant in Europe,* edited by Nicholas Deakin. London: Fabian Society.

Bonacker, Margrit. 1982. "The Social Community of Immigrants." In *Spatial*

Disparities and Social Behavior, edited by Jürgen Friedrichs. Hamburg: Christians.

Burgess, Ernest. 1926. "The Growth of the City." Pp. 51–55 in *The City,* edited by R. Park and E. Burgess. Chicago: University of Chicago Press.

———. 1928. "Residential Segregation in American Cities. *Annals of the American Academy of Political and Social Sciences* 140:105–15.

Clark, Thomas. 1987. "The Suburbanization Process and Residential Segregation." Pp. 115–37 in *Divided Neighborhoods,* edited by Gary Tobin. Beverly Hills: Sage.

Crane-Engel, Melinda. 1987. "Urban Renewal Minus Bulldozers: A Short History of Kreuzberg." *Christian Science Monitor* October 30.

Deakin, Nicholas. 1972. *Immigrants in Europe.* International Comparisons in Social Policy, no. 2. London: Fabian Society.

Dengschat, Jens. 1988. "Attitudes of Inhabitants to Gentrifying Neighbourhoods—The Case of Hamburg." Paper presented at the International Housing Policy and Urban Innovation Conference. Amsterdam.

Dengschat, Jens, and Jürgen Friedrichs. 1988. *Gentrification in Hamburg.* Hamburg: GSS.

Fanon, Franz. 1966. *The Wretched of the Earth.* New York: Harper.

Farley, John. 1987. "How Segregated are America's Metropolitan Areas?" Pp. 95–144 in *Divided Neighborhoods,* edited by Gary Tobin. Beverly Hills: Sage.

Feins, J. D., and R. G. Bratt. 1983. "Barred in Boston: Racial Discrimination in Housing." *American Planning Association Journal* 49:344–55.

Forrest, Ray, and Alan Murie. 1985. "Restructuring the Welfare State: Privatisation of Public Housing in Britain." In *Housing Needs and Policy Approaches: Trends in Thirteen Countries,* edited by Willem Van Vliet, Elizabeth Huttman, and Sylvia Fava. Durham: Duke University Press.

Gans, Herbert. 1962. *The Urban Villagers.* New York: Free Press.

Goering, John. 1986. *Housing Segregation, Race and Federal Policy.* Chapel Hill: University of North Carolina Press.

Handlin, Oscar. 1951. *The Uprooted.* Boston: Little, Brown.

Harloe, Michael. 1985. *Private Rented Housing in the United States and Europe.* London: Croom Helm.

Henderson, J., and V. Karn. 1986. *Race, Class and Public Housing.* London: Gower.

Hoffmeyer-Zlotnik, Jürgen. 1982. "Community Change and Invasion: The Case of the Turkish Guest-Workers." Pp. 114–26 in *Spatial Disparities and Social Behaviour: A Reader in Urban Research,* edited by Jürgen Friedrichs. Hamburg: Christians.

Huttman, Elizabeth. 1969. *Stigma in Public Housing in the U.S. and Great Britain.* Berkeley: Unpublished doctoral dissertation.

———. 1985. "Transnational Housing Policy." In *Home Environments,* edited by Irving Altman and Carol Werner. New York: Plenum Press.

————. 1988. "New Communities in the U.S." In *Handbook on Housing and the Built Environment,* edited by Elizabeth Huttman and Willem Van Vliet. Westport: Greenwood Press.

Huttman, Elizabeth, and John Huttman. 1989. "Types of Housing Demand and the Need for a Viable Private Rental-Housing Sector: Evidence from the United States, Great Britain, and the Netherlands." *Housing and Society* 16:16–32.

Hwang, S. S., and S. H. Murdock. 1983. "Segregation in Metropolitan and Nonmetropolitan Texas in 1980." *Rural Sociology* 48:607–23.

Ipsen, D. 1977. "Aufenthaltsdauer und integration ausländerischer Gastarbeiter (Length of Residence and Integration of Foreign Guest Workers)." *Zeitschrift für Soziologie* 4:403–24.

————. 1978. "Housing Conditions and Interests of Foreign Workers in the Federal Republic of Germany." Paper presented at World Congress of Sociology. Uppsala.

Kain, John. 1986. "The Influence of Race and Income on Racial Housing Policy." In *Housing Segregation, Race and Federal Policy,* edited by John Goering. Chapel Hill: University of North Carolina Press.

————. 1987. "Housing Market Discrimination and Black Suburbanization in the 1980s. Pp. 68–94 in *Divided Neighborhoods,* edited by Gary Tobin. Beverly Hills: Sage.

Kemeny, Jim. 1987. *Immigrant Housing Conditions in Sweden: An Analysis of Unpublished 1980 Census Data.* Gaevle: National Swedish Institute for Building Research.

Lake, R. W. 1981. *The New Suburbanites: Race and Housing in the Suburbs.* New Brunswick: Center for Urban Policy Research.

————. 1986. "Postscript: Unresolved Themes in the Evaluation of Fair Housing." In *Housing Segregation, Race and Federal Policy,* edited by John Goering. Chapel Hill: University of North Carolina Press.

Lembcke, E. 1988. *Race, Class and Urban Change.* Westport: JAI Press.

Mallach, Alan. 1988. "Opening the Suburbs: New Jersey's Mount Laurel Experience." *Shelter Force* 11:12–13.

Meuter, H. 1982. "Regional and Social Effects of Changed Conditions in Housing Supply." In *Applied Urban Research towards an Internationalization of Research and Learning,* edited by G. Hellenstern. Bonn: Bundesforschungsanstalt für Landeskund und Baum-Ordnung.

Murie, Alan, and Ray Forrest. 1988. "The New Homeless in Britain." In *Affordable Housing and the Homeless,* edited by Jürgen Friedrichs. Berlin: Walter DeGruyter.

New York Times. 1987. "Jersey Lagging in Suburban Housing for the Poor." June 1. P. 1.

Oc, Tanner. 1988. "Inner City Housing Improvement and Ethnic Minorities in Britain." In *Housing and Neighborhoods: Theoretical and Empirical Contributions,* edited by W. Van Vliet, H. Choldin, W. Michelson, and D. Popenoe. Westport: Greenwood Press.

Peach, Ceri. 1975. *Urban Social Segregation*. London: Longmans.

Rex, John. 1988. *The Ghetto and the Underclass: Essays in Race and Social Policy*. London: Avebury, Gower.

Rex, John, and Robert Moore. 1967. *Race, Community and Conflict*. London: Oxford University Press.

Saltman, Juliet. 1989. *A Fragile Movement: The Struggle for Neighborhood Stabilization*. Westport: Greenwood Press.

Sarre, Philip. 1986. "Choice and Constraint in Ethnic Minority Housing." *Housing Studies* 1:71–86.

Smolowe, Jill. 1989. "Berlin's Far-Right Surprise." *Time*, February 13.

Swedish Institute. 1987a. *Housing and Housing Policy in Sweden*. Stockholm: Swedish Institute.

———. 1987b. *Immigrants in Sweden*. Stockholm: Swedish Institute.

Tobin, Gary. 1987. *Divided Neighborhoods*. Beverly Hills: Sage.

Van Hoorn, F. J. J. H., and J. A. Van Ginkel. 1986. "Racial Leapfrogging in a Controlled Housing Market: The Case of the Mediterranean Minority in Utrecht, the Netherlands." *Tijdschrift voor Economische en Sociale Geografie* 77:187–96.

Van Vliet, Willem. 1989. *Handbook on International Housing Policy*. Westport: Greenwood Press.

Van Weesep, J. 1986a. "Dutch Housing: Recent Developments and Policy Issues." Housing Studies 1:61–66.

———. 1986b. *Condominium: A New Housing Sector in the Netherlands*. Utrecht: Geografisch Instituut, Rijksuniversiteit Utrecht.

Vaughn, Donald. 1985. "Housing and Renewal in the Inner City." Paper presented at the International Housing Policy Conference. Amsterdam.

Wienk, R., C. E. Reid, J. C. Simonson, and F. J. Eggers. 1979. *Measuring Discrimination in American Housing Markets: The Housing Market Practice Survey*. Washington, D.C.: Department of Housing and Urban Development, Office of Policy Development and Research.

3. Housing Segregation for Different Population Groups in the Netherlands

The Netherlands have long had the reputation of being tolerant to foreigners, and have welcomed such diverse groups as French Huguenots, Jews, and Eastern Europeans. During the fifties and sixties, the Dutch were considered to be a homogeneous society with people who were friendly to foreigners. Even the Dutch themselves were inclined to believe this image of their society.

At the beginning of the seventies, however, this image was defamed. Astonished, the London *Times* reported (August 12, 1972) on riots in the streets of a lower-class district of Rotterdam, with Dutch people pelting Turkish migrants' guest houses with stones, an event that did not fit the image of the Dutch. As the *Times* reported, "We are inclined to view the Dutch as reasonable, moderate-minded, non-violent, unprejudiced, progressive, neat, hardworking and friendly to foreigners." The view had two fallacies: first, Dutch society is no longer homogeneous, and second, the integration of migrants from abroad is not always without tension. As was supposed, the outburst was due to irritation about the overcrowding of single male migrants, particularly Turks and Moroccans, in guest houses. The native Dutch perception of the situation was one of unacceptable competition with migrants over the housing market. There was a feeling that old districts were threatened by the influx of too many ethnic immigrants. Due to these sentiments the Rotterdam city council decided to limit the percentage of ethnic minorities in the old neighborhoods to a maximum of 5 percent. However, a judge declared the decision to be illegal, and by the late 1980s, the percentage of ethnic minorities was about 25 percent in the city's older districts.

Under these circumstances, urban housing segregation in the Netherlands has recently drawn the attention of Dutch social scientists. Politicians fear developments in the direction of increasing segregation, leading to the ghettos for which the United States is famous. The discussion herein concerns the following questions: (1) Which ethnic minorities can be distinguished, and what is their position in Dutch society? (2) Are there indications of a certain degree of segregation of these minorities? (3) Which factors might explain this phenomenon? In relation to this, observed changes in the residential pattern of some ethnic minorities—their moves to newer residential districts—should be explained. Changes in the residential pattern might be because of an improvement of the housing situation which, in addition to improvement of government position on the housing market, would be an important indication of the government's aim to decrease the relative weak position of minorities in Dutch society. Connected with this is the question of whether there are any obstacles to improving the minorities' situations by moving them to dwelling and living environments that come closer to their housing wishes.

Ethnic Minorities

The concentration of ethnic minorities in older residential districts of large Dutch cities and the accompanying tensions between "ethnics" and the native lower-class Dutch residents led to increasing attention of the local and national governments to the ethnic minorities' positions on the housing and the labor market. In *Minderhedennota* (Report on Ethnic Minorities 1983) the national government's policy took the line that guest workers and their family members would stay permanently. It proclaimed as objectives:

1. to promote conditions for ethnic minorities to be emancipated and to participate in Dutch society through stimulation of mutual adjustment and acceptance between all population groups;

2. to diminish the backward social and economic position of ethnic minorities; and

3. to prevent discrimination against ethnic minorities and to improve their legal position.

The argument over whom to consider as an ethnic minority is arbitrary. The Dutch national government declares a group an ethnic minority when social and economic support for such a group is deemed necessary. This interpretation implies an element of keeping people subordinate. Although the groups involved may be aware of their position in society, they may turn away from the idea that the government knows what is best for them. *Immigrants* may be a more neutral term, but it does not refer to all populations described herein. The term *immigrants* refers to those foreigners who came from abroad with the intention of residing permanently in the country. From a legal point of view, Surinamese and Antillians are not immigrants. Many came to the Netherlands when Surinam and the Antilles were part of the Kingdom of the Netherlands, and consequently they did not immigrate legally. Second, Western European immigrants, compared to Southern European immigrants—for example, those from Turkey and Morocco—have a closer cultural identity with the Dutch, are not in quite as different a social and economical position as are Southern migrants, and will not be discussed as ethnic minorities herein.

In addition, one must be aware of status differences among the ethnic minorities, and even within these minorities, in Dutch societies. For example, in general Surinamese have a better position on the housing market than Moroccans and Turks, but those Surinamese who arrived earlier have a relatively better position. Although Dutch-Indonesians are not considered an ethnic minority group, a description of their integration into Dutch society fits in a comparative perspective such as the one that follows.

Dutch-Indonesians

Before the coming of Turkish and Moroccan guest workers, several hundred thousand people arrived from the Indonesian colonies. The first stream of about 100,000 Dutch-Indonesians came to the Netherlands after World War II when the Japanese occupied Indonesia. A large number of these immigrants had suffered in concentration camps. They were Dutch (*totoks*) and generally well trained and could easily find a job as the country was reconstructed, but it took time to house them because of the housing shortage after the war. The national government provided guest houses from which the repatriates gradually moved to other housing units. Clothing was supplied, and credits were given in order to buy furniture (Ellemers and Vaillant 1987).

The second stream, again about 100,000 immigrants, occurred when Indonesia became an independent state. Those Indonesians, who had married Dutch (the *Indos*), had to choose whether to stay in Indonesia and hold an Indonesian nationality or to move to the Netherlands. Around 1960, when Sukarno came into power and the feelings against the Dutch rose in Indonesia, a third group of about 40,000 immigrants left Indonesia. Although they held Indonesian nationality, they nevertheless were admitted in the Netherlands.

Generally, the first stream of Dutch *totoks* integrated smoothly into

Dutch society. Those Dutch-Indonesians who arrived later, however, experienced more difficulties in integrating; large numbers had not been in the Netherlands before, and their children spoke Indonesian instead of Dutch. To help Dutch-Indonesian housewives the government organized courses on such aspects of housekeeping as house cleaning, filling the stove, hygienics, furnishing, and budgeting.

Although research reports on integration of Dutch-Indonesians carried out by order of the Dutch government were positive about the group's integration, there are also some indications of a more problematic adjustment to the Dutch way of life. Whereas these migrants, particularly the younger families, were "realistic," accepted the new situation, and tried to make the best of it, others complained about unequal treatment and about the formal behavior and parochialism of the native Dutch.

It is striking that data are lacking about the position of Dutch-Indonesians in Dutch society today. Apparently the process of integration is considered to be fully completed. However, some social problems still exist. Dutch-Indonesians who are psychologically impaired as a consequence of having been prisoners of war in World War II desire the same acknowledgment, morally and materially, as the Dutch who became victims of the war in Europe. To date nearly 60,000 Dutch-Indonesians have applied for reparation payments from the national government. It is fortunate for them that interest in the war and its long-term effects is increasing. While aged Dutch-Indonesians, particularly those whose native tongue is not Dutch, risk becoming isolated socially, the second generation is becoming more interested in the cultural background of their parents and want to know more about their roots.

Dutch-Indonesians had the disadvantage of immigration at a time when the Dutch government, as a consequence of the war, had few resources to compensate them, whereas later Surinamese and Mediterranean immigrants with their own organizations could benefit from a more favorable economic situation.

Moluccans

The situation of the Dutch-Indonesians did not apply to migrants from the Molucca Islands, who wanted to be independent from Indonesia and fought as soldiers side by side with the Dutch. They considered their stay in the Netherlands temporary while they waited to return to the Moluccas when they became an independent state. In this they counted on the help of the Dutch government. The Moluccans had no intention of integrating into Dutch society, preferring in the past to live in segregated hut camps at the outskirts of cities and maintaining their own culture. The capture of a passenger train by a group of Moluccans was meant to put pressure on the Dutch government to give them their independent state. The estimated 35,000 Moluccans in the Netherlands today still encounter problems in integrating into Dutch society. For example, the young Moluccans who are orienting themselves more and more to Dutch society and accepting permanent residence in the Netherlands are relatively poorly trained and thus more often unemployed than Dutch youth. Although nearly all the hut camps are demolished and their former residents housed in new neighborhoods, the Moluccans' degree of housing segregation continues to remain high.

Surinamese and Antillians

To date, approximately 200,000 inhabitants of the Netherlands are persons born in Surinam or the Antilles. They are a mixed ethnic population consisting of predominantly Creoles (the black population), Javanese, and Hindus. Although there are social-cultural differences between these groups, as well as between them and the Dutch, the Surinamese and Antillians have the great asset of having learned Dutch at school. A large influx of Surinamese occurred just before Surinam became an independent state in 1975. Many Surinamese, still having Dutch passports, took the opportunity to move to the cold and wet Netherlands. The influx from the Antilles has been caused by mass dismissals at oil refineries.

Mediterraneans

Whereas the immigration of the ethnic groups described previously can be viewed as the result of the colonial past, the immigration of "Mediterraneans" (Spaniards, Portuguese, Greeks, Italians, Yugoslavs, Turks, and Moroccans) has been caused by the Netherlands' need of unskilled workers in a period of strong economic growth and industrialization. After World War II, approximately half a million Dutch emigrated, particularly farmers, because the country was considered to be too densely populated with not enough space to offer young farmers land or a job in industry. During the sixties industrialization in the Netherlands boomed, although somewhat later than it did in the other Western European countries. It became difficult for employers to find enough Dutch for less attractive manual work and so they began to recruit unskilled workers in Italy and Spain, and later in Turkey and Morocco, now the dominant Mediterranean immigrant groups in the Netherlands. Return migration proved to be much more common for Spanish and Italian immigrants than for immigrants from Turkey or Morocco. The number of Italians decreased gradually from about 20,000 during the peak immigration of the mid-seventies to 17,000 in 1988; and the number of Spanish immigrants decreased even more, from 30,000 to 18,000. Their numbers became smaller than those for immigrants from neighboring countries. In 1988, 40,000 inhabitants in the Netherlands were from the Federal Republic of Germany, 38,000 from Great Britain, and 23,000 from Belgium.

The Turkish and Moroccan immigrants' stay proved to be less temporary than the immigrants themselves and the Dutch government, the receiving country, had intended. By 1976 the recruitment of Mediterraneans ended officially. However, as a consequence of family reunions and a relatively high fertility rate the number of Turkish, and particularly Moroccan, immigrants increased considerably: the Turkish population from 53,000 in 1974 to 160,000 in 1987, and the Moroccans from 30,000 to 122,000. In general, compared with the Moroccans, the Turks have been more oriented to Western society, a result of not only greater economic development in Turkey than in Morocco, but also because a relatively large proportion (70 percent) of Moroccans come from the isolated countryside.

Overview of Ethnic Minorities in the Netherlands

To summarize, in comparison with other Western European countries, the Netherlands have had a relatively low number of immigrants considered to be ethnic minorities. Table 3.1 shows the categories of the population considered as ethnic minorities as defined by the minority policy of the Dutch government. The Turkish and Moroccan ethnic groups are the largest (160,600 and 122,700 respectively), together with the Surinamese-Antillian group (197,400). These groups are not only the largest in numbers, but also best documented with regard to their housing situation.

Segregation at the Regional Level

Although the term *segregation* is generally used to describe the pattern of distribution of residents within cities, the phenomenon can also be

TABLE 3.1.   Numbers of Ethnic Minorities
in the Netherlands (1987)

Country of nationality	
Turkey	160,600
Morocco	122,700
Spain	18,200
Italy	17,000
Yugoslavia	11,600
Portugal	7,500
Greece	3,800
Tunisia	2,600
Cape Verde Islands	2,000
Country of birth	
Dutch Antilles	45,200
Surinam	152,200
Other groups	
Moluccans	33,300
Caravan dwellers	30,000
Refugees	26,500
Gypsies	3,700
Total	636,900
Total population of Netherlands	1,468,400
Ethnic minorities as percent of total population	4.3

Source: Ankersmit, Roelandt, and Veenman (1988).

measured in the same way on a regional scale (Blauw 1980). Thus, using the index of dissimilarity (I.D.), Atzema and Buursink (1985) show that for a period of five years (1977–82) the mean I.D. for Turks and Moroccans was 39, indicating that 39 percent of all members of these groups would have to move in order to create a percentage distribution by region that was similar to the distribution of the remaining population.

A relative concentration of Turks and Moroccans can be observed in the older industrial regions of the Netherlands such as the large cities and the urban regions of Twente and Brabant. Surinamese-Antillians live concentrated in the four large cities, Amsterdam, Rotterdam, The Hague, and Utrecht. In 1986, 14 percent of the Dutch had their residence in these cities, whereas more than half (56 percent) of the Surinamese lived there. Their presence was particularly high in Amsterdam, where 24 percent of all Surinamese in the Netherlands live. Moroccans were also concentrated in the four large cities (48 percent), particularly in Amsterdam (22 percent). More than a third (36 percent) of the Turks in the Netherlands had their residence in these cities in 1986, but they were more concentrated in Rotterdam (14 percent).

Segregation at the Urban Level

As can be inferred from the preceding data, large cities in the Netherlands have relatively high percentages of ethnic immigrants. The overall percentage of Turks, Moroccans, and Surinamese-Antillians is about 15 percent of the total population in large cities. The general pattern is a concentration of ethnic minorities in the older nineteenth-century districts close to the central business district (C.B.D.). However, some differences can be observed among concentration patterns of ethnic minorities in the cities. For example, the Surinamese population in Amsterdam is not only concentrated in older residential districts, but also in some high-rise apartment buildings in the Bijlmermeer district on the periphery of Amsterdam (Van Amersfoort and De Klerk 1986).

A comparison of the segregation of ethnic minorities proves they are not segregated equally. If measured by an index of dissimilarity some differences can be shown. According to Mik's extensive study in Rotterdam (Mik 1987:96), Turks and Moroccans are more segregated (I.D. of 54 and 53, respectively) than the other Mediterraneans (Spaniards and Italians, I.D. of 47 and 29, respectively). The Surinamese and Antillians are least segregated, with an I.D. of 34, according to 1984 figures.

Although a remarkable increase of the ethnic minority population occurred in the seventies (in Rotterdam, from 4.7 percent of the population in 1972 to 12 percent in 1984), "ghettoization" is not overwhelming compared to that found in most U.S. cities. The district of Feijenoord experienced the highest percentage of ethnic minority concentration, but that was only about 40 percent of the population in 1984 (Mik 1987:98).

Explanations of Segregation

The concentration of Turkish and Moroccan immigrants in older industrial regions of the Netherlands is the consequence of the need of employers in older industries (e.g., textile, leather, and food) to recruit workers for unskilled work. In a period of increasing economic growth such as the 1960s, this work was rejected by the relatively well-trained native Dutch. Guest workers in turn looked for better-paid jobs that were unavailable in their home countries. It was hoped that the well-paid jobs would enable workers to save money for either consumption or investment in their home countries. Because the immigrants' stay was not considered permanent, employers offered temporary housing facilities, for example, a Dutch steel factory installed a boat, and other employers offered caravans. Some immigrant workers were housed in guest houses with no more than a bed, which they sometimes used in shifts.

In the seventies most immigrant workers, if they did not return to their country of origin, brought their families to the Netherlands. Better—or in any case more spacious—housing was necessary to accommodate their relatively large families. Housing preferences were restricted by what were, according to Dutch standards, low incomes, and family reunions caused moves from guest houses to apartments in the older residential districts.

The situation of the Surinamese immigrants has been different from that of the Turks and Moroccans. Because Surinam was part of the Kingdom of the Netherlands, the Surinamese had Dutch passports and knew the Dutch language, history, and geography. Thousands of Surinamese, most from upper and middle classes, came to the Netherlands in the 1950s. Most stayed in Amsterdam or another city with ample educational facilities; 7.5 percent of Amsterdam's population is Surinamese-Antillian, the highest in the Netherlands (Muus 1987:21).

In 1974, when Surinam became independent, Surinamese who feared a worsening political and economic situation moved to the Netherlands. These who had few skills preferred to live in the same neighborhoods as family and friends, areas including not only central city areas but also less desirable, hard to let, housing association subsidized units in the suburbs. The remarkable concentration of immigrants of Surinamese origin in some high-rise apartment buildings in the new residential district of Bijlmermeer is exceptional. Initially, two- or three-bedroom apartments of the "gallery" type had been designated for native Dutch families with children. But as a consequence of extra facilities such as elevators, parking garages, and parks between buildings, the all-inclusive rents became too high for Dutch families, who preferred older and cheaper apartments.

As owner of the Bijlmermeer apartment houses, the housing associations had to choose either to accept high vacancy costs or to offer the units to households who did not conform to the allocation rules that specified giving units only to families who had lived in Amsterdam for some years. As Surinamese in the early 1970s immigrated in large numbers, one housing association began to assign units to Surinamese families, and problems developed. Because of overcrowding, conflicting life-styles, a large number of unemployed young Surinamese, and the lack of social control in the large and massive-looking apartment building, one building, Gliphoeve, with a high concentration of Surinamese (90 percent in 1975) had to be renovated completely (Van Kempen 1986).

In comparison with Turkish and Moroccan immigrants, Surinamese are generally less concentrated and segregated; they are more likely than the other groups to be dispersed throughout the outer city. This can be explained by the Dutch government's policy from 1975–79 to reserve for special categories 5 percent of the units in each new housing project of rent-subsidized dwellings—in practice, mainly for Surinamese and Antillians.

Another factor that might explain lower rates of concentration and segregation among Surinamese is that they do not offer each other help in looking for housing to the degree that Turks and Moroccans do. These Mediterranean groups either look for housing in their neighborhood or give the needed information (addresses of letting offices or government offices) on behalf of family members or people from the same village or town. Mik notes that 45 percent of the Turks helped each other, whereas only 25 percent of the Surinamese do (Mik 1987:143). De Smidt also concludes that the help of friends and acquaintances was decisive in Mediterraneans finding jobs and houses (1980:168).

Changing Residential Patterns of Turks and Moroccans

The gradual increase of the proportion of Turks and Moroccans in the somewhat less rundown residential districts built from 1906–44 seems to conform to Burgess's concentric zonal theory. However, the move of immigrant workers from the zone of transition (city and districts built before 1906) to prewar lower-class districts is not because of the extension of the C.B.D. but rather to family reunions. After family reunions guest workers left guest houses and moved into the newer residential districts with apartments more appropriate for families. Changes in the composition of the population in older residential districts cannot be considered invasion and succession; such a proposition cannot be supported. The percentages of Turks and Moroccans in the districts increased only gradually in the period under investigation (1974–84) and remained below 50 percent for all ethnic minorities counted together (table 3.2). The oldest residential districts (measured by building age) have the highest percentages of Turks and Moroccans. In 1984 the percentage of Mediterraneans in the oldest zones

TABLE 3.2.   Turks and Moroccans as Percent of Total
Population in Residential Districts of Three Large
Dutch Cities

Districts	1974	1979	1984	%Change (1979–84)
Amsterdam				
C.B.D.	2.8	1.8	1.8	100
Inner-city districts	1.8	1.6	2.4	150
Districts built before 1906	1.8	5.7	8.2	144
Districts 1906–30	1.8	7.3	12.4	170
Districts 1906–30 with many housing-act dwellings	1.2	3.4	6.2	182
Districts 1931–44	0.8	3.9	7.4	190
Districts prewar high status	0.9	0.8	1.4	175
Districts 1945–59	0.5	2.4	5.6	233
Districts from 1960	0.4	0.7	1.7	243
Districts after 1971	—	—	0.1	—
Total	1.2	3.5	6.1	174
Rotterdam				
C.B.D.	10.3	5.4	5.0	92
Districts built before 1906	10.7	16.2	19.0	117
Districts 1906–30	3.8	6.9	12.5	181
Districts 1931–44	1.4	2.4	4.0	167
Districts prewar high status	0.7	0.8	1.3	162
Districts 1945–59	0.5	0.9	2.1	233
Districts 1960–79	0.4	0.5	1.4	280
Districts after 1979	—	—	0.8	—
Remaining districts	0.5	0.4	1.9	475
Total	3.4	5.2	7.6	146
The Hague				
C.B.D.	3.6	3.7	2.8	76
Districts built before 1906	7.5	9.6	12.3	128
Districts 1906–44	3.8	6.4	9.5	148
Districts prewar high status	0.5	0.6	0.8	133
Districts postwar high status	0.8	0.8	0.8	100
Districts 1945–59	0.4	0.8	2.3	288
Districts 1960–79	0.5	0.5	1.0	200
Districts after 1979	—	—	1.0	—
Remaining districts	0.6	0.6	1.0	167
Total	2.4	3.4	4.6	135

Source: Van Praag (1985).

(those built before 1906) was no more than 20 percent in any of the
large cities. However, a considerable increase occurred between 1974
and 1984 in the percentage of Mediterraneans in newer prewar and
even in the postwar districts. In the period 1974–84 the percentage of
Turks and Moroccans in the C.B.D.s decreased in all three cities (table
(3.2). On behalf of family reunion they looked for more appropriate

accommodation, which could not be found in the C.B.D.s. Authorities required the immigrants to have appropriate accommodation before allowing them to bring their families to the Netherlands. Thus Turks and Moroccans had no other choice than to rent or even buy an apartment in an old residential district. Compared to the native Dutch, they sometimes paid two or three times as much per month for the mortgage as the Dutch paid for rent (Van Hoorn and Van Ginkel 1986:190; Werkgroep Huisvesting Etnische Minderheden 1982). The increase between 1979 and 1984 in minorities in the somewhat less deteriorated districts built from 1906 to 1944 is larger than in the oldest districts, although only slightly. What is much more striking is the relative increase in the number of immigrants in the postwar districts—an increase of 200–300 percent, whereas the increase in the prewar districts varies from 117–181 percent (see last column of table 3.2). These changes can be explained by the housing associations and local authorities' policy decision to open postwar public housing stock to ethnic minorities, particularly to Turks and Moroccans. The national government monitored these authorities to prevent discrimination of ethnic minorities.

One must be cautious in assuming that the described changes of residence reflect an improvement of the housing situation among most Turks and Moroccans. First, in all three cities the older postwar districts built in the period between 1945 and 1959 still have higher percentages of Turks and Moroccans than do the ones built between 1960 and 1979. Urban renewal in the prewar districts has led to a decrease in the number of older and cheaper dwellings. In order to move to a renovated or completely new dwelling in their residential district, the Mediterranean groups had to pay higher rents. As a research report proved, Turkish and Moroccan households often preferred to move to another old, inexpensive dwelling in the same district or, if that was not available, to move to an inexpensive unit in a district still farther away from the city center (Directoriaat-Generaal van de Volkshuisvesting 1984).

It has been found that the Turks and Moroccans, especially in the postwar districts, are most likely to live in public housing apartments built in the fifties and sixties. Because of the housing shortage of the era, the quality of such housing is below present standards; the apartments usually lack modern facilities like elevators, central heating, or bathrooms. Sometimes they are poorly insulated and not sound proof.

Various groups' life-styles may cause others to move. Vacancy and turnover rates in such apartments are high, as the Dutch families that are able to afford a single family house leave. Because no other native Dutch families or singles want to live in the substandard apartments, housing authorities often assign the vacant dwellings to Turkish and Moroccan households. It is difficult to know whether this is because of the preferences of these Mediterraneans, the greater availability of dwellings, or to the hidden policy of local government or housing association officials.

The "Invasion" of Turkish Families into a High-Status District

As figures for the city of The Hague show, Turkish and Moroccan population has not increased in high-status residential districts: the percentage of Turkish and Moroccan inhabitants in these districts varies from 0.8 in The Hague to 1.3 in Rotterdam and 1.4 in Amsterdam. Although the number of families who actually moved to these districts is still low, it is interesting to note which Mediterranean families took the plunge and moved and which families did not. As an experiment, the local government of Rotterdam collaborated with a housing association to reserve some vacant apartments for Turkish families—an idea that caused considerable unrest in the high-status residential district selected. An invasion of Turkish families, and the resulting tensions between native Dutch and the Turkish families, was feared. Ultimately about sixty Turkish families did accept the offer of an apartment in the district.

Interviews with both the families who had accepted and those who had refused showed some obvious differences. As the rents of the offered apartments in the high-status district were considerably higher than the rents the Turkish families paid in the older districts, one would expect that those who accepted would have higher incomes than those who refused. However, on the average the accepting families had lower incomes. Instead, the explanation seemed to be that accepting an apartment in the high-status district was attributed to a "modern-dynamic pattern of culture" (Blauw 1985). The acceptors could be characterized as having more likely lived in the past in a Turkish city, being younger, and having smaller households, working wives, and fewer financial obligations to family in Turkey. They also were less strict in regard to religious rules, more fluent in the Dutch language, less inclined to return to their country of origin, and more willing to integrate into Dutch society (Blauw 1985; Blauw and Ravestein-Willis 1984).

Changing Housing Situation
of Ethnic Minorities

To explain the described patterns of segregation and concentration it is also necessary to have a closer look at the housing situation of the ethnic minorities. Initially Turks and Moroccans, compared to Surinamese, made a different start in their housing careers. As discussed previously, these Mediterranean groups entered the country as single workers and were housed by their employers, private companies in older industries. The Surinamese, as Dutch citizens, were looked after by the national government, which felt responsible for their housing. From their arrival in the Netherlands, 5 percent of public housing units in newly built projects was reserved for Surinamese and Antillians. While Turks and Moroccans are now moving to the districts built in the fifties and sixties, Surinamese have already moved to newer residential districts in the suburbs with better housing.

In comparing these groups' present situation with their situation ten years ago, one can say the ethnic minorities' housing situation appears more favorable. If we assume the lack of desire to change one's residence is an indication of housing satisfaction, a remarkable improvement may be observed, either because of housing improvement or because of ethnic minorities' previous change of residence. In 1981, more than 50 percent of ethnic immigrants expressed the desire to change residence within the next two years. In 1985–86 about one-fourth expressed this wish (for Dutch natives it was 10 percent). The reason given most frequently for changing dwellings was the quality of the housing; poor quality was cited by 60 percent of the Moroccans and 45 percent of the Turks and Surinamese. The next most important reason for change was the wish to have a cheaper dwelling.

Although an improvement of ethnic minorities' housing situations can be observed, there are still major differences compared to the situation of the native Dutch. Two-thirds of the Dutch live in single-family houses, whereas by 1986 only one-third of the Turks and Moroccans lived in such a house. (The figures herein are derived from the 1985–86 National Housing Needs Survey and published in Ankersmit, Roelandt, and Veenman 1988.) The circumstances of these Mediterraneans with large families present an even more obvious difference. The mean number of residents per dwelling for Turkish and Moroccan households was about twice that of the mean number for the Dutch population: 4.5 versus 2.6 (Van Praag 1986). Moroccan families in particular are often large: 41 percent have six persons or more, as opposed to 22 percent of the Turkish, 19 percent of the Surinamese, and 8 percent of the native Dutch.

Only one-fourth of Surinamese households own or rent a single-family house, perhaps because of the group's high percentage of singles (often students): 35 percent of Antillian households and 24 percent of Surinamese households are singles. Some assume that Surinamese and the Antillians on the average have a stronger preference for apartment dwellings than Turks and Moroccans.

Another striking difference between native Dutch and ethnic minorities is home ownership. Whereas 43 percent of the Dutch own their apartment or house, the percentage for ethnic minorities is much lower: 15 percent for Turks, 5 percent for Moroccans, and 14 percent for Surinamese. For Turkish home-owners in particular, the 15 percent figure is misleading and by no means a true indicator of wealth. As discussed previously, many are "emergency buyers," who in their search for housing had no other choice than buying an apartment in older residential districts. They could neither find a private rental nor get into public housing units owned by local authorities or housing associations.

Some immigrants had the chance to move to better and newer dwellings as a consequence of urban renewal in older residential districts. The newly built apartments, distributed by housing associations and local governments, were assigned on the basis of certain criteria, including living in a unit to be pulled down and the length of residence in the district. As has been discussed previously, the Mediterranean groups frequently prefer an older and less expensive dwelling to a renovated or new one.

If immigrants rent new or renovated dwellings, they often rent from a local government, which in general administers lower-quality dwellings compared to those owned by the nonprofit housing associations. Nevertheless, because housing associations are the primary landlords in the Netherlands, between 50 and 60 percent of the immigrants rent an apartment or terraced house from housing associations. In line with national policy toward ethnic minorities, the government keeps a careful watch to see that semiprivate housing associations, operating with government subsidies and under government rules, do not exclusively assign dwellings to their own members (initially the housing associations had strong affiliations with unions or religious institutions) and assign a reasonable number of dwellings to ethnic minorities. On the basis of the national housing surveys, it appears that during the first half of the eighties the housing situation of the Mediterranean groups improved (Van Praag 1986).

Differences in Housing Situations between Ethnic Groups

Monthly rents paid by Surinamese households have been higher than those paid by Turks and Moroccans. Whereas nearly 40 percent of Turks and Moroccans pay less than 250 Dutch guilder, only 25 percent of the Surinamese pay such low rents. Taking into account the average lower incomes of Surinamese, this means that they place a higher priority on housing. They are also more likely to take individual rent subsidies: 40 percent receive a subsidy, as opposed to 24 percent of Moroccans and 18 percent of Turks. (Because governmental individual rent subsidies are dependent on the proportion of income spent for rent, the higher this proportion the more rent subsidy is given, although a maximum has been fixed.) Even if Turks and Moroccans have the right to claim such a subsidy, only one-fifth of them do so. This might be caused by their unfamiliarity with the subsidy system, but may also be caused by their unwillingness to be dependent on or involved with bureaucracy.

Turks and Moroccans may expend less money on rent because they hold to the idea of returning to their country of origin and consequently want to save money for that event. They often have financial obligations to their family in the country of origin, and, of course, the cost of living for the relative large families means that they must keep down rent costs. It might also be that there are hindrances of a different kind to obtaining access to better and more expensive housing.

Obstacles to Obtaining Better Housing

Although it is understandable that Mediterranean groups stay in inexpensive apartments in older residential districts, there is no indication that they do not wish to move to better dwellings in newer districts. They do move more and more often to newer residential districts, as the figures in table 3.2 show. They are housed in three- or four-story apartments that become available as original Dutch residents move to better housing. Nevertheless, the Mediterranean groups still must wait longer on the average than do native Dutch to be assigned to a unit. The question arises of whether any hindrances are put forth by government offices to make it more difficult for Turks and Moroccans to acquire a dwelling in the public housing sector.

Legally there are no hindrances to stop Mediterranean groups from gaining access to public housing. A decision of the Rotterdam city council in 1972 to limit the percentage of ethnic minorities in residential districts to 5 percent and not let larger numbers in has been reversed. In practice, however, housing authorities likely take ethnic background into consideration when assigning dwellings. At the beginning of the eighties, housing authorities operated according to rules intended to disperse ethnic immigrants over a number of housing blocks in order to prevent concentrations. In accordance with government policy based on the rejection of discrimination and the favoring of ethnic minorities before native Dutch ("positive discrimination"), the Ministry of Housing instructed local governments to report annually about the allocation of their housing units. Unintentionally the allocation system may disadvantage ethnic immigrants because they were hampered by required residence qualifications in their early phase of immigration; male immigrants could not register as long as their families did not reside in the Netherlands.

Informal Obstacles

More problematic and more difficult to fight are informal obstacles. When housing officials fear that native Dutch residents might protest having Turks or Moroccans as neighbors, they sometimes are inclined to prejudge the likelihood of protest and overreact by not assigning a housing unit to a Mediterranean family. The known preference of Mediterranean groups to live in inexpensive apartments also might easily be abused, with officials not assigning them a housing unit if it is costly. The longer waiting times for Turks and Moroccans might be attributed to these practices, but it is also obvious that no fit exists between the demand of the Mediterranean groups and the supply of dwellings available. There is a shortage of appropriate dwellings for members of these groups. Many need more rooms than public-sector dwellings usually contain, and they are not willing to pay the relatively high rents for the new apartments and terraced houses (Kornalijnslijper 1988). The national government has tried to stimulate local governments to create larger units by subsidizing such accommodations and by combining two existing dwellings. However, local governments did not prove to be very active in doing this, although when they did accomplish such renovation the dwellings were indeed assigned to ethnic minorities.

Position on Labor Market

The housing situation of ethnic minorities in the Netherlands has been the focus of this chapter. However, it is evident that their housing situation is determined by their social and economic position in Dutch society. From research on the position of ethnic minorities in urban renewal areas, it has been found that they participated in residents' meetings but were not represented on the committees charged with executing building plans (Van der Pennen and Wuertz 1985). In general, ethnic minorities' position in the housing market is weak as a consequence of not understanding the allocation system, and as a consequence of their position in the labor market. As unskilled workers, they often are the first to become unemployed and thus require inexpensive dwellings. As the national government, as in other Western countries, retires from the housing market and tries to reduce its subsidies in the public housing sector, these ethnic minorities' prospect for housing improvement becomes more and more dependent on the flow of Dutch residents from cheap to more expensive dwellings.

Conclusion

The immigration of ethnic minorities, Surinamese-Antillian and Mediterranean, to the Netherlands is a recent phenomenon. The Mediterraneans' stay was initially considered temporary. When it appeared that after family reunions their presence would be permanent, the national government proclaimed a minority policy to better their living conditions. Surinamese are less segregated and concentrated and better accommodated, primarily because of the policy to reserve for them a fixed percentage of newly built apartment houses. Turks and Moroccans live in more segregated and concentrated areas, initially in guest houses as single workers; after family reunion they have no other choice than to buy or rent an apartment in the old residential districts of Dutch cities. When housing associations opened their housing stock to Turks and Moroccans, more and more of them moved to the substandard apartments of housing associations in the postwar districts. In general their housing situation has improved, although they still live in less desirable units. As a consequence of the changing economic situation in the Netherlands, the national government is trying to reduce the subsidies in the public housing sector, which could bring immigrants' chances for more improvement in housing quality to a standstill.

References

Ankersmit, T., T. Roelandt, and J. Veenman. 1988. *Minderheden in Nederland: Statistisch Vademecum* (Minorities in the Netherlands: Statistic vademecum). The Hague: Staatsuitgeverij.

Atzema. O. A. L. C., and J. Buursink. 1985. "The Regional Distribution of Mediterraneans in the Netherlands." Pp. 27–44 in *Contemporary Studies of Migration,* edited by Paul E. White and Bert van der Knaap. Norwich: Geobooks.

Blauw, P. W. 1980. "Segregatie: een overzicht (Segregation: a review)." Pp. 9–24 in *Soort bij soort: Beschouwingen over ruimtelijke segregatie als maatschappelijk probleem* (The same sort: Spatial segregation as a social problem), edited by P. W. Blauw and C. Pastor. Deventer: Van Loghum Slaterus.

———. 1985. "De buitenwijk: ook voor buitenlanders? (The suburb: also for foreigners?)." *Sociogische Gids* 32:271–83.

Blauw, P. W., and S. J. Ravestein-Willis. 1984. *Buitenstaanders in een buitenwijk* (Outsiders in a suburb). Rotterdam: Erasmus Universiteit.

Brouwers, Y. C. J., M. C. Deurloo, and L. De Klerk. 1987. *Selectieve verhuisbewegingen en segregatie* (Selective migration and segregation). Amsterdam: KNAG/Institute of Human Geography, University of Amsterdam.

De Smidt, M. 1980. "Concentratie, segregatie en huisvestingsperikelen van gastarbeiders in de gemeente Utrecht (Concentration, segregation and housing-perils of 'guest-workers' in the city of Utrecht)." Pp. 160–72 in *Soort bij soort: Beschouwingen over ruimtelijke segregatie als maatschappelijk probleem* (The same sort: Spatial segregation as a social problem), edited by P. W. Blauw and C. Pastor. Deventer: Van Loghum Slaterus.

Directoraat-Generaal van de Volkshuisvesting. Directie Onderzoek. 1984. *Stadsvernieuwing en minderheden* (Urban renovation and ethnic minorities). Zoetermeer: Ministerie van Volkshuisvesting, Ruimtelijke Ordening en Milieubeheer.

Ellemers, J. E., and R. E. F. Vaillant. 1987. "Indische Nederlanders en gerepatrieerden: de grootste categorie naoorlogse immigranten (Dutch-Indonesian and repatriated people: The largest category of post-war immigrants)." *Tijdschrift voor Geschiedenis* 100:412–31.

Kornalijnslijper, N. 1988. "Minderheden en structurele belemmeringen in de volkshuisvesting (Minorities and structural constraints in public housing)." *Migrantenstudies* 4:67–78.

Mik, G. 1987. *Segregatie in het grootstedelijk milieu: Theorie en Rotterdamse werkelijkheid* (Segregation in the urban environment: Theory and reality). Rotterdam: Erasmus Universiteit, Economisch-Geografisch Instituut.

Ministerie van Binnenlandse Zaken. 1983. *Minderhedennota* (Report on ethnic minorities). The Hague: Staatsuitgeverij.

Muus, Philip J. 1987. *Migration, Minorities and Policy in the Netherlands: Recent Trends and Developments.* Amsterdam: University of Amsterdam, Institute of Human Geography.

Prinssen, J., and J. Kropman. 1986. *The huisvesting van ethnische minderheden geregeld?* (Arrangements of housing of ethnic minorities? Report on the use and efforts of departmental instructions). Nijmegen: ITS.

Times (London). 1972. August 12.

Van Amersfoort, Hans, and Leo de Klerk. 1986. "Surinamers in Amsterdam (Surinamese in Amsterdam)." *Intermediair* 22:15–21.

Van Hoorn, F. J. J. H., and J. A. Van Ginkel. 1986. "Racial Leapfrogging in a Controlled Housing Market: The Case of the Mediterranean Minority in Utrecht, the Netherlands." *Tijdschrift voor Economische en Sociale Geografie* 77:187–96.

Van Kempen, Eva. 1986. "High-Rise Housing Estates and the Concentration of Poverty." *The Netherlands Journal of Housing and Environmental Research* 1:5–26.

Van der Pennen, T., and K. Wuertz. 1985. *Bouwen voor de kleurrijke buurt* (Building for a colourful neighbourhood). The Hague: VUGA.

Van Praag, C. S. 1985. "Spreiding van Mediterranen. (Spreading of Mediterraneans)." *Stedebouw en Volkshuisvesting* 65:217–24.

———. 1986. *De woonsituatie van etnische minderheden: Ontwikkelingen 1980–1985* (The housing-conditions of ethnic minorities: Developments 1980–1985). Rijswijk: Sociaal en Cultureel Planbureau.

Werkgroep Huisvesting Etnische Minderheden. 1982. *De huisvesting van etnische minderheden in Utrecht* (The housing of ethnic minorities in Utrecht). Utrecht: Gemeente Utrecht.

4. Racial Segregation in Britain: Patterns, Processes, and Policy Approaches

Black minority group segregation is a distinctive feature of many British cities. Although it does not compare in scale and degree of deprivation to North American ghettos, clusters of blacks (Afro-Caribbeans and South Asians) in Britain are well defined and have, over their relatively short history, shown few signs of dissipating. The clusters may vary in size from single blocks of flats in rented housing developments (estates) to extensive tracts of owner-occupied nineteenth-century housing in the inner city. The forces which shape them are nevertheless much the same: social, cultural, economic, and political forces all come into play. As in America, these clusters speak most forcibly of long-term social and economic deprivation underpinned by systematic discrimination and covert and overt hostility against the black population, in housing and in other spheres.

Unlike other more common forms of segregation (for example, on the basis of class, income, or life-style), black minority clustering has attracted considerable national interest and concern. Sensationalized in the media and a political issue for both the right and the left (for the former it provides substance to calls for further immigration control, while for the latter it is a symbol of social inequality and discrimination), it has provided a pivotal point for debates about race and immigration, social deprivation, and environmental decay. Places such as Liverpool "8," the London areas of Brixton, Notting Hill, and Spitalfields, Handsworth in Birmingham, Mosside in Manchester, and inner areas of various other Midland and Northern towns such as Leicester and Bradford are all well known for their black populations. Their reputation conjures up images of "problem areas," with high levels of crime, poor housing, alien life-styles, and the possibility of civil unrest—images that have prompted a common call for action from the public and the politicians, the right and the left wing. There is not, however, consensus on the appropriate course of action to pursue.

In this chapter, we look at the complex interweaving of factors at the national and the local level that produce and sustain a pattern of black residential segregation in Britain. We will argue that black segregation is the spatial manifestation not only of social and cultural differences between the indigenous and minority groups, but also of the social divisions and inequalities in British society. We focus particularly on the role of the major housing institutions in reflecting and reproducing those divisions. Finally, we consider postwar policy attempts to address black segregation and its worst consequences.

The following discussion of "black" segregation is primarily concerned with migrants from the Afro-Caribbean and what is termed *South Asia*—India, Pakistan, and Bangladesh. These countries (except now Pakistan) form part of the New Commonwealth, with which Britain has special ex-colonial ties.

Black Migrants and Settlers

The large-scale immigration of New Commonwealth and Pakistani citizens into Britain formed part of a widespread postwar movement of labor from less-developed, economically depressed countries to the advanced industrialized nations of Western Europe (Castles 1984). Expanding industrial economies, threatened by labor shortages at home, were eager to tap cheap, mobile labor forces abroad. Britain's link with the New Commonwealth countries was to provide an economic lifeline, which delayed, although it did not prevent, the contraction of many labor-intensive industries such as textiles in the fifties and sixties. An early program of direct recruitment by some major public-sector employers such as British Transport and the National Health Service provided a catalyst to the flow of workers. Afro-Caribbeans, especially those from Jamaica, were among the first to arrive, but they were soon followed by Indians and Pakistanis and then by Bangladeshis (Peach 1968; Robinson 1980). The socioeconomic position of these new arrivals in Britain was shaped by the material and ideological circumstances of their migration and by their role as a replacement population in terms of both jobs and housing. Black workers generally moved into jobs for which white workers could no longer be found and into housing that was in least demand from the white population, largely that in run-down, inner-city areas. The seeds of segregation were thus sown in those earliest days.

This international movement of labor to Britain proceeded at a rapid rate until 1962, when the first of the postwar immigration controls was introduced. The needs of the expanding economy having been satisfied, the entry of the poorly skilled migrant from the New Commonwealth was restricted (Dummett 1986). Dependents and refugees (particularly Asians from East Africa) have sustained the flow from the New Commonwealth and Pakistan over the years, but the overall level of black immigration has fallen steadily (Booth 1986). The question of black entry nevertheless continues to preoccupy the public, fueled by press speculation that Britain is being "swamped" by foreigners, and to stimulate political debate. The level of concern is exemplified by the general tenor of successive, highly selective immigration controls directed at keeping black immigrants (especially Asian dependents) out.

The number of South Asians and Afro-Caribbeans in Britain has been a long-standing preoccupation of those who advocate tighter immigration control and fear the changing character of the British nation. Their estimates have often been wildly high. In fact, the statistics show that in 1981, New Commonwealth and Pakistani inhabitants comprised fewer than 5 percent of the total population of Britain (i.e., 2.4 million). The black minorities are, however, conspicuous not only because they are residentially segregated, overrepresented both within particular parts of the country and within specific areas of the towns where they have settled, but also because "race" has become an important basis for social differentiation in Britain. The importance of this process of social categorization, together with the value-laden judgments that accompany it, will be considered later in this chapter. But first we examine the evidence and implications of black minority segregation in Britain.

Black Segregation: The Pattern

The initial settlement of the Afro-Caribbean and South Asian population in Britain was conspicuous for its unevenness at every scale, from town to town, neighborhood to neighborhood, and street to street. Black minority groups themselves were also unevenly distributed. While many Indians and Pakistanis gravitated to the small northern textile towns, more Afro-Caribbeans were drawn to the large metropolitan areas; more than two-thirds of the latter group settled in the London and West Midlands conurbations (Peach, Winchester, and Woods 1975; Jones 1978). Likewise, within the more cosmopolitan reception centers, the areas of Indian (particularly Sikh) settlement could be clearly distinguished from Pakistani and Bangladeshi areas and were indeed loosely sorted along regional and even village lines. In turn, South Asian clusters could be distinguished from Afro-Caribbean areas, which often had their own internal arrangement by island origin (Peach 1984; Robinson 1986). These patterns were to be reinforced later by a resorting of black groups as job opportunities changed.

The broad pattern of black minority settlement at the interurban level clearly reflects the material and ideological conditions under which South Asians and Afro-Caribbeans migrated to Britain, as well as the importance of cultural ties among the newcomers. As economic migrants commanding little power in the job or housing market, their early distribution mirrored the structure of the unskilled job opportunities open to them (Peach 1968). As opportunities changed, largely in response to industrial restructuring and recession, so adjustments in the interurban distribution of black newcomers were made. Most obviously, the more prosperous immigrant reception areas, notably London, experienced a growth in their black populations at the expense of those with declining job prospects. However, as the recession took hold and more of traditional immigrant employment opportunities were lost, the impetus for interurban movement declined. At that stage some South Asians and Afro-Caribbeans opted to return home, or reemigrate to the EEC countries or Canada, but most remained in the established reception areas where, even in the most affluent areas, they have become disproportionately represented among the unemployed.

While the interurban flow of migrants within Britain has been structured by the job market, the particular destinations selected by the minority who move have been influenced by ethnic and regional ties. For example, South Asians throughout the East Midlands gravitated to Leicester, with its established Asian community, whereas Afro-Caribbeans were more likely to join friends and relatives in places such as Bedford, Luton, or London. Chain migration from abroad helped to reinforce this pattern of ethnic differentiation, and distinctive focuses for the separate black minorities in Britain gradually emerged. Within the South Asian community, the Punjabi Sikh population is particularly well represented in Birmingham and in Southall (London), the East African Asians in Leicester, the Pakistani Muslims in Bradford and Birmingham, and more than one-half of the Bangladeshi minority is clustered in the East End of London. Each center plays an important role in maintaining the distinctive social, cultural, and economic life of the minority groups.

It is, however, at the intraurban level that black minority concentration and segregation in Britain are most explicit. The early pattern of New Commonwealth and Pakistani settlement within the urban areas is a familiar story; postwar immigrants throughout North America and Europe have followed similar paths. Black newcomers, poor, lacking information about their new surroundings, and victims of hostility and suspicion, were invariably forced to settle in the declining areas of cheaper housing within the inner city—the well-known twilight zones of deprivation and decay. A severe housing shortage compounded the difficulties experienced by the earliest arrivals to Britain, while overt discrimination by landlords, who not uncommonly displayed such signs as "No Coloureds, No Irish, No Dogs," further reduced their housing options. Despite appalling conditions within the rental sector, rooms let to blacks were far from cheap. Landlords willing to accommodate the new arrivals often inflated their rents through a "newcomer tax" or "foreigners levy" (Milner Holland 1965).

Structural changes during the 1960s, and even more in the 1970s, brought some amelioration in the housing circumstances of early black settlers. In particular, the introduction of antidiscrimination legislation in 1968 had a significant impact on the way in which blacks were treated, at least overtly, while developments within the structure of the housing market brought new openings for aspiring homeowners. However, neither change fundamentally undermined the early pattern of minority concentration and segregation, nor did they erode the relative deprivation suffered by the black population. While race relations legislation did curb the worst excesses of overt discrimination, it failed to tackle the more insidious forms of indirect discrimination rife within the institutions of the housing market at the time. Thus, in many towns, despite the urgent need of black newcomers for accommodation, the council (public) housing sector remained effectively closed to them because of residence qualifications and minimum registration periods on housing lists of up to five years. The limited options of blacks within the private sector were further reduced by the rules of the dominant private housing institutions, which systematically worked to the disadvantage of the black minorities; for example, building society (savings and loan bank) restrictions on inner-city lending disproportionately affected black applicants at that time, leaving them to shoulder much of the financial burden of purchase. With mortgages rationed, building societies had little interest in risky inner-city deals when there was plenty of safe business in the suburbs. These were the types of indirect discrimination that were to be addressed by the 1976 Race Relations Act, which made both direct and indirect discrimination unlawful.

It is true that the boom in suburban housing development during the 1960s and 1970s did bring some rewards for aspiring black homeowners, but only indirectly. Hostility from potential white neighbors and vendors coupled with institutional discrimination and economic constraints excluded the suburbs as an option for blacks. The surge in white movement to the suburbs did nevertheless release many cheap, older homes onto the market. Consequently, South Asians and Afro-Caribbeans were able to act (indeed, they had little choice but to act) as a replacement population, purchasing and renting the inner-city properties no longer in so much demand from the indigenous population. As white suburbanization continued, spatial polarization between the minority and indigenous groups increased, and black households began to dominate some inner-city areas numerically. This brought cries of alarm from some quarters; it was asserted that a black "take over" of the British city was just beginning. Extreme right-wing politicians (Enoch Powell prominent among them) seized the opportunity to renew the call for black repatriation. The fact that black dominance was highly localized and as much a product of white out-migration as black influx was ignored. The contribution of black minorities toward the stabilization and even revitalization of the declining inner areas was also largely unacknowledged.

It is clear that the pattern and conditions of black minority residence in Britain have changed gradually throughout the 1980s. The decade brought some great advances. The passage of the 1976 Race Relations Act, which addressed the outstanding issue of indirect discrimination, improved minority access to both the public and private housing sector and the socioeconomic status of the minority groups themselves improved slightly. As a result, black minority housing standards rose, and some residential dispersal occurred. However, large-scale movements away from the inner cities have not been forthcoming; these have instead been generally confined to the white minority groups such as Jews (Newman 1985), Poles, and Italians (King and King 1977). The prevailing trend for the South Asian and Afro-Caribbean population has been one of continuing residential concentration, segregation, and deprivation, with a growing overrepresentation within the poorest areas. This is particularly true for the Asian minority, whose potential for residential mixing has been reduced by their relative absence from the public housing sector (in 1982 only 19 percent of

Asian households lived in local authority property compared with 46 percent of Afro-Caribbeans [Brown 1984]). Black minority segregation within the public sector itself, notably in the worst quality inner-city estates, is nevertheless also evident, and inequalities prevail (CRE 1984; Phillips 1986; Henderson and Karn 1987). Furthermore, movement away from the inner city cannot necessarily be equated with access to decent housing for the minority population. Some Afro-Caribbeans have succeeded in escaping from traditional black inner areas through the public housing sector only to find themselves "dumped" on the local authorities' least popular, run-down estates on the urban periphery (Henderson and Karn 1987).

The Degree of Segregation

Many attempts have been made to quantify the level of black and white separation in British cities through indices of segregation. The most commonly applied is the index of dissimilarity, which measures the proportion of the group that would have to move in order to produce an unsegregated pattern. Although notoriously dependent upon the scale of analysis, such indices have provided a useful indication of the character of black and white settlement in different cities and of the stability of the early pattern over time. In the late 1970s, dissimilarity indices of more than 70 (at the census ward level) were commonly reported for the traditional immigrant reception areas; in certain cases, such as Bradford and Huddersfield, the indices exceeded 80 (Cater and Jones 1978). Recent work has confirmed that the intensity of segregation between the South Asian and white population is increasing across the city (Jones 1983). Furthermore, segregation is still typically acute on the local scale and is intensifying. For example, in 1978, the population of some streets in inner Leicester were up to 80 percent South Asian, whereas other streets were completely white (Phillips 1981). By the mid-1980s, many of the more ethnically mixed streets tended toward greater Asian homogeneity, and in some cases the proportion of ethnic households rose to more than 95 percent. This pattern is repeated in the other areas of South Asian settlement such as Birmingham, the Lancashire and Yorkshire mill towns, and Southall in London. The reasons underlying this spatial separation relate to tenure, to social, economic, and cultural differences, and to class and racial discrimination. We return to consider the importance of these in the following sections.

There is little doubt then that the early tendency toward black minority concentration and segregation from the white indigenous population has largely survived the passage of time. But more significantly, the early and close association between minority segregation and social, economic, and environmental deprivation has also persisted despite the passage of antidiscrimination legislation. Major disparities in housing standards of the black and the white population are evident (Brown 1984). For example, Afro-Caribbeans and South Asians are more likely to live in prewar dwellings (60 percent and 74 percent respectively) than the white population (50 percent). They are also twice as likely to live in the terraced (row house) property so commonly associated with inner-city residence in Great Britain. Overcrowding remains a particular problem among South Asians (35 percent live in overcrowded conditions compared with 3 percent of whites), and homelessness has increased greatly in recent years among black minorities, especially in London (GLC 1985). Furthermore, although central and local government-funded rehabilitation plans have reduced the wide discrepancy in the housing amenity levels between blacks and whites in terms of access to a bathroom or an inside W.C., gross differences remain in the design, building standards, and popularity of housing occupied by the two groups.

The pattern of inequality between the black and the indigenous populations living in Britain thus remains entrenched. This holds across and within tenures. Indeed, the high level of owner occupation among the South Asian population provides no guarantee of good housing or of a decent neighborhood. A third of South Asian owner-occupiers live in overcrowded accommodations and more than 80 percent live in pre-1945 properties. This has a number of repercussions, not only in terms of the quality of life they can expect, but also in terms of the high level of repair expenditure required by older property and the difficulties of attracting mortgage finance. Moreover, as differentials in the quality and the investment value of inner-city and suburban property increase, minority owners find the prospect of moving up the housing ladder receding further (Karn, Kemeny, and Williams 1985). For too many, the inner city has become a trap—a symbol of constraints upon spatial mobility and of obstacles to social and economic advancement.

Processes of Black Segregation

Residential segregation of South Asian and Afro-Caribbean minorities from the indigenous population in Britain is rooted in a number of factors ranging from the cultural to the economic, the social to the political. Here, we consider the way in which those processes have reproduced a distinctive pattern of settlement, one that can no longer be attributed to the newcomer status of the incoming groups. We argue that in the case of the black minorities in Britain, segregation in itself is not the salient issue; of greater immediate concern is the continuing association, described earlier, between segregation and deprivation. This relationship, indicative of the low standing (both economically and politically) of the black minorities in British society, is underpinned by the historical relationship between the sending and receiving countries and the contemporary circumstances of New Commonwealth and Pakistani settlement in postwar Britain. It is sustained by systematic discrimination against the black minority groups at both an institutional and an individual level.

Before exploring the bleaker aspects of black residential segregation in Britain, it is important to acknowledge the positive forces for the enduring pattern of South Asian and Afro-Caribbean segregation. There is no doubt that ethnic residential clustering has brought considerable social and cultural benefits for those settling within an alien and often openly hostile society (Hiro 1971; Kearsley and Srivastava 1974; Lee 1977; Carey and Shukur 1985). The proximity of group members has facilitated social interaction (especially important where there are language differences) and fostered mutual support, while spatial cohesion has enabled the minorities to reproduce, at least in part, their traditional way of life. This has been of particular importance for the Indians, Pakistanis, and Bangladeshis, who have been anxious to preserve distinctive religious, linguistic, and cultural traditions. Indeed, studies have shown that physical separation, which limits minority contact with the indigenous population, has been favored by South Asian minorities in the past to maintain the social and cultural exclusiveness of their group (Jeffery 1976; Khan 1977). Such evidence would seem to support Dahya's (1974) notion of South Asian "voluntary non-participation" in the receiving society, which rests on the notion of the migrant as a temporary sojourner. Cultural contamination, it is argued, would only jeopardize the returning migrant's status in the homeland.

The passing of the decades has seen some return migration, but the majority of Afro-Caribbean and South Asian migrants have stayed. As ethnic communities have taken root within the inner city, so social and cultural institutions as well as religious and educational amenities have emerged. Thriving ethnic centers, such as those of the South

Asian population in Bradford, Birmingham and Leicester, and South-all and Spitalfields in London, provide an anchor for the local minority population (Aldrich et al. 1981). Mosques and temples, ethnic shops, banks, businesses, and cinemas all reinforce the tendency for cluster-ing. Over time, the larger clusters have themselves become spatially differentiated along religious, regional, and linguistic lines. The spatial organization of the South Asian clusters in Leicester, Birmingham, and elsewhere is indicative of deep social divisions within the group. Although the distinctions may be blurred at the broadest scale, clearly defined patterns of spatial separation are often evident at the neigh-borhood and street level. The spatial polarization of Muslims and Hindus in Leicester, or in the case of Birmingham, Muslims and Sikhs, is the most explicit. In Leicester, for example, a dissimilarity index of 42.1 was calculated at the ward level between Muslims and Hindus (Phillips 1983). The pattern in part reflects the distribution of key religious institutions, with subgroups clustering around the temples and mosques. There is, however, also evidence of group avoidance (Muslims have been known to refuse council house offers because of the proximity of Hindu tenants) and exclusion, with vendors from one particular subgroup discriminating against prospective purchasers from another in order to maintain the social cohesion of their street.

Spatial divisions within an ethnic cluster are, however, less pro-nounced than those between the black and white populations. Physical segregation still has a particularly important role to play in the main-tenance of social and cultural boundaries between minority and indig-enous groups. Interviews with Asians living in central Leicester in the late 1970s indicated that nearly 90 percent of the respondents still strongly endorsed the principle of ethnic segregation from the indig-enous population for social and cultural reasons (Phillips 1981). This was especially important for the culturally exclusive Muslim popula-tion and became more so with the Islamic revival of the mid-1970s. However, the Asian minorities' reasons for wanting to live within the confines of the ethnic territory went beyond the cultural. More than a quarter were also willing to acknowledge that clustering had a wider defensive purpose; it gave them a sense of security in a potentially hostile white environment and reduced the fear of racial attack. It was thus clear that the boundaries of the black and white space were being maintained by the indigenous population as well.

The notion of the ethnic cluster as a haven, a basis for conflict avoidance, throws a different light on the role of the segregated ethnic minority territory and raises some important questions. First, to what extent might the minority group's commitment to social and cultural exclusiveness be reinforced by their experience of rejection by the dominant white British society? Ethnographic research has indicated that black ethnicity in Britain is not simply reactive (Jeffery 1976; Carey and Shukur 1985). Nevertheless, as Khan (1982) has observed, minority culture preservation must be understood in terms of the continuing interaction between the dominant ethnic majority and the subordinate ethnic minorities. South Asians and Afro-Caribbeans have long been dubbed a social problem, a threat to the nation, and have been stigmatized as alien and inferior by public officials, by the media, and in political discourse (Hartmann and Husband 1974; Rex and Tomlinson 1979; Anwar 1986). Their outsider status is confirmed on a day-to-day basis by a process of individual and institutional "social closure" against them (Parkin 1979), through which they have been deprived of the material and symbolic rewards of British society. Within this context, the minority might well opt to strengthen their cultural autonomy as both a resource and a refuge in a hostile society (Jeffery 1976; Hall and Jefferson 1976).

Second, it must be asked to what extent culture preservation is contingent upon spatial segregation? The emergence of Rastafarianism, a West Indian religious movement which has its roots in black alienation through white domination, among young Afro-Caribbeans has no necessary spatial counterpart. Also, research in Leicester has indicated that second-generation South Asians no longer regard spatial proximity as a prerequisite for social propinquity and cultural cohesion. The maintenance of community and family ties are important to the young Asians, as is access to their ethnic institutions. In this they differ only minimally from their parents. But increasing residential mobility, especially with greater automobile and telephone ownership, has overridden the perceived need to cluster for cultural reasons. Moreover, the wide-ranging provision of ethnic goods and services through minority institutions appears to have decreased the perceived cultural threat from the indigenous population and thus the need for physical isolation from them. Boundary maintenance and cultural separateness can thus now be seen to be as much an institutional process as a physical condition.

The potential for minority dispersal throughout the British city is, however, limited. As Cater and Jones (1978:88) have emphasized, "as subordinate minorities, [blacks] do not exert any real control over spatial allocation, which is a majority group preserve." White institutions, with their greater control over power and resources, still by and large determine where the boundaries to black and white space will be drawn.

Black minority segregation and deprivation is produced and sustained through widespread institutional discrimination against the South Asian and Afro-Caribbean population in Britain. The process is one of cumulative disadvantage, which arises, for example, from discrimination against black minority groups in the job market and the education system, by the police (especially in relation to racial harassment), and the judiciary, as well as in the housing market itself. The institutions of both the public and private housing sectors play a major role within this mutually reinforcing "web of urban racism" (Baron 1969). Despite race relations legislation, banks and building societies, estate agents, and public housing departments have been found to discriminate systematically against black competitors for housing resources. The black minorities are not alone in their disadvantage; housing institutions have long used a range of social criteria, such as "race," class, and gender, as a basis for allocating their resources. But as negative racial ideologies articulate with class prejudices, South Asians and Afro-Caribbeans find themselves in a position of special disadvantage.

Racial inequality in housing differs from class inequality in that racial discrimination is illegal. But it is one thing to put legal or other pressure upon an individual landlord or estate agent not to discriminate and quite another to grapple with the large and powerful institutions that dominate the housing system—local authorities and building societies. Despite the law, these institutions are still generally characterized by a lack of monitoring of the social outcomes of their policies and day-to-day decisions. There also tends to be a self-protective view on the part of senior management and lower-level officers alike that if there is no specific policy or intention to discriminate, no discrimination can be occurring. Only exceptionally is there any recognition that the major housing institutions may obstruct the achievement of racial equality and indeed tend to protect white privilege against black competition.

Housing managers are prominent among those who have attributed black segregation and deprivation to minority "choice"; the result of a "preference" for clustering and a desire to minimize housing costs. Dahya's return migration hypothesis, which is in part founded on the notion of a voluntary restriction on expenditure in the receiving country, has certainly provided some support for this view. Other authors have also described how early migrants, keen to maximize their remittances to the homeland, were prepared to cut housing costs by living in seemingly intolerable conditions (Aurora 1963; Desai 1963). However, the plausibility of this argument for ethnic segregation and deprivation has declined over time, especially as the likelihood of migrant return to the homeland has diminished. Evidence suggests that South Asians and Afro-Caribbeans are now far more concerned with housing quality and status than with the minimization of expenditure in Britain (Fenton 1977; Nowikowski and Ward 1978; Phillips 1983) and that their expectations about rent levels are very similar to those of British tenants. But the relative deprivation of black minority owners and tenants persists. It is this association between deprivation and segregation which we see as the most crucial issue. The association takes different forms and arises through different mechanisms in the various tenures.

Segregation and Deprivation in Council Housing

In the council sector, a whole series of research reports (see, for example, Duke 1970; Ward 1971; Runnymede Trust 1975; Smith and Whalley 1975; Stunell 1975; Parker and Dugmore 1976; London Borough of Lewisham 1980; Skellington 1981; Phillips 1986; Henderson and Karn 1987) has shown that black families have more difficulty in getting into council housing than whites, receive less attractive housing than whites, have greater difficulty in moving from worse to better housing within the council stock, and are heavily concentrated into the least popular estates, usually in inner-city areas. This occurs for several reasons. First, it is common for the most desperate applicants to be offered and accept a standard of housing that others would refuse. Given the bad housing conditions in the private sector, and the high level of homelessness among minority groups in some cities, black families may be more likely to accept a poor offer. Second, inner-city estates, despite their poor physical quality, remain more popular with black than white applicants because they are located close to the main centers of black communities. In areas of racial violence, locations close to other minority households also present a "safe" option. However, a growing number of black applicants are seeking suburban homes rather than inner-city properties. White and black tenants are therefore in competition for the better-designed estates. In this competition minority groups are handicapped by the fact that councils have a tendency to allocate good- and bad-quality housing according to the social status of the applicant (Henderson and Karn

1987). Because black families in Britain tend to be stereotyped as having a low status, such approaches to allocations tend to reinforce all the other factors such as low socioeconomic status, large family size, and unconventional life-styles that lead to the downgrading of black tenants.

The Housing Associations and Segregation

While segregation is a problem in inner-city council estates, it is still true that local authorities operate centralized systems of registration for housing that provide the potential for movement from inner city to suburbs, even if this potential has not yet been fully realized. In contrast, housing associations operate independently of each other, have no centralized systems of registration (and indeed have extensively improved systems of access to their waiting lists and housing), and tend to be located either in the inner city or the suburbs, not both. It is therefore difficult for people from the inner cities to use housing associations as a route out of segregated areas.

The style of operation of the housing association movement tends in fact to reinforce the pattern of black inner cities and white suburbs and of inequality in housing standards. Typically, an inner-city association will be housing large numbers of black households, but in doing so, confines them to nineteenth-century terraced housing, often in deteriorated areas (Niner and Karn 1985:154). It is not the responsibility of that association to seek alternative suburban housing for its applicants, and "a suburban association . . . may feel reluctant to put the effort into, and indeed have difficulty in building up an adequate referral system of contacts with inner city communities in order to provide better opportunities for black families" (Niner and Karn 1985:154). Although each association operating independently in this way cannot be faulted under the race relations legislation, the overall effect of the activities of the voluntary housing movement is to discriminate against black households. The only solution would be more open access and joint referrals among associations, but the voluntary sector tends to be typified by rivalry rather than collaboration.

Segregation and Deprivation in the Private Sector

Racial disadvantage and segregation in the private sector arises not only through race but also through class discrimination. As Henderson and Karn (1987:5) point out:

Racial exclusion in the private sector is largely produced through normal market mechanisms. The private market's operation is based on price and ability to pay. Price is affected by many factors other than just the physical characteristics of the property. In particular the social characteristics of areas have a dramatic effect on people's willingness to buy. As whites are so dominant numerically both in the population as a whole, and, even more so as employees in the real estate industry, white views about living near black people and sharing schools and other facilities with them are bound to have dramatic effect on the market. So the desire of whites to live in white areas produces, through competition, a bidding up of the prices in those areas. As the black population is mostly of lower income relative to the white, higher prices disproportionately exclude them. In this way class discrimination comes to articulate with racial discrimination to produce a form of discrimination through the market that any anti-discrimination legislation is powerless to touch.

Racial discrimination within private market institutions also occurs through the manipulation and withholding of information and finance from minorities (especially black) wishing to buy. This results, directly and indirectly, in the funneling of minorities into particular types of residential areas, most notably the poorest, least-desirable ones no longer popular with whites. Borrowing restrictions, for example, have imposed severe limitations on the minorities' range of housing options. Even controlling for price, house type, and location, black buyers find it more difficult than whites to borrow from building societies (Stevens et al. 1982; Karn, Kemeny, and Williams 1985). The building societies argue that this is because blacks are not saving with the societies, and that Asians in particular fail to apply for funds. However, again there is evidence that whites who do not save are more favorably treated than blacks who do not save, and that Asians experience higher refusal rates when they do apply (Stevens et al. 1982).

Those who are successful in competing for loans are more likely in the end to borrow on less favorable terms than their white counterparts, which restricts the price range of the properties they can consider (Karn, Kemeny, and Williams 1985; Sarre, Phillips, and Skellington 1989). Building society managers are quick to deny discriminatory practices, maintaining that they consider each case "on its merits" (Housing Monitoring Team 1982). But in a society where social categories such as race, class, and gender play a part in differentiating between the deserving and the undeserving, the concept of merit is far from the objective category that is implied. In the face of building society rejection (both anticipated and actual), black purchasers have turned to banks and more informal lending sources for help. Although in recent years the move to more competition in mortgage lending has probably reduced the scale of mortgage famine in inner cities, this improvement has undoubtedly been somewhat offset by the price charged for covering what is seen as added risk. Home finance has often been forthcoming, but stringent loan conditions often limit housing ambitions to the cheapest inner-city areas.

The pattern of black segregation within the inner city is also reinforced by minorities' limited access to housing information. Certain groups, especially South Asians, make relatively little use of main street realtors, both for cultural reasons and for fear of discrimination. Their heavy reliance upon friends and relatives for information, on for sale signs, and on private sales inevitably restricts their housing options. For example, Karn, Kemeny, and Williams (1985) found that South Asians relying on friends and relatives for information on housing in Birmingham looked at very few properties before buying; most bought the first they saw. Because most of these purchases are in or near the area in which their relatives live, this type of purchase can only reinforce the pattern of ethnic concentration. The use of an estate agent (realtor) would certainly provide the prospective minority purchaser with a greater range of options but would bring no guarantee of purchase. Research in Bedford showed a remarkably low success rate for black house-hunters using white estate agents, a rate that only got worse for those with greater housing aspirations (Sarre, Phillips, and Skellington 1989). Some estate agents in the town openly confessed that they actively discouraged black customers, while others admitted that they would steer them toward recognized ethnic minority areas, usually in the inner city. Other research has confirmed the entrenched and widespread nature of realtor discrimination in Britain (CRE 1988).

The private rental sector is still relatively important for black single people and even for many black families with children. Recent evidence suggests that the level of racial discrimination within this sector has declined and rejection is less blatant. However, black people are still likely to be told that the accommodation has been let when a vacancy exists and to experience discrimination at the hands of rental agencies (CRE 1980). There is also still a strong tendency for ethnic minorities, especially those with language difficulties, to avoid discrimination by renting from someone within their own group; this is especially true for South Asians (Smith 1977). Because these minority landlords have rarely been able to acquire anything other than older property within the inner areas, this rental pattern again reinforces the pattern of minority concentration, segregation, and deprivation.

Despite the wealth of evidence pointing to systematic bias, both intentional and unintentional, in the operation of the private housing market (CRE 1980; CRE 1985; Karn, Kemeny, and Williams 1985; Sarre, Phillips, and Skellington 1989), there has been little drive for institutional reform. The resistance of the private sector to change and the patchy record of the voluntary sector are likely to have particularly important implications for the stability of the pattern of segregation and deprivation, especially given the dominance of home-ownership in the British housing market (it accounts for two-thirds of the market and is growing) and government policy to promote private and voluntary renting at the expense of the council sector.

If large numbers of council housing estates, especially in the outer areas, are handed over to housing associations, opportunities for black households to move out of the most segregated areas are likely to be further curtailed. So far, government has done nothing to address the issue in its plans for transfer of council estates to private landlords, and housing associations, unlike local authorities, have no statutory duties to promote equal opportunities and good race relations. All they have to do is avoid acting in a discriminatory fashion.

Racial Harassment and Racial Violence

Race, along with social categories such as class, has clearly become an institutionalized basis for allocating resources within the housing market in Britain, with black minorities invariably faring worst. This process of racial differentiation does not, however, take place in a vacuum. It is sanctioned by popular racism, which finds its most obvious expression within the housing market through racial hostility and violence (especially on local authority housing estates), through the individual vendor's refusal to sell, and in the avoidance strategies of private purchasers. White purchasers in Birmingham, for example, were found to avoid areas where South Asians made up 20 percent or more of the population, although they were still prepared to buy into similar inner-city areas with a South Asian representation of less than 5 percent (Karn 1979).

It is, however, the fear of racial harassment and abuse that almost certainly presents the strongest force for continuing segregation within the inner city at the individual level. The extent and repercussions of violence against black people in Britain are still poorly documented.

Many attacks are not reported or are dismissed by a seemingly unsympathetic police force as having been provoked. Emerging evidence, however, indicates that while there are significant variations between locations in the level of racially motivated violence, the severity of the situation nationwide has been seriously underestimated (Runnymede Trust 1986; CRE 1987; Leeds CRC 1988). Racial violence, in its most extreme form, defines the margins of black and white space, as most clearly exemplified by the physical segregation of the Bangladeshi community in London's East End (Husband 1983). In 1979 the Commission for Racial Equality referred to the Bangladeshis living here as a "community under siege" (CRE 1979). Since then, the situation has deteriorated even further; in a fifteen-month period, one public housing authority (the Greater London Council) recorded 361 attacks on its own estates alone. The fear of violence structures the Bangladeshis' housing options in the East End. They avoid areas with active right-wing extremist groups and turn down local authority housing offers on estates with a history of racial violence. Although some Bangladeshis have endeavored to raise their housing standards by moving into predominantly white areas, a number have returned to the sanctuary of their old neighborhoods, despite their deteriorating condition (Phillips 1986).

Individual hostility has thus combined with institutional discrimination to maintain a pattern of black concentration, segregation, and deprivation. The pattern both reflects and contributes to the low social standing of the black minorities in Britain. Hostility, suspicion, and resentment of foreigners is hardly new in Britain. There is a long history of racial differentiation in British society; the British culture is steeped in negative racial images that predate mass black migration and settlement. Recurrent themes of immigrant inferiority, backwardness, and threat (particularly to the well-being of the nation) have emerged, but the colonial association of black subordination and white domination has given greater strength to racist sentiments in the case of the New Commonwealth and Pakistan population. The low status of this minority population in Britain in the 1980s was reinforced by the material circumstances of their migration. Most Afro-Caribbeans and South Asians came as economic migrants, and from the earliest days, their standing was linked inextricably to the economic fortunes of the country. As postwar conditions changed (i.e., from economic expansion to recession and decline), so the position of the migrant work force was transformed from that of essential labor to workers surplus to requirements (Castles 1984). In the 1980s, racist ideologies overlapped with economic circumstance to bring the black minorities into focus as scapegoats for Britain's social and economic malaise.

All this has had a direct bearing on the housing opportunities of South Asians and Afro-Caribbeans. As victims of particularly high levels of unemployment, the ability of the black minorities to gain access to certain parts of the housing market and to meet the financial outlays on their homes has been eroded. As outsiders, they are generally the first to fall victim to housing resource rationing, especially at times of shortage. Their limited options within the housing market reinforce the potential for continuing segregation and deprivation, unless this can be counterbalanced by government strategies for change.

Segregation: Policy Initiatives

The concentration, segregation, and deprivation of black minorities in Britain have prompted many initiatives during the postwar years, from formal legislation against racial discrimination (the 1968 and 1976 Race Relations Acts) to local strategies. These have been designed to tackle the worst consequences of minority segregation at both the inter- and intraurban level. The strategies, although apparently united in aim, have in fact differed in their definition of these consequences and their underlying causes and have therefore effectively differed in their purpose. These differences reflect the various ways in which minority segregation issues have been conceptualized. On the one hand, minority concentration and segregation has been seen as an immigrant problem, with unfortunate repercussions for the indigenous white population. On the other hand, segregation may be viewed as a white problem, the result of white racism expressed through local prejudices and institutional practices. The balance of these competing perspectives has changed over time as, in official circles at least, the former has gradually made room for the latter.

Early strategies were preoccupied with the management of the "immigrant problem." The concern was not so much to alleviate the disadvantage of the newcomers as to protect the indigenous population from the undesirable effects of an alien incursion. Fears were voiced about a build-up of crime and disease in immigrant clusters and about the threat posed to the British way of life by the concentration of great numbers of aliens. Such fears were translated at the national level into an effort to disperse incoming East African Asian refugees in the early 1970s, the objective being to divert them from towns with high inner-city concentrations of black immigrants (designated "red" areas) to less well-established immigrant reception areas (designated "green"). This national-level dispersal policy, operated under the auspices of the Ugandan Resettlement Board, was indicative of the government's attitude toward black newcomers at the time, namely that it was best not to make provision for the well-being of the refugees because this "might have been resented by the white majority as favorable treatment of the Asians" (Bristow 1976).

This national dispersal policy was supported by local efforts such as those by the Leicester city council, who, immediately before the expulsion of Asians from Uganda, placed an advertisement in the Ugandan *Argus* that read, "In the interests of yourself and those of your family . . . you should not come to Leicester." Their efforts in the long run were unrewarded; the pull of community and family ties proved too strong. Nearly a quarter (5,000 to 6,000) of the Ugandan refugees arriving in Britain in 1972 settled immediately in Leicester, often taking up lodgings with relatives (Bristow and Adams 1977). By the end of the 1970s, another 5,000 had gravitated to Leicester from their dispersed locations throughout Britain despite a general decline in job opportunities in the city. Undeterred by this past experience, the British government still has a policy of refugee dispersal (albeit less draconian), as exemplified by the officially guided settlement of Vietnamese boat people in Scotland.

These national-level dispersal policies have been mirrored within cities by attempts to disperse black groups away from inner-city areas to more suburban locations. The best-documented example of such a policy is that operated by Birmingham's council housing department between 1969 and 1975. There were undoubtedly authorities that operated (and probably still operate) ad hoc dispersal practices in the sense that allocations officers offered, or failed to offer, particular properties to black applicants on the basis of how many other black people were already in an area. Such practices have been illegal since 1968, but informal routine actions of this type have been quite common, especially in the 1960s and 1970s before local authorities took notice in any serious way of the implications of the Race Relations Acts.

The Birmingham policy was, however, much more formal. In the late 1960s, the concentration of Afro-Caribbeans and South Asians in the inner and middle rings of the city was a matter of concern to the city council, particularly in terms of service provision (City of Birmingham 1968). The city had tried to obtain central government resources to help with the costs of education, welfare, and housing for the new arrivals but concluded that another approach would also be necessary, to disperse the black population to suburban areas with less pressure on services. It was felt that racial integration would be helped by spreading black people thinly among the white population. It was this last argument which was to be used as the main rationale for the policy, although it was based not on evidence that geographical dispersal creates social integration, but rather on the hostility that white tenants expressed to having many black tenants in their area. It therefore focused on the interests of white tenants, not black.

The event that triggered the introduction of the policy happened in February 1969, when nine white tenants in a block of twelve maisonettes in the Ladywood area of the city signed a petition and threatened a rent strike to object to the allocation of a maisonette to a black family that would have been the second black family in the block. The Housing Committee rejected the petition but decided to avoid similar trouble in the future by limiting the number of black families that would be housed in any one area. The policy was never publicly announced but it was not secret, in the sense that the Housing Department did not, if asked, deny that it existed. Most tenants and applicants remained in ignorance of it, however, even when its effects began to bite.

The mechanics of the policy were that in any block, street, or estate not more than one in six properties could be allocated to black households. The five properties on either side of the one allocated to a black tenant were to be reserved for whites. If the policy had been strictly adhered to, no black family in council housing in Birmingham could ever have been allowed a black next-door neighbor. This extreme form of policy did not happen. Rather, because of the uneven way in which vacancies occurred, a guideline of one in six was used for a maximum overall density of blacks on a particular estate. When this maximum was reached, no further black families were allowed in unless a black family moved out. Because certain estates were particularly popular with black applicants, this began to occur frequently. Increasingly many black applicants at the top of the housing list found either that they were getting no accommodation offers or only offers of areas they did not want. By 1974, the tops of the two- and three-bedroom lists were completely dominated by black applicants to whom no acceptable offer had been made. Although applicants themselves were unaware of the cause of this, housing advice agencies and the Race Relations Board began to be seriously concerned about the adverse effects of the dispersal policy on the housing chances of black families.

However, the Race Relations Board could not bring an action for discrimination unless there had been a specific complaint from an individual, a feature of the legislation that was remedied under the 1976 Race Relations Act. Yet it was difficult if not impossible for a black applicant who had not received an offer to prove that the reason for this was the dispersal policy.

Eventually, in 1975, six years after the implementation of the policy, a complaint appeared in a rather extraordinary way, which illustrates the difficulty any ordinary black applicant would have had in producing similar evidence. The complainant was an Irish woman allocated a property designed "no colored." Only when she went to collect the keys did it emerge that her husband was Jamaican. Immediately the offer was withdrawn, and the woman, with the help of a housing aid center, lodged a complaint with the Race Relations Board, which subsequently ruled that discrimination had occurred. Even then Birmingham argued that the dispersal policy itself was not discriminatory because it was aimed at fostering integration and was therefore in accordance with the spirit of the 1968 Race Relations Act. The city denied knowledge of the adverse effects on the waiting time of black applicants to the housing list, although the data had been provided to the chair of housing. Ultimately the board conceded that a voluntary dispersal policy was perfectly acceptable and possibly desirable, but said that it regarded a set-ratio policy as problematic. As a result, Birmingham's dispersal policy was formally but reluctantly suspended in October 1975 (Henderson and Karn 1987:129–30).

Birmingham's dispersal policy has to be seen in the light of discussion taking place at that time about race relations and segregation. Three national reports—"Colour and Citizenship," the Report of the Institute of Race Relations (Rose 1969), the Cullingworth Report (Cullingworth 1969), and the Report of the House of Commons Select Committee on Immigration and Race Relations—all advocated dispersal as a means of improving housing conditions, assisting integration, easing the pressure on education and welfare services, and circumventing the possibility of racial conflict. They differed from Birmingham's policy in that they all emphasized that dispersal must be voluntary, but they failed to specify how this was to be achieved given the natural preference of any ethnic group to want to live close together. In fact, as Henderson and Karn note, "The whole discussion about dispersal failed to give adequate recognition to the importance of ethnic cultural infrastructure for the quality of life of Britain's black settlers. In this, all the reports revealed an ethno-centric bias which continues to pervade discussion of dispersal policies. Though in recent years there has been a growing awareness of the need to value the preferences of racial minorities, unfortunately this growing awareness of the issues has often become converted into a stereotyping of black groups, and Asians in particular, as uniformly and permanently resistant to living away from their main areas of residence" (1987:129).

Birmingham's dispersal policy was very much a product of its time. Ideas about racial segregation and discrimination were essentially simplistic. Although perhaps such approaches still predominate at both central and local government levels, a much greater level of knowledge and sophistication has developed among a minority of local authority politicians and officers. This has been most evident in inner-city local authorities with substantial proportions of black minority voters. Ironically, the concentration and segregation of Britain's black population has given this otherwise relatively powerless minority some political muscle, albeit at the local level (Anwar 1986). Black local councilors and more recently black Members of Parliament have taken their place in the political arena, and white politicians in inner-city areas can no longer neglect South Asian and Afro-Caribbean interests. Race, racism, and—more significantly—anti-racism have thus emerged as part of the local political agenda, especially in places such as inner London. This development has brought an official reappraisal of the pattern and causes of black minority segregation and deprivation, and in some local authorities at least, black people are seen as the victims rather than the purveyors of disadvantage. Thus, gradually, policies aimed at ameliorating conditions for blacks have begun to replace those aimed at protecting whites, and white institutions implicated in the production and reproduction of unequal structures have come under scrutiny.

Measures for tackling the worst consequences of minority segregation and deprivation at the local level range from area-based improvement programs designed to upgrade the conditions of the segregated minority popularity on-site, to equal opportunity initiatives aimed at promoting voluntary dispersal. Equal opportunity programs have brought a revision of housing policies and practices, staff "anti-racist" training, and, most important, the introduction of more stringent measures against racial harassment on housing estates. In some cases, equality targets for the allocation of black people to good-quality housing have also been set. These "equality targets" differ from the early quotas set by the Birmingham housing department (quotas are illegal under the Race Relations Act) in that they represent a goal rather than a threshold. Few councils, however, have moved into the controversial area of "equality targeting" for in Britain there is still, with the notable exception of more radical left-wing councils, a reluctance to embrace programs that might be construed as "positive discrimination" (Edwards 1987).

While local electoral politics has much to do with the awakened interest of these local authorities in racial equality and the problems of "ghettoized" estates of run-down properties, the activities of the Commission for Racial Equality (CRE) have been crucial in documenting both direct and indirect discrimination and requiring remedies. The CRE's inquiry into racial discrimination in the allocation of Hackney's properties (CRE 1984) was influential in bringing racial equality higher on the agenda in local authorities and giving pressure groups ammunition. It was really only during the late 1980s that the Race Relations Acts began to be treated with any seriousness by local authorities. Even in 1989, the main approach was just to avoid being investigated, but that in itself is a step forward.

Meanwhile, forces for segregation and deprivation within the private sector of the British housing market remain relatively untouched by public policy. Race relations legislation has of course opened areas of access within this sector that were completely closed off in the 1960s. It is possible for a black person to raise a loan and buy a decent house in the white suburbs, even though it may take longer and be a more expensive process than for a white purchaser. The days of blanket minority exclusion by private market institutions are also over. In part, this reflects the changing mood of these institutions in the light of antidiscrimination legislation and their fear of investigation by the CRE. The new openness, however, also undoubtedly springs from commercial considerations. During the 1980s, building societies competed to find borrowers for the record levels of savings coming in. Mortgage queues became a thing of the past. South Asians became perceived by many building societies to be good savers and hence "good business" (Sarre, Phillips, and Skellington 1989).

In the voluntary housing sector there is again the fear of CRE investigation, but there is also an added motive for taking racial equality seriously, the Housing Corporation. This controlling body for the movement has begun looking at the housing associations' approach to race as part of their management monitoring process and threatens to make it a factor in capital allocations and management allowances. This firmer approach by the Housing Corporation has made racial equality more of an issue outside the core of committed inner-city associations. However, it is still easy for associations to obey the letter of the law and yet still not provide for ethnic minorities.

Conclusions

Future trends in racial segregation in Britain are likely to be heavily affected by government housing policy to encourage home-ownership, housing associations, and private rental property at the expense of council housing. The greatest degree of segregation is experienced in inner-city home-ownership. Council housing has some fairly segregated estates in the inner cities but, other than the inner London boroughs, local authorities have offered some access to suburban housing.

The whole trend of the British housing system is to become more like the U.S. system, with greater dependence on market forces and greater segregation according to race and income. The worse the climate of race relations and the greater the prevalence of racial harassment and racial attacks, the more entrenched that pattern is likely to become. Local initiatives have brought local successes, but grounds for optimism are shaky. More often than not, equal opportunities programs look good on paper but in practice may lack both financial and political backing. More important, local initiatives have not been underwritten by a strong central government commitment to the promotion of equal opportunities or to the elimination of racism. There is nothing to compare with the centrally coordinated affirmative action programs in the United States. A revision of the cumbersome Race Relations legislation is long overdue, and attempts to introduce racial harassment legislation in 1985 and again in 1988 were thwarted in Parliament. Without such central government backing, local initiatives alone are insufficient to challenge the structural disadvantage that underlies the entrenched pattern of black segregation and deprivation in Britain.

References

Aldrich, H., J. Cater, T. Jones, and D. McEvoy. 1981. "Business Development and Self-Segregation: Asian Enterprise in Three British Cities." Pp. 170–92 in *Ethnic Segregation in Cities,* edited by C. Peach, V. Robinson, and S. Smith. London: Croom-Helm.

Anwar, M. 1986. *Race and Politics.* London: Tavistock.

Aurora, G. 1963. *The New Frontiersmen: A Sociological Study of Indian Immigrants in the UK.* Bombay: Popular Prakashan.

Baron, H. 1969. "The Web of Urban Racism." Pp. 134–76 in *Institutional Racism in America,* edited by L. Knowles and K. Prewitt. Englewood Cliffs: Prentice-Hall.

Booth, H. 1986. "Immigration in Perspective: Population Development in the UK." Pp. 109–36 in *Towards a Just Immigration Policy,* edited by A. Dummett. London: Cobden Trust.

Bristow, M. 1976. "Britain's Response to the Ugandan Asian Crisis." *New Community* 5:265–79.

Bristow, M., and B. Adams. 1977. "Ugandan Asians and the Housing Market in Britain." *New Community* 6:65–69.

Brown, C. 1984. *Black and White Britain: The Third PSI Survey.* London: Heinemann.

Carey, S., and A. Shukur. 1985. "A Profile of the Bangladeshi Community in East London." *New Community* 12:405–17.

Castles, S. 1984. *Here for Good: Western Europe's New Ethnic Minorities.* London: Pluto Press.

Cater, J., and T. Jones. 1978. "Ethnic Residential Space: The Case of Asians in Bradford." *Tijdschrift voor Economische en Sociale Geographie* 70:86–97.

City of Birmingham. 1968. *Report to the General Purposes Committee on Immigration.* Birmingham: City of Birmingham.

CRE. 1979. *Brick Lane and Beyond: An Inquiry into Racial Strife and Violence in Tower Hamlets.* London: CRE.

———. 1980. *Reports of Two Formal Investigations.* London: CRE.

———. 1984. *Race and Council Housing in Hackney: Report of a Formal Investigation.* London: CRE.

———. 1985. *Race and Mortgage Lending: Formal Investigation Report on the Allocation of Mortgages in Rochdale.* London: CRE.

———. 1987. *Living in Terror: A Report on Racial Violence and Harassment in Housing.* London: CRE.

———. 1988. *Racial Discrimination in a London Estate Agency: Report of a Formal Investigation into Richard Barclay and Co.* London: CRE.

Cullingworth, J. B. 1969. *Council Housing: Purposes, Procedures and Priorities, Report of the Housing Management Sub-Committee of the Central Housing Advisory Committee.* London: HMSO.

Dahya, B. 1974. "The Nature of Pakistani Ethnicity in Industrial Cities in Britain." Pp. 77–118 in *Urban Ethnicity,* edited by A. Cohen. London: Tavistock.

Desai, R. 1963. *Indian Immigrants in Britain.* Oxford: Oxford University Press.

Duke, C. 1970. *Colour and Rehousing: A Study of Redevelopment in Leeds.* London: Institute of Race Relations.

Dummett, A. 1986. *Towards a Just Immigration Policy.* London: Cobden Trust.

Edwards, J. 1987. *Positive Discrimination, Social Justice and Social Policy.* London: Tavistock.

Fenton, S. 1977. *Asian Households in Owner-Occupation: A Study of the Pattern, Costs and Experience of Households in Greater Manchester.* Working Paper no. 2. Bristol: SSRC Research Unit on Ethnic Relations, University of Bristol.

GLC. 1985. *Homelessness in London.* GLC Housing Research and Policy Report no. 1. London: Greater London Council.

Hall, S., and P. Jefferson. 1976. *Resistance Through Rituals.* London: Hutchinson.

Hartmann, P., and C. Husband. 1974. *Racism and the Mass Media.* London: Davis Poynter.

Henderson, J., and V. Karn. 1987. *Race, Class and State Housing: Inequality and the Allocation of Public Housing in Britain.* Centre for Urban and Regional Policy 4, University of Birmingham. Aldershot: Gower.

Hiro, D. 1971. *Black British, White British.* London: Penguin.

Housing Monitoring Team. 1982. *Building Societies and the Local Housing Market.* Research Memorandum. Birmingham: University of Birmingham.

Husband, C. 1983. *Racial Exclusionism and the City: The Urban Support of the National Front.* London: Allen and Unwin.

Jeffery, P. 1976. *Migrants and Refugees: Muslim and Christian Pakistani Families in Bristol.* Cambridge: Cambridge University Press.

Jones, P. N. 1978. "The Distribution and Diffusion of the Coloured Population in England and Wales, 1961–71." *Transactions of the Institute of British Geographers* 3:515–32.

Jones, T. 1983. "Racial Segregation and Ethnic Autonomy." *New Community* 11:10–22.

Karn, V. 1979. "Low Income Owner Occupation in the Inner City." Pp. 160–90 in *Urban Deprivation and the Inner City,* edited by C. Jones. London: Croom-Helm.

Karn, V., J. Kemeny, and P. Williams. 1985. *Home Ownership in the Inner City: Salvation or Despair?* Aldershot: Gower.

Khan, V. S. 1977. "The Pakistanis: Mirpur; Villagers at Home and in Bradford." P. 35 in *Between Two Cultures,* edited by J. Watson. Oxford: Blackwell.

———. 1982. "The Role of the Culture of Dominance in Structuring the Experience of the Ethnic Minorities." P. 197 in *Race in Britain,* edited by C. Husband. London: Hutchinson.

Kearsley, G., and S. Srivastava. 1974. "The Spatial Evolution of Glasgow's Asian Community." *Scottish Geographical Magazine* 90:49–63.

King, R., and P. King. 1977. "The Spatial Evolution of the Italian Community in Bedford." *East Midlands Geographer* 6:343.

Lee, T. 1977. *Race and Residence: The Concentration and Dispersal of Immigrants in London.* Oxford: Oxford University Press.

Leeds CRC. 1988. *Racial Harassment in Leeds 1985–86.* Leeds: Leeds CRC.

London Borough of Lewisham. 1980. *Black People and Housing in Lewisham.* London: London Borough of Lewisham.

Milner Holland Report. 1965. *Report of the Committee on Housing in Greater London.* London: HMSO.

Newman, D. 1985. "The Changing Distribution of the Anglo-Jewish Community." *Transactions of the Institute of British Geographers* 10:360.

Niner, P., and V. Karn. 1985. *Housing Association Allocations: Achieving Racial Equality.* London: Runnymede Trust.

Nowikowski, S., and R. Ward. 1978. "Middle Class and British: An Analysis of South Asians in Suburbia." *New Community* 7:1–11.

Parker, J., and K. Dugmore. 1976. *Colour and the Allocation of GLC Housing.* Research Report 21. London: Greater London Council.

Parkin, F. 1979. *Marxism and Class Theory: A Bourgeois Critique.* London: Tavistock.

Peach, C. 1968. *West Indian Migration to Britain: A Social Geography.* Oxford: Oxford University Press for the Institute of Race Relations.

———. 1984. "The Force of the West Indian Island Identity in Britain." Pp. 23–42 in *Geography and Ethnic Pluralism,* edited by C. Clarke, D. Ley, and C. Peach. London: Allen and Unwin.

Peach, C., S. Winchester, and R. Woods. 1975. "Distribution of Coloured Immigrants in Britain." *Urban Affairs Annual Review* 9:395.

Phillips, D. A. 1981. "The Social and Spatial Segregation of Asians in Leicester." Pp. 101–21 in *Social Interaction and Ethnic Segregation,* edited by P. Jackson and S. Smith. London: Academic Press.

———. 1983. "The Socio-cultural Implications of Asian Patterns of Settlement." Ph.D. diss., University of Cambridge.

———. 1986. *What Price Equality: A Report on the Allocation of GLC Housing in Tower Hamlets.* GLC Housing Research and Policy Report no. 9. London: Greater London Council.

Rex, J., and S. Tomlinson. 1979. *Colonial Immigrants in a British City.* London: Routledge and Kegan Paul.

Robinson, V. 1980. "Asians and Council Housing: Notes and Comments." *Urban Studies* 17:323.

———. 1986. *Transients, Settlers and Refugees: Asians in Britain.* Oxford: Clarendon.

Rose, E. J. B. 1969. *Colour and Citizenship.* Oxford: Oxford University Press for the Institute of Race Relations.

Runnymede Trust. 1975. *Race and Council Housing in London.* London: Runnymede Trust.

———. 1986. *Racial Violence and Harassment.* London: Runnymede Trust.

Sarre, P., D. Phillips, and R. Skellington. 1989. *Ethnic Minority Housing: Explanations and Policies.* Aldershot: Gower.

Skellington, R. 1981. "How Blacks Lose Out in Council Housing." *New Society* 55:187–89.

Smith, D. 1977. *The Facts of Racial Disadvantage*. Harmondsworth: Penguin.

Smith, D., and P. Whalley. 1975. *Racial Minorities and Council Housing*. London: Political and Economic Planning.

Stevens, L., V. Karn, E. Davidson, and A. Stanley. 1982. *Race and Building Society Lending in Leeds*. Leeds: Leeds Community Relations Council.

Stunell, J. G. 1975. *An Examination of Racial Equality in Points Scheme Housing Allocation*. Research and Information Report. London: London Borough of Lewisham.

Ward, D. 1971. *Cities and Immigrants*. Oxford: Oxford University Press.

5. Immigrant Housing Patterns in Sweden

Immigrant Traditions and Immigrant Policy

Until the 1930s, Sweden was a homogeneous country in ethnic terms; a country which had only been confronted on a few occasions with people from other cultures through immigration. The first immigration to Sweden in historic time took place in the twelfth century, when German merchants settled in trading and manufacturing towns in central and eastern Sweden. For several centuries this immigration was such a dominant feature of Swedish administration and business life that German almost became an official language (Widgren 1982).

Several hundred years later, the seventeenth century saw Scottish immigration to Gothenburg on the west coast. This was to have great influence on the West Swedish shipping and business world for a long period. During the same period Swedish mining and iron industries experienced a marked upturn as a result of the knowledge and skills brought by immigration of prominent Walloon businessmen and guest workers. The Walloons came from the area around Liège in Belgium and settled in iron-working communities, many of which have developed into important industrial centers in recent decades. Even today the number of descendants of the Walloons is estimated at around 30,000 (Widgren 1982).

The freedom of religion introduced in the eighteenth century led to a limited immigration of Jewish merchants and craftsmen who were a distinctive part of the life in some cities. During the seventeenth century there was major immigration from eastern Finland directly subsidized by the Swedish government through tax exemptions. For the whole of this century some 40,000 Finns moved to Sweden to found new communities in the unpopulated border regions between Norway and Sweden (Widgren 1982). Many of these pioneer communities still remain Finnish-speaking.

In previous centuries, however, immigration was numerically very small, limited to certain occupations, and, above all, concentrated in

FIGURE 5.1.   Immigration and Emigration, 1900–1985

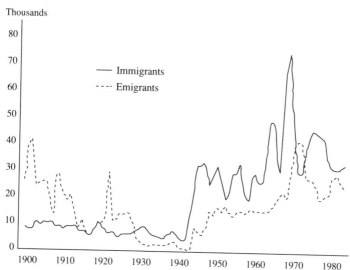

a few places in the country. For Swedes in general, there was little question of contacts with immigrants and their languages and cultures. The major contact with other nationalities came through the great emigration from Sweden, mainly to North America. From the mid-nineteenth century up to World War I, 1.2 million Swedes emigrated out of a population that totaled 5.5 million at the end of the period (Guteland et al. 1975).

In the thirties Sweden became an immigrant country, but a large part of the immigration consisted of Swedes returning home (figure 5.1). Then during World War II Sweden became the immigrant country that it is today.

Several factors account for sharply increasing immigration in the forties. As a neutral country Sweden was not involved in the war; for foreign policy reasons Sweden's borders were kept open for refugees from neighboring countries. In the forties, 60,000 Danes and Norwegians and 30,000 Estonians, Latvians, and Lithuanians fled to Sweden. In addition, 70,000 Finnish "war children" came to Sweden, as did 34,000 refugees transferred from German concentration camps (Widgren 1982).

Other reasons for the increased immigration were demographic and economic. Birth rates fell sharply in the thirties. When industry picked up again quickly after the war there was a large shortage of labor. The

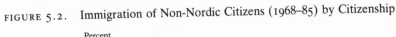

FIGURE 5.2.   Immigration of Non-Nordic Citizens (1968–85) by Citizenship

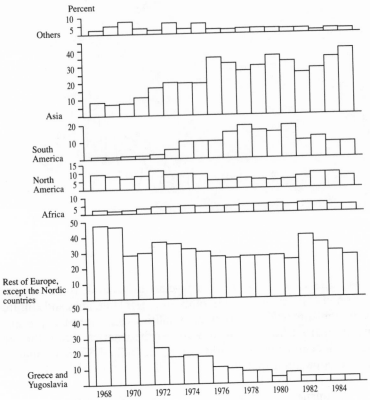

considerable flow of refugees along with reduced employment in agriculture and an increase in female participation rates were not sufficient to cover the labor need.

The Immigration Boom after World War II

In the years immediately after the war, agreements were reached with each of the Nordic countries on the abolition of visa requirements. The work permit requirement for employment in Sweden had already been abolished for Nordic citizens in 1943. In 1954, an agreement on a common Nordic labor market was signed and further increased immigration (sou 1974:69). There has been considerable migration among Nordic countries throughout the postwar period, totaling one million Scandinavians by the early 1980s (Widgren 1982). The agreement has, however, been of greatest importance for Finnish-Swedish immigration, with migration from Finland accounting for 40 percent and return migration to Finland accounting for 20 percent of Nordic migration. Finnish immigration consists primarily of blue-collar workers from rural areas, whereas immigration from the other Scandinavian countries represents a variation of social classes. At the same time, Swedish authorities and Swedish industry began active recruitment of workers in countries such as Italy, Hungary, and Austria. This action was not based on any immigration policy; the only important motive for increased immigration was labor needs.

Up to 1960, net immigration totaled 280,000 persons, the majority of whom were Nordic immigrants. Little was to be seen of foreign cultures in most places. In the sixties, immigration entered a new phase. Even more active steps were taken to recruit immigrants from more distant countries, mainly Greece and Yugoslavia (figure 5.2). Immigration from other European countries continued to be important although it fell relative to that from distant lands. Net immigration more than doubled in the sixties compared with the previous decade (Widgren 1982). Immigrants from outside the Nordic region became a more noticeable feature of Swedish society. However, immigration was to the major cities and industrial centers, where immigrants came to represent almost 10 percent of the population (figure 5.3). The forest and agricultural communities in the rural north of Sweden remained almost unaffected by immigration.

In 1968, unregulated immigration from non-Nordic countries was stopped (Widgren 1982). Parliament was unanimous in the view that immigration must be controlled to prevent "the present workforce being put out of work as a result of immigration of foreign labor" (Government Bill 1968:142). This principle still applies. Immigrants must have a work permit and a job before entering Sweden or be able to document other strong reasons for coming. As a result, actual labor participation has become less important as a reason for immigration (table 5.1). However, immigration to Sweden did not fall until the mid-seventies, with net immigration declining from a high of 40,500 persons in the sixties to about 17,000 in the seventies (figure 5.1). In the first five years of the eighties, net immigration increased again to 27,000 persons. The most common immigrant groups are refugees from all parts of the world and immigrants with personal ties to people who already live in Sweden.

The extensive immigration of the sixties and the significance it had for the development of society led to several major debates on the

FIGURE 5.3.   Residence of Foreign Citizens, Proportion of Population

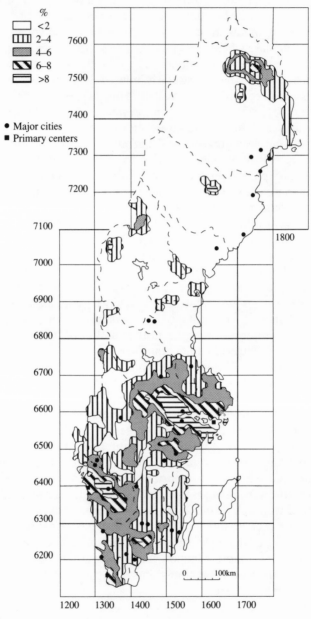

Source: SOU 1974:1.

TABLE 5.1.   Estimated Distribution
of Non-Nordic Immigration
(1968–81) by Reason for Granting
a Residence Permit

Reason	1968–75	1976–81
Employment	21,000	6,000
Political reasons	30,000	28,000
Adoptive children	5,000	9,000
Swedish descent	2,500	2,000
Visiting student	3,500	4,000
Return migration	4,000	7,000
Personal ties	61,000	43,000
Total	127,000	99,000

Source: SOU 1982:49.

need for an immigrant policy. Should immigrants assimilate and become Swedes or be integrated but still have the opportunity to retain
their distinctive culture? Would it be acceptable for the foreign part
of the population to have a lower living standard than Swedish natives?
Equality, freedom of choice, and cooperation became goals of immigrant policy. Equality was to comprise the same opportunities, rights,
and responsibilities as for the rest of the population. Freedom of
choice means the immigrants' right to decide how far they want to
assume a Swedish cultural identity. Cooperation means using various
instruments to work for tolerance and solidarity between immigrants
and Swedes. These important goals led to a series of significant measures at a juncture when the differences between Swedes and immigrants were large, not least in terms of housing standards (table 5.2).

Political refugees have a special position among immigrants. In the
sixties, the proportion of political refugees increased. In the 1968 Par-
liamentary decision on regulated immigration this was given particular
attention. It was held that organized transfers should be the main form
of refugee reception. This principle was underlined and followed up
in the 1978 decision on refugee policy, which stated that efforts should
focus on refugees in acute need of rescue. Each year a refugee quota
is fixed, the number of refugees that Sweden considers it can receive
during that year. The Vietnamese boat refugees were one such group
in the early eighties and were one of the reasons for a relative increase
in Asian immigration (figure 5.2).

In recent years refugee immigration has both increased and assumed more organized forms. The objective has been to spread refugees over the whole country to avoid the formation of large ghettos

TABLE 5.2.   Space and Equipment Standards (1975)

Nationality	Overcrowding* Norm 2 (%)	Modern Housing (%)†
Swedish citizens	6.9	94.2
Swedish-born	7.0	94.1
of which native Swedes	6.9	94.1
Second-generation immigrants	9.8	94.6
Naturalized immigrants	3.5	96.3
Foreign citizens	27.6	93.8
with Nordic citizenship	23.1	96.0
of which Finnish	25.3	96.2
with non-Nordic citizenship	32.4	91.5
of which South European	46.7	89.5
Total	7.8	94.2

Source: Living Conditions, Report no. 9, 1977.
*Norm 2: two persons per room, not counting kitchen and one other room.
†Modern housing: dwelling has central heating, hot and cold running water, W.C., shower/bath.

and to achieve fairer distribution among the local authorities, the municipalities. Thus, municipalities sign agreements with the National Immigration Board to accept a specified number of refugees each year. In 1987, only 6 of the 284 municipalities refused such an agreement. Over three years, this form of organized refugee reception has caused some 14,000 refugees to immigrate to different parts of Sweden each year: 14,460 in 1985, 14,235 in 1986, and between 11,400 and 14,600 in 1987.

In most cases, the municipalities that refused to sign agreements cited job shortages. According to these agreements, municipalities undertake to provide basic training in Swedish and Swedish social life, arrange schooling for the children and housing for the family, and gradually channel the adults into the Swedish labor market.

The Segregation of Ethnic Minorities

There are a relatively large number of studies of socioeconomic segregation in Sweden (Danermark 1984). The fact that much less research has been done on ethnic minorities is probably because we viewed ourselves for a long time as a homogenous country in ethnic and cultural terms. To date only one empirical study deals significantly with ethnic housing segregation in the proper sense, a sociological dissertation from 1984 (Andersson-Brolin). It discusses the spread of foreign citizens and foreign-born persons over the thirty districts in

Stockholm in the seventies compared with the distribution of the Swedish majority group during the same period.

Indirectly, ethnic segregation is treated in Kemeny (1985, 1987) and in our own special analyses of the 1980 population and housing census (1986). Kemeny considers immigrants' housing conditions, covering tenure, overcrowding, housing allowances, and housing standards. Our study of housing market segmentation with respect to immigrants is, of course, closely related to housing segregation in the conventional sense since segmentation by tenure and type of housing are strongly correlated with segregation in Swedish municipalities (Lindberg and Lindén 1986).

Other sources of information on immigrant housing conditions are studies of individual immigrant groups, for example, studies of Finnish immigrants (Leiniö 1974), of Yugoslavs in Sweden, and of Syrians in some Swedish cities (Liedholm 1984). Some material is also available in government and local authority studies dealing with immigrants' living conditions (Stockholm County Council, Regional Planning Office 1984, 1985; Ebbesen 1986).

The existence of ethnic housing segregation in Sweden is an undisputable fact. Figure 5.4 demonstrates the situation in Stockholm in the seventies at aggregated level. The diagram describes the percentage of Swedish and foreign citizens distributed over the thirty districts in Stockholm. To a great extent, immigrants have a different population distribution over Stockholm's districts than do Swedish citizens. The most striking feature is that 25 percent of all immigrants, primarily from Turkey, Chile, and Greece, live in the Spånga district, which only accommodates 6.5 percent of all Stockholm residents. The predominant pattern is that districts whose population expanded rapidly in the seventies and also have a majority of multi-family housing have an overrepresentation of foreign citizens, while the group is generally underrepresented in single-family housing suburbs and in older districts, especially those that are well established and middle class.

The pattern in Stockholm is perhaps also representative of other Swedish cities. One important difference in comparison with many other immigrant countries is that it is unusual to find large concentrations of foreign citizens in the central parts of Swedish cities. This is primarily because the Swedish housing market has largely succeeded in avoiding the development of slums in older housing areas. Buildings are in good condition, and the surroundings generally clean. Although rents for housing in the central and semicentral parts of cities are generally lower than for suburban housing, this has less to do with

FIGURE 5.4.   Percentage Distribution of the Whole Population and
Foreign Citizens in Stockholm's Districts, December 31, 1978

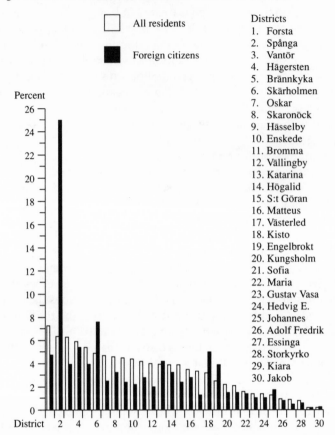

Districts
1. Forsta
2. Spånga
3. Vantör
4. Hägersten
5. Brännkyka
6. Skärholmen
7. Oskar
8. Skaronöck
9. Hässelby
10. Enskede
11. Bromma
12. Vällingby
13. Katarina
14. Högalid
15. S:t Göran
16. Matteus
17. Västerled
18. Kisto
19. Engelbrokt
20. Kungsholm
21. Sofia
22. Maria
23. Gustav Vasa
24. Hedvig E.
25. Johannes
26. Adolf Fredrik
27. Essinga
28. Storkyrko
29. Kiara
30. Jakob

Source: Andersson-Brolin 1984:95.

quality differences in the housing and more to do with the fact that
rents are set in a complicated negotiating system in which market
forces are only allowed to play a limited role. There is a high rate of
maintained residences and some of the central apartments, especially
if they are old and built in a picturesque style, become very attractive
on the market. The mobility that takes place very often is in terms of
an older generation of mainly working-class origin being replaced by
younger professionals with better incomes. Having a lease in the central sections of the city in fact represents a considerable economic asset

FIGURE 5.5.   Development of Segregation (s) in Stockholm (1970–80)

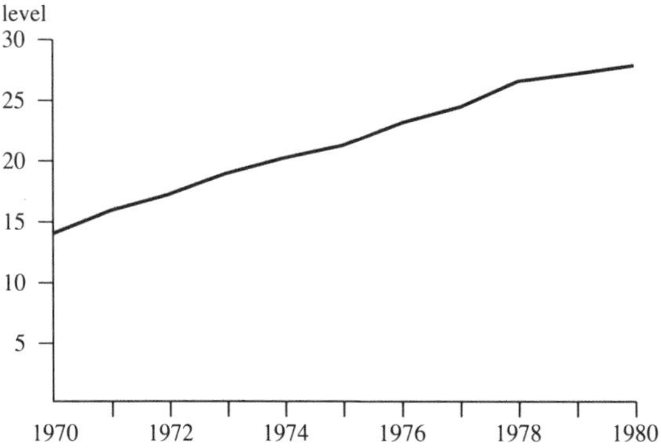

Source: Andersson-Brolin 1984:82.
Note: All foreign citizens by district.

that can be realized when the lease-holder exchanges his or her apartment for an owner-occupied house or a cooperative apartment. This is possible because of the liberal exchange rules granted to the prime lease-holder. The market is growing and, with doubtful legal status, efficiently keeps out the nonaffluent sector of the population.

Property owners have no incentive to carry out extensive subdivision of apartments or to neglect maintenance while speculating in sharp increases in land prices. This means that finding a home in the inner city is often a matter of personal contacts and of money that eventually finds its way to the pocket of the previous holder of the rental lease after complicated chains of exchange. With bank support, the market for cooperative apartments is overheated, with high sale prices. Foreign citizens, especially late arrivals, seldom have personal contacts, money, or good bank contacts, and thus it is not surprising that immigrants have largely settled in the new suburbs, as do other groups which have not established favorable positions in the Swedish housing market. Today the city center in most Swedish cities contains reconstructed and very expensive housing.

In Stockholm, ethnic segregation increased sharply in the seventies (Andersson-Brolin 1984). Figure 5.5 shows the annual development of the segregation (s) index for foreign citizens in relation to Swedish citizens calculated over the thirty Stockholm districts. A major proportion of the increase in segregation is due to the strong increase in the number of foreign citizens in Spånga district (Andersson-Brolin 1984). Throughout the decade, Spånga, with its newly built areas with a concentration of multifamily rental housing, was the easiest place in the city to find an apartment.

In most large urban areas in Sweden a pattern has developed where concentrations of immigrants live in a few newly built areas of multi-family rental housing. A survey carried out by the National Immigration Board found that some thirty housing areas in the country had a population of which 25 percent or more consisted of people with immigrant backgrounds (i.e., foreign citizens and naturalized Swedes) (Ebbesen 1986). For the housing areas in Spånga, however, more than 50 percent of the population had an immigrant background. In fact, the board's survey is a gross underestimate of the number of housing areas with concentrations of immigrants because there was not a uniform definition of the underlying geographical subdivision of the municipalities. However, one should be careful not to exaggerate the problem. One estimate from Stockholm indicates that, nevertheless, only a minority of some 30 percent of foreign-born citizens live in areas with a concentration of immigrants (in this case areas with more than 20 percent of residents born abroad) (Ebbesen 1986).

Discrimination of foreigners in the housing market cannot be advanced as the reason for the concentrations described above. It has only been possible to establish clear cases of negative discrimination for the group of foreign-born gypsies who have difficulties everywhere when trying to find homes without massive help from social services (Andersson-Brolin 1984). Undoubtedly there are more treacherous and hard-to-prove cases of discrimination of other immigrant groups, but in quantitative terms these cases are not important for segregation patterns.

Clear indications exist that ethnic segregation is largely a result of the settlement patterns of the most recent immigrant groups and that most immigrants gradually succeed in achieving both a housing standard and a location in the housing market which largely matches those of Swedes.

Housing Market Segmentation of Ethnic Minorities

Housing market segmentation and segregation are often correlated strongly in Swedish municipalities. Table 5.3 presents the segmentation (S) index for immigrants from different periods in five medium-sized Swedish cities. Note, however, that the S figures are not calculated for geographical units in the cities, but for housing units divided into eight different tenure groups. The S figures measure what we

TABLE 5.3. Immigrant Segmentation in 1980 and 1985
by Period of Immigration*

		Period of Immigration for Immigrant Population, 1980 and 1985				
S for 1980:		1969	1970–74	1975–80		Average
S for 1985:	1967	1968–69	1970–74	1975–79	1980–85	Weighted
Uppsala						
1980	—	11.5	32.5	45.0	—	26.9
1985	9.7	11.8	20.7	32.1	50.6	28.6
Linköping						
1980	—	9.6	20.1	31.9	—	16.5
1985	12.0	14.8	15.5	32.3	41.4	−24.1
Norrköping						
1980	—	9.8	30.5	51.3	—	24.5
1985	7.7	17.6	22.3	43.4	43.9	23.7
Örebro						
1980	—	12.6	25.2	39.9	—	21.2
1985	10.5	19.5	21.2	33.2	39.7	21.6
Västerås						
1980	—	9.1	23.8	37.7	—	16.8
1985	5.4	14.7	14.0	29.3	39.1	15.4

*S index calculated for housing market sectors in the five largest cities, excluding the surrounding metropolitan areas.

prefer to call the degree of segmentation rather than the degree of segregation, although in practice these phenomena are highly correlated. Housing areas are generally homogeneous in terms of ownership category, tenure, and type of dwelling. We define *housing market segmentation* as the unequal division of social groups among different forms of ownership, tenure, and type of dwelling (Lindberg 1985; Lindberg and Lindén 1986).

The various housing market sectors, which thus correspond to geographical units in conventional measurements of the degree of segregation, are: (1) rented in the public sector; (2) rented within state and local authority ownership; (3) rented in privately owned properties; (4) rented in remaining ownership categories (companies and foundations); (5) rented in cooperative housing associations; (6) cooperative in cooperative housing associations; (7) owner-occupier of houses; and (8) owner in multifamily housing. The segmentation indexes are calculated in complete analogy with the index of segregation (Duncan and Duncan 1955). Simplifications are often made in these calculations, but none are made herein.

Table 5.3 shows that the S index increases sharply with period of immigration, that is, the most recent immigrant groups, primarily those from Asia, South America, and some European countries, live more apart from other groups, including Swedes, than do earlier arrivals. This is true of the figures for both 1980 and 1985.

We can also see that there are quite large differences among cities in the degree of segmentation and that there are differences in developments between the two measurement periods. One hypothesis, which we have not yet been able to test on a larger sample, is that development is primarily determined by the degree of expansion. Cities experiencing strong population growth with large volumes of inmigration probably develop a greater degree of segmentation than cities with more orderly population growth. There is some support for this hypothesis on the limited data processed in table 5.3. Between 1980 and 1985, the population of Uppsala increased by 10 percent and the population of Linköping by 6 percent. In these cities the average degree of segmentation also increased. In Norrköping, population decreased by 1 percent, and the degree of segmentation decreased slightly there. Both Örebro and Västerås experienced weak population growth, 1 percent and 2 percent, and in these cases the changes in the average degree of segmentation are marginal.

It is particularly worth noting that the most recent immigrant group, Chileans, Turks, and Vietnamese, appears to exhibit a sharply increased degree of segmentation in rapidly expanding cities. In Uppsala in 1980, the most recently arrived immigrant group had an S index of 45. For the corresponding group in 1985 the S rating had increased to 50.6. In Linköping, the development is even more dramatic, with an increase from 31.9 to 41.4. If, on the other hand, the same groups are studied in the industrial city of Norrköping, which has experienced population decline, we see that the S rating there has decreased from 51.3 to 43.9. In the other cities, which have experienced more orderly development, the changes in S ratings between 1980 and 1985 for the most recent immigrant group are very small.

Our analysis shows that it is not possible to make a general statement that forms of tenure in immigrants' housing patterns are diverging from those of Swedes. The situation varies from place to place. Cities with high in-migration also risk high segmentation, while developments in other places are less dramatic on this point. However, the degree of segmentation decreases quickly the longer an immigrant group has lived in the country. This pattern appears to be true for all municipalities regardless of their degree of expansion.

In a multiple regression analysis of immigrant segmentation in 1980, with all 279 municipalities as analysis units, we found that four variables could "explain" as much as 52 percent of the variation in segmentation indices among municipalities. The most important variables in the ranking were a high degree of socioeconomic segmentation; a high proportion of immigrants who had immigrated in the seventies as a share of all immigrants; and a high degree of industrial employment in the municipality. Correlations for these variables were positive (Lindberg and Lindén 1986).

It is no surprise that segmentation related to socioeconomic status shows a high positive correlation with segmentation related to immigrant status. The majority of immigrants hold lower-paid service or manual jobs, especially immigrants from Southern Europe and Asia. If there is a high segmentation related to socioeconomic status one should expect to find a high degree of segmentation related to immigrant status. In our analysis we use socioeconomic segmentation as the independent variable and immigrant segmentation as the dependent variable. If the whole causal chain is taken into account, however, the matter is more complicated, since immigrant status per se is to a certain extent a cause determining the socioeconomic status a person will get.

Other factors also affect segmentation pattern. In Sweden, as in many other countries, there is a cultural factor which has at least some effect on segregation, on account of a tendency toward voluntary segregation on the part of certain immigrant groups and gypsies, and on account of the tendency of the Swedish majority to avoid housing areas with concentrations of certain ethnic minorities. Other mechanisms like selective housing allocation and discriminating behavior by landlords can also be included. Because there is often overlap between the cultural factor and a socioeconomic factor, as a great proportion of immigrants are also working class, it is, however, difficult in practice to obtain a clear understanding of the cultural factor's importance. What would be needed is data in which it is possible to hold constant immigration period, socioeconomic status, and ethnic-cultural affiliation at the same time. As yet, no such thorough analysis has been performed in Sweden.

The existence of some degree of voluntary selection is confirmed both by case studies, however, and by more everyday observation. The phenomenon is most clearly seen in the case of immigrant groups that are homogeneous in cultural terms at the same time they differ greatly from the majority population in terms of language, religion, and other aspects of cultural patterns, for example, Iranians and Turks. In a case study in Västerås, Liedholm could show a concentra-

TABLE 5.4.   Immigrant Segmentation According to Emigration
Land of Origin (1985)

	Scandinavia	North Europe	Other Europe	Asia Africa	North America	South and Central America	Swedes
Uppsala	15.7	8.6	24.7	53.2	16.7	45.4	32.5
Linköping	10.7	8.2	25.2	41.3	11.1	19.8	21.9
Norrköping	16.2	5.3	17.0	45.9	8.7	51.8	24.0
Örebro	17.1	1.9	21.8	40.2	10.1	10.0	22.4
Västerås	12.7	6.2	11.4	40.4	7.9	36.8	14.9

tion of a Christian Turkish group in a particular housing area (Lied-holm 1984). The concentration had been both steered and sanctioned to some extent by the municipal housing company which managed the area, but as time passed and the group in question set up such insti-tutions as a church and associations, the group's selection of this particular area developed a momentum of its own and continued. Liedholm shows that many, especially women and older members of the group, derived clear advantages from living close to their com-patriots. If the group had been thinly spread over the city, they would have risked being isolated socially. Yet at the same time, she could note that the group completely rejected a proposal from the housing company to bring them together in one specific part of the housing area. The group very much wanted to be integrated in Swedish society, although they wanted to be able to retain their cultural identity and social relations with their countrymen at the same time. They realized that it would be difficult to achieve integration if they were forced to live in ghettolike conditions. At the same time they reacted strongly to the company's policy of setting quotas for members of the group moving into the area as a whole. The immigrants wanted to live rea-sonably close to people from their country without living in a ghetto (Liedholm 1984).

In her Stockholm study, Andersson-Brolin (1984) also demon-strates the existence of certain ethnic concentrations which cannot be wholly explained by period of immigration and socioeconomic status and where an ethnic-cultural factor of some kind could be suspected of being the cause. Thus, for example, she found that Greeks in higher-income classes were overrepresented in the areas in Spånga with high proportions of immigrants. However, she could not establish a similar tendency for other immigrant groups.

Table 5.4, drawn from our own material, shows the degree of segmentation for immigrant groups with different ethnic origins in five major cities outside large metropolitan areas. The table shows that immigrant groups that can be regarded as "exotic" in cultural terms in relation to the Swedish majority culture also generally exhibit greater differences in their housing patterns from other groups taken together. In every case, immigrants from Turkey, the Far East in Asia, and various African countries are among the most highly segmented, primarily located in rented apartments in the public sector. They are generally followed by immigrants from South and Central America, although this does not apply to Linköping and Örebro. However, it turns out that there are only about 200 individuals from these countries in these two exceptional municipalities, while the other cities have between 600 and 1,100 each. We suspect that the low segmentation ratings for this immigrant group in Örebro and Linköping are due to a special socioeconomic structure of the group there. Probably the differences which seem to exist in the housing patterns of immigrant groups of different ethnic origin would be much smaller if the socioeconomic factor and period of immigration could be held constant.

The Housing Standard of Immigrant Households

Several studies have been able to show that differences exist between the housing patterns and housing standards of immigrants and Swedes (table 5.2; Thelander 1984). Often the concept of "cultural distance" is used to explain why immigrants differ from Swedes in various respects. Large cultural differences mean that the social and cultural context in the immigrants' land of origin differs radically from conditions in Sweden. However, such explanations are seldom of general validity. Of course, the cultural variable is important, but its content varies, even for different individuals from the same country of origin due to childhood conditions in different social classes, different cities, or geographic regions. As a result, immigrants from one country almost never replicate their own country's population in miniature.

All immigration is selective in some way. In general, both male and female immigrants to Sweden have less education and more often work in manufacturing industry than Swedes (Thelander 1984). They have probably had a poorer and economically less secure situation in their native countries, which has affected their housing situation there. There are, of course, exceptions to this general pattern. Sweden has experienced immigration of highly educated people from a number of countries, that is, people who have had an economically privileged

FIGURE 5.6.   Model of Gradual Adjustment of Immigrant Households
to Swedish Housing Patterns

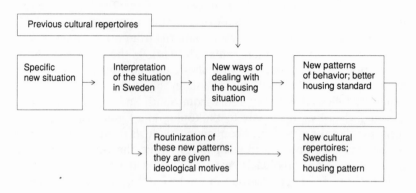

Source: Thelander 1984.

position in both Sweden and their native country. In absolute terms
these immigrants are few, and they come from a limited number of
areas, for example, North America and some Northern and Central
European countries.

It generally takes a long time for the immigrants who do choose to
stay in Sweden to make the decision to acquire Swedish citizenship.
Employment and economic resources both in their native country and
in Sweden, along with their gradual assimilation to Swedish society,
influence their choice of housing form and standard. In this process
of cultural change, new situations gradually become old and familiar
so the immigrant incorporates knowledge about what is seen as the
best solution in a particular housing situation from the point of view
of someone with a Swedish cultural background (figure 5.6). With such
a perspective, attention is shifted from the concept of cultural distance
to culture as a tool for dealing with new situations. The lower housing
standard of immigrant households is no longer a general problem,
becoming instead a stage in housing career which gradually begins to
resemble the corresponding process for a Swedish household (Thelander 1984). However, social problems associated with segregation remain despite this, with a concentration of groups in well-defined
districts of public housing rental apartments. Using this model as an
interpretive framework, we should expect immigrants to become more
like Swedes in their choice of housing type and form of tenure the
longer they stay in Sweden (table 5.5).

TABLE 5.5.   Percent of Immigrants in Different Types of Housing and Tenure According to Year of Immigration (1985)

Year of Immigration	Multifamily Housing		Single-family Housing		Percent	Base
	Rental	Co-op	Rental	Owner-occupied		
1967	39	14	5	42	100	287,606
1968–69	45	12	6	37	100	39,738
1970–74	51	11	5	33	100	85,101
1975–80	58	10	5	27	100	97,161
1981–85	67	7	6	20	100	114,829
Swedes	29	10	7	54	100	7,543,050

The shift toward a Swedish housing standard concerning type of house and tenure is slow. After twenty years in Sweden, considerable differences still exist between immigrants and Swedes. If the differences among nationalities are analyzed, great differences are found concerning the form of tenure (table 5.6). Scandinavians, other North and Central Europeans, and North Americans have a housing form which matches that of Swedes in many respects. There are also similarities among migrants from these countries in several other respects regarding housing standard, as well as other aspects of social life. Immigration from these countries has largely been dominated by well-educated people, who have taken relatively qualified positions on the Swedish labor market.

Immigration from Southern Europe and the Asian countries has long been dominated by people who hold unskilled industrial and service jobs. Despite the fact that many of these immigrants have lived in Sweden for long periods, both their cultural background in countries with a lower housing standard than Sweden and their class background probably play an important part in their slow adaptation to a Swedish housing standard. Immigration from South America largely consists of political refugees; many are young, well-educated, and have lived in Sweden for a long time, but their housing pattern is very different from that of Swedes. One likely explanation is that political immigrants hope for a return to their native country, and this delays their adjustment to a Swedish housing standard. In other instances, when it has early become obvious for other political refugees that there is little chance of returning, both the refugees' applications for Swedish citizenship, which can be made after two years in Sweden, and their

TABLE 5.6.   Form of Housing Tenure among Immigrants from
Different Countries, Compared with Swedes (1985)

	Form of Tenure					
Country of Birth	Public rental (%)	Other rental (%)	Co-op (%)	Owner-occupied (%)	Percent	Base
Scandinavia	29	18	16	66	100	304,867
North Europe	19	19	15	47	100	49,359
Central Europe	18	19	16	47	100	9,014
Eastern Europe	34	19	18	29	100	59,086
Southern Europe	45	12	12	22	100	61,929
Other Europe	24	20	18	38	100	17,806
Asia	53	12	9	26	100	70,372
Africa	52	18	12	18	100	12,055
North America	17	24	2	57	100	11,993
Central America	38	18	11	33	100	2,217
South America	54	13	10	23	100	24,293
Australia	22	24	14	40	100	73
All Immigrants	34	15	15	36	100	624,042
Swedes	16	17	13	54	100	7,538,365

adjustment to Swedish society have taken place quickly. This was true
of the fairly extensive immigration from Hungary in the late fifties
(Thelander 1984).

Housing Conditions

Housing conditions in Sweden are of high overall standard. Only 4
percent of dwellings are not modern in some respect, and lack at least
one of the following: central heating, running hot and cold water,
W.C., and bath/shower. The greater part of this stock is in single-family
housing with co-operative or private rental tenure and built before
World War II. On the other hand, differences exist among housing
types in dwelling size. The largest dwellings are in multifamily housing.
Since immigrants live in multifamily housing more often than do
Swedes, a result of their use of this house type means more overcrowded households. In 1980, 4 percent of households in Sweden were
overcrowded according to Norm 2. This figure had fallen to 2.5 percent
in 1985. Here, however, there are great differences among immigrants
from different countries (table 5.7). For countries from which immigration has been dominated by people in industrial and lower service
employment, overcrowding is considerable. These immigrants also
come from a housing market which is very different from the Swedish

TABLE 5.7.   Country of Birth of Head of Household by Percent,
Overcrowded (1980)

Country of Birth of Head of Household	Extremely Over- crowded (Below Norm 1)	Heavily Over- crowded (Below Norm 2)	Over- crowded (Below Norm 3)	Neither Over- nor Under- Crowded (at Norm 3)	Under- crowded (Above Norm 3)	Total
Sweden	0.5	3.2	13.4	20.7	62.7	100
Denmark	0.6	3.1	21.6	13.2	62.1	100
Finland	1.2	10.5	27.0	24.2	38.3	100
Norway	0.5	2.4	25.4	6.7	65.5	100
Germany	0.4	2.0	20.4	8.8	68.8	100
U.K.	1.0	4.1	29.0	6.3	60.0	100
U.S.A.	0.4	2.0	26.3	1.5	70.2	100
Estonia	0.3	2.7	23.3	11.8	62.2	100
Hungary	0.4	5.2	21.4	18.9	54.6	100
Poland	0.5	4.5	22.0	16.7	56.8	100
Greece	12.3	27.5	25.1	31.5	15.9	100
Italy	1.5	8.7	26.4	19.7	45.2	100
Yugoslavia	5.2	21.8	23.8	28.4	26.0	100
Chile	1.1	9.1	21.7	43.0	26.2	100
Turkey	10.5	30.3	21.4	32.6	15.7	100

Source: Kemeny 1987.
Norm 1: More than two persons in every room except the kitchen.
Norm 2: More than two persons per bedroom, not counting kitchen and one other room.
Norm 3: More than one person or co-habiting couple per bedroom.

market in terms of standard, for example that of Greece, Yugoslavia, or Turkey. There is probably also considerable overcrowding in these countries among the social classes these immigrants represent.

Finns in Sweden are also greatly overcrowded. In contrast to other Scandinavians there is a high proportion of reemigration among Finns. Migration between Finland and Sweden has always been extensive and different from migration with the other Nordic countries. Finnish immigration has primarily consisted of unskilled labor for Swedish industry. Immigrants are from the northern and central parts of the interior, dominated by agriculture and forestry, where the shortage of employment has been a major problem. Finland is a bilingual country, with Finnish and Swedish as official languages. Swedish is a minority language spoken by 6 percent of the population concentrated on the south and west coasts. That part of the population which has immigrated to Sweden has mostly been Finnish-speaking and have had a much greater handicap than other Scandinavians, since Finnish belongs to a different group of languages and has nothing in common with other Nordic languages. For these reasons immigration from Finland has several similarities with immigration from Southern Europe and Turkey; it is more or less involuntary, there is a language handicap, and closeness to their native country has contributed to the extensive reemigration of Finns and their slow adaptation to Swedish housing.

Summary

Sweden entered the modern era with a population that was very homogeneous in ethnic terms. In the 1920s, Sweden was still an emigrant country; the thirties saw some re-immigration of Swedes, but the influx of people with different cultural identities than Swedes was still insignificant. Since the end of World War II this picture has changed gradually. Sweden can no longer be described as an ethnically homogeneous country on the fringe of Europe; almost 10 percent of the whole population are first-generation immigrants. The proportion of households with some kind of immigrant background is considerably higher.

It is easy to show that immigrants in Sweden have a lower housing standard for every reasonable point of comparison than native Swedes. It is also a fact that segregation exists between immigrants and Swedes. Immigrants have a different housing pattern in terms of tenure, ownership category, and type of house than do Swedes on average. In an international perspective the housing situation of immigrants in Sweden hardly seems particularly alarming. However, this is not because Swedes are particularly good at solving the housing problems of ethnic minorities, but rather because housing standards in Sweden are high in general (Liedholm, Lindberg, and Lindén 1987).

However, one more unique point merits attention in an examination of current Swedish immigrant policy. For some years the government has been pursuing an active policy to spread refugee immigrants throughout the country to aid their adaptation to Swedish society. According to this policy, the government signs annual agreements with municipalities on the reception of specific quotas of refugees and the provision of housing, language training, and employment. The aim is to break the pattern which has meant that immigrants have primarily settled in metropolitan areas. Housing locations of immigrants are unevenly spread over the country. In rural areas they only make up about 1 percent of the population, whereas they can account for up to one-fifth of the population in highly industrial municipalities.

Immigrants are also segregated from the rest of the population in their housing. Stockholm had a segregation index of 30 in 1980. Corresponding data from other municipalities are not available, but there is reason to suppose that Stockholm is not atypical. In the 1970s the s index for Stockholm increased from about 15 to 30 (Duncan's index). The development in other places probably varies with the places' rate of expansion. Studies of housing market segmentation, or the distribution of different population groups across different housing market sectors, give strong indications of this. Places experiencing strong expansion exhibit high degrees of segmentation while places losing population have lower degrees of segmentation. There are in general more opportunities for households to move between segments on the housing market in the places losing population.

Discrimination can occur for a few ethnic groups, but on the whole it is of no importance as an explanation of the differences between the housing conditions of Swedes and immigrants. Rather, two factors stand out as important foundations for explanations. First, immigrants must accept that they are new arrivals in the housing market, a fate they share with other new arrivals. Thus they generally end up in newly built areas of rental housing on the outskirts of cities. Second, the immigrant group has a different composition in terms of socioeconomic class than do Swedes. On average they have less education, and they often have more poorly paid jobs than the rest of the population. A large part of immigrant segregation is therefore related to underlying socioeconomic segregation, and a result of this is large differences between the housing patterns and standards of different ethnic minorities in Sweden. In general, immigrants from the Nordic countries, North Europe, North America, and Australia have positions in the housing market that are close to those of Swedes. Immigrant groups from Southern Europe, Asia, Africa, and South and Central America, which are dominated by relatively unskilled industrial employment, have a lower housing standard on average and are more segregated and segmented than the former group. But these differences decrease gradually according to how long a group has lived in Sweden. A decisive issue on the question of the future development of immigrant housing conditions is how successful immigrants will be in the Swedish labor market. If they continue to be overrepresented in low-paid, low-status jobs, they will also be more overcrowded than the majority group in the future.

References

Andersson-Brolin, L. 1984. *Etnisk bostadssegregation* (Ethnic residential segregation). Stockholm: Swedish Council for Building Research.

Bergström, U. 1984. *Stockholmarnas levnadsförhållanden 2. Invandrarna* (Living conditions in Stockholm 2. Immigrants). City of Stockholm. Stockholm: Research and Statistics Department.

Biterman, D. 1985. *Invandrare i Stockholms län 9: Bostäder och boende* (Immigrants in the county of Stockholm: Housing and residential conditions). Stockholm: Stockholm County Council, Regional Planning Office.

Danermark, B. 1984. *Boendesegregationens utveckling i Sverige under efterkrigstiden* (The development of residential segregation in Sweden in the post-war period). Stockholm: Ministry of Housing and Physical Planning.

Duncan, O. D., and B. Duncan. 1955. "Residential Distribution and Occupational Stratification." *American Journal of Sociology* 60:493–503.

Ebessen, U. 1986. *Invandrartäta bostadsområden i utveckling* (The development of housing areas with high proportions of immigrants). Norrköping: National Immigration Board.

Government Bill. 1968.

Guteland, G., I. Holmberg, T. Hägerstrand, A. Karlqvist, and B. Rundblad. 1975. *Ett folks biografi: Befolkning och samhälle från historia till framtid* (The biography of a people: Past and future population changes in Sweden, conditions and consequences). Stockholm: Publica, Liber Förlag.

Kemeny, J. 1985. *Immigrant Housing Conditions in Urban Sweden*. Gävle: National Swedish Institute for Building Research.

———. 1987. *Immigrant Housing Conditions in Sweden*. Gävle: National Swedish Institute for Building Research.

Leiniö, T. L. 1974. *Finska invandrare i Sverige 1974* (Finnish immigrants in Sweden in 1974). Stockholm: Institute for Social Research.

Levnadsförhållenden. 1977. *Invandrarnas levnadsförhållenden 1975* (The living conditions of immigrants 1975). Stockholm: National Board of Health and Welfare/Statistics.

Liedholm, M. 1984. *Boinflytande: Förutsättningar och hinder i ett bostadsområde med etnisk särprägel* (Resident influence: Opportunities and obstacles in a housing area with a special ethnic character). Lund: Research Group on Housing and Urban Development, Department of Sociology, University of Lund.

Liedholm, M., G. Lindberg, and A. L. Lindén. 1987. "Housing Policy as an Agent of Social Welfare." Pp. 51–81 in *The Legacy and Opportunity for High Rise Housing in Europe: The Management of Innovation*, edited by M. Bulos and S. Walker. London: Housing Studies Group, Polytechnic of the South Bank.

Lindberg, G. 1985. "Den socioekonomiska bostadsmarknadssegmentationen (The socio-economic housing market segmentation)." *Ekonomi och stad-*

sutveckning. Stockholm: The Nordic Institute for Urban and Regional Planning.

Lindberg, G., and A. L. Lindén. 1986. "Housing Market Segmentation in Swedish Local Authorities: Immigrants and Swedes; Young and Old." *Scandinavian Housing and Planning Research* 3:233–48.

SOU/Swedish Government Official Report. 1974. *Orter i regional samverkan* (Communities in regional co-operation), vol. 1. Stockholm: Expert Group for Regional Development.

————. 1982. *Invandringspolitiken. Bakgrund. Delbetänkande av invandrarpolitiska kommittén* (Immigration policy: Background. preliminary report of the Committee on Immigration Policy), vol. 4g. Stockholm: Expert Group for Regional Development.

Thelander, A. L. 1984. *Bostad efter behov: Jämlikhet och integration i boendet på 80-talets bostadsmarknad* (Housing according to need: Housing equality and housing integration on the housing market of the eighties). Stockholm: Swedish Council for Building Research.

Widgren, J. 1982. *Svensk invandrarpolitik: En faktabok* (Swedish immigrant policy: A factual account). Lund: Liber Förlag.

6. Housing Segregation of Immigrants in West Germany

The influx of foreign-born population in the mid-1960s and the resulting increase in ethnic minorities constituted a new problem for the Federal Republic of Germany. Except for the integration of immigrants in the early nineteenth century, most of whom were Polish, and the integration of Germans from the former parts of the Reich after World War II, West Germany has had little experience in integrating minorities. Contrary to other European countries such as Great Britain or France, Germany lost its colonies after World War I and thus was never confronted with the problems of integrating ethnic minorities until recently. This is aside from the dramatic fate of the Jewish population during the Nazi period, which obviously documents a very extreme ethnocentrism.

Ethnic minorities in the FRG differ not only by native country and period of arrival, but also by reasons for in-migration. To analyze the status of ethnic minorities, we use the latter criterion and differentiate among three types of minorities: guest workers, refugees, and the repatriated. Throughout this chapter, we use the term *foreign-born* to designate minority members born either outside or within the FRG.

The first and major group, foreign labor or guest workers, came as a labor force and was supposed to "rotate" back to their home countries as the number of jobs decreased. Thus, they were an industrial reserve army in the Marxist sense. However, the majority stayed in West Germany and became neither immigrants nor guests. It is this ambivalent status that distinguishes them from most minorities in other European countries and creates specific problems. Second, a new group of foreign born, most of them from Asian or African countries, has come to West Germany since the mid-1980s and is composed of refugees or persons seeking political asylum. The third type of minority is the "repatriated," persons of German origin who live in Poland, the Soviet Union, or Romania. They come to the FRG by

116

emigration contracts with these countries and are treated legally as Germans; most speak little German. Regardless of the guest worker status, a multitude of scholarly studies indicates that they can be treated as immigrants in many respects such as living conditions and the stages of assimilation (Heckmann 1981). The problems of all groups are not restricted to common difficulties of assimilation and discrimination. They are aggravated by an economic recession in West Germany that is marked by rising unemployment rates, which in turn are due to larger restructuring of economies from manufacturing to information processing and services in all industrialized countries.

We will discuss herein both the specific status of the three types of minorities and their similarities with immigrants. To put problems of housing and segregation into a broader context, our analysis also pertains to the economic conditions of the minorities. First, a brief history of the guest-worker policy and corresponding population data are presented, then the economic conditions and problems in the FRG. We next analyze housing conditions and extent of residential segregation. Housing data are highly selective because the last housing census available is from 1968, and data from the 1987 census are unavailable. Finally, we make a more detailed analysis of assimilation, specifying the conditions affecting the decision to stay in the FRG or to return to countries of origin. The period under study is 1976 to 1986. Data refer to three levels: the FRG, its twelve largest cities, and the individual level to demonstrate some general problems of assimilation. The analysis refers to the two largest ethnic groups, Turkish and Yugoslavian labor migrants, of the first and second generation.

Population

Minorities in the FRG are predominantly made up of foreign laborers who came by governmental contracts to alleviate a labor shortage in the 1960s. The growing blue-collar job surplus in the early 1960s led the West German government to sign labor import agreements with several Southern European countries: Italy (1955), Spain (1960), Greece (1960), and Turkey (1961), Morocco (1963), Portugal (1964), Tunisia (1965), and Yugoslavia (1968). The foreign labor force was called guest workers because they were to work in West Germany for a limited time only and then rotate back home. However, the number of foreign residents increased from 170,000 in 1952 to 2,600,600 in 1973, and then to 4,512,700 in 1986. By the end of 1986, 31.8 percent of the newcomers were Turks, and the foreign population made up

TABLE 6.1.   Total and Foreign-born Population in FRG
(1960–86)

Nationality	1961	1970	1980	1986
Total	56,174,800	60,650,600	61,657,900	61,140,500
Foreign	686,200	2,600,600	4,453,600	4,512,700
%	1.2	4.3	7.2	7.4

Sources: 1961 and 1970: *Statistisches Bundesamt* 1983:15; 1980: *Statistisches Jahrbuch für die Bundesrepublik Deutschland* 1983:60; 1986: *Statistisches Jahrbuch für die Bundesrepublik Deutschland* 1987:60.

7.4 percent of the entire population of the FRG (tables 6.1, 6.2). In the beginning they concentrated in large cities, especially in Munich, Stuttgart, and the large cities of the Rhine-Ruhr area.

The policy of rotation was clearly based upon economic rationality, which was restricted to economic reasoning regardless of the needs of foreign laborers and their families. As the novelist Max Frisch has phrased it: "We called for laborers and there came human beings." For all, but particularly in the case of the Turks, recession conditions in West Germany proved more attractive than the best of economic ties in the guest workers' home countries. Despite rising anti-guest-worker prejudice in the German population, the social and political climate made expulsion of the workers virtually impossible. Then West Germany's economy slowed in the early 1970s and, as a consequence, in 1973 all guest-worker immigration was banned via the so-called "recruitment stop" except for close family members of those already working in the FRG. In effect, not only spouses and children joined family heads, but also brothers and sisters. For a short period, the absolute number of foreign born remained almost constant at around 3,970,000, 6.4 percent of the West German population in 1974. By 1979, the total had reached 4.1 million, 6.7 percent of the population, and it continued to climb to 4.5 million in 1986, or 7.4 percent of the population.

Even the 1983–84 federal program to promote returns to home countries by a "return subsidy" of 10,000 DM ($2,000 at the time and currently $6,000) for each household member (under the condition of recent unemployment) and a refund of the laborer's share of social security payments resulted in only 13,600 who agreed to return subsidies and 114,000 who agreed to refundings, with an estimated total of 300,000 guest workers and families who left Germany.

Thus, the idea that foreigners are "rotating guests" is no longer pertinent. The majority did not return to their home countries; they

TABLE 6.2.   Foreign-born Population in FRG, Percent by Nationality
(1960–86)

Nationality	1961	1970	1980	1986
Turkey	1.0	9.5	32.8	31.8
Yugoslavia	2.4	7.8	14.2	13.1
Italy	28.7	22.8	13.9	11.9
Greece	6.1	11.1	6.7	6.2
Spain	6.4	9.8	4.0	3.3
Portugal	0.1	1.3	2.5	1.7
Other	55.3	37.7	25.9	32.0
Total %	100.0	100.0	100.0	100.0
	686,200	1,806,700	4,453,300	4,512,700

Sources: 1961 and 1970: *Statistisches Bundesamt* 1983:27; 1980: *Statistisches Jahrbuch für die Bundesrepublik Deutschland* 1983:68; 1986: *Statistisches Jahrbuch für die Bundesrepublik Deutschland* 1987:68.

instead became immigrants. This is documented by the fact that in 1986, 66.5 percent of all foreigners had lived in West Germany longer than eight years (*Statistisches Jahrbuch für die Bundesrepublik Deutschland* 1987:68).

Since 1985, the policy of the federal government no longer explicitly stresses the goal of return, but neither does it promote an active citizenship-integration strategy. Several political moves have been made by the Social Democratic party since 1975 to give foreign labor the right to vote in local elections ("communal voting right"); all have failed to reach legislation. Moreover, applications for citizenship have been made more difficult. In June 1988, details of a plan of the Federal Department of Domestic Affairs were revealed; applications were to be restricted to those guest workers who came to West Germany before 1973 (*Süddeutsche Zeitung*, June 25, 1988, p. 1). In contrast to the federal policy, the responsibility for foreign labor and their families rests upon local administrations, which promote an integration strategy.

The term *double ambivalence* applies: the ambivalence of administrative policies corresponds to an ambivalence of the foreign laborers themselves. They pretend to want to return to their home countries eventually, but in fact they remain in Germany. Only a few of those eligible for citizenship apply. Naturalization occurred only to a minor extent; in the 1972–81 period the figure never exceeded 15,000 per year.

For the two other types of minorities, policies are split. For those repatriated it is very easy to obtain naturalization because they are

TABLE 6.3.   Applicants for Political Asylum in FRG
by Nationality (1980 and 1986)

	1980		1986	
	Total	(%)	Total	(%)
Europe	65,809	61.0	25,164	25.3
Africa	8,339	7.8	9,486	9.5
Asia	31,998	29.7	56,575	56.8
Other*	1,672	1.5	8,425	8.4
Total	107,818	100.0	99,650	100.0

Source: *Statistisches Jahrbuch für die Bundesrepublik Deutschland*
1987:69.
*Includes applicants without nationality.

regarded as "Germans," regardless of their factual links, such as language skills, to the German culture. The group is growing; 160,000
were expected in 1988. Of those obtaining citizenship in 1985, almost
two-thirds were from the repatriated German-origin group and only
14 percent were Italian, Yugoslavian, or Turkish.

A third type of minority group are those seeking political asylum
in the FRG. Their absolute number has remained fairly constant since
1980, but the countries most represented shifted from European to
Asian. In early July 1988, the Department of Domestic Affairs announced that they expected 100,000 persons to seek political asylum
in 1988; by mid-1988, 40,000 applicants had registered, 10 percent of
which obtained citizenship.

As data in table 6.1 indicate, minorities constitute a growing percentage of West Germany's total population. Because minorities are
concentrated in large cities, their share of the population in cities is
far above the national average (table 6.4). And even these figures
conceal dramatic differences among each city's census tracts. In all
cities, foreign born represent an overproportionate share of the population in two types of residential areas: those adjacent to the central
business district (C.B.D.), often areas designated for urban renewal,
and in peripheral large new housing estates built in the 1960s and
1970s. In addition, all cities have neighborhoods in which the percentage of foreign born in primary schools exceeds 60 or even 80
percent of the school population.

Hence, the general demographic trend is a decrease of the native
German population due to death rates exceeding birth rates, as well
as low fertility rates. In the cities, the decrease is also due to moves
to the suburbs and the share of foreign-born population growing both

TABLE 6.4.   Population and Percent Foreign Population,
West German Cities of 500,000 or More (1970, 1980, and 1986)

City	Population		Foreign Born (%)		
	Total 1986	% Change 1980–86	1970	1980	1986
Berlin	1,879,225	−6.0	3.5	10.7	13.7
Hamburg	1,571,267	−4.5	5.4	9.0	10.2
Munich	1,274,716	−1.9	14.0	16.4	17.3
Cologne	914,336	−6.4	9.1	13.6	15.0
Essen	615,421	−5.0	3.8	5.5	6.1
Frankfurt	592,411	−5.9	13.3	20.2	25.0
Dortmund	568,164	−6.6	3.7	8.5	8.9
Stuttgart	565,486	−2.6	13.1	17.7	18.1
Düsseldorf	560,572	−5.1	9.2	12.3	16.0
Bremen	521,976	−6.0	3.8	6.4	7.5
Duisburg	514,718	−7.8	6.2	12.2	13.0
Hannover	505,718	−5.4	6.1	9.8	9.7
FRG	61,140,500	−0.8	4.3	7.2	7.4

Sources: *Statistisches Jahrbuch Deutscher Gemeinden* 69, 1982:306; 73, 1986:272; 74, 1987:36–37, 272–74, 291, 325; *Hamburg in Zahlen*, July 1987:262, data for FRG in table 1.

by immigration and higher fertility rates. Ironically, the decrease in the German population and increase in the foreign population gives cities the advantage of receiving a higher fiscal income because tax revenues are redistributed from the federal to the local level on a per capita basis.

Employment

As in the United States, the type and speed of economic transformation in West Germany varies by region. However, the general tendency is the same for all large cities of 100,000 or more inhabitants: a decline in employment in manufacturing and an increase in service jobs.

In 1970–80, the total change in numbers of jobs was very low. Yet these totals conceal dramatic internal shifts. Manufacturing and mining jobs declined by 10.3 percent, whereas services (including construction) increased by 14.9 percent. Comparing 1970–80 with the 1980–86 period, the decline in manufacturing continued (−7.9 percent), but these losses were no longer compensated by gains in services, where jobs also declined by −0.8 percent.[1] Consequently, unemployment went up dramatically. Among the largest cities, all

TABLE 6.5.   German and Foreign Labor by Industry, in Percent (1970, 1980, and 1986)

Year/ Nationality	All Industries	Agri- culture	Mining, Manufacturing, Construction	Commerce	Transpor- tation	Insurance Banking	Services
1970							
Total	20,335,802	0.4	52.7	15.3	6.0	2.7	10.0
German	18,496,943	0.4	49.7	16.4	6.4	2.9	10.5
Foreign	1,838,859	0.9	82.8	4.6	2.1	0.4	4.7
1980							
Total	21,003,474	1.1	51.6	13.9	4.8	3.6	16.9
German	18,990,980	1.0	49.6	14.8	4.9	4.0	17.1
Foreign	2,012,494	0.8	70.0	6.5	3.7	0.7	15.0
1986							
Total	20,730,107	1.1	48.6	13.2	4.8	4.0	19.3
German	19,138,560	1.1	47.2	13.7	4.8	4.3	19.4
Foreign	1,591,547	0.9	65.4	6.7	3.8	0.8	18.4
Percent Change, 1970–80							
Total	+1.9	+0.7	+0.6	−0.9	−1.0	+1.0	+7.5
German	+2.7	+0.6	+1.2	−1.2	−1.4	+1.2	+7.1
Foreign	+9.4	−0.2	−6.2	+2.5	+2.0	+0.4	+11.7
Percent Change, 1980–86							
Total	−1.3	0.0	−3.6	−0.9	−0.1	+0.4	+2.2
German	+0.7	+0.1	−2.0	−1.0	−0.1	+0.3	+2.5
Foreign	−20.9	−0.1	−18.3	−1.2	−0.7	−0.1	−0.5

Sources: Authors' calculations from data in *Amtliche Nachrichten der Bundesanstalt für Arbeit, Jahreszahlen* 1973:18; 1979:50; May 1984:778; *Jahreszahlen* 1986:13, 20.

except Düsseldorf and Munich lost more workers than the national average, with the highest losses occurring in Duisburg.

The functional transformation of West German cities from centers of goods-processing to centers of information-processing has reduced the role these cities were once able to play as employment opportunity centers for disadvantaged and ethnic minorities. This appears especially true for cities in West Germany's Rhine-Ruhr and the Saar regions where economic transformation and resulting blue-collar job declines have been most severe since the early seventies (table 6.5).

The simultaneous transformation and selective decline of employment in the cities have contributed to a number of serious problems including a widening gap between urban job opportunity structures and skill levels of disadvantaged residents (mismatch), unemployment, and public assistance.

Mismatch

Declines in blue-collar and other entry-level jobs in central cities and growth in white-collar information-processing jobs that require substantial education or training have occurred (Kasarda and Friedrichs 1985:25). As a result, the gap between the skill levels of minority groups residing in central cities and skill requirements of new urban growth industries has widened. The result is a growing demographic-employment opportunity mismatch. *Mismatch* may be defined as a discordant distribution of labor qualifications with respect to qualifications required for available jobs (Cheshire 1979).

We find that for 1980–84, in the 67 cities of 100,000 or more inhabitants, an overall decline in jobs requiring low qualifications (ten or less years of schooling) and a rise in jobs that require high qualifications (thirteen or more years of schooling). Furthermore, since foreign labor is less qualified, the workers are harder hit by changing qualification requirements. The number of jobs for Germans with low education dropped by 11 percent compared to by 21.8 percent for foreigners (Kasarda, Friedrichs, and Ehlers 1989). This largely explains why central city unemployment rates in West Germany tend to be above the national average and inordinately high among ethnic minorities.

The request for higher qualifications will continue. A projection for the 1982–2000 period indicates that even under status quo conditions the share of jobs requiring a low qualification will drop noticeably, whereas jobs requiring high qualifications will increase (Rothkirch and Tessaring 1986).

Unemployment

Unemployment was virtually unknown to West Germany until the early 1970s; even in 1980 the total unemployment rate was only 3.4 percent. In the following years, it rose sharply, and the trend will probably continue until the late 1990s. From all economic forecasts, we have forecast that the number of unemployed will go up to 2.4 million by 1990 (Klauder, Schnur, and Thon 1985:62).

Unemployment rates vary among cities. By 1984 Duisburg, Bremen, Saarbrücken, and even Hamburg exhibited high rates, indicating the crisis in some of their industries, such as mining, steel, and shipbuilding. Düsseldorf, Frankfurt, and the southern cities of Stuttgart

TABLE 6.6.   Unemployment and Public Assistance, West German Cities of 500,000 or More (1980 and 1986)

City	Employed		Unemployment Rate			Public Assistance Recipients 1984 per 1,000 inhabitants†
	1986	% Change 1980–86	Total 1980	Total 1986	Foreign* 1986	
Berlin	732,500	+0.4	4.3	10.7	14.6	67
Hamburg	714,900	−6.8	3.3	13.3	23.7	62
Munich	656,700	−0.6	2.4	5.9	10.2	28
Cologne	413,300	−2.8	6.0	14.0	21.0	36
Essen	218,700	−6.3	5.6	14.7	21.8	45
Frankfurt	448,200	−2.5	3.0	6.5	9.4	54
Dortmund	206,500	−8.9	6.1	18.2	23.6	58
Stuttgart	360,500	−0.7	2.0	4.9	6.2	30
Düsseldorf	334,800	−2.0	4.1	12.0	15.0	53
Bremen	234,800	−6.6	5.2	15.5	24.6	70
Duisburg	191,400	−13.9	6.6	17.7	20.5	49
Hannover	281,600	−7.3	4.4	12.6	22.4	55
FRG	20,730,100	−1.1	3.8	9.0	14.2	34

Sources: *Statistisches Jahrbuch Deutscher Gemeinden* 69, 1982:306; 73, 1986:272; 74, 1987:36–37, 272–274, 291, 325; *Hamburg in Zahlen* 1987:262, data FRG: *Statistisches Jahrbuch für die Bundesrepublik Deutschland* 1987:106, 112, 416.

*The unemployment rate for foreign labor is not given in official statistics. Therefore, the unemployment rate ("Vergleichsquote") was calculated as: Unemployed / (Unemployed + Employed). Calculations based on data in *Amtliche Nachrichten der Bundesanstalt für Arbeit* 1987:96–98, 1206–1213.

†"Continuous assistance for living" only.

and Munich were below the national average. These are economically prosperous cities where both the rates for German and foreign labor are comparatively low. In contrast, in Bremen and Saarbrücken one out of four foreign employees was unemployed.

As can be seen from the data in table 6.6, foreign labor not only experienced larger losses in jobs requiring low qualifications and less increase in jobs requiring high qualifications than the Germans, they were harder hit as well by unemployment. In 1984, differences in unemployment rates even increased. By 1984, the unemployment rate for foreign labor was double that for German labor. These increasing differences are primarily due to the lower qualifications of foreign labor and their numbers in the declining manufacturing sector (Friedrichs 1985b).

Public Assistance

Paralleling unemployment rates for persons on public assistance increased in 1980–86. As with unemployment, there were considerable differences between the twelve cities. Evidently, cities with high unemployment have high quotas of persons on public assistance and vice versa. However, there are exceptions that are due to local differences in the implementation of public assistance programs. Typically, the unemployed receive unemployment "money" for one year; if unemployment continues, they receive unemployed aid for a further two years. After that period, they are on public assistance. Because more foreign than German laborers are unemployed, we would therefore expect the proportion of foreign labor on public assistance to be higher than the proportion of Germans. This is not the case; in 1984 the ratio for the twelve cities was 34.9 per thousand inhabitants for the German and 31.7 for the foreign population.[2] This discrepancy is difficult to explain, yet, two reasons can be given. First, by law, foreign born are eligible for public assistance, as are Germans. In contrast, refugees typically receive public assistance during the period between application for citizenship and decision. To receive public assistance, it has to be proven first that the person cannot be supported by his or her family. This regulation is applied in varying degrees of strictness by local authorities of the states of the FRG. Second, it is legally possible to expel foreign persons not able to finance their living costs and who instead live on public assistance. Although this is not the common practice, it might deter foreigners from applying for public assistance. Regulations to expel foreign born receiving public assistance vary among the states (Länder) of the FRG, and this—in addition to differences in the cities' economic conditions—may also account for the differences observed in table 6.6.

Housing and Segregation

It is not possible to provide a detailed account of the housing situation of ethnic minorities because of the lack of statistical data. The last available census is from 1968, and the 1987 census data were unavailable. Furthermore, it can safely be assumed that the three types of minority groups differ in their residential location. We are therefore limited to evidence from case studies and some more detailed data for Hamburg.

There are no differences in the dwelling spaces of owners, but foreign owners have only 1 percent of the total number of dwellings owned, a figure far below their share in the population. Foreign renters have smaller apartments than their German counterparts, even when controlling for household size. Most of the major group of foreigners, foreign labor, was initially located in inner-city neighborhoods near declining industrial and commercial zones, areas often designated for urban renewal. Case studies for Augsburg (Ruile 1984; Reimann and Reimann 1987), Berlin (Hoffmeyer-Zlotnik 1977, 1982), Frankfurt (Helmert 1982), Nuremberg (Märtens 1980), or Stuttgart (Loll 1982a, 1982b) have shown the disproportionate concentration of foreign born in such areas. Both Hoffmeyer-Zlotnik and Märtens demonstrate that invasion-succession processes occurred in such CBD-adjacent renewal areas, following closely the patterns observed in North American cities. In the FRG, it was foreign labor that invaded traditional working-class neighborhoods.

This situation has partially changed, and by the mid-1980s more members of ethnic minorities were found in peripheral locations such as the large new housing estates constructed in the 1960s and 1970s. The new location pattern was probably not due to achievement-integration processes, as was the dispersal Jonassen (1949) observed over time for Norwegian immigrants in New York, but to the existence of periphery social housing newly accessible to minorities.

The early German pattern of residential distribution of minorities may more adequately be accounted for by several other divergent processes. Many foreign laborers initially did not want to stay and chose cheap dwellings in order to save money to send home. In addition, German landlords were not willing to rent to foreign labor households, except those landlords owning turn-of-the-century buildings in neighborhoods in the zone of transition. These buildings very often needed repair, which had been postponed due to anticipated urban renewal. However, rent returns were highly profitable because overcrowded dwellings resulted in high rent totals.

The degree of assimilation of the newcomers can be researched for this inner-city situation from 1975 to 1979. Given the fact that the minorities arrived at different periods, we may assume: (1) residential segregation to be lower for the early period and higher for the later period minorities, and (2) segregation to decrease over time for all minorities. Both assumptions can be tested, although not with cohort data, by a study Loll (1982a, 1982b) conducted for Hamburg and Stuttgart. The study covers the period from 1974–79 and is based on census tracts as spatial units. The assumption underlying the selection of these cities was that in a city with a high share of foreign born, the pressure toward residential assimilation would be stronger than in a city with a low share of foreign born. In 1974, 16.3 percent of Stuttgart and 6.9 percent of Hamburg was foreign born.

TABLE 6.7.   Indices of Dissimilarity, Hamburg and Stuttgart (1974–79)*

Nationality	1974	1975	1976	1977	1978	1979
Stuttgart						
Italy	28.9	28.4	29.1	29.5	29.3	29.6
Spain	32.8	33.8	34.5	34.8	35.3	34.3
Greece	32.5	34.3	36.0	37.6	39.0	39.2
Turkey	34.6	32.3	34.1	34.7	34.0	34.2
Portugal	41.1	42.4	41.8	43.7	42.7	42.4
Yugoslavia	28.4	28.6	29.2	29.8	29.4	29.3
Total foreign	29.9	30.4	31.4	32.2	32.6	32.8
Hamburg						
Italy	32.2	32.8	32.4	32.0	32.7	31.0
Spain	40.2	40.4	39.4	38.1	37.9	37.1
Greece	40.4	41.5	40.6	41.0	40.4	40.3
Turkey	41.9	43.9	44.5	45.3	45.9	45.4
Portugal	51.6	52.1	50.9	52.0	52.4	52.3
Yugoslavia	34.2	35.1	35.6	36.2	36.3	36.1
Total foreign	38.7	39.3	40.5	41.0	41.5	41.5

Source: *Loll* 1982a:284.
*Number of census tracts: Stuttgart, 144; Hamburg, 180.

In table 6.7, the results of the analysis are presented, with minorities listed in the order in which the contract was signed between their respective governments and the FRG. It is apparent that trends are fairly similar in both cities, with Italians and Yugoslavians being assimilated the most when measured by residential segregation; Turks and Portuguese are the most segregated. Surprisingly, segregation does not decrease but remains on a constant level or even increases. Thus, the assumption is confirmed of a negative effect of the share of minorities on segregation, whereas the two other hypotheses, lower segregation of early period minorities and decrease of segregation over time, are not supported by the data.

To account for the stable indices of dissimilarity over time, Loll (1982a) analyzed whether spatial concentration processes occurred, but that was not the case. However, closer inspection of data revealed that in tracts that were 20 or more percent foreign-born, Germans moved out in far greater numbers than the normal mobility rate, thus increasing dissimilarity. This finding raises the question of whether these moves of German residents were due to discrimination, or, in Schelling's (1971, 1972) term, an excess of the "tipping-in point," or to higher incomes of German residents and thus their more competitive position on the housing market. (For a study of tipping processes in the FRG, see Kecskes and Knäble 1988.)

Although it is not possible to conclude which of the two explanations—or a multiplicative effect—is at work from aggregate data available, an additional analysis by Loll (1982a) supports the housing market explanation. He compared the share of Germans and the six minority groups in census tracts that had a high percentage of dwellings in substandard condition, for example without central heating or bathrooms. The share of the minorities ranged from 44 to 58 percent in such tracts, compared to only 26 percent for the total Hamburg population. Similar discrepancies were obtained when analyzing for tracts with low social status population. We may thus conclude the economic explanation to be more probable than the discrimination hypothesis.

This interpretation is further supported by housing data on the national level. As table 6.8 shows, foreign-born households of all sizes live in older buildings than do Germans; they are concentrated in buildings constructed before 1918. In addition, their dwellings are often substandard: 63.8 percent of foreign as opposed to 42.8 percent of German households lived in substandard dwellings in 1979 (Statistisches Bundesamt 1983:92). Case studies pertaining to the housing conditions of the foreign born in Augsburg (Ruile 1984), Berlin (Arin, Gude, and Wurtinger 1985; Schuleri-Hartje 1982), and Mannheim (Ipsen 1978) document a considerably higher extent of overcrowding for foreign than for German households. For example, in Augsburg the average density of 1.4 persons per room was exceeded by 72 percent of foreign, but only 15 percent of German, households (Reimann and Reimann 1987:183).

Although overcrowded dwellings are more prominent among foreign households and concentrations of ethnic minorities in specific urban areas, there are no ghettos—as defined by either a high concentration of one minority or by their inability to leave a neighborhood—in cities of the FRG. Yet, under present conditions, the housing situation of minorities is by no means satisfactory. On one hand, location decision is less constrained by discrimination or formal regulation than it was ten years previously. On the other hand, most foreign born compete with German households in the lower-priced segment of the housing market, a large part of it consisting of social housing dwellings. But it is exactly this segment of the housing market that becomes increasingly tight. Throughout the FRG, new social housing construction has declined, both in absolute and in relative numbers. Total construction of dwellings declined by half in the 1960–86 period. The situation is even more dramatic in large cities where

TABLE 6.8.   German and Foreign-born Renter Households,
by Size of Household and by Age of Building (1978)

| Household Size/ | | Construction Period of Building | | | |
Nationality	Numbers	− 1918	1919–48	1949–54	1955 +
One person					
German	4,839,000	24.4	15.3	37.3	23.0
Foreign born	231,000	36.8	10.4	32.7	20.0
Two persons					
German	4,078,000	19.5	14.9	40.4	25.1
Foreign born	215,000	36.0	12.6	29.3	22.1
Three persons					
German	2,247,000	18.2	13.0	37.6	31.2
Foreign born	216,000	37.8	12.5	29.0	20.7
Four persons					
German	1,512,000	18.8	12.5	35.9	32.9
Foreign born	197,000	38.0	13.8	26.5	21.7
Five or more persons					
German	700,000	21.8	13.9	32.1	32.3
Foreign born	138,000	44.2	13.0	24.3	18.4
Total households					
German	13,376,000	21.1	14.4	37.9	26.6
Foreign born	997,000	38.1	12.4	28.8	20.7

Source: Statistisches Bundesamt 1983:96.

the housing shortage is still a major problem. In Hamburg, for example, total new construction fell from 20,900 in 1960 to 4,512 in 1986, 88 percent of which were social housing dwellings.

When local policy changed due to the influx of foreign families, foreign labor and repatriated and refugee minorities were allowed to apply for social housing, most of which are in new housing estates located in a zone distant from the c.b.d.

The Distribution of Ethnic Minorities in Hamburg

When the recruitment of foreign labor stopped in 1973, the increase in the number of foreign born dropped to an average annual increase rate of 3.3 percent over the 1974–79 period and 3.6 percent from 1980 onward, compared to an average rate of 13.4 percent in the 1968–73 period. Most of the new immigrants were relatives and dependents of those foreign born already living in Hamburg. Changes in distribution may therefore be assumed to reflect trends in degree of segregation primarily influenced by a tendency toward assimilation. We further assume that during the period of immigration, new foreign labor set-

FIGURE 6.1.   City of Hamburg, Proportion Foreign in Census Tracts (1976)

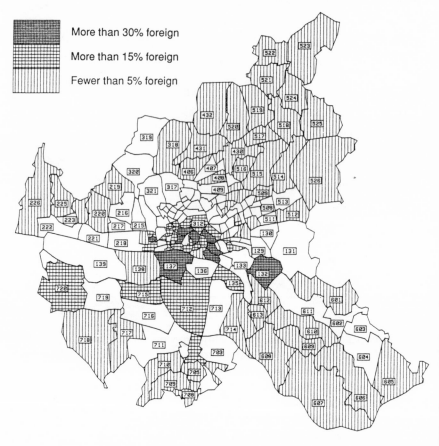

Source: Statistical Office Hamburg 1977: Statistische Berichte, Series A I4-j76.

tled in the typical "areas of first settlement" (Jonassen 1949): inner-city areas near the harbor and the central business district, areas designated for urban renewal in the 1960s and deteriorating since then.

Because the influx of new immigrants is less, we can assess the changes in the areas of first settlement. Did they attract more foreign born, or did a process of desegregation occur? In the case of assimilation, the foreign population should move from the inner-city areas toward the periphery. This trend should be reinforced by urban renewal programs which increase residential mobility.

In the "no assimilation" case, the residential pattern should tend toward increasing segregation. Both German and foreign residents would promote segregation by moving to homogeneous neighborhoods, the foreign born choosing ethnic neighborhoods and Germans moving out of mixed neighborhoods.

Unfortunately, the period under study, 1976–86, is too short to reveal trends of dispersal which—according to data reported by Jonassen (1949)—take several decades. Therefore, the analysis of the figures on residential distribution is limited to whether assimilation occurred in Hamburg in a time of economic decline and rising unemployment both among German and foreign populations.

Data. The data were taken from the annual publications of the Statistical Office of Hamburg. They refer to 1976 and 1986, with the midpoints 1981 and 1984 revealing more recent changes. Figures 6.1, 6.2, and 6.3 show the distribution of all foreign labor minorities over the 180 census tracts, as in the study by Loll (1982a). As expected, areas of first settlement were the inner-city areas near the harbor (figure 6.1). Ten years later almost the same pattern is evident (figure 6.2). The areas with low foreign population remained constant, for example, the agricultural region in the southeast and the well-off suburbs in the northeast.

In the 1976–86 period, Hamburg suffered a heavy loss of its German population, which declined by 12.5 percent. The majority of the census tracts experienced a constant decrease over the years. It is possible that the proportion of foreigners was not influenced by intracity migration of foreigners, but by out-of-the-city migration of Germans. This interpretation is supported by data showing that the census tracts with the largest decrease in German population between 1976 and 1986 are almost identical with the areas of first settlement of immigrants. In most tracts, more than half of the German population moved. These areas also lost foreign population, but because outmigration of Germans was higher than that of foreign population, the *proportion* of foreign population increased in these tracts.

This finding supports the hypothesis suggested earlier that processes of segregation are due to the behavior of the German population. It is not evident whether the out-migration of Germans is a reaction to high proportions of ethnic minorities or to low levels of the quality of life in inner-city tracts. Tracts with a constant loss of foreign population are primarily located in inner-city areas. Comparing only trends from 1981–84 and 1984–86, we find a constant decrease in many inner-city areas. This finding contradicts the assumption of increasing seg-

FIGURE 6.2.   City of Hamburg, Proportion Foreign in Census Tracts (1986)

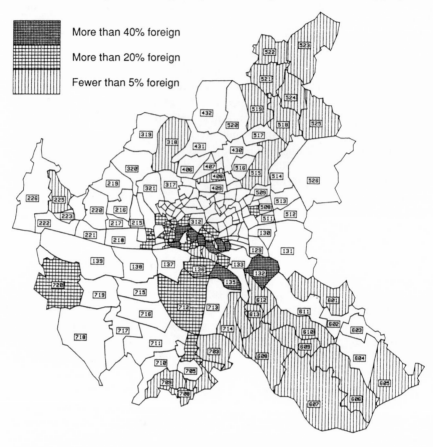

Source: Statistical Office Hamburg 1987: Statistische Berichte, Series A I4-j86.

mentation and segregation of minority population in times of an economic depression; not only high-status tracts in outlying parts of Hamburg lose their foreign population.

When comparing minorities by their absolute numbers instead of their proportions, the data reveal a constant increase in outlying census tracts of the city and in some selected inner-city areas. However, data do not show a clear trend of concentration or segregation emerging. Census tracts with the highest change in number of foreign population were those at the periphery but still inside the central city.

FIGURE 6.3.   City of Hamburg, Trends in Concentration of Foreigners

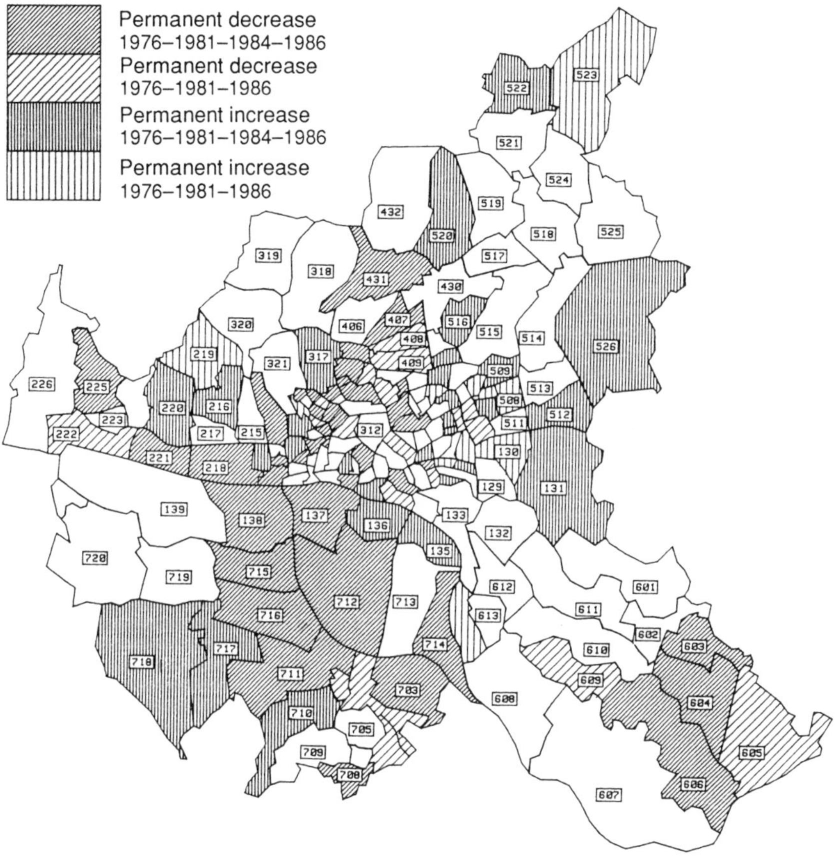

Source: Statistical Office Hamburg 1987: Statistische Berichte, Series A I4-j86.

Here a ceiling effect may be at work: tracts with extremely low figures in 1976 could easily double the number of foreign born, compared to the inner-city areas which already held a great number of foreign born in 1976.

Several tracts exhibit a constant increase in the share of foreign born from 1976 to 1981 and from 1984 to 1986. No clear pattern emerges; nonetheless, we find a concentric zone of those in the outlying tracts and three segments emanating from the inner-city tracts leading to the outlying tracts. This supports the hypothesis of an on-going process of assimilation resulting in a residential dispersion—albeit a slow one—of the foreign population.

To control for the moves of Germans we finally analyze the pattern of ethnic *concentration*, a concept that measures the proportion of total foreign population residing in a specific tract. Rising ethnic concentration in a tract indicates the tract's rising attractiveness (for whatever reason) for the foreign population, regardless of nationality.

Data reveal that the harbor area has experienced a decrease in its foreign-born resident population. This is due to expansion of the harbor into adjacent areas, which resulted in a decline of housing. In agricultural areas, the foreign-born population also decreased as the work became less attractive; assimilated Turkish workers no longer were willing to work at low-paying farm jobs. Rising attractiveness is found in tracts of the outlying regions. Although some inner-city tracts experience rising attraction, we find more inner-city tracts with decreasing ethnic concentration.

Discussion. The analysis of residential patterns in Hamburg between 1976 and 1986 has limited scope in revealing trends in residential segregation and therefore ethnic assimilation. The following restrictions apply:

The time span covered may be too short to reveal trends.

Changing proportions are primarily the result of a massive loss of German population due to out-migration and fertility decline. Without individual-level data on migration motives, it is impossible to decide whether characteristics of the social environment (e.g., number of foreign born) or of the physical environment (e.g., air pollution) were the driving force behind the out-migration.

The foreign population was not homogenous and stable over the time under study. There were some in- and out-migrations, in particular, the influx of the second type of minorities, refugees. This may introduce a bias in the aggregate analysis.

Even under these restrictions it is evident that residential patterns in Hamburg do not show a trend toward further segregation. This finding is supported by a comparison of indices of dissimilarity for the decade 1976–86. The I.D. values remained fairly constant, as the data from Loll (1982b) have already shown. In a recent study, Alpheis (1988, 1989) calculated an I.D. of 31.6 for 1976, 31.7 in 1981, and 29.8 in 1986. These calculations are based on the 180 census tracts, which can be aggregated in the seven districts of Hamburg. In only one of

TABLE 6.9.   Distribution of Foreign born in Hamburg Census
Tracts with Varying Ethnic Proportions

Tracts with Certain Levels of Foreign-born Concentration	Percent Foreign born	Percent Cumulated
0–5	8.8	8.8
5–10	30.8	39.6
10–15	20.8	60.4
15–20	12.8	73.2
20–25	9.0	82.2
25–30	6.2	88.4
30–35	1.5	89.9
More than 35	10.1	100.0
Total	100.0	

these districts did the I.D. increase over the decade under study, from
14.1 to 20.8.

Nonetheless, even in 1986, census tracts in inner-city areas remained those with the highest proportions of ethnic minorities, but
trends indicated that the direction of movement was to be outward,
thus decreasing residential segregation. Because inner-city areas are
not densely populated, the majority of the foreign population lives in
areas that have a relatively low ethnic proportion.

Taking into account the fact that the foreign population is comprised of several nationalities, none of which usually make up one-
third of the total foreign population, we conclude that residential segregation plays only a minor role, and there are no indications that
problems will be aggravated.

Housing Quality and the Individual
Process of Assimilation

Having discussed the status of ethnic minorities on an aggregate level,
we now turn to the role of housing on the individual level. Housing
is assumed to be crucial for the process of individual assimilation. It
is both an indicator and a source of assimilation—a dependent and an
independent variable. To put housing and segregation into a broader
theoretical context, we refer to a model of assimilation proposed by
Esser (1980), which builds upon prior work by Eisenstadt (1954), Taft
(1957), and Gordon (1964). Esser subsumes housing under the structural dimension of assimilation. "Structural assimilation" is assumed
to be influenced by "cognitive assimilation" such as language skills

and exogenous factors designated "pre-migration-traits" (Heiss 1969). Furthermore, Esser posits that structural assimilation influences "social assimilation" (interethnic contacts) and "personal integration" (extent of satisfaction) directly, and "identificational assimilation" (feelings of belonging) at least indirectly.

This model was tested (Esser and Friedrichs 1989) in a larger survey of Yugoslavian and Turkish labor migrants of the first and second generation.[3] The results pertaining to housing are briefly reported herein. Two indicators of housing quality were used: an additive index giving information about the quality of the dwelling unit such as central heating, hot water, and own W.C., the other indicating the quality of the building (interviewer ratings of type, age, and condition).

Among the factors influencing the quality of housing, it was assumed that cognitive assimilation (measured as a score of subjective perceived language ability) is most responsible for the type of housing chosen. In addition, the effects of years of schooling (whether in country of origin or the FRG) and the length of stay in the FRG were tested as exogenous variables. Finally, the proportion of foreign persons on the block level was introduced as a contextual variable. A strong negative correlation was hypothesized between that variable and the quality of housing.

Housing as Dependent Variable. With respect to quality of housing as the dependent variable, for the first-generation Turks we found a confirmation of the Esser model (table 6.10). Cognitive assimilation had a strong effect on both indicators of housing quality. Year of schooling had a considerable zero-order correlation with quality of housing, but no effect when cognitive assimilation was controlled. Specific skills such as language ability were more relevant for Turks of the first generation than was the unspecific variable "education." Surprisingly, length of stay had no impact on housing quality. The hypothesis of a strong negative correlation with the contextual variable, percent foreign born in the block, was confirmed. The overall explanatory power of the model is only moderate, with the adjusted R^2 around .12.

The same holds true for the Turks of the second generation. Coefficients were almost identical except for the effect of length of stay on the quality of the dwelling, indicating a more or less "automatic" movement of young Turks toward assimilation regardless of their skills.

Results for first-generation Yugoslavians yielded a different picture. Years of schooling was more relevant than specific cognitive skills for

TABLE 6.10.   Results of Regressions of Housing Quality

Turks, First Generation ($N = 470$, $mpn = 337$)

Regression of BUILD on	(r)	B	beta	Regression of DWEL (r with BUILD: .51) on	(r)	B	beta
COG	(.33)	0.16	.30	COG	(.28)	0.09	.24
YSC	(.23)	0.01	.01	YSC	(.22)	0.02	.04
LST	(.03)	− 0.01	− .02	LST	(.04)	− 0.01	− .00
PFB	(− .22)	− 0.02	− .19	PFB	(− .25)	− 0.02	− .22
Const.		7.08		Const.		2.60	
adj. R^2			.13	adj. R^2			.12

Turks, Second Generation ($N = 463$, $mpn = 298$)

Regression of BUILD on	(r)	B	beta	Regression of DWEL (r with BUILD: .50) on	(r)	B	beta
COG	(.27)	0.15	.23	COG	(.28)	0.10	.22
YSC	(− .04)	− 0.04	− .03	YSC	(− .08)	− 0.03	− .03
LST	(.16)	0.01	.03	LST	(.23)	0.04	.12
PFB	(− .24)	− 0.02	− .22	PFB	(− .19)	− 0.01	− .16
Const.		6.96		Const.		1.90	
adj. R^2			.11	adj. R^2			.11

Yugoslavians, First Generation ($N = 482$, $mpn = 414$)

Regression of BUILD on	(r)	B	beta	Regression of DWEL (r with BUILD: .53) on	(r)	B	beta
COG	(.19)	0.03	.05	COG	(.32)	0.10	.25
YSC	(.23)	0.13	.19	YSC	(.29)	0.07	.16
LST	(.10)	0.02	.05	LST	(.03)	− 0.02	− .07
PFB	(− .37)	− 0.04	− .35	PFB	(− .27)	− 0.02	− .24
Const.		8.01		Const.		1.92	
adj. R^2			.18	adj. R^2			.18

Yugoslavians, Second Generation ($N = 431$, $mpn = 302$)

Regression of BUILD on	(r)	B	beta	Regression of DWEL (r with BUILD: .48) on	(r)	B	beta
COG	(.16)	0.07	.08	COG	(.22)	0.08	.15
YSC	(.11)	0.11	.11	YSC	(.03)	0.02	.03
LST	(.14)	0.04	.08	LST	(.17)	0.01	.05
PFB	(− .33)	− 0.03	− .30	PFB	(− .33)	− 0.02	− .29
Const.		6.85		Const.		2.75	
adj. R^2			.12	adj. R^2			.13

BUILD: Building's quality   YSC: Years of schooling
DWEL: Dwelling's quality   LS: Length of stay
COG: Cognitive assimilation   PFB: Percent foreign on block-level

the quality of the building, and both variables proved relevant for the quality of the dwelling unit. Length of stay had no effect, contrary to the results obtained for the Turks of the second generation. Again, the explanatory power of the models was very moderate; the model better explains quality of the dwelling (R^2 = .12) than quality of the building (R^2 = .06). The models for the Yugoslavians of the second generation exhibit similar results, and even lower R^2 values.

Summarizing the results, we find the signs of coefficients in the models to be in the expected direction. The most influential variable is cognitive assimilation; for Yugoslavians there is also an influence of schooling. The total explanatory power of the models is not very strong (R^2 = .05 to 0.12) when the contextual variable is excluded. Those who have the best language skills live in the better houses or dwellings. The proportion of foreign born at the block level is, as expected, negatively correlated with quality of housing. Turks show less variation in housing quality with ethnic proportion on the block level than do Yugoslavians.

A multiple classification analysis, with the four subsamples as grouping criterion and cognitive assimilation, years of schooling, and length of stay as co-variates, yielded additional insight into the housing situation. Turks generally had lower quality housing than Yugoslavians. But controlling for the three co-variates resulted in a pattern showing that the members of the first generation live in better quality housing than the members of the second generation. Hence, after controls we find no difference between first-generation Turks and Yugoslavians.

The differences observed can predominantly be attributed to a generational effect. Members of the first generation should usually have housing of better quality than members of the second generation when asked at the same time (since both groups are cohorts and differ in age and position in life-cycle). Aside from this generational (or life-cycle) effect, there is an interaction effect between generation and nationality. Turks of the second generation have a remarkable lack of higher quality housing than would be expected from their status after controlling for language skills. They live in worse conditions than do Yugoslavians of the same age and skills.

Housing as an Independent Variable. Earlier we argued that the guest-worker minority is trapped in a situation of double ambivalence concerning whether to return to their home country or whether to stay in the FRG, an ambivalence imposed both by government policies and by the attitudes of the migrants themselves. In the Esser and Friedrichs study (1989), the propensity of guest workers to return and the role quality of housing has on this attitude was analyzed. According to the

Esser model, the re-migration orientation is assumed to be influenced above all by personal integration, measured as the degree of satisfaction (overall, school/work, residence).

Propensity to return, or re-migration orientation, was measured by intended length of stay, scaled from "1 = wishing to stay for good" to "7 = wishing to return within the next 12 months." Nearly 67 percent of the respondents fell into category 2 of this scale: "I will return, but don't know when." This result lends support to our diagnosis of individual ambivalence. (However, in terms of multivariate analysis, it has the consequence of little variance to be explained.)

Regressions of re-migration orientation on various variables, including both housing quality and "personal integration," yielded only very low R^2 values (maximum: .07). Analyses for both generations of Turks reveal almost no influence of housing quality when personal integration is controlled. Housing quality has possibly only indirect effects. Results for Yugoslavians show a different pattern. Personal integration has no effect on re-migration orientation of the first generation, for both generations no coefficient in complex models exceeds beta = .20.

Overall, the analyses of housing support the model of assimilation proposed by Esser (1980). Quality of housing as an indicator of structural assimilation is primarily influenced by cognitive assimilation and only to a minor extent by years of schooling. In contrast, we found no relation between housing and the propensity to return to the home country.

From these results we conclude that skills—whether specific (language) or unspecific (years of schooling)—have significant effects on housing conditions. Comparing first- and second-generation guest workers we find increasing cognitive assimilation, and therefore we forecast that migrant descendants will improve their housing standards as they improve their cognitive skills.

Conclusions

Reviewing the analyses presented, the conclusion to be drawn is that the process of integration of minorities advanced during the 1980s. Despite spatial concentrations in two types of areas (center-of-business-district-adjacent turn-of-the-century renewal areas and peripheral new social housing estates) and, for the first area, often substandard quality of housing, indices of segregation remain low when compared with Great Britain or the United States. Language skills, participation in higher education, and performance in schools have improved steadily. However, prospects may change, among other reasons because of these achievements, which increases competition with Germans and among minorities. Future economic problems will be exacerbated, and social polarization among Germans and among the foreign born will increase. What follows are the prospects among the various minorities. [*Ed. note*: Friedrichs and Alpheis wrote this conclusion in 1988–89 before the Wall came down and Germans from the East poured into the FRG.]

The composition of minorities changes. The number of guest workers can be assumed to remain fairly stable; in contrast, the number of refugees and the repatriated will increase. These shifts in the proportion of different minority types may have two effects. First, attitudes and prejudices will change, with social distance toward the "traditional" guest-worker minorities possibly decreasing,[4] and distance toward refugees from Asia and Africa increasing. As of 1982, social distance (percent in population disliking a given ethnic minority) was lowest for Yugoslavians (19 percent) and Italians (20 percent) and highest for Turks (48 percent), Pakistani (47 percent), and North Africans (42 percent) (SWS Meinungsprofile 1983).

Second, to house the growing number of repatriated, the Christian Democrat-headed Department of Housing announced in mid-1988 a new social housing program that, when implemented, may alleviate effects on quality. [Though with the increased influx of persons in 1990, it will hardly alleviate the supply problem.] Typically, new social housing is of better quality. Third, allocation of these dwellings cannot be restricted to the repatriated. Perhaps the German population will move into these dwellings, leaving behind a growing share of minority households in older social housing estates.

Furthermore, the situation in the labor market may become more complicated because members of the second and third generation are better educated, enabling them to apply for a broader range of jobs. Under such circumstances, competition between foreign and German labor will become stronger and, in turn, hamper assimilation or even result in stronger discrimination, as is the case in France. The crucial question then becomes whether competitive minority members, when applying for a job, will be judged according to their skills or discriminated against on account of their ethnicity.

There seems little doubt that as long as first-generation masses of less-educated minorities remain concentrated in economically transforming cities, their employment prospects will continue to deteriorate. The spatial mobility of foreign labor will decrease as well. Their families—and often their married children—are in the FRG, often living near the rest of the family. This reduces the propensity to return to the home country

(Wilpert 1987). In addition, second- and third-generation labor migrants no longer have to take any job just to save money for themselves or to send it to relatives in their home country.

By all measures, the FRG has become a multiethnic country, a fact at best accepted in social interaction but by no means legally recognized. So far, state and individual adjustments—both from Germans and from the foreign born—to this situation are only adequate. The melting pot will not be achieved in the foreseeable future.

It is surprising that under such circumstances very little discrimination is based on ethnicity. Right-wing movements have so far gained considerably less power in the FRG than in France, the Netherlands, or Denmark. The reasons for this may be found in a specific aspect of recent German history: the terrifying consequences of anti-Semitism.

Before the Wall came down, as long as there was no dramatic change, it could be said that the assimilation burden was only imposed on a small cohort of immigrants: the nowadays well-accepted Italians, who came in the 1960s; the Turks, who immigrated in the late 1970s and early 1980s; and the refugees of the late 1980s and 1990s. They had to solve their problems of adjustment to West German society without public assistance. The unfortunate aspect of most minority members' situation is that they acquire skills desirable for an industrial society as society changes from manufacturing to services and knowledge-intensive new industries, demanding from them additional efforts of training and adjustment if they intend to stay in the FRG.

Notes

1. Figures based on authors' own calculations of special material from the Federal Agency of Labor for 1970; *Amtliche Nachrichten der Bundesanstalt für Arbeit, Jahreszahlen* 1981:13; *Jahreszahlen* 1987:12. Data refer to June 30 of respective years.

2. Calculations refer to *all* forms of social assistance, the ratio is recipients per 1,000 German or foreign inhabitants. Figures are from *Statistisches Jahrbuch Deutscher Gemeinden* 1985:24; 1986:272.

3. The study, conducted in 1984, was a large survey of Turkish and Yugoslav labor migrants in five cities of the FRG: Munich, Nuremberg, Duisburg, Essen, and Hamburg. The sample comprised 1,846 persons, evenly divided between Turks and Yugoslavs, and members of the first and second generation. In each city, three residential areas (high-medium-low proportion foreign) were selected and further divided into two subunits by their propor-

tion of foreign-born. Within each of these thirty subunits, sampling of households was at random.

4. Written in 1988–89.

References

Alpheis, Hannes. 1988. "Does Ethnic Concentration Really Matter?" Paper presented at the Conference on Urban Minorities in France, Great Britain, the United States, and West Germany: Problems and Patterns. Nancy: June.

———. 1989. *Kontextanalyse. Die Wirkung des sozialen Umfeldes, untersucht am Beispiel der Eingliederung von Ausländern* (Context analysis: The influence of social environment, research into immigration of foreigners). Opladen: Westdeutscher Verlag.

Arin, C., Siegfried Gude, and H. Wurtinger. 1985. *Auf der Schattenseite des Wohnungmarktes: Kinderreiche Immigrantenfamilien* (Drawbacks of housing market: Immigration families with many children). Basel: Birkhäuser.

Cheshire, Paul C. 1979. "Inner Areas as Spatial Labour Markets: A Critique of Inner Areas Studies." *Urban Studies* 16:29–43.

Eisenstadt, Shmuel N. 1954. *The Absorption of Immigrants: A Comparative Study Based Mainly on the Jewish Community in Palestine and the State of Israel*. London.

Esser, Hartmut. 1980. *Aspekte der Wanderungssoziologie* (Aspects of immigration sociology). Darmstadt/Neuwied: Luchterhand.

———. 1982. "Sozialräumliche Bedingungen der sprachlichen Assimilation von Arbeitsmigranten" (Spacial requirements for language acquisition of guest workers). *Zeitschrift für Soziologie* 11:279–306.

Esser, Hartmut, and Jürgen Friedrichs. 1989. *Kulturelle und ethnische Identität bei Arbeitsmigranten im interkontextuellen, intergenerationalen und internationalen Vergleich* (Cultural and ethnical identity of guest workers in an contextual, generational and international comparison). Opladen: Westdeutscher Verlag.

Friedrichs, Jürgen. 1985a. "Die Zukunft der Städte in der Bundesrepublik Deutschland" (The future of cities in the Federal Republic of Germany). Pp. 2–22 in *Die Städte in den 8oer Jahren* (Cities in the eighties), edited by Jürgen Friedrichs. Opladen: Westdeutscher Verlag.

———. 1985b. "Ökonomischer Strukturwandel und Disparitäten von Qualifikationen der Arbeitskräfte" (Economical structures and disparities of qualifications of laborers). Pp. 48–69 in *Die Städte in den 8oer Jahren* (Cities in the eighties), edited by Jürgen Friedrichs. Opladen: Westdeutscher Verlag.

Gordon, Milton M. 1964. *Assimilation in American Life: The Role of Race, Religion and National Origins*. New York: Oxford University Press.

Heckman, Friedrich. 1981. *Die Bundesrepublik: Ein Einwanderungsland?: Zur Soziologie der Gastarbeiterbevölkerung als Einwandererminorität* (The Federal

Republic of Germany: An Immigration Country? Toward the sociology of guest-workers as an immigration-minority). Stuttgart: Klett-Cotta.

Heiss, Jerold. 1969. "Factors Related to Immigrant Assimilation: Pre-Migration Traits." *Social Forces* 47:422–28.

Helmert, Uwe. 1982. "Konzentrations- und Segregationsprozesse der ausländerischen Bevökerung in Frankfurt am Main" (Concentration and segregation processes of foreign population in Frankfurt am Main). Pp. 265–93 in *Ausländer in Bundesrepublik Deutschland und in der Schweiz* (Foreigners in the Federal Republic of Germany and in Switzerland), edited by Hans-Jürgen Hoffmann-Nowotny and Karl-Otto Hondrich. Frankfurt: Campus Verlag.

Hoffmeyer-Zlotnik, Jürgen. 1977. *Gastarbeiter im Sanierungsgebiet* (Guest-workers in redeveloped districts). Hamburg: Christians.

———. 1982. "Community Change and Invasion: The Case of the Turkish Guest-Workers." Pp. 114–26 in *Spatial Disparities and Social Behavior: A Reader in Urban Research*, edited by Jürgen Friedrichs. Hamburg: Christians.

Ipsen, Detlev. 1978. "Wohnungssituation und Wohninteresse ausländerischer Arbeiter in der Bundesrepublik Deutschland" (Housing situation and housing interests of foreign workers in the Federal Republic of Germany). *Leviathan* 4:558–73.

Jonassen, C. T. 1949. "Cultural Variables in the Ecology of an Ethnic Group." *American Sociological Review* 14:32–41.

Kasarda, John D., and Jürgen Friedrichs. 1985. "Comparative Demographic-Employment Mismatches in the U.S. and West Germany." Pp. 1–30 in *Research in the Sociology of Work*, Vol. 3: *Unemployment*, edited by Richard A. Simpson and Ida Harper Simpson. Greenwich: JAI Press.

Kasarda, John D., Jürgen Friedrichs, and Kay E. Ehlers. 1989. "Urban Industrial Restructuring and Minority Problems in the U.S. and West Germany." Pp. 153–80 in *The Dispossessed: Racial Minorities and the Coming of the Post-Industrial City*, edited by Malcolm Cross. Cambridge: Cambridge University Press.

Kecskes, Robert, and Stephan Knäble. 1988. "Bevölkerungsaustausch in ethnisch gemischten Wohngebieten: Ein Test der Tipping-Theorie von Schelling" (Population exchange in mixed ethnic residential districts: A test of the tipping-theory of Schelling). Pp. 293–309 in *Soziologische Stadtforschung* (Sociological urban research), edited by Jürgen Friedrichs. Opladen: Westdeutscher Verlag.

Klauder, Wolfgang, Peter Schnur, and Manfred Thon. 1985. "Arbeitsmarktperspektiven der 80er und 90er Jahre" (Perspectives of the labor-market in the '80s and '90s). *Mitteilungen aus der Arbeitsmarkt- und Berufsforschung* 18:41–62.

Loll, Bernd-Uwe. 1982a. "Zur Assimilation von Ausländern in Hamburg und Stuttgart" (Toward assimilation of foreigners in Hamburg and Stuttgart). Hamburg in Zahlen 9:281–91.

———. 1982b. "Guest-Worker Assimilation in West Germany." Pp. 127–39 in

Spatial Disparities and Social Behavior: A Reader in Urban Research, edited by Jürgen Friedrichs. Hamburg: Christians.

Märtens, Hans W. 1980. "Gastarbeiter in einen city-nahen Mischgebiet" (Guest-worker in a mixed suburb). *Bauwelt* 13:553–55.

Reimann, Helga. 1987. "Die Wohnsituation der Gastarbeiter" (Housing situation of guest-workers). Pp. 175–94 in *Gastarbeiter: Analyse und Perspektiven eines sozialen Problems* (Guest workers: Analysis and perspectives of a social problem), 2nd rev. ed., edited by Helga Reimann and Horst Reimann. Opladen: Westdeutscher Verlag.

Reimann, Helga, and Horst Reimann. 1987. *Gastarbeiter: Analyse und Perspektiven eines sozialen Problems* (Guest workers: Analysis and perspectives of a social problem), 2nd rev. ed., edited by Helga Reimann and Horst Reimann. Opladen: Westdeutscher Verlag.

Rothkirch, Christoph von, and Manfred Tessaring. 1986. "Projektionen des Arbeitskräftebedarfs nach Qualifikationensebenen bis zum Jahre 2000" (Projections of the need of labor force on qualification levels until the year 2000). *Mitteilungen aus der Arbeitsmarkt- und Berufsforschung* (Notes of the labor-market and profession research) 19:105–18.

Ruile, A. 1984. *Ausländer in der Großstadt* (Foreigners in the city). Augsburg: Universität, Lehrstuhl für Sozial- und Wirtschaftsgeographie.

Schelling, Thomas C. 1971. "Dynamic Models of Segregation." *Journal of Mathematical Sociology* 1:143–86.

———. 1972. "A Process of Residential Segregation: Neighborhood Tipping." Pp. 150–84 in *Racial Discrimination in Economic Life,* edited by Anthony H. Pascal. Lexington: Heath.

Schuleri-Hartje, Ulla-Kristina. 1982. *Ausländische Arbeitsnehmer und ihre Familien: Teil 1: Wohnverhältnisse* (Foreign workers and their families. Part 1. Living conditions). Berlin: Difu.

Schütte, Wolfgang, and Waldemar Süss. 1988. *Armut in Hamburg* (Poverty in Hamburg). Hamburg: VSA.

Statistisches Bundesamt. 1983. *Strukturdaten über Ausländer in der Bundesrepublik Deutschland* (Data of structures of foreigners in the Federal Republic of Germany). Stuttgart: Kohlhammer.

Süddeutsche Zeitung. 1988. June 25.

SWS-Meinungsprofile. 1983. "Einstellungen zu den Ausländern in der BRD" (Attitude toward foreigners in the FRG). *Journal für Sozialforschung* 23:471–502.

Taft, Ronald. 1957. "A Psychological Model for the Study of Social Assimilation." *Human Relations* 10:141–56.

Wilpert, Czarina. 1987. "Zukunftorientierungen von Migrantenfamilien" (Future orientations of migrant families). Pp. 198–221 in *Gastarbeiter: Analyse und Perspektiven eines Soziales Problems* (Guest-workers: Analysis and perspectives of a social problem), 2nd rev. ed., edited by Helga Reimann and Horst Reimann. Opladen: Westdeutscher Verlag.

7. Urban Housing Segregation of North African "Immigrants" in France

The Anglo-American concept of *ethnic minority*, that is, a social group identified (and stigmatized) by its physical appearance (Rex 1986), applies to North Africans in France. However, even in scientific literature, it is usual to call them "immigrants," and even "second [or third] generation immigrants," although they are no longer immigrants but residents. Linguistic usage represents this population as foreign and temporarily in France, when in fact most of them are settled. In the 1982 Census, 80.5 percent of the foreigners had already been in France at the time of the previous 1975 census. For Algerians, the ratio was of 87.8 percent. More recent statistical data are missing, but observers agree that the foreigners' length of stay in France has been increasing.

North Africans, or Maghrebines, are the most important minority in France: Algerians, Moroccans, and Tunisians together comprise 38.4 percent of the foreigners in France (1982 Census). But these data are an underestimate, and George considers that North Africans constitute about half of the French foreign population (1986a:18). Algeria, Morocco, and Tunisia are usually considered as former French colonies, but for historical reasons they had different juridical statuses, inducing statistical inaccuracies. Morocco and Tunisia have always been national states different from France, which gave them its "protection." This was not the case for Algeria; from 1848 to 1963, it was considered a French territory. Algerians were French nationals, although they were "non-citizens" (Borella 1987:43–45). With the independence of Algeria in 1963, the *Harkis* (Algerian soldiers serving in the French army) had to leave Algeria and settle in France with their families. They are registered as French, and George estimates their number at around 500,000 (1986a:19). French nationality and citizenship, however, do not protect them from the same discrimination experienced by "true" Algerians. Housing is one example.

145

FIGURE 7.1.   North Africans in the total population of the French
départements (counties) in 1982 (George 1986:66)

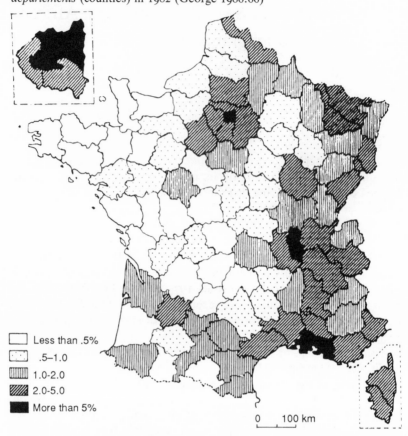

Less than .5%

.5–1.0

1.0-2.0

2.0-5.0

More than 5%

0   100 km

Algerians arrived in France first and are numerically the largest
foreign group. According to the 1982 Census, Algerians number
796,000, Portuguese, 765,000, and Moroccans, 431,000; numbers of
Tunisians are far behind: 181,000. Even after independence, Algerian
immigration remained high. Algeria had a surplus unemployed population in rural areas, and from 1945 to 1973, France had a tremendous
need for an unskilled labor force. Most Algerian immigrants were
workers unaccompanied by family. For opposite reasons, French and
Algerian governments agreed on considering immigration as temporary and on preventing families' migration. France was facing a severe
housing crisis, and also had no interest in supporting the costs of child
care; Algeria feared a definitive loss of an important fraction of its

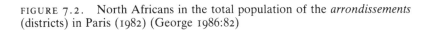

FIGURE 7.2.   North Africans in the total population of the *arrondissements* (districts) in Paris (1982) (George 1986:82)

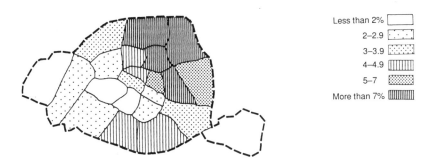

Less than 2%

2–2.9

3–3.9

4–4.9

5–7

More than 7%

young adult population (Blanc 1984). The pattern began to change in 1974, and familial immigration is now predominant.

Moroccan immigration is more recent and has been growing rapidly, with family immigration predominant: from 10,700 in 1954 to 260,000 in 1975 and 431,000 in 1982 (George 1986a:37). Tunisian immigration has occurred regularly for several decades but represents a small proportion of all immigrants.

Spatial Distribution of North Africans

Most North African labor is in low-level employment in building, public works, and industry; Algerians also work in services, and Moroccans in agriculture (George 1986a:47). The regional distribution of North Africans coincides fairly closely with the industrial map of France. Usually entering through Marseilles, "the gateway to the Orient," a fraction of the North Africans settle there, but others go north to the highly industrial areas of Lyons and Paris, or to the mines and iron industries of northern and eastern France (figure 7.1).

North Africans in France are concentrated in physically dilapidated areas, but according to two different patterns. In the traditional pattern of ethnic minority housing location, they are concentrated in dilapidated buildings in inner-city areas. However, a new pattern has developed: North African families are numerous on suburban public housing estates, built in the sixties and already dilapidated (Blanc 1985). This pattern is clear in metropolises such as Greater Paris,

FIGURE 7.3.   Foreigners in Greater Lyons (1982) (George 1986b)

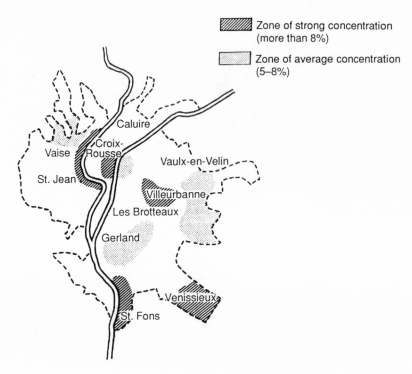

Lyons, and Marseilles. In Paris, 110,000 North Africans represent one-third of the foreigners in the city. Most are concentrated in old housing in formerly industrial and working-class districts of the north and east of the city (figure 7.2). In the industrial suburbs close to Paris (for example, Nanterre, Saint-Denis, and Aubervilliers), and more clearly in industrial suburbs far from Paris (for example, Poissy and Argenteuil), they concentrate in large public housing estates planned for reducing the distance between residence and place of work.

After Paris, Lyons has the greatest concentration of North Africans (80,000). Some live in the inner city (Croix-Rousse), but most live on suburban public housing estates such as Vénissieux and Villeurbanne (figure 7.3). Marseilles also has a high concentration of foreigners (figure 7.4). Although figure 7.2 (Paris) shows North Africans only whereas figures 7.3 and 7.4 (Lyons and Marseilles) show foreigners together, only Marseilles has high concentrations (more than 40 percent) in two areas: the city's center, in unhealthy housing near the

FIGURE 7.4.   Foreigners in Greater Marseilles (1982) (George 1986b)

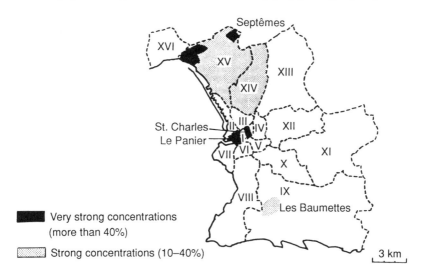

harbor (Saint-Charles), and especially in large public housing estates in the northern suburbs.

According to the traditional pattern, ethnic minorities are grouped in unhealthy buildings in the inner city, where they live alongside other ethnic groups and the indigenous population of the same socioeconomic status. This is true for Algerian single workers, who want to reduce their expenses, either to send money to their families abroad or to save in the hope of returning to their native land. Thus they "choose" dilapidated housing for its low cost. Regarding their stay in France as temporary helps them to endure bad housing conditions. For example, 14.7 percent of French households have neither a shower nor a bath, but 29.2 percent of the North Africans lack these facilities (1982 Census).

The emphasis on economic conditions should not lead to cross-cultural misunderstanding: some elements of comfort which appear today absolutely necessary for Western middle classes have a different value both in North African and popular cultures (Féraud-Royer 1987). For example, a private bath (or shower) is not necessary when the public bath is the favorite place for social communication.

As they live in dilapidated areas, North Africans adapt space to their own ways of life and cultures. They re-create social networks on a family or village basis, and shopkeepers who sell goods from their country of origin play a key role (De Rudder 1987). Communities are useful for newcomers: they act as a "staging-post," helping them to find their way in the host country (Pétonnet 1982).

The pattern of North Africans living on suburban public housing estates is recent, but the tendency is toward rapid growth as a result of the convergence of three evolutions: economic, demographic, and urban. The economic crisis which began in 1973 with the oil crisis directly affects immigration policies. In 1974, France (and other European countries) stopped the immigration of new workers; the only admission were families joining their heads already working in France. This policy had unexpected consequences: Algerian workers, shuttling between their jobs in France and their families on the other side of the Mediterranean, did not dare to leave France. Because they were afraid of being refused reentry, they sent for their families to come and live with them in France. The policy of restricting entry to immigrants may not be the primary cause for the arrival of the families, but it has certainly accelerated it. In order to get residency permits for their families, North African workers need "decent" housing. For this reason and two others, they apply for public housing: they are more aware of their rights to it, and they have no other choice given the level of rents on the free market. This occurred in the mid-seventies, when public housing organizations faced a severe crisis. Large suburban public estates built in the sixties had a high rate of vacancies; the French who could afford to left public housing in order to acquire suburban property through state-financed incentives. At first, public housing organizations were happy to fill their empty flats with foreign families who regularly paid their rents. As a result, in 1982, 13 percent of French households were tenants of a public housing organization, but 25 percent of foreigners were public housing tenants. The proportion of North Africans in public housing is high: 34 percent for Algerians and 40 percent for Moroccans (1982 Census:50, 98). However, taking the effect for the cause, many now tend to claim that North Africans "invaded" public housing and forced the French to move (Blanc 1985). An element in the high vote for Jean-Marie Le Pen in the 1988 presidential campaign was his sharp criticism of the invasion of France by Arab immigrants. His proposal of reserving public housing for nationals is unrealistic: tenants who moved out of public housing, even when they gave the excess of Arabs in the neighborhood as a reason, will certainly not return. The primary effect of Le Pen's proposal would be an increased vacancy rate, but it is an effective chauvinistic political proposition. When North African workers left inner-city slums to settle with their families in suburban public housing, more recent illegal immigrants often took their places, among them black Africans (De Rudder 1987).

The Effects of Housing Improvement Schemes for North Africans

Before 1974, areas affected by programs against unhealthy housing were those with high concentrations of North Africans. But the eradication of unhealthy housing is an alibi for restructuring inner-city areas, and re-housing is usually outside the renewed area, which acquires more prestigious commercial and urban functions (Castells and Godard 1973). The official policy consisted in re-housing North African families in suburban *cités de transit,* where social workers were supposed to teach them the urban way of life on a public housing estate. But these so-called "transit cities" stigmatized their residents, and it has been extremely hard for them to get into better housing (Pétonnet 1982). The majority of North African unaccompanied workers received accommodation in suburban guest-worker *foyers* (hostels), where they were concentrated without regard to nationality. This made it hard for residents to communicate with one another and led to difficulties. *Foyer* residents had a very long rent strike, from 1974 to 1980, because rents were too high and also because of the paternalistic and authoritarian style of management. Many North Africans have thus preferred to look for re-housing individually in inner-city areas not yet renewed. With the reduction of unaccompanied workers, these guest-worker *foyers* faced a financial crisis and have been opened to foreign students and others in order to survive (*Le Monde,* May 4, 1988).

In 1974, the policy of banning of new immigration coincided with measures in favor of those who were already in France, specifically for improving their housing conditions. Under the supervision of the Housing Department, 20 percent of the funds spent by employers for helping their employees in housing had to be applied to the housing of "immigrants." But the National Commission for Immigrants' Housing is uncertain about how best to use its resources. Because there is a risk of provoking new urban segregation by funding specific housing for "immigrants," some suggest that it is better to fund housing organizations, public or private, in order to encourage them to accept ethnic minorities. This orientation tends to prevail, but its justification is unclear. The extra funding is supposed to cover the overheads in order to ensure foreigners' true inclusion in the housing market, but its real use is uncertain.

At the same time, new schemes of urban development are evolving. Instead of clearing out an area for new construction, the trend is to restore existing buildings and modernize housing. Since 1977, in inner-city areas as well as on suburban public housing estates, the modernization of housing policy aims at giving low-income population a chance to stay. An agreement between the central state and the landlord, either private or public, provides that modernized housing will have a higher rent but, as a counterpart for state funding and for a period of nine years, rent increases are regulated and former tenants who want to stay have priority. On the other hand, the centralized government is committed to helping low-income tenants who cannot afford this moderated rent increase. They receive an *aide personnalisée au logement* (APL), or personal housing aid, which may also be given to low-income families wanting to acquire a new suburban property. When a landlord modernizes housing at his or her own initiative, low-income tenants have no right to APL. The right is limited to housing improvement plans that have state partnership, and APL is an instrument of centralized government urban policy. The effects of housing modernization policies are different in the inner city and on suburban public estates. Furthermore, long-range effects contradict the short-range ones. In inner-city areas, only a small fraction of low-income residents stay in modernized housing. Many are suspicious of the "APL dream": they consider it as a trick and look on their own for other affordable housing. Many North Africans move, although they often have large families, giving them the right to a substantial APL. "In certain cases, the more or less explicit aim of the [modernization] operation was to reduce the foreign population" (Mollet 1987:23). Every low-income household that stays in a modernized inner-city area, thanks to APL, faces long-term threats; what will happen after nine years when the landlord recovers the freedom of fixing rents? In the case of large families, when children grow older they will no longer be taken into account, and consequently APL will be reduced or suppressed. In gentrified inner cities, state intervention slows down the exclusion of low-income and poor households, but it does not eliminate it.

On suburban public housing estates since 1977 revitalization programs have been called *habitat et vie sociale* (HVS), housing and community life, and—since 1982—*développement social des quartiers* (DSQ), social development of communities. The introduction of APL produces opposite effects: low-income families live in a modernized apartment, and—thanks to APL—pay a lower rent. But families with incomes slightly above the official level of poverty have no right to APL, so their rents increase greatly (often from 40 to 50 percent), and they try to move out. APL produces new segregation, concentrating the poor on modernized suburban public housing estates, but with the same uncertainties for the future that they would have in inner-city areas. As far as North Africans are concerned, they are often the victims of discriminatory practices. In accordance with the so-called "tolerance level," some local authorities and some public housing organizations believe that public housing modernization cannot be effective without a reduction in the number of ethnic minorities in their proportion of residents. This aim is more or less openly acknowledged in certain operations (Blanc 1985:78).

Conclusion

Compared with Great Britain, France has a very timid policy for decreasing racial discrimination. The French law of 1972 condemns direct racial discrimination but ignores indirect racial discrimination (Blanc and Bloch-Sturm 1984:181). Many local authorities do refuse North African applicants after they reach a certain proportion of these residents, but such practices are off the record, leaving no possibility of taking the case to court.

My intention herein has not been to present too dark a picture. In many places, particularly in DSQ operations, measures in favor of North Africans are taking place. But it often seems as if no one agency publicly wants to announce that something is being done for them. The official policy is to help the poor with housing problems regardless of their nationality or ethnic origin. In practice, racial discrimination remains; compared to other groups with the same socioeconomic status, North Africans encounter more difficulty in finding suitable housing.

References

Blanc, Maurice. 1984. "Immigrant Housing in France: From Hovel to Hostel to Low-Cost Flats." *New Community* 3:225–33.
———. 1985. "Le logement des immigrés et la dévalorisation de l'espace (Housing of immigrants and the depreciation of space)." *Espaces et sociétés* 46:71–82.

Blanc, Maurice, and Danièle Bloch-Sturm. 1984. "L'Habitat des 'noirs' et la lutte contre la discrimination raciale en grande-Bretagne (Housing of 'blacks' and the struggle against racial discrimination in Great Britain)." *Espaces et sociétés* 45:173–91.

Borella, François. 1987. "Nationalité et citoyenneté en droit français (Nationality and citizenship according to French law)." Pp. 27–51 in *L'Etat de droit,* edited by Dominique Colas. Paris: Presses Universitaires de France.

Castells, Manuel, and Francis Godard. 1973. *La renovation urbaine à Paris* (Urban renovation in Paris). Paris: Mouton.

Census. 1982. *Recensement général de la population de 1982: Sondage au 1/20°. France metropolitaine. Les Etrangers* (Counting of the population in 1982: Gauging of 1/20°. Urban France. Foreigners). Paris: INSEE-La Documentation française.

De Rudder, Véronique. 1987. *Autochtones et immigrés en quartier populaire* (Natives and immigrants in the popular district). Paris: L'Harmattan.

Féraud-Royer, Marie-Rose. 1987. "Conversations publiques (Public conversations)." *Les Annales de la recherche urbaine* 34:5–14.

George, Pierre. 1986a. *L'Immigration en France: Faits et problèmes* (Immigration in France: Facts and problems). Paris: Armand Colin.

———. 1986b. "Les Etrangers en France (Foreigners in France)." *Annales de géographie* 529:273–300.

Le Monde. 1988. "Dans le foyers pour travailleurs immigrés: La SONACOTRA se separe de 844 salariés (Immigrant workers in focus: The SONACOTRA parts from 844 wage-earners)." May 4.

Mollet, Albert. 1987. "OPAH et evolution des quartiers anciens (OPAH and evolution of old districts)." Pp. 2–30 in *Les notes de l'observatoire de l'habitat ancien.* Paris: Agence Nationale pour Amélioration de l'Habitat.

Pétonnet, Colette. 1982. *Espaces habités: Ethnologie des banlieues* (Inhabited spaces: Ethnology of suburbs). Paris: Galilée.

Rex, John. 1986. *Race and Ethnicity.* Milton-Keynes: Open University Press.

8. Housing Segregation in Switzerland

The question of the spatial concentration of the foreign immigrant population has been less of an issue in Switzerland than it has in the United States or in most Western European countries. The lack of interest in the topic, which drew considerable attention in other countries, is attributed chiefly to two reasons. First, within the general public, the discussion concerning guest workers still focuses on the risks seen to be inherent in the presence of a whole population of foreigners in Switzerland, that is, on issues such as the "overforeignization" and the "preservation of traditional Swiss traits." Within this context, problems of spatial distribution have been treated only on a broad national and regional level and have centered around the question of cantonal or regional quotas for guest workers. Second, the tendency toward the formation of ghettos in cities, that is, the segregation of foreigners, is relatively weak in Switzerland.

The discussion that follows will be concerned primarily with underprivileged guest workers from poorer European countries. Although a number of refugees live in Switzerland, people who had to leave their home country because of political, religious, or ethnical persecution, their situation is not the same as that of the guest worker's. Living and housing conditions are again different for the privileged foreigners who have chosen freely where to live and are attracted to Switzerland for one or another reason, including the possibility of working for international organizations and the Swiss economy in higher qualified positions.

Nationality and the Large-scale Spatial Distribution of Foreigners[1]

Switzerland has always been viewed as a country with a high percentage of foreign-born population. Even in 1988, 15 percent of the population is foreigners. Tables 8.1 and 8.2 show that between 1970 and 1980 both the ratio and the total number of foreigners living in Swit-

155

TABLE 8.1.   Foreign Residents in Switzerland, According to Nationality and Continent of Origin

Continents of origin and nationalities in absolute numbers and as percent of foreign population	1970		1980		1980 as Percent of 1970
	Number	Percent	Number	Percent	
Europe	1,021,764	94.6	889,995	94.2	87.1
Germany	118,289	11.0	87,913	9.3	74.3
France	55,841	5.2	47,570	5.0	85.2
Italy	583,855	54.0	418,989	44.3	71.8
Austria	44,734	4.1	32,135	3.4	71.8
Lichtenstein	1,935	0.2	1,838	0.2	95.0
Great Britain	14,746	1.4	15,378	1.6	104.3
Yugoslavia	24,971	2.3	60,916	6.4	243.9
Spain	121,237	11.2	107,510	11.4	88.7
Czechoslovakia	12,966	1.2	14,398	1.5	111.0
Turkey	12,215	1.1	38,626	4.1	316.2
Others	30,975	2.9	64,722	7.0	208.9
Africa	5,121	0.5	11,039	1.2	215.6
America	18,425	1.7	20,455	2.2	111.0
Asia	8,327	0.8	21,883	2.3	262.8
Australia, Oceania	1,063	0.1	1,299	0.1	122.2
Unknown			303	—	—
Refugees	25,376	2.3	32,756	3.5	129.1
Total foreign residents	1,080,076		944,974		87.5
Percent of total population	17.2		14.8		

Note: The 1970 census identified refugees only as refugees; they are also accounted for as nationals in the 1980 census.

zerland dropped considerably. More than two-thirds of this decrease, however, is due to naturalization (primarily of German, Austrian, Hungarian, and Czech immigrants), whereas just under one-third is because of outward migratory movement of guest workers, especially in the late 1970s due to government policies, and because of the natural demographic evolution. Among the countries included in table 8.1, the absolute figures for Italian, German, and Austrian nationals—who represent a high percentage of the foreign resident population—clearly fell, while the number of Yugoslavians, Turks, Africans, and Asians more than doubled between 1970 and 1980.

The diminution in foreign population which occurred between 1970 and 1980 was evenly distributed between the cantons; the increase in the cantons of Obwalden and Geneva constitutes an exception. The fact that between 1970 and 1980, the proportion of foreigners in Zurich, Geneva, and Lausanne increased is because population losses for these large cities were greater for Swiss nationals than for foreigners.

TABLE 8.2.   Foreign Residents in Swiss Cantons and Cities
(more than 100,000 Inhabitants)

	1970		1980		1980 as Percent
Cantons	Number	Percent	Number	Percent	of 1970
Zurich	210,104	19.0	184,189	16.4	87.7
Bern*	101,672	10.3	69,631	7.7	—
Lucerne	30,143	10.4	26,149	8.8	86.7
Uri	2,698	7.9	2,212	6.5	81.2
Schwyz	10,771	11.7	9,202	9.5	85.4
Obwalden	1,597	6.5	1,762	6.8	110.3
Nidwalden	2,356	9.2	1,772	6.2	75.2
Glarus	6,834	17.9	6,333	17.2	92.7
Zug	10,720	15.8	10,368	13.7	96.7
Fribourg	16,806	9.3	14,349	7.7	85.4
Solothurn	34,305	15.3	26,976	12.4	79.6
Basel-Stadt	41,362	17.6	35,508	17.4	85.8
Basel-Land	38,639	18.9	31,114	14.2	80.5
Schaffhausen	3,947	19.1	11,107	16.0	79.6
Appenzell A. Rh.	7,209	14.7	5,657	11.9	78.5
Appenzell I. Rh.	1,090	8.3	974	7.6	89.4
St. Gallen	58,834	15.3	52,054	13.3	88.5
Graubünden	24,091	14.9	19,910	12.1	82.6
Aargau	80,031	18.5	67,215	14.8	84.0
Thurgau	34,043	18.6	28,087	15.3	82.5
Ticino	67,504	27.5	66,085	24.9	97.9
Vaud	115,552	22.6	106,998	20.2	92.6
Valais	21,254	10.3	19,895	9.1	93.6
Neuchâtel	36,695	21.7	27,837	17.6	75.9
Geneva	111,819	33.7	112,639	32.3	100.7
Jura*	—	—	6,651	10.2	—
Cities					
Zurich	73,997	17.5	65,308	17.7	88.3
Basel	38,786	18.2	33,233	18.2	85.7
Geneva	58,511	33.7	55,916	35.7	95.6
Bern	22,532	13.9	18,342	12.6	81.4
Lausanne	31,154	12.7	29,552	23.2	94.5

*Between 1970 and 1980, part of Canton Bern became independent and formed the new
Canton Jura.

Both in 1970 and in 1980, Geneva, as the site of numerous international organizations, was the city and the canton with the highest proportion of foreigners in Switzerland.

Housing Conditions of Foreigners

Only the results of the 1980 census are analyzed in the light of indicators such as ownership, residential density, facilities available, period of house construction, and annual rent. All four main groups

TABLE 8.3.   Dwelling Situation and Housing Conditions of Different Subgroups
in Native and Foreign Resident Population (1980)

	Swiss			Total Foreigners		
	One Person Household	Family Households		One Person Household	Family Household	
		With Change	Without Change		With Change	Withou Change
Conditions of property						
Apartments in one-family houses	8.9	22.4	27.1	2.8	8.5	10.1
Other owner-occupied apartments	17.1	37.7	43.5	4.8	11.9	10.7
Rented apartments	76.6	54.3	48.5	92.1	84.7	84.7
Cooperative-owned apartments	3.3	5.3	4.6	0.8	1.6	2.5
	100.0	100.0	100.0	100.0	100.0	100.0
Number of persons per room						
Less than 0.5	76.8	47.0	8.7	56.8	25.6	2.8
0.51–1	23.2	51.5	74.0	43.2	65.1	57.6
1.01–2	—	1.5	16.9	—	9.1	38.0
More than 2 per room	—	—	0.4	—	0.2	1.7
	100.0	100.0	100.0	100.0	100.0	100.0
Facilities						
Apartments with own kitchen	89.2	98.2	98.6	77.0	94.4	97.8
Apartments with own bath	88.5	94.8	96.4	83.1	92.7	94.2
Apartments with central or remote heating	86.6	87.2	87.2	88.8	89.8	89.3
Period of construction						
Apartments in houses built before 1947	44.5	42.1	36.0	39.6	34.0	33.0
between 1947–70	40.0	41.4	40.5	42.5	44.5	45.4
after 1970	15.4	16.5	23.5	17.9	21.5	21.7
	100.0	100.0	100.0	100.0	100.0	100.0
Annual rental rate in Fr. (where known)‡						
less than 3600	39.0	22.4	13.9	43.3	26.3	22.6
3601–7200	53.5	59.9	60.0	47.5	55.9	60.3
7201–10800	6.0	13.5	19.3	6.7	12.0	12.0
more than 10801	1.4	4.3	6.8	2.5	5.8	5.1
	100.0	100.0	100.0	100.0	100.0	100.0

*Total number of Germans, French, Austrians, British, Americans, and Dutch.

†Total number of Italians, Spaniards, Yugoslavians, Turks, Portuguese, and Greeks.

‡Comparison of rental rates can be effected for normal tenancy and for cooperative buildings only. It was not possible to obtain information about the rental rate of a relatively large number of occupied apartments. In order to dampen the statistical influence of the availability of facilities on the rental rate, I took into account only those apartments and shares in cooperative buildings which had their own kitchen and whose rental rate was recorded in the 1980 census.

defined in table 8.3—Swiss, total number of foreigners, "privileged Westerners," and "underprivileged guest workers"—are further subdivided into single and family households without and with children. For statistical reasons only German, French, Austrian, British, American, and Dutch citizens are included in the category "privileged Westerners." Italians, Spaniards, Yugoslavians, Turks, Portuguese, and Greeks are included under "underprivileged guest workers."

	Privileged Westerners*			Underprivileged Guest Workers†	
One Person Household	Family Households With Change	Without Change	One Person Household	Family Households With Change	Without Change
4.2	16.8	24.4	2.0	4.3	5.1
7.7	22.7	25.6	2.8	6.2	5.6
89.4	74.2	70.3	93.8	90.0	89.5
1.0	1.8	2.4	0.7	1.4	2.5
100.0	100.0	100.0	100.0	100.0	100.0
65.2	42.0	6.8	52.2	16.5	1.3
34.8	54.3	76.4	47.7	71.4	50.8
—	3.7	16.4	—	11.9	45.8
—	—	0.4	—	0.3	2.0
100.0	100.0	100.0	100.0	100.0	100.0
82.6	97.9	98.4	74.0	93.1	97.6
92.4	98.0	98.8	74.8	89.1	92.4
94.2	95.0	95.7	83.1	85.9	86.5
30.8	24.9	21.6	49.0	41.0	37.9
46.6	44.6	43.5	37.7	43.8	46.3
22.5	30.5	34.9	13.3	15.2	15.8
100.0	100.0	100.0	100.0	100.0	100.0
28.7	11.8	7.6	57.5	35.2	27.6
56.8	53.2	52.4	38.7	57.3	63.4
10.6	21.5	24.6	2.9	6.0	7.5
3.9	13.5	15.4	0.9	1.5	1.4
100.0	100.0	100.0	100.0	100.0	100.0

From the point of view of housing, guest workers are greatly un-derprivileged compared to the Swiss—and to the privileged Western-ers. This is most clearly shown in the low proportion of owners (5 percent for guest workers, as opposed to 33.6 percent for the Swiss in 1980) and the very high proportion of tenants (90.6 percent against 59 percent), together with the high proportion in overcrowded dwellings with more than one person per room (31 percent against 7.8 percent).

The differences in the facilities available and in the distribution of the households in dwellings dating from the three construction periods are less marked. However, the fact that, in 1980, more than 25 percent of one-person guest-worker households lived in dwellings without baths and kitchens seems significant.

As far as the classes of annual rental rates, important differences existed between the Swiss and guest workers in 1980: 25.2 percent of all Swiss households and 35.3 percent of all guest-worker households paid less than SFr. 3,600 per year; 17.2 percent of all Swiss households, but only 7.8 percent of all guest-worker households, paid a rent of more than SFr. 7,000 per year.

The Role and the Significance of Foreigners
in the Swiss Housing Market

Foreigners in Switzerland are both a work force and a resident population; as such, they have "underlayered"[2] the employment system and the housing market. Their presence has been a specific prerequisite for upward job mobility and social ascent of the native population. Without foreigners, the Swiss housing market would have developed very differently after World War II, not only in terms of the growth in the income available to households, but also of the evolution of needs and preferences concerning housing. The employment and residential underprivileging of guest workers has been and still is the reverse side of upward mobility in the native population. Relative to the housing market, foreigners must not be considered as only demanding, but also as guaranteeing the occupancy of dwellings which would either remain empty or be leased under different conditions to native tenants. Some sectors of the Swiss housing market were influenced by this aspect, insofar as the relative market value of buildings used as residential dwellings was higher than it would have been under other types of utilization. In other sectors, adjustments which would otherwise have been required, that is, structural renovation of available buildings, were delayed. It thus appears that the presence of foreigners is ambivalent in that it both accelerates and delays the dynamic evolution of the housing market.

The transition zone of contemporary Swiss cities still contains numerous old buildings not equipped with the facilities usually considered standard. They are comparatively less attractive than the average, well-equipped Swiss dwelling. A concentration of underprivileged guest workers exists in this segment of the Swiss housing market. It

TABLE 8.4.   Index of Dissimilarity (I.D.) for the Swiss and Eight Other Nationalities in Zurich*

	1.	2.	3.	4.	5.	6.	7.	8.	9.	10.
1. Germans	*	17	33	11	15	27	33	31	21	13
2. French	+1	*	38	22	14	32	35	36	27	26
3. Italians	+6	+4	*	24	40	15	17	12	12	28
4. Austrians	+1	+2	+3	*	23	20	28	25	14	10
5. British	−4	−2	0	−2	*	34	36	37	29	26
6. Yugoslavians	+7	+6	−9	+4	+4	*	21	18	11	22
7. Spaniards	+8	+9	−5	+6	+6	−1	*	14	16	32
8. Turks	+6	+9	−3	+7	+4	−2	−6	*	14	27
9. Total foreigners	+5	+3	0	+5	+1	−4	−1	−1	*	17
10. Swiss	0	+2	+3	−1	−4	+1	+2	+1	+1	*

Note: Top right half of the table: 1980 I.D.; bottom left half of the table: difference between 1980 I.D. and 1970 I.D.
*Calculated for thirty-four districts of the city of Zurich, on the basis of the 1970 and 1980 census.

was no coincidence when, at the end of the 1970s, immediately after numerous guest workers returned home, that a considerable intensification occurred in the renovation of buildings situated near the centers of Swiss cities.

Foreigners play an equally important role as guarantors of the leasing potential of new dwellings. In this context, not only guest workers, but also refugees and "privileged Westerners" must be considered. An above-average proportion of foreigners are found in many housing estates built in the suburbs and on the periphery of cities; they are also overrepresented in some rural areas. Foreign nationals who came to Switzerland as a group (e.g., the refugees who left Hungary in 1956 and Czechoslovakia in 1968) are still likely to live in areas where, at the time they entered the country, many new buildings were under construction and hard to let. There is also a clear link between the increasing difficulties met by owners after 1980 in finding tenants and the fact that the supply of migrants had come to a standstill.

Housing Segregation between Swiss and Foreigners in Zurich

With its 360,000 inhabitants, Zurich is the largest city in Switzerland. Both in 1970 and in 1980, the proportion of its foreign population was around 17.5 percent (table 8.2). The absolute values in the index of dissimilarity (I.D.), calculated following Duncan and Duncan's method,[3] are relatively low (table 8.4). Helmert (1982), computing this index for Frankfurt, arrived at I.D. values that are approximately

10 percentage points higher than those for Zurich, taking corresponding pairs of nationalities.[4] Many American cities have an index of
dissimilarity between blacks and whites that is above 70 percent (Taeuber and Taeuber 1965).[5]

The German and the Austrian residents in Zurich are most likely,
both in 1970 and 1980, to adopt a residential behavior similar to that
of the Swiss. During the same period the French, the Italians, the
British, the Spaniards, and the Turks adopted a residential behavior
clearly dissimilar from that of the native population. The high degree
of dissimilarity found for the British and for the French may be attributed to their being overrepresented in "good" districts, whereas
the high index arrived at for the Italians, the Spaniards, and the Turks
is due to their being overrepresented in less-popular residential areas
in the zone of transition.

Indeed, between 1970 and 1980 the degree of spatial dissimilarity,
or housing segregation, between the Swiss and all foreigners has not
increased significantly, that is, from 16 to 17 percent. However, this
global trend included contradictory partial trends which, if taken separately, are remarkable: A cross-comparison between the nationalities
in the privileged and those in the underprivileged group shows that
almost all I.D. values have increased between 1970 and 1980. The
increase in the I.D. values of underprivileged nationalities, that is,
computed cross-wise against these for the Swiss, was relatively low
due to the large absolute number in this last group and to a consequent
lack of influence on their small-scale spatial distribution. As opposed
to this, the I.D. values of underprivileged nationalities computed
against those of the French, the British, the Germans, and the Austrians increased considerably.

All I.D. values within the underprivileged nationalities decreased
between 1970 and 1980, whereby the large group of Italians living in
Zurich is characterized by more extreme changes.

The preceding empirical results corroborate the notion that social
conditions can be reflected spatially. The causes of the housing segregation for foreign residents in Zurich are now discussed in greater
detail, along with the fact that this segregation is less pronounced than
in other cities of Europe.

In order to analyze the origin of housing segregation, we have developed a model in which the average rental price, together with the
degree of accessibility and the attractiveness of specific city areas are
defined as independent variables.[6] On the basis of this housing segregation model, various statistical tests were computed to demonstrate

the dominant significance of the accessibility of dwellings as a determinant for the percentage of foreign residents in each district. Accessibility itself was shown to correlate negatively with the number of properties owned by state and building cooperatives because in Switzerland these proprietors seldom rent their apartments to foreigners. Accessibility also correlated negatively with the stability of the resident population.

In contrast to popular opinion, our study showed that on average foreigners did not live in cheaper dwellings than did Swiss of similar socioeconomic status. They looked for apartments which they were able to afford and selected the cheaper among these. Both variables, "accessibility of dwellings" and "rental rate," could explain around 50 percent of the variance concerning the percentage of foreigners in the different city districts. The remaining variance was to be attributed to aspects of attractiveness that cannot be easily defined.

Four causes may contribute to the fact that housing segregation in Zurich is relatively low compared to U.S. and Western European cities:

1. Zurich's population lives in a relatively limited spatial area; this complicates the differentiation of clearly demarcated city districts that would each have a homogeneous population.[7]

2. The majority of Zurich's Swiss population reacts relatively "mildly" to the intrusion of foreign minority groups. It is significant in this context that the foreign minority in Zurich includes a large proportion of Italians and Spaniards who look less "foreign" than the Turks in West Germany or the blacks in the United States.

3. Zurichers seldom move from their present apartments; there is a marked rootedness of the native population. Thus they do not create much space for new foreigners. The overaging and thus low mobility orientation of the local population in areas of the zone of transition influences the low degree of housing segregation, together with the fact that Switzerland has not been submitted to the type of migratory movements which the war provoked in other countries. Foreigners who came to Zurich in the 1950s and 1960s found a local population who, for the most part, had been born, grew up, and still lived in its "home" district.

4. In Zurich, the conditions for capital invested in real estate tend to differ from those found in foreign cities known for their stronger degree of housing segregation. The renovation of older buildings can be expected to bring a reasonable, or at least adequate, yield because these are greatly appreciated by many local residents who can afford

higher rents. It seems, furthermore, that relatively efficient official records of the presence of foreigners, together with measures designed to prevent abuses relative to tenancy, have contributed to an impeding of the practices which would promote housing segregation.[8]

A Prospective View of the Potential for "Ghettoization"

Housing segregation between privileged and underprivileged foreign nationalities has clearly increased from 1970–80 but only slightly between the underprivileged and the Swiss. It is, however, not clear whether this trend will persist in the future. It is true that the contrasts between "good" and "bad" residential areas within specific cities and regions will become sharper. A number of important arguments related to the evolution of the income level may be formulated, which would suggest that housing segregation will continue to increase. The labor market is evolving toward a polarization between income levels and between those with and without job security. A consequence may be a considerable broadening of the span between "have's" and "have not's" and, therefore, an increase in housing segregation. The builders' and investors' future strategy will likely involve a greater differentiation in offerings in terms of price, facilities, and environmental attractiveness. The fact that for numerous households the rent-income ratio (the rent proportionate to the family budget) is already reaching an unacceptable level may also induce the state to intervene, which would be "un-Swiss" but likely to reinforce the housing segregation.[9]

Considering, however, that Switzerland has adopted an immigration policy that allows very few newcomers into the country and that guest workers who have been in Switzerland for some time will tend to assimilate at an employment and at a residential level, we may infer that although dissimilarities based on nationality will decrease, global housing segregation will simultaneously increase due to other dimensions such as social class, age, and household structures.

Until now, the coexistence of native and foreign residents in the housing market did not involve too many problems because the two groups had clearly different aspirations. Swiss immigration policy of the 1960s contributed to these groups "politely sharing" the housing market in so far as it was based on a "rotation model" which allowed foreigners to come and leave the country on a continuous basis. With this temporary status guest workers created a demand for residential opportunities which were not attractive to the Swiss.[10] Switzerland's present immigration policy aims at restricting the number of newcomers while attempting to integrate and assimilate the foreigners who already live in the country. Together with the gradual appearance of "new relative poverty" among the Swiss population, the policy will contribute to native and foreign residents having to compete for dwellings more than was the case in the past.

Notes

This chapter is a revised and abridged version of two articles by the author: *Segregation zwischen Schweizern und Ausländern in der Stadt Zürich*, DISP No. 75 (Zürich: ETH, 1984), and "Wie wohnen die Ausländer?" in *Wohnen in der Schweiz, Schriftenreihe Wohnungswesen* 34 (Bern: 1985). See also the author's "Sozialökologische Analyse der kleinräumigen Ausländerverteilung in Zürich," in *Ausländer in der Bundesrepublik Deutschland und in der Schweiz*, edited by H.-J. Hoffmann-Nowotny and K.-O. Hondrich (Frankfurt and New York: Campus Verlag, 1982).

1. The data relevant to questions of small-scale segregation are collected in Switzerland only every ten years, in connection with the census. No non-aggregate data are available for the period 1981–88.

2. The concept of "underlayering" is developed in H.-J. Hoffmann-Nowotny, *Soziologie des Fremdarbeiterproblems* (Stuttgart: Campus Verlag, 1973).

3. The "index of dissimilarity" developed by O. Duncan and D. Duncan (1955) is defined as

$$\text{ID} = 1/2 * \left\{ \sum_{i=1}^{k} |100^* a_i/A - 100^* b_i/B| \right\}$$

whereby a_i and b_i represent the absolute number of people belonging to the first and to the second group in district i and A, and B the absolute number for these groups in the whole city. The eight nationalities were taken into account for which data was easily available concerning the period studied. Large numbers of Czechoslovakians and Hungarians who live in Zurich were not included in the study.

4. U. Helmert's contribution in *Ausländer*, ed. Hoffmann-Nowotny and Hondrich, 265–67.

5. About methodical problems concerning the comparative study of segregation, see in particular H. F. Taeuber and A. Taeuber, *Negroes in Cities* (Chicago, 1965), and C. F. Cortese, R. F. Falk, and J. K. Cohen, "Further Considerations on the Methodological Analysis of Segregation Indices," *American Sociological Review* 41 (1975):630–37.

6. See my detailed remarks in *Ausländer*, ed. Hoffmann-Nowotny and Hondrich, pp. 341–53.

7. In this sense, a large enough population or spatial extension are necessary, although passive, prerequisites for segregation.

8. It would be difficult to prove this thesis empirically because no comparative studies exist that would take into account at an international level the unknown number of foreigners staying illegally in the country or the overcrowding of living space by foreign tenants (and native landlords). Sales and tenancy practices that encourage segregation—such as the famous "blockbusting" found in American cities or the speculative turning into slums of whole districts—have not occurred on a large scale in Zurich.

9. In Geneva, with its international organizations and many well-off foreign residents, as in some tourist resorts with numerous secondary residences, measures for the protection of the indigenous population have already been taken (e.g., rental price control and laws prohibiting the sale of real estate to foreigners or the building of further secondary residences).

10. Regarding Swiss immigration policy, see J. M. Niederberger, "Die politisch-administrative Regelung von Einwanderung und Aufenthalt von Ausländern," in *Ausländer,* ed. Hoffmann-Nowotny and Hondrich. See also BIGA (Department of Trade and Industry), *Grundzüge und Probleme der schweizerischen Arbeitspolitik* (Bern 1980).

References

Arend, M. 1982. "Socialökologische Analyse der kleinräumigen Ausländerverteilung in Zürich (Socioecological analysis of foreigners spread over Zürich)." Pp. 294–374 in *Ausländer in der Bundesrepublik Deutschland und in der Schweiz* (Foreigners in the Federal Republic of Germany and in Switzerland), edited by H. J. Hoffman-Nowotny and K. O. Hondrich. Frankfurt and New York: Campus Verlag.

———. 1984. *Segregation zwischen Schweizern und Ausländern in der Stadt Zürich* (Segregation between Swiss and foreigners in the city of Zürich). DISP No. 75. Zurich: ETH.

———. 1985. "Wie wohnen die Ausländer? (How do Foreigners live?)." *Wohnen in der Schweiz, Schriftenreihe Wohnungswesen* (Living in Switzerland, Scientific Journal of Housing) 34. Bern.

BIGA (Department of Trade and Industry). 1980. *Grundzüge und Probleme der schweizerischen Arbeitspolitik* (Foundations and problems of Swiss labor politics). Bern.

Cortese, C. F., R. F. Falk, and J. K. Cohen. 1975. "Further Considerations on the Methodological Analysis of Segregation Indices." *American Sociological Review* 41:630–37.

Duncan, O. D., and B. Duncan. 1955. "A Methodological Analysis of Segregation Indexes." *American Sociological Review* 20:201–17.

Helmert, U. 1982. "Konzentrations- und Segregationsprozesse der ausländerischen Bevölkerung in Frankfurt am Main (Concentration and segregation processes of foreign population in Frankfurt am Main)." Pp. 256–93 in *Ausländer in Bundesrepublik Deutschland und in der Schweiz* (Foreigners in the Federal Republic of Germany and in Switzerland), edited by H. J. Hoffmann-Nowotny and K. O. Hondrich. Frankfurt and New York: Campus Verlag.

Hoffmann-Nowotny, H. J. 1973. *Soziologie des Fremdarbeitersproblem* (Sociology of the guest-workers problem). Stuttgart: Enke Verlag.

Hoffmann-Nowotny, H. J., and K. O. Hondrich. 1982. *Ausländer in der Bundesrepublik Deutschland und in der Schweiz* (Foreigners in the Federal Republic of Germany and in Switzerland). Frankfurt and New York: Campus Verlag.

Niederberger, J. M. 1982. "Die politisch-administrative Regelung von Einwanderung und Aufenthalt von Ausländern (The political-administrative regulation of immigration and residence of foreigners). Pp. 11–123 in *Ausländer in der Bundesrepublik Deutschland und in der Schweiz* (Foreigners in the Federal Republic of Germany and in Switzerland), edited by H. J. Hoffmann-Nowotny and K. O. Hondrich. Frankfurt and New York: Campus Verlag.

Taeuber, H. F., and A. Taeuber. 1965. *Negroes in Cities*. Chicago: Aldine Publications.

II

Policies and Programs
Related to Housing Segregation
in Western Europe

[*Editorial note*: In this section the emphasis moves from overview descriptions of housing segregation in Western European countries to illustrations of policy directions. Cihan Arin describes the policy of dispersal for West Berlin and Ger Mik that for Rotterdam. In both cases problems with the policy and alternatives to the policy are discussed. The underlying notion of stopping concentration of minorities by demanding dispersal differs from the American approach of giving access to all housing. In the Netherlands the new alternative to dispersal policy, that of increasing resources to inner-city deprived areas, is not foreign to American policymakers. Nor are the policy decisions that cause a concentration of minority households in public (social) housing, a situation Elizabeth Huttman describes in her chapter on European social housing. She also compares such housing with its American counterpart.

In his introduction to this section Alan Murie reminds us of the framework policymakers use in housing matters related to minorities in Europe—how they see minorities as marginal persons who lack the same status as the native born. He points out the powerlessness of these minorities and the controls the government uses over them, citing both British and continental examples. In his chapter Arin also points out government controls in terms of regulations on housing standards in West Berlin. E.D.H.]

9. Introduction to the Policies in European Countries

The introduction to Part I of this book has already outlined a range of issues relating to housing segregation in Western European countries. This introduction to the policy section contributions relating to Western Europe will not cover the same ground. Instead, it focuses on identifying key issues relating to migration and segregation in Europe, issues taken farther in the following chapters. Rather than summarize or refer to them in detail, the aim of this introduction is to establish some of the questions and issues for subsequent discussion and provide an overview relevant to the individual contributions which follow.

European history is one of continuous migration. Movements to Europe from other continents, movements between European countries, and movements from Europe to other continents predate the modern nation state and industrialization. Political and economic changes, invasion, war, and religious and political persecution have contributed to large-scale population movements which have left their mark on at least the older cities of Europe. Furthermore, what is regarded as internal migration, especially that associated with industrial development and the movement from rural to urban areas, has added to the population profile. European cities prior to recent migration did not have homogeneous populations. While recent migration has added new diversity, it is a false image to perceive postwar migrants arriving in homogeneous cities. Cities already had districts where earlier waves of migrants had settled.

However, the postwar period has involved different elements. Long-established black communities did exist in some cities but were relatively small. Postwar migration involved a much larger scale of Afro-Caribbean and Asian migration, especially from former colonies. While issues of racism and discrimination had affected previous migrants, new migration has made these issues more prominent in many cities. But postwar migration has not only consisted of movement from former colonies. As Hammar (1985:142) states, "Postwar migration to and within Europe has been characterized as a movement from South to North, although such postwar migration would be better characterized as a movement from the periphery to the center." In these terms, the chapters that follow all refer to countries at the center. These countries have been affected by migration from other European countries: from Ireland to Great Britain; from Finland to Sweden; and variously from Southern Europe (Portugal, Spain, Italy, Yugoslavia, and Greece) as well as Turkey and North Africa to Switzerland, France, the Netherlands, and the Federal Republic of Germany. These flows of migration are affected by geographical location, although changing and unequal patterns of economic development are also involved.

In some cases, the origins of migrants are very different. In Britain, the pattern has been of settler migration from former colonies, especially in South Asia and the West Indies. In Germany, on the other hand, European migrants have dominated. In early phases Italian migrants were most apparent. Yugoslavs and Turks were important later, with Turks forming by far the largest groups. A continual flow of refugees and migrants from Eastern Europe has also been important in Germany—and has become more important in recent years. In the Netherlands and France, both colonial and European/Turkish migrants have been important.

For migration from former colonies, economic development is also an important factor. Patterns of migration to Britain, to the Netherlands, and to France in particular reflect their colonial heritage but also reflect economic circumstances and the demand for labor. While patterns of migration have been affected by laws on citizenship which gave rights (subsequently revised) to those in the colonies and by groups seeking refuge from the post-colonial settlement (Moluccans in the Netherlands, Algerians in France) and sometimes by subsequent changes in political control (Ugandan Asians in Britain), the underlying influences on the scale of migration have related to the demand for labor in the postwar full-employment period. With the higher unemployment which developed in Europe since the mid-1970s this influence has begun to act to reduce the flow of migration. At the same time, governments have sought to restrict migration for a variety of political and other reasons.

The demand for labor which has affected this flow is generally portrayed as a spontaneous movement (as against a planned or managed migration), reflecting economic push and pull factors and individual decisions. However, there are elements which are less "spontaneous," including the lateral recruitment agreements between Germany and Italy (1955), Spain (1960), Greece (1960), and Turkey (1961) (see Esser and Korte in Hammar 1985) and direct recruitment by employers. The scale of the resulting movement varies. It is highest in Switzerland, which is also striking for its large flow of nonresident "border-commuters." Foreign citizens residing in Switzerland in 1983 were 14 percent of residents and more than a fifth of the labor force. Foreign citizens in West Germany comprised 8–9 percent of residents and of the labor force; in France, 6–7 percent of residents and of the labor force; in Sweden, 5 percent of each, and in the Netherlands, 4 percent of each (Hammar 1985). Such statistics involve definitional problems. In Great Britain, 3–4 percent of residents and of the labor force in 1983 were foreign citizens, but the percentage of people born outside the country is significantly higher.

Given all this, the most important feature of the postwar migration in Europe has been that it has been a response to demand primarily for low-skilled and sometimes menial work. Such work is low-paid. It is often (and increasingly so in a period of rising unemployment) insecure, with poor standards of safety and limited trade union organization. Furthermore, many migrants (and especially those regarded as guest workers rather than settlers) have limited political rights and power. These two things are generally reflected in the housing situation of minority ethnic groups, most of whom are postwar migrants. As the chapters in this volume demonstrate, migration was not managed in the sense of providing programs to house migrants. In general, migrants had to compete with others to find housing. They had limited bargaining power in both market and bureaucratically managed sectors. Consequently, they tended to be only able to obtain housing of the worst standard in terms of physical condition, overcrowding, and security (Delcourt 1976). Their economic and political powerlessness left them prone to exploitation and discrimination in housing. In most cities the sectors of the housing market which they were able to move into were concentrated spatially—especially in older, decaying, inner-city neighborhoods. Where special arrangements did emerge, they have generally been regarded as involving lower standards of housing. Thus in Germany "in the 1960s immigrant workers were mostly housed in dormitories provided by the employer; bad or even inhumane living conditions often prevailed" (Esser and Korte in Hammar 1985, p. 192).

In France during the 1950s the construction of the so-called *bidon-villes* involved creating slum housing similar to the improvised settlements usually associated with third-world cities. And the *foyers* which replaced the *bidonvilles* and initially provided homes for single persons retained their original character; "the residents lived like soldiers in barracks or students in a boarding school, with former soldiers as supervisors and many restrictions in personal liberties" (Verbunt in Hammar 1985, p. 149). Initial "reception" areas sometimes used in each of the other countries referred to in the following section have involved similarly low standards.

If this situation is best understood in terms of the economic and political powerlessness of new migrants, there is another factor. In many European countries postwar migration was regarded as a temporary migration of guest workers. The situation was and is probably most apparent in Germany, and the term *gastarbeiten* comes from there. The *gastarbeiten* were welcome as migrant labor who would return to their country of origin and to their families and communities—and not bring their families with them. Various aspects of housing and migration policy relate to this. Temporary workers needed temporary, low-standard housing and did not qualify for voting and citizenship rights. They would be subject to different and restrictive regulation and control as a result. Not all European countries made this assumption to the same extent, and in some cases migrants were expected to settle. Nevertheless, most countries have experienced a move from a minority ethnic group population of workers (often males) to a phase of family growth or family reunification. At the same time the workers' status has remained marginal; an aging population and rising unemployment have drawn attention to the way in which these minority ethnic groups are treated under social security and social welfare systems. In some cases entitlements are minimal and linked to policies for deportation or encouragement of return migration.

Real differences in policy exist among countries on these matters. Nevertheless, certain distinctions among minority ethnic groups are apparent. In addition to differences between settler migrants and *gastarbeiten,* or those subject to work permits and restricted residence, there are various groups of refugees and illegal migrants. These groups have different legal status and political, economic, and housing rights. Furthermore, for countries in the European Community there are important distinctions between migrants within the Community and those outside.

One important perspective on the treatment of minority ethnic groups relates to these differences and to trends in policy toward immigration control and regulation. Rising unemployment and political exploitation of racism contributed to a tendency for European countries to develop new immigration policies, to increase control, and to change nationality laws. While these policies have generally restricted entry (even associated with family reunification), they have also tended to develop the system of *gastarbeiten* as a system of control. It is argued that the demand for migrant labor now is for temporary, flexible, and casual work, and this fits with seeking temporary residents where labor costs will be lowest. Even if this version of the link with economic change is not regarded as convincing, there is no doubt that new legislation tends to restrict settler migration and favor temporary migrants who have very few citizenship rights and, partly as a result of this, have limited political and economic power. For example, the European Community's preparations for establishing a single European market involve regulations relating to migrant workers. This gives people a status as migrant workers but not as settler migrants. A free market in labor does not involve providing rights for migrant workers to settle and leaves them insecure and powerless. The emerging situation leaves migrants and refugees more subject to racism and discrimination (Sivanandan 1988). Thus the position of minority ethnic groups has not improved over time. Indeed in some respects it has gotten worse and may get still worse in the future. The number of disenfranchised migrants in Europe's democracies is a serious issue. The regulation of illegal migrants can be used to justify checks and procedures which are only applied to nonwhite migrants.

All of these factors are reflected in the housing experience of minority ethnic groups. Economic and political marginality contributes to marginality in housing. Demands for housing rights are difficult to promote and impossible for some refugees, illegal or temporary migrants. Consequently, minority ethnic groups continue to be disproportionately concentrated in the lowest-demand housing, which tends to be spatially concentrated. The explanation for the social segregation of minority ethnic groups starts with a recognition that their economic position tends to put them in a weak bargaining position in relation to the private housing market or to public or voluntary housing sectors. It continues by recognizing the general consequences of political marginality and the more extreme problems faced by some disenfranchised categories. It is carried one step farther by acknowledging the way in which housing markets and housing market organizations generally operate in favor of individuals and households according to their occupational, income, and asset characteristics.

Finally, it is argued that minority ethnic groups are affected by various direct and indirect racial discriminations, the most difficult elements to detail. They require the use of time-consuming qualitative research into processes and decision making rather than simple, quick surveys. Where such methods have been used, the ways in which discrimination occurs emerge as complex consequences of a range of sometimes conflicting management and other pressures rather than simple expressions of the racism of individual managers. Such discrimination almost certainly occurs in all European countries. Discrimination could only be assumed not to explain part of the disadvantaged position of minority ethnic groups *where appropriate research* had been carried out and such processes had not emerged. These explanations emphasize labor market position, political power, and housing market processes, as well as the constraints affecting households. This is not to deny some degree of choice. However, in many cases it is evident that the housing choices available to minority ethnic groups are only in terms of similar dwellings and similar locations. The tenure and price structure of the market relates to spatial patterns, and choices are restricted by tenure and price. While it is important to recognize that some members of minority ethnic groups are in stronger positions, either because of successful careers or because past housing decisions have increased bargaining power in housing, in general the framework of opportunity remains restricted. All evidence suggests that this also applies to second-generation households.

Given this, a final aspect of policy development and state intervention relates to the position of minority ethnic groups—the general direction of housing policy. Rather than special schemes and projects, it is the general tenure and price structure of the market which is important. Policies which improve the quality or supply of the housing available to minority ethnic groups are crucial. The continued decline in the number and condition of affordable dwellings in the private rented sector has an initial impact. Except in Britain, home ownership tends to be too expensive for those on lower incomes, and in Britain cheaper properties are usually in either low-demand areas (where jobs are limited) or are in poor condition. The focus of attention therefore tends to be on the social rented sector. In the past this sector was often closed to minority ethnic groups by residential qualifications and other rules and procedures relating to allocation. This situation has changed, in part because of concern to remedy discriminatory policies, in part because minority ethnic group households have moved into "need" categories where they do qualify for housing, and in part because some social housing agencies have experienced increasing problems in letting some of their properties. Increasing vacancy rates and difficult-to-let housing became a phenomenon in Britain, Germany, France, Sweden, and the Netherlands; the response was to broaden access and relax rules governing allocation. The outcome of all this was that although households from minority ethnic groups increasingly moved into the social rented sector, they tended to move into the least desirable and most difficult to manage estates. A wider choice of tenure often involved only a choice among the least desirable properties.

Against this background, the erosion of social rented housing in some countries is important. If investment in the social rented sector had remained high and involved new high-quality housing, the benefits would have begun to reach poorer households and those in minority ethnic groups. Segregation would have been affected, but not eliminated. In general, unemployment and cuts in public expenditure have resulted in a trimming of social rented housing. But the social rented sectors in different countries are on different trajectories. In both Britain and Germany, the prospects are of a decline in the size of the sector and privatization of the most desirable properties. In contrast, however, in the Netherlands investment has been maintained at a higher relative level, and the social rented sector will continue to grow. The consequences of these developments for segregation and housing choice cannot be taken for granted. They depend on the way in which housing is managed and allocated as well as on the economic and political experience of different households. They also depend on how other policies change or develop.

All of these issues are important in considering issues of segregation in Europe. As was stated in chapter 2, there are important differences in the background to issues in Europe and America. The way the issues are discussed and researched often varies, too. As the chapters of this volume make clear, the particular features of immigration, of the nature of minority ethnic groups, where they come from, and their rights and status, are significantly different. In particular, the definition and treatment of migrants as *gastarbeiten* rather than as settler immigration is fundamental. Any drift toward this approach (as appears to be the tendency), and the increasing numbers of illegal and disenfranchised immigrants raise real issues about racism. This approach adds to the marginalization of minority ethnic groups, which is basic to understanding their general situation in respect of housing and social segregation.

References

Delcourt, J. 1976. *The Housing of Migrant Workers: A Case of Social Improvidence?* Brussels: Commission of European Communities.

Hammar, T. 1985. *European Immigration Policy.* Cambridge: Cambridge University Press.

Sivanandan, A. 1988. "The New Racism." *New Statesman and Society* 4:8–9.

10. Housing Segregation and Policy in the Dutch Metropolitan Environment

The study of housing segregation on an ethnic, minority, or nationality basis was, until recently, primarily an Anglo-American exercise. Research in the Netherlands has been quite rare, principally because of the absence of large-scale immigration apart from immigration of Indonesian residents entitled to Dutch citizenship in the period after Indonesian independence after 1950. Segregation can be described in two ways: as the process by which persons with common characteristics group themselves in a certain place, or at a moment in this process when a certain concentration of a population group is indicated.

The arrival of a number of Mediterranean (primarily Turkish and Moroccan) migrants, Surinamese, and Dutch Antilles' residents, and their concentrated settlement pattern in central parts of Dutch cities, have attracted the attention of Dutch researchers. The first analyses in the Dutch context were published in 1972 (Verdonk 1972; Drewe et al. 1972). Nevertheless, it was not before the second half of the seventies and the first half of the eighties that the number of studies increased considerably. From the beginning, Dutch researchers were involved in policy discussions concerning the way in which public policy should cope with segregation (the term *segregation* herein indicates residential or housing segregation) as a social problem. In scientific circles as in society, there was no consensus of opinion about the question. Specifically, discussions on advantages and disadvantages of spatial dispersal of minority groups to non-central city areas created much debate (for example, Van Praag 1980, 1981; Drewe, Hulsbergen, and Mik 1982). From the beginning, housing segregation was considered a social problem, that is, as a phenomenon that engenders negative consequences for the population groups involved. The situation in American cities, where part of the black population lives together in ghettolike districts, strongly contributed to this negative image of housing segregation. Attention in Dutch research was fo-

179

cused both on segregation as a spatial process and as a spatial form. Whether segregation in itself should be considered a social problem, or whether it is a spatial development—a concentration of disadvantaged minorities who have problems that have no causal relationship to the development—is a question yet to be answered.

The number of migrants from abroad present in the Netherlands is a matter of definition. When we define migrants as minorities from Mediterranean countries, Surinam, and the Dutch Antilles, Moluccans, refugees, gypsies, and caravan dwellers, the minority population in the Netherlands composes about 4.5 percent of the Dutch population (chapter 3) (Penninx 1984). This percentage is low compared to surrounding countries. Belgium, the Federal Republic of Germany, France, and the United Kingdom show percentages of 7 to 8 percent (Entzinger 1982).

The origin of immigrant groups in the Netherlands is more varied than that in the surrounding countries. In most continental European countries immigration has been composed of labor migrants and their families. In the United Kingdom, however, most immigrants are from former colonies in the West Indies, South Asia, and Africa. The Netherlands take an intermediate position with both Mediterranean labor migrants as well as migrants from former colonial areas. Moreover, the zenith of immigration in the Netherlands was later than elsewhere, largely because of the arrival of Surinamers around 1975. Additional family reunion migrations of Mediterraneans occurred at a later date than in surrounding countries.

The four largest Dutch cities, Amsterdam, Rotterdam, The Hague, and Utrecht, have become societies with a larger ethnic and cultural plurality than before. Of all foreigners in the Netherlands at the beginning of 1984, 35 percent lived in these four cities compared to 13.3 percent of total population. Specific groups however show a higher rate of attraction toward these largest cities. For the Mediterraneans as a whole, 332,532 in early 1984, 55.4 percent lived in one of the four cities of the Randstad—as did 62.2 percent of the Surinamers, who totaled 192,000. On the other hand, the small Antillian population group of 43,500 was less concentrated in the four largest cities, with only 28.3 percent living there; the same is true for the Moluccans.

Housing Segregation Policy
in the Four Large Dutch Cities, 1970–87
The National Policy Context

In more than one respect the 1983 government report on minorities (Minority Report) was a turning point in government policy concerning foreign presence in the Netherlands (Ministry of Interior Affairs 1983). A comparable 1970 report was dominated by the idea that official recruiting of foreign workers from the official recruitment countries should be supported and accomplished as effectively as possible. Problems of adaptation and integration were mentioned, but were far from the foreground of attention. The 1970 report was written during a period when the number of foreign workers in the prosperous Netherlands totaled about 80,000 (Ministries of Social Affairs and Public Health et al. 1970).

In 1983 the new government report documented the broadening of policy toward those population groups considered to belong to a minority. The emphasis on workers disappeared, with minorities instead described by membership in one or another of the defined minority groups, those from Mediterranean countries, Surinam, the Dutch Antilles, and Molucca, as well as refugees or gypsies. There was reason for this change in point of view. The number of immigrants living in the Netherlands increased considerably, and a large proportion took no part in the labor process. This is a consequence of the economic crisis and the changed age and sex composition of the immigrant population.

Although the situation in 1970 was not too bright, the 1983 Minority Report was published in a period in which minorities came under heavy pressure, not only because of increasing unemployment among the minority population, but also because of increasing racism. The psychological burden for minorities is likely to be much greater than commonly expected. In the period 1970–84 a number of shifts occurred in national policy and found expression in the 1983 report: (1) a shift from a specific to a more general policy; (2) a shift from a nearly exclusively labor market-oriented policy to a wider attention toward integration and the combating of deprivation; and (3) a shift from recruitment of foreign workers to creating possibilities for voluntary re-migration.

The three shifts are strongly related. Policy around 1970 was largely aimed at recruitment of foreign workers to solve the absolute and structural shortage of labor in the Netherlands. Presence of foreign workers was considered temporary, even though early research results showed the necessity of taking into account long-lasting or permanent stays of at least a portion of the immigrant population (Ned. Stichting voor Statistiek 1971). As a consequence, national and local policy was focused on the labor market: recruitment in the Mediterranean countries (especially Turkey and Morocco) was an essential element. Policy also had a strong ad hoc character: measures were taken when problems were identified. This has changed considerably; the primary objective of the Minority Report is now to create a society in which members of minority groups, individually and as group members, have a position equivalent to native Dutch inhabitants and equal chances to develop. Key words are "integration," while maintaining "cultural plurality" and "re-migration" possibilities for those who so wish. This development is a logical consequence of the now-permanent presence of minorities in the Netherlands, a situation due in part to the almost-completed stage of family reunion.

The shifting focus of national policy to an emphasis on stimulating integration and acting against deprivation of all population groups has been accompanied by the use of spatial instruments. A dispersal policy was never actual on the national level, except for those of Indonesian background; such a policy was discussed more at the local level. From the Minority Report it appears that dispersal as a housing policy is not to be stimulated from the national point of view; nevertheless there is a spatial dimension in the Minority Report, primarily in terms of the proposed deprivation area policy. In seventeen municipalities, in a number of districts where an accumulation of problems in the field of employment, housing, welfare, and education have been identified, an area-oriented scheme is proposed, with extra funds and attention given to the districts by local authorities. This scheme is not focused upon minorities, but on the population as a whole inside the districts, which generally have high percentages of minority groups. The basis of definition of these areas' boundaries has been on such criteria as a high percentage of low-income groups, a high percentage of people depending on social aid, and a high percentage of minority groups. It is meant as an area-based antideprivation policy focused on all population groups in those areas and on several aspects of deprivation. The problem is that local municipalities have limited financial resources available to implement the policy.

The Local Policy Context

Discussions about segregation on the Dutch local level have primarily centered on the field of housing. Most of the financial means for housing has been furnished by the central government, although most allocation of the funds has been a municipal task. In the first half of the seventies dispersal of migrants to more peripheral (somewhat suburban) districts was the dominant force in municipal housing policy (Van Praag 1980, 1981). The start of this policy was marked by the so-called "5 percent rule" in Rotterdam in 1972 (suspended in 1974 by the national government). In the Netherlands permits for cheap housing are a long-standing fact of life, dating from the chronic housing shortage of the early postwar years. Housing regulations in Rotterdam were changed so that migrants were unable to get a housing permit in districts where more than 5 percent of the population consisted of members of minority groups (Mediterraneans and migrants from Surinam and the Dutch Antilles). As a follow-up to criticisms of the 1972 policy, the Rotterdam municipality council adopted a policy in 1979 which was designed to disperse migrants voluntarily over the city: a so-called "clustered deconcentration" (B and W Rotterdam 1979, 1980). The clustered deconcentration of 1979 meant a specific policy for migrant groups by decreasing their number in old city districts and increasing on a voluntary basis their number in eight newer and more peripheral districts of the city where better housing should be available. This deconcentration should, according to the Rotterdam plans, be clustered; each peripheral district should hold its own nationality group. The dispersal policy has created many emotional discussions, and even a lawsuit between Rotterdam and a grouping of migrant organizations. Rotterdam abandoned its dispersal policy in 1983 as agreed in a published protocol between the city and the migrant organizations. This meant a radical change-over of Rotterdam policy that has resulted in a municipality moving toward walking in step with the other three large Dutch municipalities that changed their policies.

The municipality of Amsterdam also began to change its policy. In 1974 the city council proposed that the municipality management implement a dispersal policy to stimulate integration of ethnic minorities and prevent the formation of ghettos (B and W Amsterdam 1974). In 1978 this policy principle was abandoned completely as a consequence of much severe criticism. Plans for closing some districts to immigrants from Surinam and the Mediterranean countries, and limiting the number of members from these groups in other districts to one family per apartment building, were rejected by the municipality council. The conclusion was that housing allocation on the basis of place of origin or color was not a good policy. From 1978 on, no distinction has been made between native Dutch inhabitants and migrant groups in housing allocation. Thus in Amsterdam the policy of dispersal was rejected.

The municipal government of The Hague came to a similar conclusion. On the basis of an exploratory report, the municipality council decided in 1980 that the housing problems of migrants should be solved, as much as possible, by creating open housing facilities. Several general principles were laid down: the right of everyone to live where he or she wanted, the same rules for everybody, and the rejection of forced dispersal (Municipality of The Hague 1980). In 1982 an additional principle was added: the rejection of forced concentration (B and W The Hague 1982). The report "Cultural Minorities" of 1982 emphasized free access of all groups to housing, including building certain housing types for groups for which a shortage is identified. Dispersal on a voluntary basis was recommended in the same report.

In Utrecht, after discussions that seemed to be leading to a dispersal policy in 1982, the ultimate policy decision was for a complete rejection of dispersal (B and W Utrecht 1982). No differentiations are made in Utrecht between original Dutch and low-income migrant groups. Groups—like ethnic minorities in certain cases—with extra problems can receive extra facilities in the housing field, such as access to larger houses when larger families are concerned. When granting such facilities, consequences for other low-income groups, including Dutch inhabitants, must be taken into account. The closing of districts in the city is rejected, while measures will be taken to improve living conditions in areas where migrants are concentrated (ROVU 1982).

In the period 1972–83 the change in policy was accomplished in part by the availability of more research results and the strong influence on policy of the more outspoken and emancipated organizations representing minority groups and their Dutch sympathizers. The changes are from a dispersal policy for minority groups toward a policy aimed at abolishing deprivation of both migrant and Dutch inhabitants in the field of housing and other aspects of life, a policy in which dispersal is no longer a major component. Abandoning dispersal policy in the four larger Dutch cities leads to a policy of considering both original Dutch and migrant groups as comparable and as sharing a number of problems. From then on, minority policy was considered to be part of a more general antideprivation policy. Nationally, the 1983 Minority Report ended the dispersal policy for minority groups as a part of a

TABLE 10.1.   Population by Nationality and Ethnic Origin in Rotterdam (1972–84)

	Jan. 1, 1972		Jan. 1, 1976		Jan. 1, 1980		Jan. 1, 1984	
	Number	Percent	Number	Percent	Number	Percent	Number	Percent
Mediterraneans	19,307	2.9	27,194	4.4	36,242	6.3	42,219	7.6
Surinamers/								
Antillians*	±12,000	1.8	16,187	2.6	19,850	3.4	24,472	4.4
Other foreigners	7,213	1.1	8,385	1.4	10,654	1.8	14,075	2.5
Other Dutch	631,540	94.3	563,013	91.6	512,441	88.5	474,587	85.5
Total	670,060	100.1	614,769	100.0	579,187	100.0	555,353	100.0

Source: Demografische Gegevens Rotterdam, various years, Stichting Sociale Belangen Surinamers 1972.

more general housing policy because of the similarities of social and economic behavior between minority groups and Dutch inhabitants. Policy on a local level therefore developed from a dispersal policy as panacea for housing problems of ethnic groups to an antideprivation policy applied to both the original Dutch and the ethnic deprived groups.

Segregation in Rotterdam

Rotterdam is an example that illustrates the type of housing segregation both in a metropolitan context and a local policy (table 10.1). A series of research projects was carried out in Rotterdam by a group of scholars from Rotterdam and environs during the seventies and eighties. The results provide a full documentation of spatial development of housing segregation in the Rotterdam urban context, its causes and consequences, and the reaction of public policy. These research results also influenced the above-mentioned policy discussions (Drewe et al. 1972, 1975; Hulsbergen and Mik 1980; Mik 1980, 1982, 1983, 1987).

Analysis of the theory (Mik 1987) has led to twenty-one hypotheses that constitute the basis for the research in Rotterdam. These hypotheses concern spatial patterns of segregation in Rotterdam, variables related to segregation, and changes in the spatial context. Testing of these hypotheses was accomplished by the following:

1. A description of spatial patterns for 1972, 1976, 1980, and 1984 by way of dissimilarity indices, percentages, homogeneity indices, and a specially developed segregation index S, which can be calculated as

$$S_i = \frac{B_i}{O_i} \times \frac{B_i}{T_i}$$

FIGURE IO.I.   Percentage of Mediterraneans, Surinamers, and Antillians in the total population of Rotterdam, per city district in quintiles as of January 1, 1976 (city average = 7.0%)

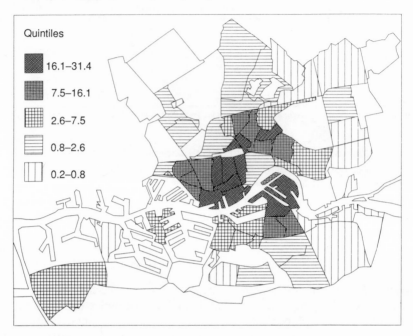

Source: Institute of Economics and Geography, Erasmus University, Rotterdam.

in which B_i is the number of immigrants (B) in a certain area i (grid square or city district), O_i indicates the size of that area, and T_i is total population size of that area (for a broader discussion of this index, see Mik 1983).

2. A sample survey was conducted in 1977, based on interviews with 150 Turkish, 150 Spanish, 142 Surinamese, and 151 Dutch heads of households; it focused on areas of high, medium, and low segregation in Rotterdam. The survey was a stratified spatial sample from grid squares of 100 by 100 meters.

3. A multiple regression analysis was done on data by city district for 1976 and 1984.

Spatial Patterns

Based on the measures in 1972, 1976, 1980, and 1984, segregation of immigrants is found to occur, especially in the older districts around

FIGURE 10.2.   Percentage of Mediterraneans, Surinamers, and Antillians in the total population of Rotterdam, per city district in quintiles as of January 1, 1984 (city average = 12.0%)

Source: Institute of Economics and Geography, Erasmus University, Rotterdam.

the central business district, on both sides of the river, the Nieuwe Maas (figs. 10.1 and 10.2). City districts are divided over five groups (quintiles) with the same number of districts but different group boundaries. Immigrants are concentrated in three areas, to the north, west, and south of the central business district (c.b.d.). A "gap" in the ring, the east side of the CBD, can be identified. The highest concentrations of Mediterraneans are located on the north and south sides of the city center, whereas concentrations of Surinamers and Antillians are located on the west side. In addition, Surinamers and Antillians are distributed over a larger number of districts than are the other groups.

Levels of segregation have changed in the period 1972–84 in the various city parts. Table 10.2 shows these tendencies by way of dissimilarity indices. This index can be interpreted as the percentage of the population group that would have to move to other city districts

TABLE 10.2.   Dissimilarity Indices

	Dissimilarity indices			
	Jan. 1, 1972*	Jan. 1, 1976†	Jan. 1, 1980†	Jan. 1, 1984†
Surinamers and Antillians	—	44	38	34
Turks	50	53	56	54
Moroccans	61	57	56	53
Spaniards	52	50	48	47
Yugoslavians	63	54	54	48
Portuguese	53	55	55	47
Italians	32	30	30	29
Greek	42	37	36	34
Other foreigners	22	25	32	31
Mediterraneans	49	51	52	50
Med./Sur./Antill.	—	48	47	44
All Med./Sur./Antill./ other for.	—	43	44	41

*Dissimilarity indices for immigrant groups versus Dutch, including Surinamers and Antillians.
†Dissimilarity indices for immigrant groups versus Dutch, excluding Surinamers and Antillians.

if the same spatial distribution is to be reached as that of the group being compared. This distribution is not meant as a policy option because free choice of location does not have to lead to proportional distributions; nevertheless, the dissimilarity index is a simple and illustrative design to indicate situations of segregation.

In the seventies, segregation increased modestly for Mediterranean groups, while in the same period segregation of Surinamers and Antillians decreased somewhat. In the first half of the eighties the decrease continued for West Indian immigrants, while the level of segregation for Mediterraneans decreased slightly. At the same time, a certain dispersal of immigrants can be identified as a consequence of a movement to a second ring of older districts further from the CBD, while a modest number of immigrants live in even some of the peripheral districts. Although in some districts close to the CBD the number and proportion are declining, many districts around the CBD show considerable levels of immigrant concentration. Nevertheless, movement is somewhat away from the city center and to the second ring of districts.

Outward growth from the concentric zone around the CBD on the north bank of the city is primarily sectoral to the northern half of the city, with movement in a western and northern direction. In the southern part of Rotterdam, growth is more concentric than sectoral. An infiltration-invasion process (a slow and later accelerated in-migration of members of minority groups in certain districts, as observed in some

American cities) cannot clearly be recognized, although a number of districts have more than average growth over a long period, leading to relatively high percentage of immigrants. In no city district did a major succession of an immigrant group replacing Dutch inhabitants occur. Feyenoord on the south bank of the river, close to the city center, was the district with the highest percentage of immigrants, 39.6 percent in 1984. This percentage is the total proportion for all different foreign and ethnic groups, however; there was no institutionalization of immigrant presence and no major cultural ghetto. Compared to American examples, areas of concentration are small.

There are no ghettos in Rotterdam, that is, institutionalized residential areas of a certain immigrant group. Nor are there ethnic neighborhoods, that is, areas of some size that predominantly are residential areas for a particular immigrant group. Nevertheless there are areas of considerable concentration where certain immigration groups are represented more strongly than in the city as a whole without being the majority of the population in that area.

Factors Related to Segregation

The sample survey identified a number of factors related to segregation. The survey results gave information on the relationship between socioeconomic status, an element in this process as it is elsewhere, and the degree of individual segregation. A higher degree of segregation existed for immigrants with a lower income and educational position. Professional status did not influence the degree of segregation of persons, however, except for the unemployed. It is also clear that inhabitants of the older districts, both immigrants and original inhabitants, are at the same lower class level in the population and have a similarity of income, education, and professional status.

The presence of cheap, low-quality housing is a second factor related to segregation. In areas with high and medium degrees of segregation, most immigrants live in old apartment houses; areas with a low degree of segregation have better housing. Immigrants in the areas of highest segregation live in the smallest number of rooms, have the worst housing facilities, and pay the lowest rents. It appears also that in the areas with the most segregation more immigrants live in public housing, a consequence of the lack of other possibilities for this population group.

A factor that plays a special role in bringing about a concentrated pattern for immigrants in Rotterdam is the way in which many obtain their dwellings. From the sample survey it appeared that a third of the Spaniards, almost half of the Turks, and a fourth of the Surinamers (compared to 14 percent of the original inhabitants) found their dwellings with the help of their fellow countrymen. In two out of every three such cases, immigrants found a house in the neighborhood of the countryman who helped him to find it. This was especially true for the Turks. The hypothesis that orientation toward the home country would lead to segregation proved not to be entirely true. From the interview responses, the data showed that more than 90 percent of immigrants, regardless of their location in areas of high, medium, or low segregation, plan to remain in the Netherlands for five years. Other variables, chosen as criteria for establishing orientation toward the home country (recent visits to the home country and the rate of family reunion), show more correlation with the degree of segregation.

There was no doubt from the survey results that prejudice (measured by asking the respondents their opinion about twenty-three positive and negative qualities of ten nationality groups) is a reality in Rotterdam. It is, however, not true that there is a simple relationship between degree of prejudice and level of segregation. It appears that Dutch prejudice against immigrants is highest in areas of medium segregation, especially prejudice toward the black Surinamers. However in these areas of medium segregation more positive opinions by Dutch are also found. The explanation can be twofold: either the measurement scale of segregation and the geographic scale of occurrence of prejudice are not the same, or prejudice is highest in areas where concentrations of immigrants are increasing.

The survey also identifies a common group identification among immigrants of the same nationality in areas of higher segregation, especially among Turks. There is a relationship between level of segregation and the perception of problems, especially those concerning housing. This is true for both immigrants and for the Dutch. The difference is that immigrants mention the housing problems most in areas of high segregation, the Dutch in areas of medium segregation. Nevertheless, housing problems are the most serious problem for all interviewed groups.

Much attention was paid to the group-linked factor of integration in Dutch society. Results indicate that integration into the Dutch society does not vary with the degree of housing segregation levels. To make the concept of integration operational, it was divided into four dimensions: instrumental integration (knowledge of Dutch language and knowledge and use of facilities), economic integration (association between education and position in the labor market), cultural integration (way of spending leisure time), and social integration (contacts between immigrants and original Dutch inhabitants). None of the variables chosen for these integration dimensions correlated with the degree of housing segregation, thus the degree of integration by these measurements is the same on each housing segregation level. This result is remarkable considering the fact that much of the literature presents findings in which the degree of segregation and levels of assimilation are considered to correlate with each other (for example, Duncan and Duncan 1955; Duncan and Lieberson 1959; Lieberson 1961, 1963; Lancaster 1967; Timms 1969). However, some research results have been published that criticize this all too easily accepted result of a relationship between segregation and assimilation. Kennedy (1944, 1952) criticized the relationship based on her intermarriage research among ethnic groups in New Haven in which religious affiliation seemed more important than ethnic variables (with a critical reaction of Peach in 1980, 1981a, 1981b). Robinson (1980) concludes in a survey of South Asians in the United Kingdom that, despite greater spatial dispersal, marriage patterns showed that marriage remained within one's own ethnic group. Similar results came from Clarke (1971), whereas Taeuber and Taeuber (1964, 1965) in a study of 207 American cities showed that the relationship between spatial and assimilation variables for the black population were different from those of other ethnic groups. Jackson (1981) came to similar conclusions, as do Jiobu and Marshall (1971). This was especially true for the black population in the United States, which remained segregated despite socioeconomic upgrading. The Rotterdam results support the point of view that the relationship between segregation and levels of integration is by no means self-evident. There is, on the contrary, no relationship at all in the Rotterdam context. This is shown for the variable knowledge of Dutch language. The ability to speak Dutch is, for all levels of housing segregation, similarly low (43 percent in low-segregation areas and 35 percent in high-segregation areas). Comparable results were found for other dimensions of segregation. Finally, the survey showed that migration of *Dutch* inhabitants to other districts seems to be more a consequence of bad housing conditions than of high levels of minority concentration.

Changes in Spatial Context

The survey indicates the situation as of 1977. Since 1977, spatial patterns have evolved, and therefore changes in the spatial context have

TABLE 10.3.   Multiple Regression Analyses for 1976 and 1984,
with the Percentage of Mediterraneans, Surinamers, and
Antillians as Dependent Variable

Regression Variables Based on District Data	1976		1984	
	Coefficient	t-value	Coefficient	t-value
Constant	+ 181.54	+ 2.43	− 0.50	− 0.14
Receivers of social help (%)	+ 0.27	+ 2.14	—	
Unemployment (%)	—		+ 0.33	+ 2.50
Age 20–34 (%)	+ 0.55	+ 3.56	—	
65 and older (%)	—		− 0.46	− 3.63
Average building year	− 0.10	− 2.67	—	
Housing density	—		+ 0.09	+ 3.25
Out-migration Dutch (%)	—		+ 0.77	+ 6.44
In-migration Dutch (%)	+ 0.64	+ 4.12	—	
R^2	0.84		0.81	

— = No statistical significance in that year.

been analyzed for the period between 1976–84 by using a number of variables from statistical data in the field on socioeconomic aspects of the Rotterdam population: age-structure, living conditions, and migration per city districts. These variables were studied using computer-made maps, correlation coefficients, and regression techniques to provide an insight into the changes that have taken place in the physical and socioeconomic environment of segregation patterns.

A summary of a multiple regression of the chosen variables, as far as statistically significant, is presented in table 10.3. Variables involved are not to be considered as causes of segregation. They indicate the spatial context, that is, the kind of environmental milieu in which the percentage of migrants is likely to be higher or lower. The coefficients are to be considered as the best possible estimation, based on values for the 58 residential districts of Rotterdam.

In 1976, the context for the degree of segregation is determined by four variables: percent who are receivers of social help (+), percent 20–34 years of age (+), and average building year (−); because of the composition of data, a minus sign indicates that when the percentage of migrants increases, the average building age is also higher, as is the percentage in-migration of Dutch (+). Together they explain 84 percent of the variation in the percentage of migrants. By 1984 the context changed. Percent unemployment (+), percent more than 65 years of age (−), housing density (+), and the percent of out-migration of Dutch (+) are the most important variables involved, together accounting for 81 percent of the context.

Along with the cartographic analyses of the variables, the following picture is revealed. The regression analyses on the district level indicates that dispersal of immigrants to districts with a higher socioeconomic level has not occurred, but that dispersal was to districts with comparable low levels. This also explains the sectoral growth in the northern part of Rotterdam, where immigrant groups have avoided districts with a higher socioeconomic level. Age structure of the concentration districts changed between 1976 and 1984. Dispersal of immigrants and change of the spatial distribution of age groups has made the concentration districts younger in age structure. Housing conditions in newer concentration districts are not essentially different from the belt around the CBD.

Mobility plays an important part in the spatial context. In 1984 departure of original inhabitants from the second ring of older districts around the CBD was higher than in 1976, leaving opportunities for immigrants to settle in the second ring.

The conclusion from the regression analysis is that despite a certain spatial dispersal of immigrants between 1976 and 1984, immigrants move within a limited choice and environment limited by socioeconomic and housing quality characteristics. Mobility characteristics of the Dutch inhabitants enable immigrants to move within this environment.

Regression analysis also shows that spatial distribution of municipality controlled housing, orientation to home country, location of employment, and level of facilities are *not* significant factors in the spatial context of segregation. These variables were included in the analysis but did not appear to show influence according to the multiple regression technique.

Conclusions and Policy Recommendations

As far as spatial patterns are concerned, Rotterdam has similarities to those observed through research in many other cities. In Rotterdam, concentrating around the city center can be recognized, concentration that has gradually expanded and partially spread over a larger area. Both zonal and sectoral patterns can be identified. However the migration history of Rotterdam migrants is too short to make full comparison possible. It is however clear from the analysis results that the large migrant concentrations found in American cities, particularly of the blacks, are not reproduced in Rotterdam.

The spatial dispersal of migrants is limited, however, as far as residential milieu and area's socioeconomic level are concerned. Dispersal takes place to districts with comparable low levels of segregation. Migrants in this study did not succeed in infiltrating higher quality and more peripherally located parts of the Rotterdam housing market.

This analysis confirms, in part, research results from studies elsewhere abroad, and in part differs with these results. Residential environment and socioeconomic status have a comparable role in Rotterdam, as has been recognized elsewhere. A fellow countryman's influence in obtaining a dwelling is especially valid in Rotterdam, although not absent elsewhere. The role of orientation to the country of origin as a voluntary element in segregation may be present in Rotterdam, but interview responses do not fully support this hypothesis. Prejudice and rate of integration in Rotterdam show remarkable differences in their relation to segregation compared to studies in other countries. The relation between segregation and prejudice is by no means simple, showing highest prejudice in areas of medium segregation but also showing positive opinions by Dutch inhabitants in these areas.

Regarding the goal of integration, the Rotterdam results do not support research results accepted elsewhere of a relation between segregation and assimilation measured by language ability. Integration of members of minority groups in Rotterdam is similarly low for all levels of segregation. With respect to the relationship of group formation among immigrants to segregation and the reasons for out-migration of Dutch inhabitants away from districts, the Rotterdam results also do not support other studies. Survey results show a common group identification among immigrants of the same nationality (especially Turks) in areas of high segregation. Migration of Dutch to other districts would appear to be more a consequence of bad housing conditions than segregation. Studying the policy in the Netherlands toward housing segregation and the results of the Rotterdam analysis leads to the following policy recommendations:

1. From the results of analysis it may be concluded that immigrants and lower-class Dutch share many similar problems and characteristics. Hence they should be treated as one group.

2. Policy should not be aimed at spatial instruments, but at causes of spatial distributions. From the analysis it is clear that phenomena such as prejudice and integration show no simple relationship to levels of segregation. Therefore, dispersion policies cannot contribute to solving these problems.

3. Policy should be aimed at a redistribution of resources, in its broadest sense, toward lower-class Dutch and immigrants.

4. Since the sample survey in 1977, unemployment for both immigrants and the Dutch has become much more serious. This emphasizes the importance of a redistribution of resource policy.

5. It is necessary to improve access for low-income immigrants and low-income Dutch to districts with better housing environments.

6. Urban renewal in the concentration areas continues to be necessary for lower-class immigrants and low-income Dutch groups.

7. The newly developed state policy of support for deprived areas provides a good instrument for improving situations in concentration areas for both immigrant and Dutch inhabitants. Lack of financial resources poses serious problems however for implementation of this policy.

8. Specific measures are necessary for typical immigrants' problems, such as mutual integration, higher than average unemployment, and the status of women.

9. Prejudice deserves great attention from policymakers. Fighting prejudice is by no means simple. Dispersal of immigrants provides no solution; a "deprived area" policy and employment measures should go together, supported and implemented by strong financial resources.

References

Blalock, H. M. 1972. *Social Statistics* 2nd ed. New York: McGraw Hill.

B and W Amsterdam. 1974. *Nota opvang en begeleiding rijksgenoten* (Report on reception and guidance of Antilleans and Surinamese). Amsterdam: Municipality of Amsterdam.

B and W Rotterdam. 1979. *Leegloop en toeloop: Nota over de bevolkingsbewegingen in Rotterdam* (In- and out-migration: First report on population movements in Rotterdam). Rotterdam: Municipality of Rotterdam.

———. 1980. *Leegloop en toeloop, een eerste vervolg: Nota over de bevolkingsbewegingen in Rotterdam* (In- and out-migration: Second report on population movements in Rotterdam). Rotterdam: Municipality of Rotterdam.

B and W The Hague. 1982. *Evaluatie huisvesting etnische minderheden* (Evaluation of ethnic minorities' housing). The Hague: Municipality of The Hague.

B and W Utrecht. 1982. *Rompnota minderhedenbeleid* (Policy report on ethnic minorities). Utrecht: Municipality of Utrecht.

Clarke, C. G. 1971. "Residential Segregation and Intermarriage in San Fernando, Trinidad." *The Geographic Review* 61:198–218.

Drewe, P., G. A. Van der Knaap, G. Mik, and H. M. Rodgers. 1972. *Segregatie in Rotterdam: Een vooronderzoek naar theorie, gegevens en beleid* (Segregation in Rotterdam: An explorative study on theory, data and policy). Rotterdam: Nederlands Economisch Instituut.

———. 1975. "Segregation in Rotterdam: An Explorative Study on Theory, Data and Policy." *Tijdschrift voor Economische en Sociale Geografie* 66:204–16.

Drewe, P., E. D. Hulsbergen, and G. Mik. 1982. "Het overschatte belang van spreiding: migranten en hun huisvesting (The overestimated importance of spreading)." *Intermediair* 44:19–23.

Duncan, O. D., and B. Duncan. 1955. "Residential Distribution and Occupational Stratification." *American Journal of Sociology* 60:493–503.

Duncan, O. D., and S. Lieberson. 1959. "Ethnic Segregation and Assimilation." *American Journal of Sociology* 64:364–74.

Entzinger, H. B. 1982. "Migratie- en minderhedenbeleid in Europees perspectief (Migration and ethnic minority policy in European perspective)." Pp. 20–39 in *Immigrant en Samenleving, Mens en Maatschappij* (Immigrant and society, man and society), edited by J. M. M. van Amersfoort and H. B. Entzinger. Deventer: Van Loghum Slaterus.

Hulsbergen, E. D., and G. Mik. 1980. *Enquête onder allochtonen en autochtonen. I Resultaten. II Bijlagen. Segregatie in Rotterdam* (Inquiry of foreigners and natives. 1 Results, 2 Appendix. Segregation in Rotterdam). Rotterdam: Economic Geographic Institute, Erasmus University of Rotterdam.

Jackson, P. 1981. "Paradoxes of Puerto Rican Segregation in New York." Pp. 109–26 in *Ethnic Segregation in Cities,* edited by Ceri Peach, Vaughn Robinson, and Susan Smith. London: Croom-Helm.

Jiobu, R. M., and H. H. Marshall, Jr. 1971. "Urban Structure and the Differentiation between Blacks and Whites." *American Sociological Review* 36:638–49.

Kennedy, R. J. R. 1944. "Single or Triple Melting Pot? Intermarriage Trends in New Haven 1870–1940." *American Journal of Sociology* 49:331–39.

———. 1952. "Single or Triple Melting Pot? Intermarriage in New Haven." *American Journal of Sociology* 58:56–59.

Lancaster, Jones F. 1967. "Ethnic Concentration and Assimilation: An Australian Case Study." *Social Forces* 45:412–23.

Lieberson, S. 1961. "The Impact of Residential Segregation on Ethnic Assimilation." *Social Forces* 40:52–57.

———. 1963. *Ethnic Patterns in American Cities.* Glencoe, Ill.: Free Press.

Mik, G. 1980. *Segregatie in Rotterdam: Feiten en beleid* (Segregation in Rotterdam: Facts and policy). Rotterdam: Economic Geography Institute, Erasmus University of Rotterdam.

———. 1982. "Residential Segregation as a Social Problem: The Case of

Rotterdam." Pp. 175–201 in *Migrant Workers in Metropolitan Cities,* edited by J. Rex and J. Solomos. Straatsburg: European Science Foundation.

———. 1983. "Residential Segregation in Rotterdam, Background and Policy." *Tijdschrift voor Economische en Sociale Geografie* 74:74–86.

———. 1987. "Segregation in the Metropolitan Environment: Theory and Rotterdam Reality." Dissertation, Erasmus University of Rotterdam.

Ministries of Social Affairs and Public Health, Law, Economic Affairs, Culture, et al. 1970. *Nota buitenlandse werknemers* (Report on foreign workers). The Hague: Staatsuitgeverij.

Ministry of Interior Affairs. 1983. *Minderhedennota* (Report on ethnic minorities). The Hague: Staatsuitgeverij.

Municipality of The Hague. 1980. *De huisvesting van migranten in Den Haag* (Housing of foreigners in The Hague). The Hague: Municipality of The Hague.

Nederlandse Stichting voor Statistiek. 1971. *De buitenlandse arbeider in Nederland* (The foreign worker in the Netherlands). The Hague: Staatsuitgeverij.

Peach, C. 1980. "Ethnic Segregation and Intermarriage." *Annals of the Association of American Geographers* 70:371–81.

———. 1981a. "Conflicting Interpretation of Segregation." Pp. 19–33 in *Social Integration and Ethnic Segregation,* edited by P. Jackson and S. J. Smith. Institute of British Geographers, Special Publication 12:19–33.

———. 1981b. "Ethnic Segregation and Ethnic Intermarriage." *Ethnic Segregation in Cities,* edited by C. Peach, V. Robinson, and S. Smith. London: Croom-Helm.

Penninx, R. 1984. *Migration, Minorities and Policy in the Netherlands: Recent Trends and Developments.* The Hague: Ministry of WVC.

Robinson, V. 1980. "Patterns of South Asian Ethnic Exogamy and Endogamy in Britain." *Ethnic and Racial Studies* 3:427–43.

ROVU. 1982. *Woon- en leefsituatie ethnische minderheden in Utrecht* (Housing and living situation of ethnic minorities in Utrecht). Utrecht: Department of Research, Municipality of Utrecht.

Taeuber, K. A., and A. F. Taeuber. 1964. "The Negro as an Immigrant Group." *American Journal of Sociology* 69:374–82.

———. 1965. *Negroes in Cities.* Chicago: Aldine Publishing.

Timms, D. W. G. 1969. "The Dissimilarity between Overseas-Born and Australian-Born in Queensland: Dimensions of Assimilation." *Sociology and Social Research* 3:363–74.

Van Praag, C. S. 1980. "Spreiding en spreidingsbeleid (Spreading and Spreading Policy)." Pp. 41–78 in *Huisvesting van ethnische minderheden: Cahier 3* (Housing of ethnic minorities: Notebook 3), edited by R. Spreekmeester and V. D. M. Evers. The Hague: Nederlands Instituut voor Ruimtelijke Ordening en Volkshuisvesting.

————. 1981. "Allochtonen: huisvesting en spreiding (Foreigners: housing and distribution)." *S.C.P. Cahier 22* Rijswijk: Social and Cultural Planning Bureau.

Verdonk, A. 1972. *Vreemdelingen in Rotterdam. Een statistische analyse van enige aspecten* (Foreigners in Rotterdam: Statistical analysis of some aspects). Rotterdam: Erasmus University.

11. The Housing Market and Housing Policies for the Migrant Labor Population in West Berlin

We don't want to begin with a disconsolate wailing about the moral and material plight of the workers and poor, and also not with a description of their miserable housing and with the disastrous results of their unnatural living conditions. We assume that the sore spot which exists for the whole human society is adequately known.—C. W. Hoffmann, *Berliner Gemeinnützigen Bau-Gesellschaft*, 1852

These are the words of the founders of the first "non-profit construction company" in Berlin (*gemeinnützige Baugesellschaft*), which aimed to improve the "moral and material" living conditions of the working class according to its "real needs." The quotation from over a century ago is a reminder of long experience with the housing plight of the working class and of measures to remedy the situation. In spite of this experience, we still speak of a housing plight among working-class people in West Berlin and in many other large German cities. The difference is that most of the new victims of the existing housing plight are members of the guest-worker population, who are at the bottom.

A discussion of the housing desegregation policy of the Berlin Senate necessarily requires an introduction to the social, economic, and cultural status of the so-called guest worker population, with particular emphasis on their situation in the housing market and on the debate over the so-called ghetto phenomenon.

But first it is necessary to clarify precisely which group we are discussing. In the debate on labor migration after World War II in the Federal Republic of Germany (FRG), many different terms have been used to define the labor migrants. *Guest worker* has been the most popular, a term which corresponded to the official policy of recruit-

This chapter was written in 1988 before the 1989 opening of the Berlin Wall and free travel by East Germans. At that time West Berlin was a special entity.

ment of foreign workers at the beginning of labor migration. This policy was based on the assumption that the recruitment of a foreign labor force was a temporary necessity that led to the formation of the "rotation principle." The term *guest* thereby implied the temporary character of the recruitment. Later, this policy was "corrected," and the rotation principle gave way to the "integration principle" of the migrant labor population. The latter evolved because of its more realistic response to the interests of employers who sought continuity of labor productivity. But the term *guest workers* has not lost its popularity, and many people discuss the "integration of the guest workers" without noticing the concept's inherent contradiction. In spite of the fact that the FRG defines itself as a "non-immigrant country with immigrants," according to Commissioner for Alien Affairs of the Berlin Senate Barbara John, such terms as *foreign workers, migrant workers, immigrants,* and later even, *ethnic minorities,* have found use, especially within sociological discussion.

In this chapter, the term *migrant laborers* or *migrant labor population* is used because the other terms seem to lack the necessary precision. The term *foreign workers* is too general and does not imply the existing difference between foreigners coming from Western countries, above all from the countries of the European Community (EC) and those who come from such Southern European countries as Turkey. The former have the automatic right to a residence permit and a work permit (*Aufenthaltserlaubnis resp. Arbeitserlaubnis*) in the FRG and West Berlin; the latter—particularly after the "recruitment stop" at the end of 1973—are allowed neither to stay nor to work within the FRG and West Berlin unless they are officially permitted. But the main problem with the term is that it does not indicate the mass labor migration process which took place after World War II. The term *ethnic minorities* suggests the fact of mass migration and the process of the formation of ethnic colonies in the cities of FRG and in West Berlin. It also suggests that this group is more likely to be citizens of Southern European countries because there is no mass migration from Western European industrial countries. Yet two fundamental arguments make it difficult to use this term in regard to the labor migrants' situation in the FRG and West Berlin. First, at present, most ethnic minorities in the traditional countries of immigration like the United States, Canada, Australia, and Sweden are accepted—surely after long struggles—as a part of the society. For the most part, they obtain the rights of citizens, above all the right to vote, whereas the migrant laborers in the FRG and West Berlin from such countries as Turkey and Yugoslavia are far from having these rights to citizenship. In fact, they are denied many basic human rights.

Second, the more important argument is that the term *ethnic minority* puts together and equalizes two essentially different groups of foreigners who live more or less permanently in the FRG and West Berlin—the migrant labor population just described and the refugees who seek asylum, most of whom are from Poland, Iran, Iraq, and other Middle Eastern countries. The right of asylum, of taking refuge in a sanctuary, is a very old human right; it is older than the civil society and older than the phenomenon of state. It is not comparable with any other right; it guarantees the security of the life of a person. It cannot be bilateral between states; it is and must be absolutely unilateral to save individuals. A totally different field concerns the so-called foreigners' rights and the laws that regulate their legal residence and work status; it has to do with the importation of foreign labor for economic growth.

Insisting on the distinction between these two groups of foreigners and the related different fields of policy is very important at present in the FRG and West Berlin; the increased interest began with the "phase of family reunification." When migrant laborers started to bring their family members and the settlement process of "foreign" population began, the tendency was to perceive all foreign-looking persons as "foreigners" and to devise a "foreigner problem" for the German society. This conscious concealment of the difference between these two groups, ignoring the need for and the right of asylum of the one group and forgetting the active recruitment of foreign labor by the German government of the other groups, has led to talk about "overcrowding by foreigners," about the "foreign influx to Germany," and even about a "foreign infiltration." All of these cursory arguments contribute to an atmosphere propitious to the growth of neoracism. In spite of the fact that asylum is—or was—a constitutional right in the FRG, such an atmosphere has made it politically convenient for the conservative government to hinder obtaining asylum, even to the point of sometimes making it almost impossible. Fewer than 5 percent of all foreigners in the FRG are those who seek asylum.

This chapter discusses the West Berlin housing situation of migrant laborers who were recruited originally to contribute to the economic stability and growth of West Germany. In this context, the suggested clear distinctive terminology *migrant laborers* seems to be important to make clear which group is described. In addition, the term *under-privileged foreigners* is used to indicate those foreigners who come from Southern European countries such as Turkey or Yugoslavia due to the fact that in some legislation and regulations there are special restrictions for this group. They are also referred to as "foreigners from the main recruitment countries."

The Position of Migrant Laborers on the West Berlin Housing Market

It is first necessary to discuss the West Berlin housing market in general and the policies of the Berlin Senate in this context, in order to be able to evaluate the legal and social conditions of migrant laborers and the discrimination they face in housing.

West Berlin Housing Market as of 1988

West Berlin has had a special status that originates from the Allied agreements on the occupation of Germany after World War II. The city has had a four-power administration that was established in 1945. Thus, it is rightly not a part of the FRG, although politically and practically it has been considered an exclave of the FRG surrounded by the German Democratic Republic, as a "land" (state) of the FRG. [*Ed. note*: This changed in 1990 with the reunification of West and East Germany.]

This "half city" had, nevertheless, almost two million inhabitants in 1988 and has been the largest German city. It also has had the largest number of foreigners, more than 240,000 persons, 12.5 percent of the total population. Nearly half have Turkish citizenship. Until 1987, the population of West Berlin had been decreasing slightly but it began to increase during 1987 and 1988 due to the "resettlement" of the German-origin people from the Eastern bloc countries in the FRG and West Berlin. Since the October 1989 opening of East Germany, the influx has increased still more. The results of the census published at the beginning of December 1988 showed that the number of households increased relatively more than the increase of the population; in 1988, it was about 1.1 million. The proportion of one-person households has been relatively high. In 1988 these constituted about 50 percent of all households, most of which were pensioners with low incomes. Together, one- and two-person households comprised 80 percent of all households in West Berlin.

The size of West Berlin's housing stock totals about 1.07 million units, and among them a half million units are so-called "old units" built before 1949; four out of ten were built even before World War I, primarily in the 1860s and 1890s. Within the old unit segment, about 90,000 of the half million units can be described as extremely substandard, that is, without the basic amenities of toilets, central heating, baths, or showers. Another 140,000 units have toilets but no central heating, baths, or showers. About 280,000 units urgently need rehabilitation or renovation. Furthermore, almost a half of the million units built after World War II belong to the public housing sector (*sozialer Wohnungsbau*). For both the old units and the public units there are rent regulations; only about 80,000 are free financed, that is, nonsubsidized rental units not directly under rent regulation. Many public units are being converted into free-financed units due to the ending of public subsidies, a process that will continue in the future so that public housing stock will decline gradually. Thus, West Berlin is a city of tenants; 86 percent of all units are rental units (in the FRG, 40 percent of the housing stock is owner-occupied). A larger proportion of the housing stock consists of small units; almost two-thirds are one- or two-room units, excluding kitchens. Based on the fact that an enormous proportion of all households in West Berlin consists of low-income households, the low-rent housing supply must be guaranteed. Present development, however, is in the opposite direction.

Because there are different market segments with very different conditions, it is difficult to discuss the West Berlin rental housing market in general. Due to the fact that the largest segment consists of old, often substandard, units, these have an important function in the housing supply. Until the end of 1987, rent control existed for the old units, thus guaranteeing reasonable rents. In spite of the fact that rent control has ended, a considerable part of the old housing stock still constitutes the most inexpensive segment of rental housing stock. It can easily be argued, however, that with the dissolution of rent control for old units, these rents, which have already started to increase, will escalate enormously [and with the East German influx will even more]. Second, the phenomenon of gentrification will gain ground as it did in Munich and Hamburg, where rent control was ended in the 1970s.

The rents in the recently built public housing sector are fairly high due to the existing public housing financing system (subsidization of the so-called cost rents, which primarily consist of the interest rates from the private credit market). These high rents, in turn, cause vacancies, particularly in larger public housing units.

Within this background, one can speak of two dualistic developments. The first is the disparate development of increasing rents on

the one hand, and sinking real incomes on the other. This development first affects single-income large households, which often have
more than two children.

The second is the structural dualistic development. The dominant
proportion of rental stock in West Berlin is comprised of small units,
due to the existing financing system; the production of larger units,
even within public housing, causes high rents unaffordable for the low-
income households who urgently need larger flats. The only affordable
large units are to be found within the stock of old units but landlords
prefer to rent these to households with double incomes and no children. Thus, low-income large households are often bound to reside in
small apartments which causes overcrowding. Under "free market"
conditions, as long as there are no measures to move the high-income
small households into adequate smaller apartments, the structure of
housing stock does not meet the demands of the low-income large
households. The result is that an enormous demand exists for larger
apartments with inexpensive or moderate rents within the West Berlin
housing market. [With the influx of East Germans since October 1989
this demand is increasing.]

A partial housing shortage thus exists within particular segments of
the West Berlin housing market. Most affected by the partial housing
shortage is the migrant labor population, such as Turks, Yugoslavians,
and Poles, most of whom have large, single-income households with
many children. [East German households arriving since 1989 have also
been greatly affected by this shortage.]

Migrant Laborers as Participants in the Housing Market

In West Berlin, two more or less distinct periods of recruitment of
foreign labor can be described. The first period was during the mid-
1960s, especially 1964–66; the second, more remarkable, period was
from the beginning of the 1970s until the middle of 1974. Most of the
newcomers in the second period were Turks, whereas in the first they
were Yugoslavs and Italians. The shift from migration to settlement
also began to become apparent in the second period. Migrant laborers,
who were initially housed by their employers as single, employed persons, usually in huts or hostels on the work site, began during the
second period to participate in the housing market as tenants (chapter 6). Thus, it was during this period when concentrations of labor
migrant population became noticeable in specific areas of the city.

The position of the migrant labor population within the West Berlin housing market is determined by several factors. First and probably most important is the legal framework that consists of many discriminatory regulations. It is well known that migrant laborers are subjected to various legal restrictions in the FRG and West Berlin. Characteristic of the legislation in this field are vague and elastic formulations in laws and regulations that allow considerable freedom of interpretation by the authorities concerned (foreigners' police) and give them great power. The existence of two different permits, the residence permit and the work permit, and the linkage between them, indicates the ambiguous situation of migrant laborers. Two examples illustrate the degree of legal discrimination that exists. The key formulation is to be found in the National Foreigners Law (*Ausländergesetz*) of 1965: "a residence permit may be granted, if it does not harm the interests of the German Federal Republic." Furthermore, according to the national "regulation of implementation" of this law: "Foreigners enjoy all the basic rights with the exception of the basic rights of freedom of assembly, freedom of association, freedom of movement, free choice of occupation, place of work and place of education, and protection from extradition abroad." This quotation shows that there is a system of institutionalized discrimination toward migrant laborers established by the state and related to the needs of the labor market.

These examples can be extended to almost every aspect of daily life. The most important discriminatory measures existing in the housing market should be briefly mentioned. Three regulations seem to be important in this context:

"A ban on entry and settlement" (*Zuzugssperre*) is a Berlin regulation, initiated in 1975, that prohibits underprivileged foreigners, primarily Turks and Yugoslavians, from moving into three of a total of twelve boroughs (*Bezirke*) of the city, Kreuzberg, Tiergarten, and Wedding. The three boroughs are traditionally working-class housing districts. The ban was legislated by the social democrats–liberal coalition and is still retained by the conservative Senate. The main argument politicians used for this measure was that the concentration of the foreign population in these boroughs would "overload the social infrastructure, isolating them within their subculture, and hindering their integration." Since the legislation of *Zuzugssperre*, the proportion of the foreign population in the "banned" boroughs has remained relatively constant. Table 11.1 provides an overview of the development of the foreign, including Turkish, population in the banned boroughs. As may easily be assumed, there is a slight increase at the end

TABLE II.I.   Development of the Foreign Population in Selected
Boroughs of West Berlin

Boroughs	Jan. 1, 1975	Jan. 1, 1976	Jan. 1, 1978	Jan. 1, 1982	Jan. 1, 1984
Kreuzberg					
Total population*	152.1	143.7	142.1	141.6	139.6
Foreign population*	41.5	37.9	33.0	40.2	40.0
Turkish population*	28.1	25.5	21.6	26.8	27.0
Foreign population†	27.3	26.4	23.2	28.4	28.7
Turkish population†	18.5	17.7	15.2	18.9	19.3
Tiergarten					
Total population*	87.2	82.9	80.3	78.0	76.0
Foreign population*	15.6	14.6	13.2	16.7	16.5
Turkish population*	7.7	7.3	6.3	7.9	7.7
Foreign population†	17.8	17.6	16.4	21.5	21.7
Turkish population†	8.9	8.8	7.8	10.1	10.2
Wedding					
Total population*	161.3	152.6	150.1	143.8	143.6
Foreign population*	31.2	29.1	26.0	30.2	29.9
Turkish population*	20.8	19.4	17.1	20.2	19.6
Foreign population†	19.3	19.1	17.3	21.0	20.8
Turkish population†	12.9	12.7	11.4	14.5	13.7
Reinickendorf					
Total population*	242.7	240.5	245.7	241.6	238.1
Foreign population*	9.0	8.9	9.9	13.5	14.4
Turkish population*	2.3	2.4	2.9	4.9	5.1
Foreign population†	3.7	3.7	4.0	5.6	6.0
Turkish population†	0.9	1.0	1.2	2.0	2.1
West Berlin					
Total population*	2,126.0	2,086.8	2,028.8	1,990.7	1,956.6
Foreign population*	190.5	185.5	189.9	245.9	245.0
Turkish population*	87.9	85.5	85.5	118.3	117.4
Foreign population†	9.0	8.9	9.4	12.4	12.5
Turkish population†	4.1	4.1	4.2	5.9	6.0

Sources: Arin 1979:150ff.; Senator 1985:76ff.
*Figures in thousands.
†Figures in percent.

of the 1970s and beginning of the 1980s because of increasing family
reunification in that period. The experience in the last thirteen years
shows that the ban regulation resulted in no dispersion effects of the
migrant labor population. It would be naive to believe such a dispersion could come about because spatial concentration in these areas is
due to the existing mechanisms of the housing market. Furthermore,
since the legislation at the end of 1973 of another ban regulation on
entries of non-EEC workers to the FRG and West Berlin, labor immigration of these groups to West Berlin has been curtailed. The
residential mobility was taking place only within the city, among the

boroughs—a fact that could be considered up to 1989 as the main reason for the stagnation of the migrant labor populations of West Berlin boroughs. The only explanation for this continuing mainte- nance of the *Zuzugssperre* regulation might be the political tendency to follow the mass assumption that there exists institutionalized dis- crimination and stigmatization against migrant laborers.

The Housing Supervision Law (*Wohnungsaufsichtsgesetz*) is a na- tional law initially thought to protect tenants against deteriorating housing conditions. According to the law, certain minimum standards must be guaranteed. For example, there must be a minimum housing space of 9 square meters for each adult and 6 square meters for each child under six. In case the minimum standards are not fulfilled, the apartment has to be declared as uninhabitable and must be vacated. The law does not define responsibility for the replacement, so it is up to tenants to find a new apartment when theirs is declared uninhab- itable. As a result, migrant laborers, at least until late 1989, have been automatically blamed when housed in an overcrowded apartment, yet this is often due to existing housing market discrimination. Violation of any law may be a cause for deportation.

"Obligation to verify occupancy in a legally conforming apartment" (*Nachweispflicht angemessenen Wohnraums*) is a national regulation that declares underprivileged foreigners obliged to verify that they reside in a legally "conforming" apartment in a non-banned borough in order to extend their residence permit or to get a permit to bring their family members from their country of origin. The basis of the definition of legal conformity of an apartment is the Housing Super- vision Law. The respective office for alien control, which is in charge of this decision, often checks the lease to determine the legal con- formity of an apartment. Thus, migrant laborers are more interested in getting a "proper" lease than an apartment per se. Often they have to pay bribes to get the necessary apartment, or at least the lease for one.

The second group of factors that underlines the existing housing plight of migrant laborers concerns their weak position with regard to German tenants due to ethnic and social discrimination. Housing de- mands of the migrant labor population concentrate on inexpensive three-to-five-room rental units, exactly the segment of the housing market where the biggest demand exists, with demand increasing after the 1989–90 influx of East Germans. The results are diverse. In most of the cases, migrant laborers have to accept apartments which cannot be easily rented. These are small, badly maintained, substandard units in damp, run-down, and cramped buildings that have shortcomings in sanitation and lack other amenities; they are located in the traditional proletarian areas. Lack of space is another characteristic of the miserable housing conditions. Whereas the average ratio of the number of rooms per person in West Berlin is 1:32, the corresponding ratio in case of migrant labor households is 0:6. In large Turkish households (with three children and more), the ratio is lower. Moreover, migrants often also are forced to pay excessive rents due to ignorance of their legal rights or difficulties in dealing with authorities, as well as a general anxiety about getting involved in conflicts and a desire to avoid trouble.

The Desegregation Policy of the Berlin Senate

The basic element of the desegregation policy of the Berlin Senate as of 1989 was the "ban" legislation (*Zuzugssperre*). One additional aspect of this measure is the quota recommendation of the Berlin Senate to nonprofit or public housing companies. This recommendation proposes that a certain percentage of the rentable apartments be made available to foreigners. The first recommendation was undertaken by the social democrats–liberal coalition in 1978, which recommended that 10 percent should be made available for foreigners. This corresponded with the proportion of the foreign population within the total population of the city in that year. It was, indeed, soon clear that this recommendation would not lead to any useful tangible results. First, nonprofit or public companies interpreted the recommendation in relation to their entire stock of housing. Because most already had enough substandard apartments rented to foreign residents, it was not difficult for them to declare that at least 10 percent of their tenants were foreign. Furthermore, many companies began to use this recommendation against foreigners: they refused foreigners as tenants using the recommendation in buildings where 10 percent or more of the households were already foreign. In a building with a total of 18–20 apartments, two already occupied by foreign households, foreigners had no chance of obtaining an apartment. This was based on the argument of serving "better integration," referring to the official policy of integration.

In 1982, the Christian democrat–liberal coalition made some changes in the recommendation: the quota was elevated to 15 percent, and this percentage was to refer to a particular housing settlement and not to the whole housing stock of a company. Experience shows that this policy was not effective in providing better access to apartments, nor was the housing supply of migrant laborers improved by the recommendation. The renting policy of the big housing companies did not change within the old unit segment of the housing market. These companies own 18 percent of the older stock, and neither they nor private landlords were motivated to rent to the migrant laborers due to the recommendation. It is not obligatory that they do so.

Within the public housing sector, foreigners did indeed obtain a slightly increased share of rentals, but the main reason seemed to be that, especially in the case of recently built apartments, there have been rental problems due to relatively high rents and the income limits set in this sector. In public housing settlements built since the beginning of the 1980s within the project of International Building Exhibition (*Internationale Bauausstellung Berlin* [IBA]), 10 to 15 percent of the public housing apartments have been rented to foreigners. Of course, these were not rented to the migrant laborers, but to Western foreigners or to "exotic" foreigners from the Far East. Both property owners and the Berlin Senate did not miss the chance to show the world how "liberal" and "multicultural" their rental policy was. This was possible due to the fact that the term *foreigners* was not clearly defined in the recommendation.

Despite the acrobatics of this public relations policy, a serious evaluation of the Berlin Senate's housing policy regardless of the political parties in power, indicates that since the "ban" legislation the housing supply of migrant laborers has worsened rather than improved. The suspicion arises that the goal has always been to make the miserable living conditions of migrant laborers as invisible as possible instead of improving their housing accommodations. The political tendency in the housing sector has always been the distribution of migrant labor among the boroughs instead of improving the housing conditions of the neighborhoods. The only exception is the urban renewal applied by the IBA since the early 1980s in the borough of Kreuzberg. This "banned" borough has a high proportion of migrant laborers, and the basic principle of the urban renewal of IBA is a "careful renewal for and with the people." Due to this project, housing conditions of approximately two thousand migrant families, most of whom were Turks, were being improved by the end of 1988; IBA has renovated a total of four thousand apartments. Politically, however, IBA is a thorn in the side of the Berlin Senate; its participatory urban renewal practice loses ground rather than gains and the following questions remain open.

1. What is the reason for keeping the Housing Supervision Law in its present form? Migrant laborers can hardly make use of it, since with it they are at risk of losing their apartments or residence permits. It is a simple act to obligate landlords to relocate tenants in case an apartment is declared uninhabitable due to overcrowding or the lack of maintenance for which the landlords are obligated.

2. How is it possible to improve the housing supply for a group by prohibiting them from moving into areas where they have the best chance of finding an apartment? The restricted boroughs are exactly such areas.

3. Were any concrete measures undertaken (aside from the recommendations) to improve the housing supply of migrant laborers? The fact is that the Berlin government could influence policies and actions in regard to almost half of the housing stock if it wanted to.

Since provision of an adequate housing supply must be assumed as a constitutional assignment of the state, the Berlin government has the authority to take action. However, in the case of migrant laborers the Berlin government has freed itself from the task, delegating it back to the affected group, the migrant laborers. The government makes them responsible for settling the problem, with the sanction of punishment if they do not or cannot meet these conditions. It seems as if the primary focus of the policy is to keep the existing discriminatory system, and keep migrant laborers in as uncertain a position in the housing market as in the labor market.

The German Debate on "Ghettoization" in West Berlin

It is not possible to fully analyze the debate over the new ghetto phenomenon in the FRG and West Berlin. But it seems important to mention some aspects of the debate with reference to the spatial concentration patterns of the migrant labor population in West Berlin (fig. 11.1).

The most important aspect of this debate is the public assumption of the interrelation between the "integration" of labor migrants to the German society and the spatial concentration of them in specific areas of the city. Most politicians declare that there should be a contradiction between spatial concentration and integration. Thus, concentration, or the "ghetto," is assumed to be something negative, and "integration" something positive. Each politician's understanding of integration is different, but there seems to be a minimum consensus on the desegregation policy as a "measure of integration." Based on

FIGURE II.I.   Distribution of the Migrant Labor Population in
West Berlin by Boroughs

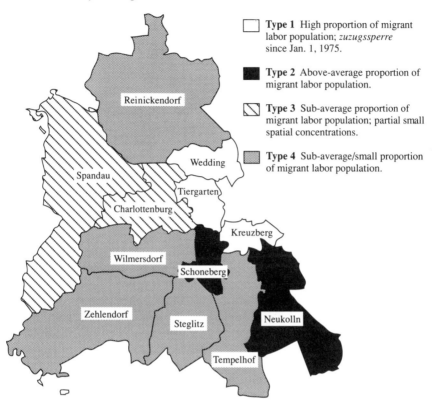

Type 1 High proportion of migrant labor population; *zuzugssperre* since Jan. 1, 1975.

Type 2 Above-average proportion of migrant labor population.

Type 3 Sub-average proportion of migrant labor population; partial small spatial concentrations.

Type 4 Sub-average/small proportion of migrant labor population.

this pseudo-contradiction, the main goal should be an equal spatial distribution of migrant laborers in the city. This short-sighted policy overlooks the fact that social problems can never be mastered through spatial measures, and that restrictive political methods are the worst possible way to mitigate social problems. Furthermore, one of the results of existing political propaganda is that migrant laborers carry the brunt of the responsibility for their unsatisfactory housing conditions. The argument is that they prefer to live in such low-rent areas and within their own subcultures. Thus, it is unavoidable that they are most affected by urban renewal as inhabitants of the urban renewal areas; they are "renewal gypsies." This is the practical side of the ghetto discussion.

Within the social sciences, the approaches of social and human ecology and the explanations of the Chicago School (basically of Park and Burgess) predominate. These approaches find processes of succession and invasion in areas of concentration and define quantitative limits of ethnic proportions as indicators of these processes. Integration being a positive goal, they, too, assume that ghettoization is a negative factor in the process of integration.

There is not space here to discuss the hypotheses of social and human ecology; general criticisms of these are known. As far as the German and the West Berlin cases are concerned, a solid empirical basis is lacking to substantiate this line of argumentation. Furthermore, not enough consideration is given to fundamental differences between American society and European societies, particularly the FRG, where the role of the state is traditionally much different and stronger. The phenomenon of ghettoization is not a natural event; it has much to do with the housing and urban renewal policies of the state, with each country's historical experiences with ethnic minorities. These aspects cannot be neglected. Finally, within the social sciences the predominant position in the debate is in favor of preventing spatial concentration of the migrant labor population, a tendency that corresponds to the predominant policy.

At this point it is necessary to put forth some arguments which concern the determinants and effects of the spatial concentration and the segregation of migrant laborers. A distinction must be made between voluntary and enforced segregation; these are closely related to the social and economic status of a group. The lower the socioeconomic status, the more enforced is the segregation, and the converse is so. The social mobility of a person or group is an indicator of the possibility for spatial mobility. The migrant laborers in the FRG and West Berlin are primarily victims of enforced segregation. It is not incidental that they reside in the traditional proletarian areas, this is a reflection of historical continuity.

Thus, the underlying determinants of the spatial concentration of migrant labor population are to be traced to the mechanisms of the capitalist housing market and the corresponding housing policies of the state, rather than to the social and cultural preferences of the migrants. The predominant policy and the social scientific debate reverses the cause and effect of the process of spatial concentration.

If the definition of integration is considered to be the process of developing social competence, that is, the ability to deal with various situations and problems in the civil society as a process of development, then integration does not contradict the spatial concentration of the migrants. On the contrary, concentration contributes to strengthening personal and collective identity and the formation of ethnic consciousness and awareness because the process of concentration also renders possible the formation of social and cultural networks in the daily life.

In this case, the perception of ethnic visibility in an area as a presumed negative feature of the area must be doubted. Instead, it indicates the existence of prejudices and resentments against labor migrants. Many of the existing features in the areas of concentration of the labor migrants could be seen positively: the existence of families with children, local business and shopping possibilities, forms of communication, and utilization and even appropriation of public spaces. Neighborhoods with these features are always presented as intact neighborhoods. If this positive perception is overlooked in migrant concentration areas, it is only because of the fact that the people in question are not Germans. The serious question exists of the existence of a subtle racism in the minds of those who complain about such areas.

There are, indeed, points to criticize in the concentrated areas of migrants, such as miserable housing conditions in rundown buildings. Thus, the question is not whether the inhabitants of these areas are Turks or not. Nor is it the improvement of the "social structure," as is demanded in certain circles, or how to distribute Turks equally in West Berlin. The question is how to improve material housing conditions in these areas for their inhabitants.

Even to be able to pose the question supposes that one has achieved a certain level of consciousness that allows a perception of the existing multicultural situation as a matter of course. That means, first, definitely overcoming implicit or explicit racism. The only way to deal with existing social and cultural problems adequately is acculturation, or interculturation. This implies no hierarchic assumption of different cultures and subcultures and is a long and laborious process.

Cultural pluralism in this sense is at present a goal that can be reached only within a political process. The first step of the process is the assertion of equal rights for the migrant labor population with no exceptions. This is also an indicator of the ability and courage of a society's democracy. Concerning the FRG and West Berlin, the question is still open, whether society ever seriously aims to show such courage.

References

Arin, Cihan. 1979. *Analyse der Wohnverhältnisse ausländischer Arbeiter in der Bundesrepublik Deutschland—mit einer Fallstudie über türkische Arbeiterhaushalte in Berlin Kreuzberg.* Berlin: Technische Universität.

———. 1982. "Immigrants as Inhabitants of Urban Renewal Areas." Pp. 89–98 in *Housing and Labour Immigrants,* edited by Friedemann Kunst. Berlin: Technische Universität.

Arin, Cihan, Sigmar Gude, and Hermann Wurtinger. 1985. *Auf der Schattenseite des Wohnungsmarkts: Kinderreiche Immigrantenfamilien.* Basel: Birkhäuser.

Der Regierende Bürgermeister von Berlin, Senatskanzlei/Planungsleits (ed.). 1980. *Wohnraumversorgung von Ausländern und Entballung überlasteter Bebiete durch städtebauliche Massnahmen.* Berlin.

Senator für Gesundheit, Soziales und Familie, Ausländerbeauftragter (ed.). 1985. *Miteinander Leben. Bilanz und Perspektiven.* Berlin.

12. Subsidized Housing Segregation in Western Europe: Stigma and Segregation

A large segment of the rental housing in Western Europe is social housing operated either by local authorities or by subsidized housing associations or private investors. Thus it is appropriate to focus on the degree of segregation of minorities in such rental housing in different European countries and on the causes of this segregation. In Britain, 27–28 percent of the housing stock is council housing; in the Netherlands, it is more than 40 percent; in Sweden, a high proportion is still local authority housing or new-town rentals; in France a large proportion is HLM subsidized rental units; and in West Germany, while less than in the other countries, there are still many social housing units.

Accommodations in social housing has come slowly for immigrants to these countries. Some have been moved in early due to urban renewal or slum clearance. More recently, some have gotten in because they are homeless, because of increased vacancies in unpopular housing estates, and because of the fact of long-time residence in an area.

In this chapter I will document how difficult it is for immigrants to get into social housing, and more important, their concentration in some estates, those not popular with the native population. Examples of these estates that are both stigmatized and have a large foreign-born population are Bijlmermeer outside of Amsterdam; Stonebridge estate, Hackney; an outer-area social housing estate in Hamburg; and, to a lesser degree, some outer-area new towns near Stockholm and Malmö. The bad reputation of certain social housing has long been evident in the United States (Huttman 1969, 1972; Rainwater 1970), to the point where programs and legislative directives have been begun to try to rectify the situation.

In evaluating the American public housing, I, on the basis of many years of housing research that includes a major study of stigmatization in public housing, conclude that it will be very difficult to reverse both stigmatization and segregation. Goering (1986:198), although more optimistic, admits that "there are also some PHAS [public housing authorities] where it is difficult, if not impossible, to achieve significant levels of desegregation. PHAS that have an overwhelming minority or an all-white population in occupancy and on their waiting lists have few options to achieve system-wide desegregation." I am more optimistic about a turn-around for stigmatized and segregated housing estates in Britain, the Netherlands, Sweden, France, and West Germany, in part because the problem in those countries is fairly recent and only effects some housing estates in a minor way.

Postwar housing accommodations for immigrants, including guest workers, were for decades in the private rental sector and most still are. Because government officials and the public on the Continent saw these groups as short-term contractual workers, primarily single persons hired for a specific job, it was hard to realize the changing situation by the 1970s. Workers, first housed in barracks and other employer-provided accommodations or hostels for single men, began, in the 1970s, to bring their wives, children, and other relatives and to move to private rental apartment accommodations. They were becoming long-term residents, and their children were moving toward adulthood. Governments, still under the myth that they were a temporary part of the community, made little provision for workers' housing. Housing for the immigrants was not only substandard, but also was usually in areas of some degree of immigrant concentration. Growth of these segregated areas is slowing and some immigrants go home. Actual decrease has been slight or nonexistent, however, as immigrant families arrive and increase through high birth rates and refugees also arrive. During the 1970s the growth was great; Bonacker (1982) reports that in the port area of Hamburg 13 percent of the residents were immigrants in 1970, in contrast with 73 percent eight years later. Such an increase also occurred in the Netherlands, where immigrants, especially Turks, Moroccans, and Surinamese, have been concentrated in poorer, inner-city areas (see chapters 3 and 10). Earlier Indonesian arrivals were somewhat more assimilated into different areas of the city and different towns. In Paris, Lyons, Marseilles, and other large French cities, they were concentrated in private rentals in certain areas and in industrial suburbs (chapter 7).

In Britain, South Asian and West Indian populations arrived as permanent immigrants, as did those who came later from Kenya, and concentrated in certain areas. This postwar immigration had greatly decreased by the 1970s due to immigration laws (chapter 4). By 1980, many immigrants had been in Great Britain and Germany for more than ten years, some for even twenty years (chapters 4 and 6). In fact, a second generation was coming of age that would want separate homes and feel entitled to social housing.

Karn (1986) finds that in Britain most immigrants lived in private units and that more still lived in lower-standard housing units than did whites. She discusses distinct differences among various minority groups, with "Indians and Pakistanis on average living in worst conditions and most concentrated in owner-occupied pre-1919 houses. They are much more segregated than are Afro-Caribbeans" (p. 5). Oc (1988) considers South Asians involuntary owners, forced to make high payments on deteriorated housing. He also finds that many West Indians are trapped in poor-quality private furnished units; Karn (1986) finds them highly represented in London's homeless population housed in bed and breakfast accommodations under conditions "totally unsuitable for families." Yet by 1986, Karn points out, some West Indians were moving into council housing (chapter 4).

Greater Access to Social Housing in the 1980s

General access to social housing became more of a fact in most countries in the late 1970s and the 1980s. Earlier, minority groups were generally not considered for social housing (except in Sweden), in part because they did not meet residential qualifications and were not thought of as permanent members of the community who should get what was still considered in the 1960s and early 1970s as a desirable housing commodity—a standard, often fairly new, unit at a subsidized rent. When I studied British council housing in the late 1960s, I found council housing popular, with long waiting lists that allowed local authorities to carefully select those they considered most eligible in terms of housing need, residence, and status in the community of stable, working-class families. The criticism of the allocation system was that the poor, the female-headed households, and transients were excluded (Huttman 1969). In the Netherlands the situation was the same, with some exception made for Indonesian immigrants or those cases in which special housing was provided for new immigrants (chapters 3 and 10).

Another exception was in those cases in which urban renewal or slum clearance occurred in substandard inner-city areas that had a high concentration of immigrants. To clear the land, a city was obligated

to re-house these residents. The West Berlin government in an un-
planned way found it necessary to re-house immigrants. Reporting on
the Kreuzberg district slated for urban renewal, Hoffmeyer-Zlotnik
reports (1982) that ethnic colonies developed there just because the
buildings, as old and run-down housing slated to be torn down, were
more available than others. Rents were cheap and landlords negligent.
He reports (pp. 121, 124) that although the influx of Turkish households, including many illegal workers, first went unnoticed by the authorities, by 1973 authorities "saw themselves increasingly confronted
with the hitherto unseen problem of providing a large number of apartments for Turkish families living in condemned buildings. Otherwise,
urban renewal could not have continued. . . . The proportion of Turkish residents in the partially-renovated blocks [in the center of the
colony] is higher than can be expected for new apartments built by
construction firms for so-called 'social' or low-income housing (*sozialer
wohnungsbau*) even though the state-owned or partially state-owner
low income housing construction companies make sure that German
low-income families move into state-subsidized housing." Meuter
(1982) describes the concentration of foreign households in an inner-
city area of Cologne undergoing urban renewal and gentrification and
reports that these households were moved to outer-area social housing
that was unpopular with native Germans because of its isolated location, rather than desirable social housing. By the 1980s, some immigrants lived in social housing in most German cities, and access was
increased. This was also true in Great Britain, France, the Netherlands, and Sweden.

Stigmatization of Social Housing

Another development began earlier than the opening of *some* social
housing (the least desirable) to ethnic minorities in Northern European countries and that was the stigmatization of some public housing
in the 1970s. Such stigmatization was an even earlier postwar phenomenon in the United States. Unlike Northern European social housing,
intended for a wide range of the working class and often built above
the standards of existing workers' housing (especially in the Netherlands), American public housing was built as low-quality units that
would not compete with private housing and would be for the poor
only (Huttman 1972). The size of the buildings, often high-rise, caused
many criticisms, as did their architecture and design, which made them
look institutional and identified them as housing for the poor. Build-

ings had a stripped-down, mean, and skimpy appearance, with little trim or landscaping. As projects of several buildings located in the worst locations, such as industrial areas, they stood out as undesirable places. Because tenants had to be very poor, as Moore describes one project, "From the very beginning the project was the embodiment of urban poverty, tenants from the former slum dwellings . . . all the tangled problems rooted in generations of destitution found in big city slums everywhere abound in Blackmoor. . . . Relief [welfare] is an assumption; crime, unemployment, and delinquency are routine; broken windows, broken bottles, and broken spirits are commonplace" (1969, 38).

The maintenance problem was worst in the early 1970s, when housing authority revenues from rents decreased after the Brooke Amendment, which required authorities to take no more than 25 percent of a household's income for rent and that a certain proportion of the tenants have very low income. Hartman (1975) reports that a number of projects, near bankruptcy, cut services and maintenance. Poor management policy, including the rent policy (Welfeld 1985), has also hurt projects. Funds for operating costs and maintenance, the modernization projects of the 1970s, as well as services have always been inadequate (Meehan 1979); the Reagan administration restricted already meager help to long-term visible projects. Reagan policy for this 1 percent of the public housing stock was either to starve it or try to sell it (Pit and Van Vliet 1988); the administration definitely did not support the building of new public housing (Hays 1985).

Demolition in the 1970s was the solution for the most deteriorated projects such as Pruitt-Igoe in St. Louis, the worst of the high-rise units. Even the poor found it unacceptable; those who had not moved, generally black, female-headed households with no place to go, found crime a daily problem, due in part to the large teen-age population. Rainwater (1970), in giving the characteristics of Pruitt-Igoe, states that "the elevators are dangerous . . . the laundry areas aren't safe . . . the children run wild and cause all kinds of damage." For similar projects we would add that drug dealers dominate, holding drug wars on project grounds and causing unfortunate residents to live in fear of being caught in gun-fire.

What went wrong? Yinger (1986:293) partly blames the "large conspicuous housing projects as labeling residents, giving them a social stigma." The lack of maintenance and upkeep by authorities added to architectural deficiencies; lack of security control added to lawlessness. I think that underlying causes were government policies that limited entry to only the poorest. Projects became large, isolated ghettoes of the poor, usually blacks and Hispanics (chapter 18) who, with their low incomes, were the most likely to qualify for and accept such housing.

This stigmatization was also due to the location of the projects, often in run-down ghetto areas (Goering 1986), with local public opposition making other areas unavailable (Huttman 1969). Gray and Tursky (1986) report that for the standard metropolitan statistical areas (SMSAS) they studied, most of the central city public housing was in minority areas—Portland was the exception. In four SMSAS, 79 percent or more of the units were in minority areas. This site location inequality was revealed in the major Supreme Court decision on local housing authorities' role in "creating and maintaining racially separate housing projects" (*Lucille Young v. Housing Authority* [1983]).

Stigmatization of Social Housing in Europe and Developing Ethnic Segregation

For some social housing estates in some countries of Western Europe one could clearly say stigmatization, while unlikely in the 1960s, existed by the 1980s. As Priemus (1986:157) has pointed out, "problems on post-war usually large scale housing estates are making themselves apparent in the United States, Great Britain, France, Sweden, Norway, the Netherlands and Denmark." In fact, reports on the issue have been commissioned by governments in many countries (Great Britain, West Germany, the Netherlands, for example) to try to deal with these problem estates. Demolition of some high-rise buildings has either been suggested or carried out to resolve what are considered incurable problems (Friedrichs 1987; Bulos and Walker 1987; Priemus 1986).

It is clear in these countries that stigmatization comes before some degree of ethnic concentration. Priemus, in the Prak-Priemus model (1985), calls this the "decay process" in some postwar housing estates: first, technical decay, then social decay and financial decay. Social decay results in part from technical decay, which includes concrete and foundation defects, poor finish, noise pollution, dampness, and the massive size of projects. Other factors have been location and size and housing type.

Technical decay causes the better-off to leave and vacancies to occur. Vacancies have also been caused, as Prak and Priemus (1985) point out, by such external factors as high unemployment, over-building, and high rents (with the latter a major problem), and—for France and Great Britain—good mortgage terms. Social decay occurs because high vacancy rates mean less selectivity of tenants. In addition, when an estate has been a third empty, as in some Dutch and British buildings, they have a negative image (Priemus 1986; Bulos and Walker 1987). As Priemus states, vacancies cause more vacancies. Vacancies attract vandals and addicts and, when many empty units are not adequately maintained, residents feel unsafe and that they are in a deteriorated building. Social control is reduced to a minimum when a dwelling is empty. This all causes more residents to leave the estate.

Financial decay, Priemus points out, has been loss of rent due to vacancies, increased need for maintenance and renovation due to high turnover and empty unkept units, and increased management costs. Financial decay stems from technical decay and then affects social decay, mainly vacancies and change in social composition of the tenant group. As the estate or one building gets a bad image, it is hard to find tenants to replace those leaving. Selectivity standards are lowered. The most pronounced example of lowered selectivity standards is Bulos and Walker's account of Killingworth Towers, near Newcastle, which advertised for tenants in the Durham prison. From 1974 on, these twenty-seven towers of maisonettes were in trouble, not so much because of technical decay as the loss of most tenants above the second floor due to the ruling that no families could live at higher stories. The out-migration of families and children was not replaced by enough single people and childless couples; turnover and vacancies were high (Bulos and Walker 1987). In the Netherlands, too, tenants replacing out-migrants are often single, Priemus reports (1986). Because stronger social groups (economically better-off) have been able to find accommodations elsewhere, weaker social groups (problem families, singles, and ethnic minorities), who have had little choice of housing, have continued to live in or move on to estates. With such a social group, an estate has a deteriorating image, and its tenants have become stigmatized. Priemus adds that once such a stigmatization occurred, it is extremely difficult to breach the negative spiral. In my study of stigma in American public housing (1969), I found the same thing, which affected residents' employment opportunities and their credit ratings.

Stigmatization means high vacancies, which often means that authorities are more willing to offer units to minorities and in fact limit their offer of housing to these hard-to-let estates, as data show for Great Britain, West Germany, France, Sweden, and, to some degree, the Netherlands. In other words, native British, German, French,

Swedes, and Dutch either refuse or move out of unpopular social housing, and minorities, considering the units better than those in their crowded and expensive slum areas, move into such units in large numbers.

It should be added, however, that renting the units to minorities (and single people and the aged) is not the only solution for these unpopular, deteriorating buildings. In addition to renting to minority tenants, if decay continues to the point where maintenance is expensive and vacancies cause the estate to run in the red, demolition or alternative uses are considered. Turning the buildings over to private management has occurred in Britain (Bulos and Walker 1987), with such management often renovating and renting to the middle class if possible (Friedrichs 1987). Demolition is continually on the authorities' minds, and tenants have favored it—two-thirds in Friedrichs's study (1987) of one outer-area Hamburg project. Bulos and Walker name eleven housing authorities in the United Kingdom where demolition was either undertaken or proposed. For example, by 1986 in Manchester, 1,018 flats in a mixed high- and low-rise estate had already been demolished. Birmingham had a high number either demolished in 1986 or scheduled to be. Surprisingly, Bulos and Walker found that many of these tall buildings had no obvious or definite structural faults or failures. They add (p. 15): "some authorities are taking this opportunity to demolish the tall blocks without proper consideration of the financial, technical and human costs this entails."

The most likely solution, however, is to offer these unpopular units to persons, usually minorities, in desperate need of housing, and this is a form of government-assisted segregation.

The Situation in Great Britain

Stigmatized estates have long existed in each major city in Great Britain. In fact, since a high-rise building collapsed in the late 1960s in Ronan Point, many prospective council tenants have been reluctant to live in high rises, and high-rise construction decreased (Ash 1980). The situation of hard-to-let estates in Britain, Ash reports, became much more serious in the late 1970s. In 1982 the U.K. Department of Environment (DOE) published its report "Priority Estates Project: Improving Problem Council Estates," following its 1980 study of the problem, and Power of DOE produced another report in 1984. The types of problems that have existed in such estates varied somewhat from place to place as the DOE study found. Evidence exists of problems on estates of many different architectural types and styles, as Power points out, but a number of authors feel that nontraditional industrialized buildings, often very large in size, are the type that cause dissatisfaction. Of the thirty difficult-to-let estates the DOE surveyed (1980), unattractive buildings were a major problem in ten and large size in fourteen. A number had major structural defects such as damp or condensation (fifteen), noise (nine), outdated fittings (thirteen), and unpopular design (five), often associated with industrial design. Coleman (1985) bases her attack on state-built mass housing on problems of design in these hard-to-let estates (using Southward for her data). In her controversial report she states of the construction: "Industrially built housing often suffered from major structural defects, like concrete cracking up or large blocks falling off buildings."

Ash writes (p. 103) that "many of the blocks were hurriedly built by unfamiliar industrialized methods and used materials which had not been adequately tested. On some estates condensation and water made living conditions worse than in houses classified as slums" (1982, A-11).

Coleman also complains about noise (as do Anderson, Bulos, and Walker 1982), inadequate control of ventilation, out-of-service lifts, the spatial layout of the estate, and its walkways. Thus, poor quality and maintenance of council housing high rises may be the real first problem, as well as their locations in unpopular outer areas. Money was never sufficient for maintenance, and as the estates' reputations dropped, less was done. With unpopularity, stage two, social decay, occurred. Poor families that Spicker (1987) describes as causing stigma, "problem families" and large households, were assigned to the estates, and vandalism, litter, and general upkeep got worse. The 1980 DOE report cites poor repair service as a major problem in nineteen estates; physical neglect in twenty; lack of caretaking in seventeen of thirty; and vandalism in twenty of thirty. Bulos and Walker (1987) report that some high rises were so bad that they were demolished. Ash, as an early DOE researcher on high rises and families and early critic of such use, laments that "altogether hundreds of millions of pounds have been wasted on public housing intended to eliminate the housing shortage quickly and cheaply but without due regard either for sound methods of construction, consumer needs and preferences, or cost" (1980, 97). In the Borough of Hackney, London, six blocks of the worst estate, Stonebridge, was demolished (Commission for Racial Equality 1984). However, not only high-rise but also newer, low-rise housing was considered unsatisfactory in design. The commission reports that on the Holly Street Estate completed in Hackney in 1970–71, the design faults of low-rise blocks included poor sound insulation (which caused tenant friction), long internal corridors used by children as play areas, large open spaces with no tenant responsibility, and inadequate drainage. The pattern of allocation added a high density of children (40 percent under sixteen in some blocks), which led to major vandalism problems and caused a situation in which "outstanding maintenance work on the estate was said to be reaching crisis proportion" and, in addition, "the heating ducts in the low-rise blocks had become infested with Pharoah ants" (CRE, 1984). In other housing authorities, pre-1919 properties still existed and were considered undesirable, as Henderson mentions for Birmingham (1984).

In Great Britain, most undesirable housing has been in inner-city estates in poorer areas, although Taylor (1979) reports depressed housing for an area of Killington new town. Housing estates can be too close to public facilities, such as Edinburgh's Martello Court, with its continuous balconies in semipublic areas (Bulos and Walker 1987). With the very large stock of public housing (still around 27 percent of the stock versus around 1 percent in the United States) there are a variety of locations for social housing in British cities; some sites are in very good areas like Hampstead or in outer areas like Kingston. The problem exists in areas of slum clearance.

In general, housing units on desirable sites are becoming less available because the units are sold to tenants (Sarre 1986; Forrest and Murie 1985). Even the move to sell whole estates or portfolios of properties to privately financed housing trusts and appropriate bodies of landlords will likely decrease availability due to purchase of the better-location properties. With higher socioeconomic level tenants buying council units in better locations (Williams, Sewel, and Twine 1986), poor tenants are left in residual council housing (Forrest and Murie 1985). This means, based on Spicker's argument that it is the poverty of the tenants that causes estates to be depressed and not just architecture and size (1987), there will be more stigmatized estates. Of course one could say certain estates—because they were built for poor tenants or were built in slum clearance areas of a city or were high rise—got only tenants who were very poor or considered as problem families. As Spicker reports, "the construction of some estates for the tenants of the slums meant that those estates carry from their inception, a particular stigma" (1987, 288). Spicker emphasizes that tenants' poverty is the major source of stigma for many estates, not design and maintenance, although he sees these as contributing factors. However, like Priemus, I feel that the cause first lies in the technical decay, the design and location that made some housing estates unattractive to many of the very large working-class population housed in council units in the 1960s. Then the less desirable and lower-socioeconomic-level households were put in such units and the stigma became greater. And *then* home maintenance declined, both by tenants who, Spicker points out, lack resources to do it (even rubbish disposal or heating) and by local authorities who see less need to expend money on such estates. The DOE study did find social factors to be a major problem on most of the thirty estates studied, with problem families the major problem on twenty estates (1980, 4). The situation has worsened since 1980, with greater implementation of the Homeless Persons Act.

Authorities concentrate homeless in the undesirable estates and also female-headed households formerly not commonly housed. In Hackney, for example, this homeless group has relative priority because they must be re-housed and the council hopes to minimize the costly use of bed-and-breakfast hotels (CRE, 1984). Local authority allocation personnel, with a review of housekeeping standards, rent records, and other data on the applicant assign those with low standing to depressed estates. Rex and Moore (1967) once documented such grading (no longer formally done) by gatekeepers of council housing. Rex described housing classes, with those deemed more worthy by local housing authority personnel as assigned to the best council housing. In the competition for a scarce good, which council housing was then considered, the higher status, the more worthy, and long-time area residents, were more successful. Such competition is somewhat lacking now; many native British prefer not to be in council housing but to buy. Yet the many native British who still live in council housing want the better, more acceptable estates, so it is harder for minorities, newcomers, and those less desirable to live there.

Segregation of Minority Groups on Stigmatized Estates in Great Britain

Local authority allocation personnel for many years avoided housing West Indian and South Asian minorities for a variety of reasons, including lack of residence, family composition, and concern over white reaction (Henderson and Karn 1986). Sarre (1986, 82) says for Bedford: "A particularly interesting entrant into the minority housing market in the 1960s was the local authority. In the case of Bedford, it is particularly remarkable how slow was the penetration of deprived groups into a sector of the market intended to provide housing on the basis of need. A number of factors contributed to this result. First, the blanket rejection of non-native applicants in the 1950s both encouraged minorities to seek other alternatives . . . and created an expectation of unfavourable treatment which persisted after the sector was formally opened up by the Race Relations Act."

Oc (1987) states that many blacks have a limited prospect of ever obtaining a mortgage or a council house; Henderson and Karn also document their difficulty in getting council housing. Several factors against their consideration have been residence qualifications (now relaxed in some authorities such as Birmingham) and—for South Asians—their home ownership, which disqualifies them from waiting lists unless their home has been demolished or rehabilitated by authorities (Henderson and Karn 1986), events now unlikely with less clearance. Other factors hurt them: for South Asians, it is the extended three-generation family; for West Indians, the single-parent family; and for both, the large family (Sarre 1986). The latter factors also cause local authority officials to place people on stigmatized estates when they do house them; the need for large units and the desire for inner-city ones also determine placement.

It is more likely that West Indians use council housing, feeling it better housing (Sarre 1986); many South Asians buy old units (Oc 1987). By the late 1980s, more than a third (more in some areas) of the West Indian population was in council housing. In Hackney, the CRE (1984) reports that these groups have difficulty obtaining council housing. With West Indians and Asians constituting 19.5 percent of the Hackney population, 60 percent of West Indians and 23 percent of Asians were in council housing; 56 percent of all households were in 1977. Most areas have many fewer immigrants in council housing, and most immigrants are put in depressed estates. Karn states that "access to council [public] housing was difficult for new arrivals, because of obstacles such as residential qualifications. However, over the years they were able to gain access to the *least popular* council estates in inner-city areas. As a result they now live predominantly in those parts of cities which suffer from the worst housing conditions, the most deteriorated physical environment and the greatest poverty" (1986:2). Even in areas of high minority concentration, West Indians and Asians were put in estates with particularly bad reputations, such as Stonebridge and Holly Street in Hackney, rather than dispersed. Here, of all the new property allocated to waiting list applicants, 88 percent went to whites, whereas 45 and 46 percent respectively were black (West Indian or Asian) in the two old estates with bad reputations. In Bedford, Sarre (1986) reports the majority of this group was allocated to the least-favored run-down interwar estates in the vicinity of the Amphill and Elstow Road minority areas.

Henderson and Karn (1986) describe the marked segregation of South Asians in a very few areas. Less aggressive than West Indians, South Asians give housing authorities fewer location choices, which affects the age of the property they receive and compounds their segregation. Some have been housed in unpopular high-rises, but many authorities will no longer allow any families in such housing. Many local authorities have held oversimplified assumptions that all West Indian and Asian council housing applicants want inner-city locations. Karn reports that this is not entirely untrue; she adds that "a growing number of black applicants are seeking suburban homes rather than inner city flats. White and black tenants are in competition for better designed estates" (1986:3). She finds that some housing officers allocate on basis of social status, giving blacks bad-quality housing. Officers who try to reverse these tendencies find that white tenants take matters into their own hands and use racial harassment to exclude blacks.

Officers of housing authorities not only place blacks on stigmatized or depressed estates to avoid negative white reactions (a problem that helped end Birmingham's 1969–75 race policy), but also because they need to fill the vacancies on the hard-to-let estates, and West Indians and Asians are the easiest to move. If "decants," those being re-housed due to house demolition or such, or homeless, these groups are given little preference. Even when they are, studies show their first choice is met far less often than it is for whites, such as in Hackney or Birmingham (CRE 1984; Henderson and Karn 1986), or the interviewer does not record their real choice. These officers have the day-to-day need to fill units promptly, which Henderson and Karn feel leads to their making judgments quickly on the likelihood of a property being accepted. They use their stereotype about the types of properties that different groups will accept, not what they prefer. Segregation is also assisted by the fact that whites can easily transfer out of depressed estates, while blacks have trouble making transfers, such as in Hackney and Birmingham (Karn 1986).

Stigmatized Estates and Segregated Housing in the Netherlands

In the Netherlands, as Priemus (1986) points out in his report on high-rise buildings in the huge housing association stock and the limited local authority stock, some estates, or parts of estates, have poor reputations. A few, such as Linnaeustratt (Leeuwarden), have been demolished; others are in trouble, with serious construction and physical faults and high maintenance and operative costs (Prak and Priemus 1985). Their design was not satisfactory (Priemus 1986; Koopman 1985). About 60 percent of the 350,000 high-rise dwellings were built in 1964–74. Van Kempen (1986) reports that these high rises comprise about 10 percent of postwar housing stock.

The Dutch central government, concerned over the housing shortage in the 1960s, saw such industrialized systems of mass housing, primarily two- and three-bedroom apartments of the "gallery" type, as cheap and quick solutions (Van Kempen 1986; Priemus 1986). The government, through its financing and controlling role, pushed the design on local bodies, primarily housing associations, as well as the massive concentration of the buildings; this happened although the public continued to have a low opinion of the high-rises and preferred older housing association units (Huttman 1985, 1972). The new units' higher rents, even with rent subsidies to people with lower incomes, also made them unpopular.

Social decay, the Prak and Priemus term, set in. The unpopularity of the high-rises caused people to move away from them. Housing association authorities, faced with high vacancies, then became more lenient in taking in nontraditional groups, or as Priemus (1986) says, weaker socioeconomic groups, often problem cases. Priemus also mentions that residents were asked to live side by side with other groups with extremely different norms, values, and cultures. The effect of the decaying processes on these few undesirable estates with technical problems is that the number of tenants better-situated socioeconomically decreases while the proportion of "weaker" tenants (ethnic minorities, young people, and recipients of benefits) increases. He says in extreme cases one may even speak of ghettoization.

Rejection of this housing by many Dutch led to an in-migration of foreign born, groups with difficulty in getting subsidized housing. Grunfeld states that "the way in which the housing market operates in the Netherlands leads to a concentration of low-paid ethnic minorities not in the highly subsidized low rent corporation dwellings, but in privately owned old houses" (1982:6). He also feels that the media in the Netherlands "usually focuses on the substandard dwelling of segregated minorities . . . from Mediterranean countries and . . . Surinam and Molukkan people." In unpopular Bijlmermeer they had a chance for better housing, as they did in other estates with poor reputations. Bijlmermeer, according to Van Kempen, attracted households that did not conform to allocation rules of the municipality, perhaps because the high rents of Bijlmermeer were not incorporated into the regular housing distribution, and individual housing associations managing different buildings could make up their own rules and also allocate flats. Started in 1968, the area by 1970 had a very large proportion of people who were single, newly married, co-habitants, and foreign-born, including Surinamese. Although in Amsterdam Surinamese comprised 3.7 percent of the population, more than 11 percent of the Bijlmermeer population was Surinamese (Van Kempen 1986). Because apartments were designed for large families, with three- and four-bedroom units, they are suitable for such families; in Gliphoeve and other blocks there were also clandestine tenants and overcrowding. Again, overcrowding and the low status of many tenants led to poor upkeep, vandalism, and a deteriorating living climate, as well as petty crime and drug addiction (Prak and Priemus 1986; Huttman 1985). Van Kempen states that the massive high-rise development lacked social control; tenants did not maintain the buildings.

Such circumstances led to an increasing unpopularity of areas that had increased concentration of minorities in certain parts of Bijlmermeer because of the allocation rules of particular housing associations. The result included an increase in Surinamese tenants, especially for the association that ran Gliphoeve 1; by 1975 the development was a ghetto, with 90 percent of the tenants from Surinam (Biervliet 1976). In Gliphoeve 2, managed by another association with stricter allocation rules, vacancies were high. Van Kempen states that Surinamese "squatted" in a hundred vacant dwellings by June 1974. More white flight then occurred, although the area never became overwhelmingly black; vandalism, deterioration of buildings, and crime increased even more. In 1984, Gliphoeve 2 was vacated for renovation, Van Kempen states—an interesting way to work with segregation and a deteriorating environmental problem. Bijlmermeer had areas with good reputations as well as bad; considerable transfer occurred among blocks, even in the early days, and it increased in the 1980s. Van Kempen states that the segregation among blocks became more pronounced, inducing new movement. Vacancies grew, and more foreign born and singles were taken from Amsterdam, as were one-parent families—43 percent of the new tenants. Since 1982, vacancy rates increased rapidly to 23 percent by 1985, but at far different rates for different estates, again indicating segregation of certain groups.

By 1988 Bijlmermeer was improving, renamed and rehabilitated— and even made more secure from crime through youth centers, design, and other factors. In general, in the Netherlands in the last few years, as Mik states (chapter 10), government policy is to have minorities on many estates; each housing association must have a quota of immigrants in its new housing and reserves a percentage of its units for minorities (chapters 3 and 10). Other government policies may affect segregation. For example, in new public housing projects, built on urban renewal and in-filling sites in The Hague, inhabitants of the neighborhood are given priority so many ethnic minority residents, as well as single people and two-person households who lived in the area before renewal are returning (Van Kempen and Van Weesep 1988). This priority selection, while certainly fair to former inhabitants, can mean a concentration of them in the new housing.

Segregation of West German and Swedish Social Housing

Evidence exists that social housing in both West Germany and Sweden has been unpopular in some cases. The cause seems to be location in the suburbs, the opposite of the British situation for many cases, although some hard-to-let British estates have been in outer areas (DOE 1980). For example, Meuter (1982) reports that Cologne's outer-area social housing has been unpopular. After the inner city's rehabilitation and gentrification, this social housing filled with immigrants from that area, many of whom could not pay the rent. Andernacht (1987 interview) reports that in Frankfurt, with its large minority population, an estate located far out of the city and with the poor architecture typical of 1970s' high-rises was primarily occupied by minorities because Germans did not like it. An estate of equally poor 1970s architecture has not suffered unpopularity because of its better location. The problem of unpopular estates varies by city. It is a major problem in Hamburg, one that Friedrichs (1987) studied in detail for one outer-area estate (Mummelmannsberg, built between 1972 and 1984, with 18,228 inhabitants in 1985). One of the new group of housing estates built on massive scale, supposedly to save as construction costs rocketed, these large estates were to house low-income tenants. Most were owned by nonprofit housing organizations. Part of the reason that they became unpopular, Friedrichs states, is because scarcity in the general housing market was over, although not in the submarket of low-cost housing, and thus many Germans had other choices. Equally as important, the financing system of social housing, related to high construction costs resulted in a higher increase in rents than in the private sector. In addition, the high-rise concrete buildings were disliked. Thus a growing tendency existed, with an above-average number of vacancies, to rent to problem families causing selective out-migration of the better-off. Most tenants considered the estate stigmatized. All this came before the concentration of foreign immigrants on the estate; by 1985, a fifth of the inhabitants were foreign-born, many of them refugees from Asia and Poland. Because more Germans moved out than foreign born between 1980 and 1985, the foreign-born population increased 80 percent (Friedrichs 1987).

In Sweden, outer new towns in the Stockholm area are not as popular as inner new towns such as Vallingby, as I observed in 1978 and 1986. Lindberg (1978) reports the industrialized method of building massive housing as the cause of this unpopularity. Minorities have moved into the vacancies in these Stockholm outer-area dwellings as they have also done in Malmö, so that a majority of households are Yugoslavian or Turkish.

For Sweden, Lindberg and Linden (1986) find, for many local authorities, housing segregation (separated dwellings between households in geographical space) decreasing, and yet housing market segmentation (the legal and financial relationships to housing, such as tenure type) increasing and related to Swedish integration policy (chapter 5).

As these authors, and also Arnell-Gustafsson (1982) report, anti-segregation housing measures are used in many Swedish municipalities. In cities such as Orebro, Linköping, Gävle, Sandviken, and Uppsala, there is construction of housing estates where privately owned cooperatives and rented flats are integrated. These areas have a varying mixture of housing types, apartment sizes, and tenure forms (Arnell-Gustafsson 1982). The number of immigrants has increased in local authority flats, but they are much less likely to live in owner-occupied housing (chapter 5). For long-term Finnish immigrants this situation is less segregated than for recent Yugoslavian and Turkish immigrants.

Swedish local governments are not alone in antidiscrimination efforts. In Birmingham, England, a racial dispersal policy was used between 1969 and 1975 to place immigrants in council housing estates;

the opposition of British natives was a factor that worked against the policy. In the Netherlands, integration of Indonesians into a wide spectrum of Dutch housing was a government effort in the early postwar years. Bagley (1972) reports that the Dutch, after first housing these early postwar immigrants in boarding houses, dedicated 5 percent of the new houses (200 units) to housing them in different areas. The Indonesian immigrants were housed all over Holland, a major and costly distribution effort at a time when housing was in short supply.

Dispersal is again a major issue in the Netherlands; some cities have tried and, like Birmingham, moved away from it (chapter 10). Dispersal in West Berlin is also controversial (chapter 11). In the United States, public housing dispersal is being attempted (mandated by HUD), but the Starrett decision (chapter 19) has made implementation difficult. Thus, in many countries, some degree of segregation exists in social housing, with the concentration often caused by unpopularity of the housing.

References

Andernacht, F. 1987. Interview with E. Huttman at International Housing Conference of ISA Working Group on Housing. Hamburg. September.

Anderson, R., M. Bulos, and S. Walker. 1982. *The Future of High Rise Housing.* London: Polytechnic of the South Bank.

Arnell-Gustafsson, U. 1982. "On Strategies Against Socio-Economic Residential Segregation." *Acta Sociologica* 25:33–40.

Ash, J. 1980. "The Rise and Fall of High Rise Housing in England." Pp. 95–123 in *The Consumer Experience of Housing,* edited by G. Ungerson and V. Karn. London: Gower.

———. 1982. "The Effects of Household Formation and Life Styles on Housing Need in Britain." Paper presented at the World Congress of Sociology. Mexico City.

Bagley, C. 1972. "Dutch Housing, Race and Integration Policies." Pp. 25–29 in *Immigrants in Europe,* edited by N. Deakin. London: Fabian Society.

Biervliet, W. 1976. *Bewonersonderzoek. Gliphoeve I* (Inquiry of Tenants, Gliphoeve I). Part 1. Amsterdam: Bijlmermeer.

Böhning, W. 1972. *The Migration of Workers in the United Kingdom and the European Community.* London: Oxford University Press.

Bonacker, M. 1982. "The Social Community of Immigrants." Pp. 102–113 in *Spatial Disparities and Social Behavior,* edited by J. Friedrichs. Hamburg: Christians.

Bulos, M., and S. Walker. 1987. *The Demolition of High Rise Housing.* London: Polytechnic of the South Bank.

Coleman, A. 1985. *Utopia on Trial: Vision and Reality in Planned Housing.* London: Shipman.

Commission for Racial Equality. 1984. *Race and Council Housing in Hackney.* London: CRE.

Deakin, N. 1972. "European Minorities." Pp. 2–7 in *Immigrants in Europe,* edited by N. Deakin. London: Fabian Society.

Farley, J. 1983. "Metropolitan Housing Segregation in 1980: The St. Louis Case." *Urban Affairs Quarterly* 18:347–59.

Forrest, R., and A. Murie. 1985. "Restructuring the Welfare State: Privatisation and Public Housing in U.K." Pp. 15–31 in *Housing Needs and Policy Approaches: Trends in Thirteen Countries,* edited by W. van Vliet, E. Huttman, and S. Fava. Durham: Duke University Press.

Friedrichs, J. 1987. Comments on tour of Hamburg housing.

Goering, J. (ed.). 1986. *Housing Desegregation and Federal Policy.* Chapel Hill: University of North Carolina Press.

Gray, R., and S. Tursky. 1986. "Location and Racial/Ethnic Occupancy Patterns for HUD-Subsidized Family Housing in Ten Metropolitan Areas." Pp. 235–52 in *Housing Desegregation and Federal Policy,* edited by J. Goering. Chapel Hill: University of North Carolina Press.

Grunfeld, F. 1982. "The Problem of Spatial Segregation and the Preservation of an Urban Society." Paper presented at the World Congress of Sociology. Mexico City.

Hartman, C. 1975. *Housing and Social Policy.* Englewood Cliffs: Prentice-Hall.

Hays, R. A. 1985. *The Federal Government and Urban Housing.* Albany: State University of New York Press.

Henderson, J. 1984. "Race and the Allocation of Public Housing in Britain." Paper presented at the American Sociological Association Meeting. San Francisco.

Henderson, J., and V. Karn. 1986. *Race, Class and Public Housing.* London: Gower.

Hoffmeyer-Zlotnik, J. 1982. "Community Change and Invasion: The Case of Turkish Guest Workers." Pp. 114–26 in *Spatial Disparities and Social Behavior,* edited by J. Friedrichs. Hamburg: Christians.

Huttman, E. 1969. "Stigma in Public Housing: Comparisons between Britain and the U.S." Ph.D. diss., University of California, Berkeley.

———. 1972. "Pathology of Public Housing." *City Magazine* Fall:2

———. 1985. "Transnational Housing Policy." Pp. 148–63 in *Home Environments,* edited by I. Altman and C. Werner. New York: Plenum.

Huttman, E., and J. Huttman. 1973. "Self-Containment and Socio-Economic Balance: Dutch and British New Towns." *Growth and Change: Journal of Regional Development.* January.

Karn, V. 1986. "Race and Housing in Britain." Paper presented at the World Congress of Sociology. New Delhi.

Koopman, J. 1985. "Opening Remarks." Pp. 3–11 in *Post-war Public Housing in Trouble,* edited by N. Prak and H. Priemus. Delft: Delft University Press.

Lindberg, G. 1978. "Cooperative Housing in Sweden." Paper presented at the World Congress of Sociology, Uppsala.

Lindberg, G., and A. Linden. 1986. "Housing Market Segmentation in Swedish Local Authorities: Immigrants and Swedes, Young and Old." Paper presented at the World Congress of Sociology. New Delhi.

Meehan, E. 1979. *The Quality of Federal Policy Making: Programmed Failure in Public Housing.* Columbia: University of Missouri Press.

Meuter, H. 1982. "Regional and Social Effects of Changed Conditions in Housing Supply." Pp. 141–48 in *Applied Urban Research: Towards an Internationalization of Research and Learning,* edited by G. Hellstern, F. Spreer, and H. Wollman. Bonn: Bundesforschungsanstalt für Landeskund und Raumordnung.

Moore, W. 1969. *The Vertical Ghetto.* New York: Random House.

Oc, T. 1988. "Inner City Housing Improvement and Ethnic Minorities in Britain." Pp. 123–37 in *Housing and Neighborhoods: Theoretical and Empirical Contributions,* edited by W. van Vliet, H. Choldin, W. Michelson, and D. Popenoe. Westport: Greenwood Press.

Pit, F., and W. van Vliet. 1988. "Public Housing in the U.S." Pp. 199–224 in *Handbook on Housing and the Built Environment.* Westport: Greenwood Press.

Power, A. 1984. *Local Housing Management: A Priority Estates Survey.* London: U.K. Department of the Environment.

Prak, N., and H. Priemus. 1985. *Post-war Public Housing in Trouble.* Delft: Delft University Press.

Priemus, H. 1986. "Post-war Public High Rise Estates: What Went Wrong with Housing Policy, with the Design and with Management." *Netherlands Journal of Housing and Environmental Research* 1, no. 2:157–86.

Rainwater, L. 1970. *Behind the Ghetto Walls.* Chicago: Aldine.

Rex, J., and R. Moore. 1967. *Race, Community and Conflict.* London: Oxford University Press.

Sarre, P. 1986. "Choice and Constraint in Ethnic Minority Housing." *Housing Studies* 1:71–86.

Smith, D. 1976. "The Facts of Racial Disadvantage." *Political and Economic Planning.*

Spicker, P. 1987. "Poverty and Depressed Estates." *Housing Studies* 2:283–92.

Taylor, P. 1979. "Difficult to Let, Difficult to Live in and Sometimes Difficult to Get Out of." *Environment and Planning* 2.

United Kingdom. Department of the Environment. 1980. *An Investigation of Difficult-to-Let Housing.* London: HMSO.

———. 1982. *Priority Estate Project 1982.* London: HMSO.

Van Kempen, E. 1986. "High-Rise Housing Estates and the Concentration of Poverty." *Netherlands Journal of Housing and Environmental Research* 1, no. 1:3–26.

Van Kempen, R., and J. Van Weesep. "Low-Income Households and Threshold Housing in Large Dutch Cities." *Netherlands Journal of Housing and Environmental Research* 4, no. 4:321–35.

Welfeld, I. 1985. "Public Housing: Managing or Mainstreaming." Paper presented at the International Housing Conference. Amsterdam.

Williams. N., J. Sewel, and F. Twine. 1986. "Socio-Economic Characteristics of Purchases of Council Houses." Paper presented at the National Swedish Institute of Building Research Conference. Gaevle.

Yinger, J. 1986. "On the Possibility of Achieving Racial Integration." Pp. 290–312 in *Housing Segregation and Federal Policy,* edited by J. Goering. Chapel Hill: University of North Carolina Press.

III

Housing Segregation
in the United States:
An Overview

13. Introduction

The following overviews illustrate the situation of comparative housing segregation in America, as well as particular policies and programs and special issues. It is not intended that the following accounts be inclusive in their coverage of all the aspects of American housing segregation, but rather provide data on the overall situation and case studies of segregation in particular cities to allow contrast with the situation in Western Europe.

The material in this section illustrates a variety of research methods and a variety of issues, both for European readers and American readers. In chapter 14 Johnston fully illustrates a variety of research focuses and methods, including historical research, index of dissimilarity data, income and housing price analysis, data on mortgage practices, and complaints to fair housing groups concerning discrimination. This chapter provides a historical orientation to the situation of blacks in the South, their movement to the North, and the situation they faced there. Johnston discusses degrees of segregation, decrease, the introduction of discrimination laws, and changes in the institutional practices of realtors and lenders. He also reports on the importance of these institutions and government agencies in the early days in producing segregated housing. The Gary, Indiana, area is used as a case study, in which the author draws on many statistics and studies, material on the degree of segregation, mortgage lender practices, and housing discrimination cases. This broad picture contrasts with the type of European data focused on previously.

Chapter 15 focuses on blacks' situation in the South, including Texas. McDaniel provides the history of a group long in this country and focuses on blacks' changing residential locational situation from after the Civil War to the present. He mentions the immediate post-Civil War movement from rural areas, in part a "push" situation due to mortgage foreclosures, no wills, and white takeovers and racial hatred, as well as a "pull" from the attractions of cities. He describes blacks' integrated residential location, as servants in the cities, in the

early post-Civil War period, but then the change to segregated communities demanded by local and state laws at first and later by racial
zoning and covenants. McDaniel then discusses blacks' movement to
the suburbs and provides a case history, in some ways similar to Johnston's but in other aspects different. McDaniel's description of Houston includes the history of segregated areas of the city, their growth
from enclaves in city wards to whole wards, and the invasion of surrounding areas. He briefly covers the role of realtors and local authorities in subdivision and public housing siting. He mentions lawsuits
as attempts to stop segregation and provides pessimistic predictions
about segregated black suburbs.

Gordon and Mayer discuss the segregation of another major group,
Hispanics (chapter 16). They focus on Phoenix but make comparisons
with data on other cities. They look at the degree of concentration of
Hispanics and blacks in Phoenix over time, but exclude the suburban
areas where they say half of the Anglos live. Their measure for segregation differs from that normal dissimilarity measure used by Taeuber and others. Gordon and Mayer use vital statistics, death and birth
records, to identify ethnic status and describe their findings in terms
of Burgess's theory of rings of the city.

They then move on to their main focus, comparing the situation of
Hispanics and blacks to Anglos in terms of housing cost and housing
quality. From their detailed data, Gordon and Mayer make the analysis by income group and ethnic group. Their primary question is, Do
Hispanic and black Phoenix renters and owners of similar income pay
more and have worse housing than do Anglos? For this analysis they
develop useful housing quality measures. Some of the measures differ
from European ones, such as the measure "more than one bathroom"
and "air conditioning"; other measures such as "age of building" and
"crowding" are similar. The emphasis on housing cost, broken down
for renters and owners of particular income, is also seldom examined
in European countries.

The overview chapters on American housing segregation are followed by several on specific policies, programs, and issues. The subject
of segregation in public housing is covered in detail by Goering and
Coulibably; the chapter can be compared to chapter 12's discussion of
stigmatized social housing in Western Europe. Next, the issue of
movement of the American black population to the suburbs is discussed by Huttman and Jones, including the historical situation, financial ability to move, desire to move to integrated areas, and

reasons blacks are in segregated suburban areas. The process of re-segregation is discussed, as are integration maintenance efforts and controversy. In chapter 21, Saltman describes the efforts of several nonprofit organizations in different cities to maintain integrated communities. Keating discusses community efforts to open up the suburbs in Cleveland.

The comparisons in the American portion of the book with the European part are not entirely satisfactory. The American studies are of the main groups, blacks and Hispanics, usually covered in housing segregation research. However, blacks differ from new immigrants, and even many Hispanics in the United States differ from other new immigrants to America; only part of their group is comprised of recent arrivals. For Western Europe the studies are of fairly new immigrants, although some have been in their host countries since the 1960s and have grown children. Second, the status and rights of some of the European immigrants, guest workers, is different from that of American blacks and most of the Hispanic group, although there are some illegals. The fortunes of the European ex-colonial group, the German-origin group, and the refugee group are somewhat closer to the status of blacks, Hispanics, and European immigrants to the United States.

Comparison between American research reports and those of the European scholars is also affected by their somewhat different focus. The Americans emphasize different measurements for concentration of minorities (dissimilarity indices more than proportion minority), measuring income level, and centering on suburban developments. American researchers also center on buyers as well as renters, the former a group seldom covered in Europe because of its small number (except for some coverage of it in Great Britain). American researchers also put more emphasis on institutional factors in discrimination, for example, realtors and lending institutions, although some emphasis is put on these in Great Britain. Second, Americans view discrimination laws, directives, and complaints more than do European researchers, in part because they are more prevalent.

These differences are not major obstacles to comparison, but only emphasize actual differences in the American and European situations, as well as differences in researchers' focus. The American material also points out some fruitful methodological approaches that European researchers can follow. Europeans focus on the spatial approach in terms of concentrations and use maps. They pay less attention to discrimination and causes than do American researchers.

European researchers, on the other hand, pay considerable attention to job situation in relation to housing situation. They also detail government policy on such matters as dispersal of immigrants, improvement of housing conditions, and immigrants' housing allocation in social housing.

14. Housing Segregation in the Urban Black Population of the Midwest

Early Forms of Racial Separation

Racial segregation in housing is a persistent problem of American society. Analysts view it as a fundamental element in maintaining the subordination of minorities and the separation of black and white America. Housing segregation impedes black progress in employment and education. It is a cornerstone in maintaining "two societies, one black, one white—separate and unequal" (*Report of the National Advisory Commission on Civil Disorders* 1968:1). Our understanding of the situation is enhanced by historical perspective. For much of American history, blacks were slaves and overwhelmingly concentrated in the South. From 1790 to 1860, the total black population living in the South increased from 91–95 percent. It may come as a surprise that 53 percent of all "free people of color" also lived in the South; between 8–14 percent were freed slaves.

Under slavery, most blacks lived in proximity to whites. A few plantations maintained separate quarters, away from the main house, however, most slave-owning families had only a few slaves. These people often lived close to the white families, and warm, personal relationships tended to spring up between black women and white children and among the children themselves. Nevertheless, most Southerners neither owned slaves nor lived in areas where slaves were a part of daily life. Slavery was the elaborate system of etiquette and economies that nurtured separation. Residential segregation was neither necessary nor functional for the system. Blacks "knew their place," and it was a social position of inferiority, not a spatial location.

With the Emancipation Proclamation and the end of the Civil War, ex-slaves were free to leave the South, but a mass exodus did not occur (table 14.1). The end of hostilities and the implementing of a decree did not markedly alter the economic infrastructure of the country. The industrial North could not economically absorb a large num-

243

TABLE 14.1.   Distribution of the Black Population, by Region
for Selected Years (1790 to 1975)
(figures in millions)

Area	1790	1870	1910	1940	1960	1970	1975
United States	1	5	10	13	19	23	24
Total (%)	100	100	100	100	100	100	100
South	91	91	89	77	60	53	52
North	9	9	10	22	34	39	39
Northeast	9	4	5	11	16	19	18
North Central	—	6	6	11	18	20	20
West	—	—	1	1	6	8	9

Source: U.S. Department of Commerce, Bureau of the Census, The Social and Economic Status of the Black Population in the United States: An Historical Overview, 1790–1978, USGPO 1979:13.

Note: In this table and the others that use regional distinctions, the regions are defined as noted. Readers are reminded that not all of these areas were part of the United States for entire periods represented in all tables. South: Alabama, Arkansas, Delaware, District of Columbia, Florida, Georgia, Kentucky, Louisiana, Maryland, Mississippi, North Carolina, Oklahoma, South Carolina, Tennessee, Texas, Virginia, and West Virginia. North and West: This designation refers to the Northeast, North Central, and West regions combined. Northeast: Connecticut, Maine, Massachusetts, New Hampshire, New Jersey, New York, Pennsylvania, Rhode Island, and Vermont. North Central: Illinois, Indiana, Iowa, Kansas, Michigan, Minnesota, Missouri, Nebraska, North Dakota, Ohio, South Dakota, and Wisconsin. West: Alaska, Arizona, California, Colorado, Hawaii, Idaho, Montana, Nevada, New Mexico, Oregon, Utah, Washington, and Wyoming.

ber of unskilled agricultural workers, however, the beaten and disorganized South had no new opportunities to offer. Consequently, most blacks stayed where they had always been.

With Reconstruction came a few political and social rights. However, as many Americans are still learning, these changes rarely have immediate and appreciable impacts on gut matters—food, shelter, jobs, and wages. In practical life emancipation was replaced by the oppression of Jim Crow. Former slaves became sharecroppers and tenant farmers. The credit system and white domination of nonagricultural work, politics, and education guaranteed that the surplus value of black labor would continue to sustain Southern landowners. This system continued without threat until the advent of World War I.

The War Periods

The war itself did not produce a mass migration from the South; there were other "push" factors. The boll weevil economically destroyed many cotton farmers and with them the systems of tenancy. Blacks had to look elsewhere for work. At the same time, political and social repression was on the rise, and the North provided an opportunity to escape the yoke of Southern racism.

The drain of workers caused by the war and the reduction in immigration from Southern and Eastern Europe produced a need for labor in the North. The need was so acute that labor recruiters often solicited Southern blacks to migrate. Once relocated, the problem of housing became acute. Northern blacks were segregated as much by class as by race and occupied the same areas as poor whites. They, like the immigrants from Italy, Greece, Poland, and other Eastern European countries, lived near the areas that provided work. Southern blacks also settled in areas occupied by their Northern counterparts. Soon these became black areas which migrants increasingly sought because they knew people would help them find housing and acclimate to the new area. Later, as European xenophobia and ethnocentrism were transformed into American racism, the mixed areas began to cleave along racial lines. This separation was intensified and institutionalized by the business practices of a growing, professionalized community of realtors. As all-black areas grew and became more common, the belief increased that residential integration was a dangerous economic threat to white communities. In response to black "infiltration," whites formed neighborhood protective associations and used restrictive covenants as mechanisms for excluding blacks. Covenants took many forms. However, their intent was clear and usually they read something like this:

no persons of any race other than ——— (race to be inserted) shall use or occupy any building or any lot, except that this covenant shall not prevent occupancy by domestic servants of a different race domiciled with an owner or tenant. . . . Hereafter no part of said property or any portion thereof shall be . . . occupied by any person not of the Caucasian race, it being intended hereby to restrict the use of said property . . . against the occupancy as owners or tenants of any portion of said property for resident or other purpose by people of the Negro or Mongolian race.

Covenants contributed to housing shortages for those most in need: the domestic poor, foreign-born laborers, and, most acutely, racial minorities.

The Federal Housing Administration (FHA) was created in 1934 to increase opportunities for the 30 percent of the country that lived in low-quality housing. According to Abrams (1955), Helper (1969), and the U.S. Commission on Civil Rights (1973:4–8), the new agency was influenced by older housing interests and staffed by representatives from the real estate industry. This led to the unhappy situation in which the racial values and practices of realtors became incorporated into federal housing policy. Realtors had institutionalized society's racism into the guiding principles of their professional conduct. The National Association of Real Estate Brokers (NAREB) articulated into its Code of Ethics the widely held idea that property values go down when blacks move into a neighborhood. Article 5 of the Code reads: "A Realtor should not be instrumental in introducing into a neighborhood a character of property or use which will clearly be detrimental to property values in that neighborhood." As Helper notes, to get the full impact of the article one must realize it was amended to that wording in 1950. From 1924 to 1950, it was Article 34 of Part III, "Relations to Customers and the Public" and read: "A Realtor should never be instrumental in introducing into a neighborhood a character of property or occupancy, members of any race or nationality, or any individuals whose presence will clearly be detrimental to property values in that neighborhood." When these statements are viewed in relation to the FHA's *Underwriters Manual* (1938), which states that "If a neighborhood is to retain stability it is necessary that properties shall continue to be occupied by the same social and racial classes," the ideology and domain assumptions of the real estate industry spreading to the government process are evident. In 1955, the *Manual* was revised, and race is not mentioned. However, "resident's homogeneity and compatibility" were stressed as desirable (Helper 1969, 201–23).

By 1940 a variety of factors had coalesced to form a foundation for racially separate communities in the North: the housing decisions of early black migrants; the transformation of Eastern and Southern European ethnocentrism to include racism; the normal business practices of realtors, restrictive covenants, and neighborhood protective agreements; and the shaping of federal housing policy by the ideology of the real estate industry. To these we can add the effects of rapid social change as the result of twelve million blacks moving into the cities of the Northeast and North Central United States between 1910–40. This wave of migration produced economic, social, educational, and political uncertainties in the receiving cities. A new fear emerged in the North as whites struggled to come to grips with changing realities of neighborhoods, jobs, and school. The anxiety often resulted in violence (Van der Zanden 1966:202–26; *Report of the National Advisory Commission on Civil Disorders* 1968:218–35) and nascent patterns of racial separation were reinforced by a mix of fear, frustration, and conflict.

These anxieties, uncertainties, and the social structures that maintained them, would grow from 1940–60 as an additional seventeen million blacks came to the cities of the North and West. Gunnar Myrdal (1944) described the social structure of the times as reflecting an American dilemma. Specifically, race relations mirrored a perplexing clash between the equalitarian values of the society and a deeply embedded institutional racism. Industrial growth, the curtailment of immigration, and the drain on workers by World War II again produced an acute need for labor. Large numbers of blacks responded. Their arrival exacerbated a housing shortage that had started with World War I, grew during the depression, and become chronic in the 1940s. To the shortage, a pattern of racial succession was added. In Northern and Western industrial cities when a few blacks moved into adjacent white areas (often as a result of blockbusting activities), their presence catalyzed white flight. Rapidly, white neighborhoods were transformed into black areas. This pattern was typical, and the black pile-up in central cities resulted in the intense growth of the modern black ghettos (Duncan and Duncan 1957; Taeuber and Taeuber 1965; Clark 1965; *Report of the National Advisory Committee on Civil Disorders* 1968).

The ghettos were not only an ecological, social arrangement, but also a political one. Blacks leaving the South had hoped for a better life in the North. They sought economic mobility and new opportunities for their children. It was not long before their hopes dimmed in the reality of the ghetto. At night, the black professional, the white-collar worker, and the laborer all came home to the ghetto. At this time one could not work his or her way out of being black: doctors, lawyers, accountants, and laborers lived in black neighborhoods. Politically, this arrangement had several unintended consequences. A large number of blacks were concentrated around the central cities in the metropolitan areas of the North and West. There was a growth of black racial awareness, that is, a realization that barriers were based on race, not economics or lack of achievement. A substantial number of educated black leaders also lived in the ghetto communities. From the standpoint of a social movement, numbers, awareness of an issue, rising frustrations, and leadership were all present in dozens of larger cities—the crucibles from which black political power and the black revolt would flow.

The shortage of black housing intensified after World War II. Returning veterans, assisted by the VA mortgage program, demanded new, single-family dwellings. As their families grew, the demand increased for uncrowded housing located away from the central cities. This new market of buyers fueled a boom in housing. However, it was one largely restricted to whites. For blacks the situation was different: their population was increasing but less housing was available. The initial result was increased density in black areas. As Taeuber and Taeuber (1965) have shown, racial succession depends on increasing blacks and decreasing whites in the central cities.

Postwar Decline in Levels of Segregation

The situation began to change in the 1960s; gradual decline began in segregation indices for most major black cities (table 14.2). Taeuber's (1987) analysis of the data for 1970 and 1980 shows a general decline in segregation measures for these cities. Taeuber uses an index of dissimilarity to describe the changes; he assumes that race is not related to choice of residence and that blacks will be distributed in each block in proportion to their representation in the city as a whole. When this condition prevails, the segregation index is zero. If whites and blacks live in completely segregated blocks, the index is 100. The value of the index is that it indicates what percentage of black residents would have to change the block on which they live for unsegregated distribution to occur (Taeuber and Taeuber 1965:27–30; cf. Cortese, Falk, and Cohen 1976; Taeuber and Taeuber 1976; Duncan and Duncan 1955; Jahn, Schmid, and Schrag 1947). The average score for all cities in 1970 was 87, and it dropped to 81 in 1980. Twenty-one of the cities experienced a drop of more than 2 points. Several others, for example, Dallas, Houston, Richmond, Columbus, Gary, and Oakland fell by 10 points or more. When trends were examined for 109 cities from 1940–80, the mean segregation indices showed segregation went down from 85 in 1940 to 82 in 1970, and then an index of 76 in 1980 for all 109 cities.

These data further substantiate the general tendency toward declining segregation in large cities. Taeuber's (1987) analysis of thirty-eight metropolitan areas showed similar results. Thirty-six had lower segregation scores in 1980 than in 1970. The average decline was 9 points. The greatest reductions were in the South and West, the lowest were in Northern areas with large numbers of blacks. Southern declines are interesting and reflect a variety of factors. Older Southern cities are less segregated than newer ones. The paternalistic pattern of the Old South does not require spatial separation to maintain social distance. However, if paternalistic patterns give way to a competitive

TABLE 14.2.   Residential Segregation Measures for Cities with Black Population of 100,000 or More

City	Segregation Index of Dissimilarity			Percent Black
	1960	1970	1980	1980
New York	79	77	75	25
Chicago	92	93	92	40
Detroit	89	82	73	63
Philadelphia	89	84	88	38
Los Angeles	84	90	81	17
Washington	80	79	79	70
Houston	92	93	81	28
Baltimore	91	89	86	55
New Orleans	85	84	76	55
Memphis	86	92	85	48
Atlanta	92	92	86	67
Dallas	88	96	83	29
Cleveland	91	90	91	44
St. Louis	93	90	90	46
Newark	77	76	76	58
Oakland	81	70	59	47
Birmingham	89	92	85	56
Indianapolis	91	90	83	22
Milwaukee	92	88	80	23
Jacksonville	95	94	82	25
Cincinnati	91	84	79	34
Boston	86	84	80	22
Columbus	89	86	75	22
Kansas City	92	90	86	27
Richmond	92	91	79	51
Gary	94	84	68	71
		90	80	23

Sources: Data for 1960 are from Karl E. Taeuber and Alma F. Taeuber, *Negroes in Cities: Residential Segregation and Neighborhood Change* (1965); data for 1970–80 are from Karl Taeuber, "Residence and Race, 1619 to 2037" (1988).

race relations model, as in the newer cities, then neighborhood segregation becomes an important factor for maintaining social separation (van den Berghe 1967; Roof, Van Valley, and Spain 1976). This difference between old and new cities is also reflected in white attitudes toward blacks. Middleton (1976) has shown that racial prejudice scores are higher in the old Confederate states than either the Southern border states or the South as a whole. Certainly the subculture of Southern racism persists and still makes the region distinct. Given these attitudes it is clear that the lower rates of segregation in some old Confederate cities (Memphis and New Orleans) reported by Taeuber (1965) must be due to other factors. The old pattern of "back-yard" separation is still found in some metropolitan areas of the South. While it is quite prevalent in the cities of the Old South, it is not entirely absent from the newer ones. Additional black gains in education, jobs, and income, for most of the last twenty years, has been slower in the South. Economic competition is more frequently found in the newer cities, but it coexists with a strong traditional pattern of racial separation. Consequently, spatial segregation does not have the same social significance in the South as it does in the North. This does not mean that segregation is not high, for it is, with the D higher in many Southern cities than in other cities up to 1970.

In the North, neighborhood segregation is fundamental for maintaining social distance. Black advances in education, income, and occupations increase the competition for status; neighborhood, rather than etiquette or tradition, becomes the bulwark for maintaining social distance. Taeuber's insights on the cities of the North is illustrated dramatically when he observes (1988:16) that "the Milwaukee area was the second most racially segregated area in the United States—less than one-half of 1 percent of the suburban Milwaukee population was black in 1980."

The only place that had a lower percentage of blacks living in the suburbs was in Lake and Porter counties, Indiana. The distribution of the black population in northwest Indiana is 125,000 in the central city areas and only 909 in the suburbs. The 1980 census shows that the population of Lake and Porter counties, less Gary, Hammond, and East Chicago, was 357,322. Divide that into the 909 suburban blacks and one has a suburban population about one-fourth of 1 percent black. This makes northwest Indiana one of the most highly segregated areas in the country. The second part of this chapter explores the case of Gary and Lake County, Indiana, and identifies the mechanism through which the pattern of separation is maintained. Such a case study is an example of the U.S. process of segregation, one fairly different from the process in Europe.

The Dynamics of Ghettoization

Three traditional explanations of racial separation exist in housing. One favors economic factors; blacks and other minorities are separated from whites because of differences in wealth and income. Advocates maintain minorities lack the necessary assets to purchase and maintain housing in white areas. Others say racial separation is a result of culture and personal preference. Specifically, blacks and whites live in separate communities because they have distinctive ways of life and prefer to be among those most like themselves. A third explanation views separation as a result of an institutionalized system of discrimination by home-owners, realtors, mortgage banks, and others. In this account, the real estate industry is believed to have incorporated racially biased practices into normal business routines. Examples are redlining by banks and insurance companies, discriminatory housing policies of the federal government, differential advertising, and steering by realtors.

Institutional Factors

Blacks, although increasing in number, have been unable to break out of the ghetto due to institutional factors, that is, the real estate industry's discriminatory practices, especially those related to buying property. The real estate industry consists of builders, realtors, appraisers, insurance companies, lending institutions (government and conventional), mortgage bankers (secondary market), buyers, and sellers. As an institution, the industry has established a set of practices which define proper, legitimate, and expected ways of doing business in order for each element to reach its goal or desired end. This institution exists in a system of laws and regulations which defines its relationship to the society as a whole.

The focus herein is on realtors and lending institutions and their relationships to buyers and sellers. The concern is with how these relationships contribute to racial and ethnic separation. Traditionally, Americans depend on private industry to meet housing needs. The housing industry has long operated on the assumption "that residential segregation is a business necessity and a moral absolute" (U.S. Commission on Civil Rights 1973:3). The foundation for this belief originated in part from the industry itself; federal, state, and local governments have historically contributed to this widely held perception.

Contemporary manifestations of the exclusionary practices of realtors and lending institutions are called redlining, which exists when "there is a lack of activity on the part of an insurance company or a lender to extend credit or coverage to certain urban neighborhoods because of their racial composition, the annual change in racial composition and the age of structures in a neighborhood regardless of the credit worthiness or insurability of the potential buyer and policy holder or the condition of the individual property" (Hutchinson, Ostas, and Reed 1977:463). In addition, insurance companies redline by cost of coverage, by requiring inspections in some locations and not others, and by selective placement of agents. Redlining by mortgagees takes the form of higher down payments for similar ventures in different neighborhoods, higher interest rates with shorter periods of maturation in some areas, refusing to make loans below a particular amount, and applying more rigid structural standards than used on comparable properties in other neighborhoods. When these practices become part of normal business routine, the socioeconomic characteristics of the targeted area change. Substantial disinvestment by conventional lenders, accompanied by FHA/VA domination of the market, often leads to decline in housing stock and quality of neighborhood life.

Steering blacks and whites into different neighborhoods is a form of discrimination used by realtors. Other practices are those which sustain racial zoning, the use of sub rosa racial covenants, and the exclusion of black realtors from all multiple listing services and real estate boards except those serving black or minority areas.

Federal Nondiscriminatory Policies

Significant federal actions did not challenge these practices until 1962, when President John F. Kennedy issued an Executive Order directing federal departments and agencies to prevent discrimination in sale, lease, or occupancy of federally supported residential property. Although laudable for its goals, the impact of the order was limited. It did not extend to conventional loans and covered only FHA and VA loans issued after 1962. Thus, all previously existing housing units under FHA and VA financing were immune to the nondiscrimination mandate.

Although Kennedy's Executive Order covered only 1 percent of the nation's housing stock, a similar infelicity affected Title VI of the 1964 Civil Rights Act. Title VI prohibited discrimination in any program receiving financial assistance from the federal government. However, conventional loans and previously closed federal loans were excluded. The impact of Title VI was limited to only .5 percent of the nation's housing stock. More comprehensive coverage came under Title VIII of the 1968 Civil Rights Act, which prohibited discriminatory practices by all real estate brokers, builders, and mortgage lenders. Under Title VIII, 80 percent of the nation's housing came under the Federal Fair Housing Law (U.S. Commission on Civil Rights 1973:6).

Each title has different penalties and mechanisms of enforcement. Title VI and Kennedy's Executive Order carry substantial penalties for violation but cover only a small proportion of the housing stock. Title VIII has broad applications but weaker enforcement practices (litigation and voluntary compliance), and HUD has not used financial leverage to assure compliance (U.S. Commission on Civil Rights 1973:6). Enforcement of Title VIII by HUD is based on housing complaints. Because of a backlog (five months in 1972, two years in 1980), HUD refers complaints to state and local civil rights agencies for investigation. Fair housing laws have produced change in the written ideology of realtors. A recent Code of Ethics included a nondiscriminatory clause; Article 10 reads: "The REALTOR shall not deny equal professional services to any person for reasons of race, creed, sex, or country of national origin. The REALTOR shall not be a party to any plan or agreement to discriminate against a person or persons on the basis of race, creed, sex or country of national origin" (National Association of Realtors 1979).

In May 1972, realtors developed the "Code for Equal Opportunity in Housing" to demonstrate publicly their commitment to open housing. An affirmative marketing agreement between HUD and realtors mandating changes in advertising, office procedures, and training of personnel was developed in November 1975. The voluntary nature of this agreement, and the fact it is primarily used for realtors found culpable of steering, limits its impact.

The Ghettoization of Gary, Indiana

This investigation begins with a color-blind analysis of Lake County, Indiana, a method that allows computation of what the distribution of blacks would be if income alone determined where they lived. More than 99 percent of Lake County blacks live in Gary, East Chicago, and Hammond. The color-blind approach starkly reveals a minority market economically qualified for housing outside central cities. The extent to which this distribution is a product of personal choice or the normal business practices of the housing industry is then considered. Consequences of exclusion are discussed in the concluding section.

The Area and Its People

Lake County is located on the southern shore of Lake Michigan and borders the Chicago metropolitan area. It is a heavily industrial region

TABLE 14.3.   Black Population of Lake County Indiana by Cities and Towns (1970–80)

Lake County City or Town	Percent Black 1970	Number Black 1970	Percent Black 1980	Number Black 1980
Gary	52.8	92,695	70.8	107,644
Hammond	4.3	4,677	6.4	5,995
East Chicago	27.4	12,881	29.7	11,802
Remainder of Lake County	.8	1,761	.2	610
Whiting	0	1	0	0
Munster	.1	10	.1	23
Highland	0	2	.1	29
Griffith	.7	79	.2	28
Lake Station	.5	54	0	3
Hobart	0	12	2.0	43
New Chicago	0	0	1.7	56
Merrillville	Not Incorporated		.1	36
Schererville	0	0	1.7	36
St. John	0	0	0	0
Dyer	0	0	.2	16
Cedar Lake	0	2	0	1
Crown Point	0	0	0	0

Sources: U.S. Department of Commerce, Bureau of the Census, *Census of Population and Housing: Census Tracts—Gary, Hammond, East Chicago SMSA*, PHC (1)-79, 1970; U.S. Department of Commerce, Bureau of the Census, *Census of Population and Housing: Census Tracts—Gary, Hammond, East Chicago SMSA*, PHC 80-2-169, 1980.

that produced a substantial portion of the nation's steel and employed a large number of workers in oil refineries and other industries. Gary, at the hub, is a steel city. In 1900, when U.S. Steel selected it as a mill site, the township had only 1,408 residents. But the area grew quickly and men seeking work in the mills came from every walk of life. By 1910 most of the labor force was Eastern and Southern European immigrants; only a few blacks lived in Gary. However, as the result of intense labor recruiting, two world wars, strikes, and shifting opportunities for whites, the black population of the city grew substantially. In 1970 more than 50 percent of Gary was black and the city had a black mayor.

By the 1920s blacks and Eastern Europeans had shared the slums for a generation and experienced a minimum of tension and strife. However, political, social, and demographic changes coalesced to produce an increasingly wary, hostile, and racially separate city and county (table 14.3). A 1983 study of fair housing in northwest Indiana by the State Advisory Committee to the U.S. Commission on Civil Rights concluded that "The most obvious characteristic of these cities

TABLE 14.4.   Household Income for Lake County, Indiana
(1980)

Categories (in $)	Total	White	Black	Proportion
5,000	20,252	11,756	8,496	.4195
5,000–7,499	10,131	6,964	3,167	.3126
7,500–9,999	9,034	6,550	2,484	.2749
10,000–14,999	17,831	13,547	4,284	.2402
15,000–19,999	20,308	15,458	4,850	.2388
20,000–24,999	24,573	19,801	4,772	.1942
25,000–34,999	36,517	30,296	6,221	.1704
35,000–49,999	21,922	17,912	4,010	.1829
50,000+	8,803	7,672	1,131	.1285

and towns in Northwest Indiana is the almost total separation of black and white populations" (3). Table 14.3 demonstrates the extent of separation; the suburbs had a very low black population.

Color-blind Housing Market

The following analysis of Lake County is based on a method developed by Raymond E. Zelder (1968, 1970). Zelder postulates that in a color-blind housing market the distribution of blacks per census tract within an area should be equal to their distribution by income group for the area as a whole. One applies this method to the income distribution of blacks and whites within a specific area (county or city). Then the proportionate distribution of black families by income can be computed (table 14.4).

We next postulate that in a color-blind market, blacks will live in communities in proportion to their economic similarities to white residents. To the distribution of white families by income in an area such as Crown Point or Merrillville we apply the areawide proportion of blacks by income. This yields the number of black households we could expect in those communities if only income determined area of residence. The expected figure is then compared with actual numbers of blacks in the area to determine over- or under-representation. The results of this analysis for 1970–80 are reported in table 14.5. The analysis shows that blacks are overwhelmingly found in Gary and East Chicago. In 1970, almost 71 percent more blacks lived in Gary than one would expect based on income characteristics of white Gary residents. By 1980, this trend had intensified. During the intercensal period Gary's population declined from 175,415 to 151,593, a 13.4

TABLE 14.5.   Color-Blind Analysis of Lake
County (1970–80)

Community or Town	1970	1980
Crown Point	− 24.3	− 32.1
East Chicago	27.4	26.4
Gary	70.6	82.6
Griffith	− 20.5	− 31.9
Hammond	− 21.9	− 29.5
Highland	− 20.3	− 30.1
Hobart	− 22.7	− 32.8
Lake Station	− 28.7	− 33.9
Merrillville	− 20.6	− 32.2
Munster	− 19.0	− 28.7
Schererville	− 23.0	− 30.4
Remainder of Lake County	− 24.9	− 33.6

Note: Negative numbers indicate the percent of black under-
representation; positive ones the amount of black overrepresentation.

percent loss. However, the black population increased by 16 percent,
whereas whites declined by 53 percent. These racial shifts accompanied by rapid housing development in South Lake County, Schererville, Merrillville, and Munster intensified the pattern of racial segregation noted in 1970.

While blacks live disproportionately in the hub cities of East Chicago and Gary, they are underrepresented substantially in the other
cities and towns of the county. If income alone determined residence,
one would expect that Crown Point, with a population of 16,455, to
be approximately 32 percent black. Instead of 5,266 blacks, there were
only 158 according to the 1980 census. This is even more remarkable
when one learns that 152 of these people were in the county jail and
the convalescent home, which are located at the northern boundary
of the city. The same is the case for all of the other cities and communities of the region. Of the 5,933 economically eligible blacks, only
twenty-three actually lived in Munster in 1980; only thirty-six lived in
Merrillville. While these data support the previously observed pattern
of racial segregation (e.g., State Advisory Committee to the U.S.
Commission on Civil Rights 1983; Taeuber 1987a, 1987b), they clearly
reveal that differentials in income do not explain it.

The foregoing analysis demonstrates that racial separation in housing is not the result of economic differences. Many believe that differences in cultures and preferences of whites and blacks lead to self-

selected segregation. That is, racial separation results from a desire to live with one's co-ethnics, regardless of differences in social class. Segregation results from the value people place on living with those who are racially and culturally most like themselves. If true, we have a powerful explanation for racially separate communities. [In the European studies in this volume, the cultural aspects were important in some cases but not in others.]

In Lake County separation is so pronounced one wonders if cultural preferences could be this strong. Studies of similarly segregated cities show a substantial portion of both whites and blacks would tolerate and be comfortable in more racially balanced communities (Farley, Bianchi, and Colasanto 1979:97–113; Saltman 1979; Lake 1979:441–46). In response to the question, "If a Negro, with just as much income and education as you have, moved into your block, would it make a difference to you?," the responses of national samples of whites was clear. Those not objecting to a black neighbor increased from 35–72 percent between 1942 and 1968. Responses in 1968 from fifteen key cities to the same question showed a similar openness. Fully 49 percent of whites sampled would not mind "at all" having a black neighbor. This subsample is composed of residents of cities not in the South and with large black populations: Baltimore, Boston, Chicago, Cincinnati, Cleveland, Detroit, Gary, Milwaukee, Newark, New York, Philadelphia, Pittsburgh, St. Louis, and Washington, D.C. (Pettigrew 1973:21–53). Furthermore, 62 percent of white respondents in these cities felt "blacks have a right to live wherever they can afford, just like whites." White attitudes are one side of the issue; what about black willingness to live in integrated settings? Blacks in the same cities were asked, "Would you personally prefer to live in a neighborhood with all negroes, mostly negroes, mostly whites, or a neighborhood that is mixed half and half?" They responded as follows: fewer than 13 percent chose all or mostly black neighborhoods, and only 1 percent selected mostly white neighborhoods, but 48 percent favored the half-and-half arrangement. For Detroit, 74 percent preferred the mixed neighborhood (Pettigrew 1973:21–51). A later study of Detroit (Farley, Bianchi, and Colasanto 1979:97–113) found 83 percent of blacks interviewed favored a 50–50 racial mix. Whites were generally not as accepting of this arrangement. The Detroit data show 44 percent of white respondents would be "somewhat to very comfortable" in a neighborhood composed of five black families for every nine white. Twenty-six percent of whites reported the same response for neighborhoods with eight black families per six white. These data suggest that whites and blacks are becoming less resistant to integrated neighborhoods.

Other research shows blacks and whites make housing decisions along similar lines. Both are property and status conscious. Concern for property values, school quality, and their children's peers and possible mates are major considerations. Similar reasons were also given for changing homes. Robert Lake (1979) found that 20 percent of both groups moved for job-related reasons, 30 percent because homes were too small, and another 33 percent due to a change in life-cycle. For both, the suburban move was motivated by a desire for home ownership. Location and accessibility to place of work were also important, but internal neighborhood characteristics such as schools, recreational facilities, and community status predominate for blacks. Whites give more weight to an easy commute (Lake 1979:441–46). The importance of schools is great for both races, and each is willing to travel greater distances for jobs, shopping, and recreation to insure acceptable schooling for their children.

These studies suggest that the racial separation typical of Lake County is not maintained by black preferences. In addition, whites are becoming more open to integrated neighborhoods when blacks are of similar class and educational backgrounds. However, these changes in attitude may not be as typical for northwestern Indiana as they are for other similar Midwestern minority cities.

Gary is, in many ways, unique. U.S. Steel's concern was profit, not community planning. U.S. Steel and the Gary Land Company were initially active in housing production. The needs and philosophy of the corporation quickly divided the new town; on the north side were the scenic communities of the business and skilled classes, while the "other Gary" was inhabited by unskilled immigrants and blacks (Lane 1978:34–37). Blacks were among the builders of the mill and town, but did not arrive in large numbers until World War I; before then Eastern and Southern Europeans were the main labor force. During World War I, as a result of Southern labor recruiting and the closing off of immigration, blacks increased substantially in number and as a proportion of the population.

At first, blacks were simply another ethnic group to the Europeans. Although no rigid color line prevailed, ethnic groups were separated by language, culture, and strong ethnocentric feelings. However, racism did not evolve spontaneously from European ethnocentrism, it was fueled by Gary's business and government elite. As early as 1909 they sponsored "clean out the Negro campaigns" to keep "worthless" and "jobless" Negroes away from the city (Betten and Mohl 1974:53–55) and taught immigrants (through the press, public announcements, and example) that being a true American involved accepting segregation and the subordination of blacks. Thus ethnocentrism began to be transformed into racism (Lane 1978:69–72; Betten and Mohl 1974:53). Political and economic leaders, almost without resistance, established a pervasive pattern of segregation in Gary. Schools, parks, recreational areas, stores, communities, churches, buses, YMCAS, restaurants, and even cemeteries conformed to the pattern. With help from government and U.S. Steel, realtors eventually ghettoized Gary. White realtors refused to sell blacks homes outside of the central city. U.S. Steel built only segregated housing, and private sales to white owners carried deeds with restrictive covenants. Even the federal housing projects begun in 1930 would remain racially segregated until 1957 (Betten and Mohl 1974:57–58; Lane 1978:278–82; Brook 1975:35–45). Such practices not only established a dual housing market, but also one in which 60 percent of black housing lacked bathrooms or hot water.

Betten and Mohl concluded that by World War II Gary had a clearly defined black ghetto with segregated services and overt discrimination—all with the support and blessing of local government. Area politicians developed municipal policies and realty codes that buttressed racial segregation. Opinion leaders preached racial inferiority, reinforced it by example, and inculcated these values and practices into the Americanization of immigrants (Betten and Mohl 1974:60–64). This produced and sustained the pattern of misunderstanding, hostility, and resentment that Michael Novak so forcefully presents in *The Rise of the Unmeltable Ethnics* (1972).

The growth of the black population and their ghettoization in the central cities of Lake County has continued unabated from the 1950s to the 1980s. As previously noted, from 1970–80 white flight intensified from the central cities of Lake County. The white population of Gary declined and black population increased, as was the case for other hub cities. Hammond lost 10,021 whites (18.4 percent of the population) and grew from in-migration of both black and Hispanic residents. The white population of East Chicago dropped by almost 16,000, a 46 percent decline. At the same time all other towns and communities in Lake County had fewer than 1 percent black residents, and most had experienced substantial population growth (Bureau of the Census 1980).

The ghettoization of Gary was accompanied by white anger and resentment. As a former resident of Gary's Glen Park area who was selling and moving away stated, "You work all your life for somethin, and then they start movin' in and suddenly you don't have anything— it's not yours anymore. First person that makes me any kind of half-ass offer on that house now, it's his and I'm gone. With one exception—I'm not sellin' to no goddam colored, I'd put a torch to it first" (Frady 1969:40).

An ethnic woman expressed another dimension: one of questioning anxiety and uncertainty based either on xenophobia or racism.

Mr. Hatcher, We are a big group of women, who would like to know a few answers. . . . We have nothing against colored people but we would not like to have them live next door to us. Yet it seems that the colored people are always pushing. . . . Please can you explain to us why the black people want to be near us when we don't want them deep from our hearts and never will. . . . God give them strength and let each one of the colored realize that we have nothing against them or ever to do them any harm. We just don't want them to try to mingle with us. . . . Again please answer our questions. Thank you. God Bless You. (Frady 1969:41).

In 1974, important stores in downtown Gary closed their doors, among them Sears, Radigan's, a large furniture store, W. T. Grant, and Gordon's Department Store. The Holiday Inn across the City Hall closed in 1975. Native-born white realtor Daniel W. Barrick expressed the feelings of some whites when he observed that "it seems like everyone wants to leave. I feel like an outcast in my own hometown. I don't want to live here. I don't like working here. And most of all, I feel that they don't want me here" (Lane 1978:303).

Blacks' desire for improved housing, schools, and community services has been consistent throughout the 1980s. Different polls report better than two-thirds desire more integrated housing or a balanced racial community. Their goals are the services, schools, and opportunities that such housing brings (Crile 1970; Weisman 1974; Allen 1975; *Post-Tribune* 1985). With integration comes a better quality of life.

Whites are now more reluctant to leave their neighborhoods when blacks move in. Having borne the financial penalties of flight once, they are less willing to leave as a few black families appear. Most stay to maintain property values, rather than out of egalitarian beliefs (Allen 1975). Thus blacks' desire for improved chances may coalesce with whites' desire to avoid financial loss. There is little doubt that the symbiosis will initially be hostile. However, attitudes of blacks and whites have changed and become more accepting over the years; there is reason to hope that initial hostility will give way to a sense of community.

In Gary institutional factors, that is, discrimination of realtors, lending institutions, and builders, have kept segregation alive. Federal laws that try to end such practices have already been described. The effects of Title VIII on Gary and Lake County will be explored using the summary report of the Indiana Committee on Civil Rights (1983) and the records of the Northwest Indiana Open Housing Center to assess the extent, type, and disposition of cases in response to fair housing laws.

Complaints of discrimination in housing can originate from several sources. Individuals can file a report with a Human Relations Commission. In areas without a commission, residents may go to the Northwest Indiana Open Housing Center, the state's Civil Rights Commission, or the director of Fair Housing and Equal Opportunity (HUD, Region V, Chicago). There are only three Human Relations Commissions in Lake County, those in Gary, Hammond, and East Chicago. Towns and communities with fewer than 1 percent black population have no mechanism for filing fair housing complaints. Crown Point, for example, has no commission, no written complaint process, no ordinance to deal with discrimination in housing, and almost no black residents. While it grew by 5,524 people between 1970–80 only six were black. The mayor contended that "fair housing isn't a problem in this city" (Indiana Advisory Committee to the U.S. Commission on Civil Rights 1983:11). Likewise, Merrillville grew by 1,700 residents between 1970–80, but blacks declined from sixty-seven to thirty-six during the period. Merrillville had no formal complaint procedures and no ordinance prohibiting discrimination. Therefore, no complaints were filed for violation of the state's Fair Housing Law. Many take this lack of complaint, due to no mechanism, to mean no problem. However, absence of complaints does not indicate lack of steering or other forms of discrimination. In a four-part series, "The Racial Makeup of the Suburbs" (Allen 1975), two area realtors were interviewed. Broker John Mangos stated, "If I sold a black a home in Merrillville, I'd be on the ——— list with everybody"; Phil Ensalaco observed that "I think there could be economic reprisals against realtors [if they sold to blacks]."

In Hobart, absence of complaints was again taken as absence of discrimination. However, a Hobart official stated to a *Post-Tribune* reporter that real estate people likely resisted selling property to blacks. "They know what people in Hobart want. I would hate to be the first realtor [sic] to have one move in . . . [a black family] wouldn't be welcomed with open arms in Hobart" (Allen 1975). By implication neither would the realtor who sold them a home.

Schererville had the largest growth rate of any municipality in Indiana between 1970 and 1980. Population grew by 261 percent from 1970 to 1980—a net gain of 9,546 residents, thirty-six of whom were black. The town manager reported no awareness of housing discrimination, but no mechanisms existed for complaints to be received or processed (Indiana Advisory Committee to the U.S. Commission on Civil Rights 1983:14–16).

Complaints from Lake County residents to state and federal agencies are few (Indiana Advisory Committee to the U.S. Commission on Civil Rights 1983:18–19). However, the Northwest Indiana Open Housing Center received and investigated more than 160 complaints from 1980–85. The majority were settled between parties, but several resulted in court cases. These are analyzed and discussed in the following section.

Purposive Sampling of Northwest Indiana Housing Complaints and Their Dispositions

The cases for this analysis are from the Northwest Indiana Open Housing Center (NWIOHC) located in Gary. The NWIOHC is one of four local agencies which processes and litigates housing discrimination complaints in the region. The others are the Hammond Human Relations Commission (HHRC), the East Chicago Human Rights Commission (ECHRC), and the Gary Human Relations Commission (GHRC). Each HRC only has jurisdiction within its boundaries. The Open Housing Center has wider jurisdiction and often takes cases from the area HRCS.

A total of thirty-three files were reviewed from NWIOHC. Approximately 53 percent of the complaints were related to refusal to rent or sell property to individuals; black females were the most affected subgroup. Eviction (14.7 percent), racial violence (17.6 percent), and foreclosures or mortgage or breach of purchase agreement (14.7 percent) were near equal in occurrence. The largest percentage of complaints were filed by black and interracial families, followed by single black females. From the thirty-three files reviewed, only two complaints were filed by whites, both of whom were female. One of these

TABLE 14.6.   Disposition of Housing Complaint
Cases, Lake County

Disposition	Federal Court[1]	Agency[2]	Total
Favorable[3]	10	4	14
Lost	4	0	4
Pending[4]	4	7	11
Withdrawn[5]	0	4	4
Total	18	15	33

1. "Federal Court" includes all cases which were filed in federal court. Not all cases were litigated; negotiated settlements occurred more often than the issue of a final order based on the merits of the claim.

2. "Agency" includes all complaints with the NWIOHC and those cases in which the NWIOHC works with the Indiana Civil Rights Commission or other agencies.

3. "Favorable" includes all agreements, settlements, and final court orders.

4. "Pending" includes cases at various stages; some were filed more recently than others. Others were in the process of pretrial litigation activities, for example, deposition or recently filed complaints in federal court.

5. "Withdrawn" includes those claims where the complainant actually withdrew the complaint or in which the complainant failed to proceed further with the claim.

complaints alleged sexual discrimination. The limited sample indicates that the Lake County residents who seek assistance on discrimination are most often black families and black females. Few whites seek help. As seen in table 14.6, eighteen of the thirty-three cases were closed. Of the eighteen, fourteen (77.8 percent) were disposed of in favor of the complainant. Twelve of the fourteen favorable outcomes occurred through settlement, either before trial or during trial. It appears that the agencies are effective in finding agreeable solutions for their clients without having to proceed fully through trial.

The four cases in which complainants lost were all tried in federal court. In the first, the court found that the black female plaintiff was not entitled to damages because there had been no racial discrimination. The court found the plaintiff had a "bad attitude," was "rude and arrogant," and accordingly was determined by the defendant to be lacking in sincerity when she presented herself as a potential tenant.

In the second case, the actions of a white defendant accused of arson against the home of a black family in the predominantly white community of Hobart were found not to be racist in origin. An interesting and, to a sociologist, elusive principle underlies this decision. The white female plaintiffs in the other cases lost their plea because of a late filing (exceeding the 180-day limitation) under Title VIII.

TABLE 14.7.   Ratio of Conventional to Federally Insured Loans by Town and Year with Rank Ordering

Areas	1978 Ratio	1978 Rank	1979 Ratio	1979 Rank	1980 Ratio	1980 Rank
Cedar Lake	18.13	9	10.63	8	5.50	11
Crown Point	28.29	8	21.20	6	7.03	8
Dyer	14.78	10	14.50	7	6.36	9
East Chicago	5.51	16	3.87	14	3.06	14
Gary	.25	21	.25	19	.21	20
Griffith	6.69	15	6.59	12	2.24	16
Hammond	1.60	18	1.49	16	.93	18
Highland	9.76	12	6.91	11	5.90	10
Hobart	2.07	17	1.05	18	1.03	17
Lake Station	.88	19	1.17	17	.77	19
Lake Village	—	—	—	—	—	—
Le Roy	—	—	—	—	—	—
Lowell	.40	20	—	—	.10	21
Merrillville	12.00	11	8.86	9	3.83	13
Munster	146.00	1	87.50	3	11.86	4
New Chicago	7.00	13	4.13	13	4.50	12
North Haydon	—	—	—	—	8.00	7
St. John	95.00	4	122.50	2	51.30	2
Schererville	38.83	7	8.15	10	11.25	5
Schneider	77.00	6	—	—	—	—
Shelby	—	—	—	—	—	—
Whiting	6.92	14	3.38	15	2.89	15
Winfield	143.00	2	65.00	4	59.00	1
West Chicago/other	124.50	3	145.00	1	9.30	6
Calumet	93.00	5	51.00	5	30.00	3
Total Number Cities		21		19		21
Average per Year	2.83		2.12		1.62	

These data show that the agencies and laws have a significant effect on bringing about the goal of open housing. Of the adjudicated complaints, 77.8 percent resulted in favorable disposition for the complainants. Two of the four lost cases were halted because of procedural inadequacies and failure to meet statutory time limitations for filing.

Mortgage Lending in Gary and Lake County

The results of a study of mortgage lending activity for the City of Gary and twenty other Lake County communities for 1978–83 follows. Lending activity in the county was determined from three interrelated but independently maintained sets of data. Conventional lending activity was reported on the Home Mortgage Disclosure Statements (HMDA) by lending institutions doing business primarily in conven-

1981		1982		1983		Totals	
Ratio	Rank	Ratio	Rank	Ratio	Rank	Ratio	Rank
1.54	16	4.38	9	1.62	12	5.16	13
10.90	6	4.19	11	1.18	14	6.71	9
9.00	7	2.47	13	1.85	10	6.21	10
2.60	13	2.44	14	1.36	13	3.09	17
.31	19	.15	19	.14	21	.23	23
2.72	12	2.89	12	1.76	11	3.51	15
1.04	17	.98	18	.73	17	1.20	20
5.67	9	4.32	10	2.15	9	5.47	12
1.56	15	1.42	17	.37	20	1.22	19
.55	18	1.50	16	.43	19	.85	22
—	—	—	—	1.00	15	1.00	21
—	—	—	—	3.00	7	3.00	18
.05	20	—	—	—		.06	24
2.82	11	1.95	15	.58	18	4.20	14
25.00	3	7.33	6	5.75	6	18.22	6
4.00	10	5.00	8	8.00	5	5.68	11
—	—	—	—	—		8.00	8
109.00	1	12.70	3	14.33	3	49.86	4
5.88	8	9.09	4	2.54	8	9.13	7
—	—	—	—	—	—	77.00	3
—	—	—	—	—	—	—	—
2.00	14	5.60	7	.95	16	3.11	16
43.00	2	30.00	2	24.00	1	364.00	1
16.70	5	38.00	1	12.83	4	28.39	5
19.00	4	9.00	5	17.00	2	109.50	2
	20		19		21		24
1.56		1.63		.96		1.87	

tional loans. Federally insured loans (FHA/VA) were reported only in aggregate form or dump codes on the HMDA statements. To obtain a geographically useful description (by census tract or town) of activity in this lending market one must go beyond HMDA and examine the original records of the transactions, which are stored by the FHA and the VA at their regional offices in Indianapolis. Mortgages did not report the transactions by census tracts as mandated by the HMDA law; the FHA/VA offices accepted the statements with only addresses and towns reported. Therefore, all of the transactions had to be coded into appropriate census tracts. The final data set consisted of 23,502 cases, which represented all reported mortgage transactions for the period of interest in Lake County. Countywide, there were 15,316 conventional loans, 5,880 FHA loans, and 2,306 VA loans.

The data presented in table 14.7 are reported in ratio form and

rank order. The ratios express the number of conventional loans received per FHA or VA loan. For example, if a community has a ratio
of 5.51, they received five and one-half conventional loans for each
insured loan. A ratio of .25 would mean that for each insured loan
the community received only a quarter of a conventional loan, or one
conventional loan for every four insured loans. The community conventional loans/insured loans (c/I) ratios are rank-ordered in the last
column.

The ratios are interpreted as follows: the larger the number, the
higher the socioeconomic status (SES) of residents and the community
area. The smaller the number, the lower the SES of the community
and residents. This interpretation is consistent with the ethos of the
Housing and Urban Development Act of 1968, which guides the lending practices of the FHA and VA. The 1968 Act charged HUD with the
responsibility for directing programs toward older urban neighborhoods in an effort to provide home ownership for lower-income families. These loans require a lower level of financial assets, little status,
and small down-payment. They also provide lenders with 100 percent
insurance against loss on the transaction. One can see that the housing
market and class composition of a community are substantially affected by the types of mortgages it receives. Financial institutions have
a significant effect on the social and economic structure of a community by withdrawing conventional mortgages and replacing them with
federally insured financing (table 14.7). The data reflect a general
downward trend in conventional to insured loan ratios for all of Lake
County. The position of the City of Gary has remained relatively
unchanged over the six years. Gary is at the lower end and has not
fared better than twentieth out of the twenty-one communities.
Clearly the city is at a serious disadvantage in obtaining conventional
mortgages.

As observed, the pattern and type of mortgage affects the socioeconomic character of a community. Reluctance to provide conventional mortgages may set in play a process which in time redefines the
demographic and economic quality of community life. Such a process
can be described as (1) withdrawal of conventional loans leading to
(2) an increase in the number of insured loans, creating (3) changes
in the SES of an area, which can lead (4) to property deterioration and
(5) the decline of housing stock, creating (6) an area's povertization
and (7) a decline in property value, increased poverty, and social unrest.

This sequence has affected the quality of life in the metropolitan hub of Lake County. The City of Gary is well along in the cycle. Indeed, the c/I ratios for Gary suggest that it may well have completed one pass through the cycle and is experiencing a second. East Chicago has undergone some change in SES, but the process has not advanced beyond that. Hammond is at the beginning of the cycle and should make every effort to reverse the process before it negatively affects the quality of housing and community life. NWIOHC is taking an active role in reducing the rate of withdrawal of conventional mortgages from the hub cities. By early 1987 they had filed lawsuits against ten area banks; three have gone to trial, two were won by the Housing Center, and the remaining seven were pending.

Racial Separation and Housing Quality

Good evidence exists that economic differences between blacks and whites do not account for patterns of racial separation in Lake County or the United States (Taeuber and Taeuber 1965:78–95; Roof, Van Valley, and Spain 1976). Although money is not the reason, racial attitudes and the practices of the housing industry are important elements. Northwest Indiana is one of the most highly segregated areas in the United States. What consequences does segregation of this magnitude have on the region and the country as a whole?

Blacks and other minorities are overwhelmingly concentrated in central cities, a racial distribution that also reflects home ownership patterns. Nationwide, blacks owned 44 percent of the housing units that they occupied in 1975. The highest percentage of home ownership (49 percent) was in the South, and the lowest (29 percent) in the Northeast (Bureau of the Census 1979:137). In Lake County, blacks occupy 17 percent of owner-occupied housing, but 99.7 percent of these homes are in the hub cities. Hispanics account for 3 percent of owner-occupied housing, but 76 percent of their holdings are in Gary, Hammond, and East Chicago. Whites live in 80 percent of owner-occupied housing, but only 10.6 percent is in Gary, 4 percent in East Chicago, 22 percent in Hammond. Of the 94,290 white units, 59,780 (63.4 percent) are located out of the central cities.

Central city housing is the oldest in the country. Substandard units with inadequate plumbing, electrical problems, poor heating, and no air-conditioning abound. As flight and decline in the economic base increases, the number of abandoned and boarded up housing units give vivid testimony to the erosion of community. To reinforce the plight and difficulties of these towns and cities, investment dollars and new construction money is moving away. Nationwide, most new homes are built out of the central cities, a trend clearly evident in Lake County. Analysis of the 1970–80 period shows that 7,011 new, single-family dwelling units were built. Only 5.5 percent were in Gary, 1.2 percent in East Chicago, and 6.4 percent in Hammond; 86.9 percent of new constructions occurred outside these areas. Far southern Lake County accounts for 30 percent, and the towns of Merrillville, Munster, Shererville, and Crown Point another 39.1 percent.

Conventional mortgage financing has also moved away from central cities. In Lake County, for every four FHA/VA mortgages that came into Gary, only one conventional mortgage was made. This compares with approximately a 6:1 conventional to FHA/VA mortgage rate outside the metropolitan hub (Johnston 1985). Such patterns of investment feed the process of neighborhood decline and deterioration of housing stock.

While the open housing laws appear adequate to the needs of minorities in northwest Indiana, the absence of reporting mechanisms in the white communities where discrimination most frequently occurs often blunts their effectiveness. Minorities in hub cities continue to be poorly housed and live with its ramifications: poor schools, inadequate public services, rising crime and vandalism, and the deterioration of the spirit, mind, and self-image that accompany housing segregation. Lyndon Johnson (Ferman, Kornblum, and Haber 1965:422) graphically captured the meaning of this condition when he observed its consequences for those who must endure it:

> It means a daily struggle to secure the necessities for even a meager existence. It means that the abundance, the comforts, the opportunities they see all around them are beyond their grasp. Worst of all, it means hopelessness for the young. The young man or woman who grows up without a decent education, in a broken home, in a hostile and squalid environment, in ill health or in the face of racial injustice—that young man or woman is often trapped in a life of poverty.
>
> . . . He faces a mounting sense of despair which drains initiative and ambition and energy.

The human and social cost of segregation and the diminished life chances that accompany it are often plainly visible to travelers on the tollroad in Lake County. They, along with Anthony Brook (1975:51), can plainly see that "Gary never solved the old problem of reconciling profit with humanity." Unfortunately, this failure is still sadly typical of the country as a whole.

References

Abrams, Charles. 1955. *Forbidden Neighbors: A Study of Prejudice in Housing*. New York: Harper.

Allen, H. Linn. 1975. "Special Report: Racial Makeup of the Suburbs." *Post-Tribune* June 14–17.

Betten, Neil, and R. A. Mohl. 1974. "The Evolution of Racism in an Industrial City, 1906–1940: A Case Study of Gary, Indiana." *Journal of Negro History* 59:51–64.

Brook, Anthony. 1975. "Gary, Indiana: Steel Town Extraordinary." *Journal of American Studies* 9:35–53.

Clark, Kenneth B. 1965. *Dark Ghetto: Dilemmas of Social Power*. New York: Harper and Row.

Cortese, Charles F., Frank Falk, and Jack M. Cohen. 1976. "Further Considerations on the Methodological Analysis of Segregation Indices." *American Sociological Review* 41:630–37.

Crile, George. 1970. "Housing, Jobs Get Top Priority in Hatcher Administration." *Post-Tribune* August 27.

Duncan, Otis D., and Beverly Duncan. 1955. "A Methodological Analysis of Segregation Indices." *American Sociological Review* 20:210–17.

———. 1957. *The Negro Population of Chicago: A Study of Residential Succession*. Chicago: University of Chicago Press.

Farley, Reynolds, Howard Schuman, Suzanne Bianchi, Dianne Colasanto, and Shirley Hatchett. 1978. "Chocolate City, Vanilla Suburbs: Will the Trend Toward Racially Separate Communities Continue?" *Social Science Research* 7:319–44.

Farley, Reynolds, Suzanne Bianchi, and Dianne Colasanto. 1979. "Barriers to the Racial Integration of Neighborhoods: The Detroit Case." *Annals of the American Academy of Political and Social Sciences* 441:97–113.

Ferman, Louis A., Joyce L. Kornblum, and Alan Haber. 1965. *Poverty in America*. Ann Arbor: University of Michigan Press.

Frady, Marshall. 1969. "Gary, Indiana." *Harpers* 239:35–45.

Helper, Rose. 1969. *Racial Policies and Practices of Real Estate Brokers*. Minneapolis: University of Minnesota Press.

Hutchinson, Peter M., James R. Ostas, and J. D. Reed. 1977. "A Survey and Comparison of Redlining Influences in Urban Mortgage Lending Markets." *Journal of the American Real Estate and Urban Economics Association* 5:463–72.

Indiana Advisory Committee to the United States Commission on Civil Rights. 1983. *Fair Housing Enforcement in Northwest Indiana*. Washington, D.C.: U.S. Government Printing Office.

Jahn, Julian, Calvin F. Schmid, and Clarence Schrag. 1947. "The Measurement of Ecological Segregation." *American Sociological Review* 12:293–303.

Johnston, Barry V. 1985. "Patterns of Mortgage Lending in Lake County, Indiana 1976–1980." Unpublished report prepared for the Human Rights Commission and City of Hammond.

Lake, Robert. 1979. "Racial Transition and Black Ownership in American Suburbs." *Annals of the American Academy of Political and Social Sciences* 441:142–56.

Lane, James B. 1978. *City of the Century: A History of Gary, Indiana.* Bloomington: Indiana University Press.

Meddleton, Russel. 1976. "Regional Differences in Prejudice." *American Sociological Review* 41:94–116.

Myrdal, Gunnar. 1944. *An American Dilemma.* New York: Harper and Row.

National Association of Realtors. 1979. "What Everyone Should Know About Equal Opportunity in Housing." NAR: Chicago Pamphlet 111-799.

Novak, Michael. 1972. *The Rise of the Unmeltable Ethnics.* New York: Macmillan.

Pettigrew, Thomas. 1973. "Attitudes on Race and Housing: A Socialpsychological View." Pp. 21–84 in *Segregation in Residential Areas,* edited by Amos H. Hawley and V. P. Rock. Washington, D.C.: National Academy of Sciences.

Post-Tribune. 1985. "Expert States Housing Separation Not a Result of Choice." July 3.

Report of the National Advisory Commission on Civil Disorders. 1968. New York: Bantam Books.

Roof, Wade C., T. N. Van Valley, and Daphne Spain. 1976. "Residential Segregation in Southern Cities 1970." *Social Forces* 55:59–71.

Saltman, Juliet. 1979. "Housing Discrimination: Policy Research, Methods, and Results." *Annals of the American Academy of Political and Social Sciences* 441:186–96.

Taeuber, Karl A. 1987. Interview. *Post-Tribune* April 26:1 and 3.

———. 1988. "Residence and Race: 1619 to 2037." Working Paper 88-19. Madison: University of Wisconsin Center for Demography and Ecology.

Taeuber, Karl A., and A. F. Taeuber. 1965. *Negroes in Cities: Residential Segregation and Neighborhood Change.* Chicago: Aldine Publications.

———. 1976. "A Practitioner's Perspective on the Index of Dissimilarity." *American Sociological Review* 41:884–89.

U.S. Commission on Civil Rights. 1973. *Understanding Fair Housing.* Washington, D.C.: U.S. Government Printing Office.

U.S. Department of Commerce, Bureau of Census. 1970. *Census of Population and Housing: Census Tracts—Gary, Hammond, East Chicago SMSA.* Washington, D.C.: U.S. Government Printing Office.

———. 1979. *The Social and Economic Status of the Black Population in the United States: An Historical View, 1790–1978.* Washington, D.C.: U.S. Government Printing Office.

———. 1980. *Census of Population and Housing: Census Tracts—Gary, Ham-*

mond, East Chicago SMSA. Washington, D.C.: U.S. Government Printing Office.

Ven den Berghe, P. L. 1967. *Race and Racism.* New York: Wiley.

Van der Zanden, James W. 1966. *American Minority Relations.* 2nd Ed. New York: Ronald Press.

Weisman, Joel D. 1974. "Every Major Problem Seems More Acute in Gary." *Post-Tribune* December 2.

Zelder, Raymond E. 1968. "Racial Segregation in Urban Housing Markets." Unpublished paper presented at the University of Chicago Conference on Housing.

———. 1970. "Racial Segregation in Urban Housing Markets." *Journal of Regional Science* April:93–105.

15. Housing Segregation of Blacks in the South

Historical Background

In the South (Louisiana, Oklahoma, Virginia, Georgia, Kentucky, South and North Carolina, Alabama, Texas, Mississippi, the District of Columbia, Florida, Tennessee, Maryland, West Virginia, and Delaware), residential segregation—de jure and de facto separation of people's living quarters by some demographic feature like race (Lake 1981)—is a major fact of life. Its contemporary form is the result of a peculiar combination of personal ("push") and sociocultural ("pull") factors. Immediately after the Civil War, during Reconstruction and immediately thereafter, most blacks remained in the South and most were rural. Housing or residential segregation was obvious, but most blacks owned their own property. However, Pennick (1983) indicates that push factors accounted for black ownership of land in the South decreasing from more than fifteen million to fewer than four million acres since 1910. Specifically, blacks lost more than eleven million acres to whites during the past seventy years, a rate of more than 150 thousand acres per year. Pennick cites six of these push factors: (1) extreme white racism in the rural South; (2) blacks' ignorance of the inherent benefits of land ownership; (3) the failure of many blacks to make wills; (4) the inability of heirs to decide how to divide property; (5) delinquent tax payments; and (6) mortgage foreclosures.

The third push factor, the failure of many blacks in the South to make wills, needs some comment, for it caused their land to become heir property. (Heir property is an estate to which a number of surviving relatives are entitled, by default, when no will exists.) Who were heirs was a question the state laws decided. This brings up the fourth push factor, the inability of heirs to decide how to divide property. One disadvantage to owning heir property is that no heir has title to a specific piece of property, but only has a certain percentage of interest in the title to the whole property. The interest can be sold, but a specific piece of property cannot. This did not pose too much of a problem when there were only a few heirs and they could agree among themselves on how to divide the property.

However, when there were many heirs (or some died and their interests descended to their children and grandchildren), it became almost impossible to devise a plan with which everyone agreed. When heirs could not decide, any heir (or another person who had acquired an heir's interest) could petition the court to decide. The court could decide how the land was to be divided, but usually it decreed that a partition sale be held. This was an auction of the property at which anyone who had an heir's interest could buy more or all of the property, and the proceeds from the sale were divided among the heirs according to the interests held. Rarely did the sale bring what the property was really worth, and usually the property was bought by a white person or a group. In the case of the last two push factors, the failure of blacks to pay property taxes and mortgage foreclosures, there was always a white land speculator who was ready to take advantage of them.

Pull factors involved the attractiveness of urban areas. Immediately after the Civil War, there was considerable black migration to nearby Southern cities. Even though the subsequent great black urban migration, from the mid-1900s through the 1940s, was directed at Northern cities, at its peak in the 1970s, more than half of all blacks were still in the South, and most of them were urban. A return migration during the 1980s increased the Southern urban population of blacks to the point that almost 90 percent of all blacks live in urban areas, with 53 percent of them in the South.

Southern Urban Blacks in General

Residential segregation plagued Southern cities ever since blacks began to move voluntarily into them in appreciable numbers. In the late 1800s, black residence in Southern cities was circumscribed under the banner of servitude, and blacks lived as servants throughout white neighborhoods. Other ethnic groups were the objects of legal residential segregation. But soon after the turn of the century, with an increase in the black influx into the cities, legal residential segregation was aimed at blacks. For example, a 1912 state law in Virginia directed all of its communities to be divided into clearly identified racially segregated districts, with severe legal penalties for cross-racial residence.

Although such ordinances were declared unconstitutional in 1917, racial zoning and racially restrictive covenants assumed prominence.

The former lasted well into the 1950s; the latter was made illegal with a lawsuit in 1948 (*Shelley v. Kramer*) and the 1968 Fair Housing Law in the Civil Rights Act. Under the covenants, home or property buyers promised not to sell or rent to families or individuals of a certain race, ethnicity, or religion. The covenants' unconstitutionality can be determined by the courts, but they are virtually unenforceable; therefore, the covenants are still sometimes included sub rosa in real estate contracts. Since racially restrictive zoning and covenants reinforced social practices so strongly before they were declared unconstitutional, the segregated residential patterns established under them still exist with the help of powerful formal and informal mechanisms.

Until about 1950, federal housing programs (as formal mechanisms) tended to reinforce the racially restrictive patterns mentioned above at the local levels in the South. In fact, during the 1930s, while intensifying its efforts to build public housing projects throughout Southern cities to house low-income people, principally blacks, the federal government indicated explicitly in its policy that "if a neighborhood is to retain its stability, it is necessary that properties shall continue to be occupied by the same racial classes" (U.S. Commission on Civil Rights 1973). This policy tarnished the implementation of the FHA and VA federally insured loan program for home ownership, the home ownership subsidy program through section 235, public housing policies, and the section 8 rental assistance program.

Since 1950, however, the policies of federal programs shifted with (1) the policy of the FHA not insuring mortgages covered by racial covenants; (2) a 1962 presidential executive order guaranteeing non-discrimination in FHA and VA housing and insurance programs; (3) the 1964 Civil Rights Act prohibiting discrimination in any program receiving federal assistance; (4) Title VIII (the Fair Housing Law) of the 1968 Civil Rights Act prohibiting discrimination by real estate brokers, builders, and mortgage lenders; and (5) the 1968 Supreme Court's declaration as constitutional an 1866 civil rights law barring all racial discrimination in both public and private housing (*Jones v. Mayer*).

Despite these policy shifts, federal programs continued to practice or operate in a discriminatory manner, thus facilitating the institutionalization of residential segregation in the South. Frequently, the U.S. Department of Housing and Urban Development (HUD) was charged with moving too slowly or continuing programs that were discriminatory (U.S. Commission on Civil Rights 1973). In sum, policies and practices were inconsistent; consequently, the proportion of blacks living in inner cities in the South rose from 1960 to 1970, while the smaller proportion of blacks living in the suburbs remained relatively constant. Residential segregation increased in the inner cities and increased only slightly in the suburbs, even throughout the 1980s. Desegregation in Southern suburbs is generally merely transitory.

Even with overall improvements in recent years in home ownership (Matney and Johnson 1983), density of living units, new construction, and quality as measured by plumbing facilities, Southern urban blacks remain quite a distance behind their white counterparts at all income levels. Yet, blacks pay a larger share of their income for shelter (Bureau of the Census 1985). Since it subsumes some of the most difficult aspects of intergroup relations in the South, housing was the last major area covered by civil rights legislation. In fact, even though President Kennedy's Executive Order of 1963 was oriented toward the integration of federally assisted housing, it covered only 7 percent of the housing market in the South. It had to be supplemented and reinforced by the 1968 Federal Fair Housing Law and a critical Supreme Court decision (*Jones v. Mayer*) which outlawed all racial discrimination in housing. Neither of these, however, has been able to stem the tide of persistent residential segregation (Schnare 1978).

Residential segregation by race, the most prominent characteristic of black housing in the South, has resulted from the actions of individual property owners encouraged by real estate organizations, laws, and the FHA. Although a professed fear that blacks jeopardize property values accounts for most of the segregation, such fears have not been validated in studies done in the South in Baltimore, Houston, Kansas City, and Louisville. The myth, however, continues to be the basis of segregation action—appraisers downgrade black-occupied housing and white homeowners sell in a panic. This is followed by a surge of black buyers willing to pay exorbitant prices for what they consider as better housing. In fact, blacks pay about 15–20 percent more for comparable housing (Yinger 1978; Bullard 1984).

Residential segregation in the South has remained relatively constant since the 1950s. Some found a slight decline in the 1970s, but this may have been due to a tight housing market making it difficult for whites to move out (Sorensen, Taeuber, and Hollingsworth 1975; Van Valey, Roof, and Wilcox 1976). Even, at best, the decline is only moderate in some Southern cities, with most residents still living racially apart. Blacks continue to be concentrated in central cities and whites in the suburban fringes. When the residential pattern conforms to a multiple-sector or multiple-nuclei format with the upper classes

TABLE 15.1.   Houston's Black Population by Ward, 1870–1910

Ward	Total Population	Black Population	Percent Black	Percent of Total Black Population
		1870		
1	738	250	33.9	6.8
2	1,638	474	28.9	12.8
3	2,812	1,075	38.2	29.1
4	3,055	1,314	43.0	35.6
5	1,139	578	50.7	15.7
	9,382	3,691		
		1890		
1	1,980	777	39.2	7.5
2	3,341	1,262	37.8	12.2
3	7,366	2,661	36.1	25.6
4	8,761	3,682	42.0	35.5
5	6,109	1,997	32.7	19.2
	27,557	10,379		
		1910		
1	6,954	1,390	20.0	5.8
2	7,572	2,335	30.8	9.8
3	24,705	7,662	31.0	32.0
4	16,772	6,366	38.0	26.6
5	16,854	4,967	29.5	20.8
6	5,943	1,209	20.3	5.1
	78,800	23,929		

Source: Wintz 1982.

moving further away from the central city, it merely increases the size of the fringe areas where black neighborhoods expand into adjoining white neighborhoods.

Given the above, black movement into the suburbs in the South conforms to two patterns: (1) black movement into adjacent white suburbs that are or become "transitional," and (2) black movement into all-black suburbs that radiate out from black lower-class neighborhoods. Actually, only about 8 percent of the Southern suburbs is black compared to about 25–30 percent of the central or inner cities. More than 60 percent of all Southern urban blacks still live in the inner cities, an increase from the 1970s to the 1980s (Matney and Johnson 1983). Entry into the suburbs is hardly random; therefore, even Southern black suburbanization represents ghettoization and spillover across municipal boundaries. In black suburbia, the quality of housing and maintenance is less than it is in comparable white neighborhoods; in 1982, nearly one out of four blacks who lived in the suburbs was below the poverty line (Bureau of the Census 1985).

TABLE 15.2.   Black Population in Houston,
1850–1980

Year	Total Population	Black Population	Percent Black
1850	2,396	533	22.2
1860	4,845	1,077	22.2
1870	9,382	3,691	39.3
1880	16,513	6,479	39.2
1890	27,557	10,379	37.7
1900	44,633	14,608	32.7
1910	78,800	23,929	30.4
1920	138,276	33,960	24.6
1930	292,352	63,337	21.7
1940	384,514	86,302	22.4
1950	596,163	125,400	21.0
1960	938,219	215,037	22.9
1970	1,232,802	316,551	25.7
1980	1,594,086	440,257	27.6

Source: Wintz 1982.

A good example of how residential segregation evolved in the South can be seen in the case of Houston, Texas: a city unfettered by industrial zoning thus allowing residential patterns to seek their own course.

Houston Case Study

The inner city of Houston is composed of six wards (fig. 15.1). The black residential pattern from 1870 to 1910 is summed up in table 15.1; however, by 1980, with tremendous expansion and suburbanization, the pattern had changed to the one reflected in figure 15.2 and table 15.2. While the total population of Houston increased from 2,396 in 1850 (about twenty years after its inception) to well over a million and a half in 1980, the proportion of blacks changed only moderately. In 1850, 533 blacks (or 22.2 percent of the total population) lived in Houston; by 1980, it had increased to 440,257 (or 27.6 percent). The largest proportion occurred in 1870 and 1880 (39.3 percent and 39.2 percent, respectively) with a gradual decline thereafter. The absolute number of blacks, however, has been quite large; and, as can be seen from table 15.1 and figure 15.1, they have been segregated differentially throughout the city.

According to Wintz (1982), after the Civil War Houston had no ordinance segregating residential areas. However, based on severe

FIGURE 15.1.   Wards of Houston

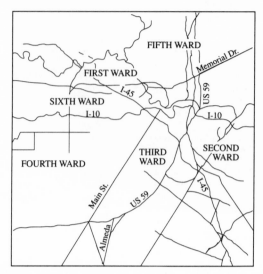

Source: Wintz 1982.

legal discrimination in other areas and custom, blacks tended to con-
gregate in specific areas, gradually leading to the emergence of fairly
well-defined black neighborhoods. Segregation deepened during the
period of 1875 to 1930 almost to the point of forming two societies
connected only by economic necessity. While blacks continued to immigrate from rural areas to each of the city's wards, the largest black
enclaves developed in the Fourth Ward's Freedmantown, the original
urban settlement of blacks immediately southwest of downtown, the
Third Ward southeast of downtown, and the Fifth Ward northeast of
the central business district (fig. 15.1). These wards remained predominantly white for a long time; as late as the 1920s, blacks comprised
no more than 30 percent of these wards, but the many residentially
segregated black neighborhoods within them were almost 100 percent
black.

Given the rural orientation of the newly arrived blacks and the fact
that they were not concentrated in a single ghetto, each black neighborhood had a small-town quality until well into the twentieth century.
As the black population grew, new enclaves developed within the
wards and some expanded beyond their de facto segregated boundaries to create some separate black-governed suburbs (good examples
are Independence Heights, which was incorporated in 1927, and Pleas-

FIGURE 15.2.   Principal Black Residential Areas (1980)

Residential Areas
 1. Acre Homes
 2. Briargate
 3. Third Ward
 4. Fourth Ward
 5. Fifth Ward
 6. Carvercrest (Piney Point)
 7. Carverdale
 8. Chasewood
 9. Clinton Park
10. Hiram Clarke
11. Independence Heights
12. Kashmere Gardens
13. Pleasantville
14. Riceville
15. Riverside
16. Scenic Woods
17. Settegast
18. South Park
19. Studewood Heights
20. Sunnyside
21. Trinity Gardens

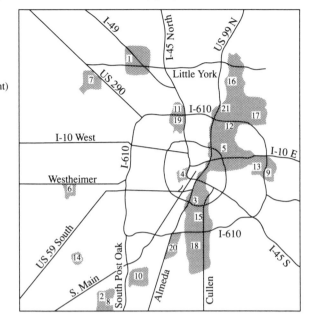

Source: Wintz 1982.

antville). This precipitated a move by realtors as early as the 1920s to develop subdivisions which offered the black middle class segregated, middle-class homes. These homes, in an environment which was much better than the older inner-city neighborhoods, were built on the fringes of older neighborhoods.

While most blacks during this period occupied poor, overcrowded housing in substandard neighborhoods, a significant percentage owned their homes, from 20 percent in 1910, to 32 percent in 1930, to 22 percent in 1940. Efforts to improve the quality of black housing culminated in the establishment in 1938 of the Houston Housing Authority. This allowed Houston to participate in the development of federally funded low-income housing projects. In 1929, Mayor Will Hogg noted in a city planning report that three main black areas existed in inner-city Houston: principally in the Third, Fourth, and Fifth Wards. Apparently, he wished to eliminate the remaining pockets and consolidate blacks, for he said in the report: "These Negroes are a necessary and useful element in the population, and suitable areas with proper living and recreation facilities should be set aside for them.

TABLE 15.3.   Black Neighborhoods
in Houston (1970)

Neighborhoods	Percent Black
Third Ward	96.0
Fourth Ward	84.3
Fifth Ward	94.7
Sunnyside: Scottcrest	97.2
South Park: Macgregor	76.5
Pleasantville	88.6
Total: wards	94.5
Total: new neighborhoods	85.1
Total: City of Houston	25.7

Source: Wintz 1982.

Because of long established racial prejudices, it is best for both races that living areas be segregated" (*Report of the City Planning Commission* 1929).

The Houston Housing Authority targeted two housing projects for blacks (Cuney Homes in the Third Ward and Kelly Courts in the Fifth Ward), providing low-income housing for almost four thousand blacks by 1945. Two other projects were built for whites—Irvington Courts and San Felipe Courts. The latter was built in a large part of a black neighborhood, Freedmantown, which was cleared of blacks in 1938 to make room for the white project. Displaced blacks adjusted by increasing the population density in existing black neighborhoods, an increase exacerbated by the continual in-migration of blacks from rural Texas and Louisiana. By the 1970s, the three wards were almost all black (table 15.3); the Housing Authority had built eleven housing projects (five of which were in black neighborhoods) and was planning four more; and the white housing project built in a black neighborhood (now called Allen Parkway Village) had long since reverted to blacks. Because inner-city blacks were so severely concentrated, some moved into and created new black segregated suburban neighborhoods (table 15.3).

With regard to suburbanization, black movement was circumscribed by zoning substitutions. Houston had tried without success to get a zoning ordinance (proposed in 1929 by Will Hogg) passed in 1936, 1938, 1943, 1957, 1958, and finally in 1962. Each time, it was approved by the conservative upper classes but met with opposition from the more numerous middle and lower classes. Simultaneously though, in response to the inner-city zoning ordinance's repeated defeats, developers outside the city zoned their own rapidly increasing suburban subdivisions with long-term renewable deed restrictions and covenants (table 15.1, fig. 15.2) which specified the type of residents permitted to live there. Furthermore, a multiplicity of contiguous incorporated bedroom suburbs (e.g., West University, Bellaire, and Southside Place) developed their own zoning laws.

Thus, blacks tended to suburbanize near or around their own inner-city neighborhoods and force "transition" in adjacent white neighborhoods by fringe encroachment. This would precipitate "white fright and flight," exacerbated by mercenary white realtors, thus creating an immediate saturation of the previously white neighborhoods by blacks. Such white-to-black transition started in South Park in the early 1960s and was completed in that area by the late 1960s (fig. 15.2). Subsequently, a trend was established in the early 1970s of blacks moving from the South Park area to Windsor Village (all-white until 1965) on South Post Oak (fig. 15.2). White realtors showed by their behavior that they did not believe in integrated areas; they created "areas in transition." The same was happening in Brentwood, Cambridge Village, Heathercrest, and Westbury. Realtors predicted that Riceville (fig. 15.2) in Meyerland would be next in line. These and similar patterns occurred in other areas and were facilitated by soliciting and steering on the part of white realtors (Houston *Post* May 27, 1973), the operational arms of racial discrimination in housing. Such movement included both home buying and apartment rental.

With regard to apartment rental, a study was conducted in Houston by the League of Women Voters to test compliance with the 1968 Fair Housing Act. The study found that racial discrimination existed in 52 percent of the apartments included. Specifically, discrimination was highest in the south central area of Houston (64 percent); the next highest was in the northwest (62 percent), followed by the southwest (45 percent), and finally, the northeast (42 percent). There was a surprisingly high incidence of overt discrimination, but no incidence of admitted quota renting (Houston *Post* June 13, 1973).

In 1974, Houston ranked sixteenth among 109 major cities in black-white segregated housing ("The Council on Municipal Performance," Houston *Post* October 25, 1974). Shreveport was ranked as the most segregated. The measure used was based on the percentage of blacks that would have to move for them to be randomly distributed throughout a geographic area. The Council on Municipal Performance noted that segregation had declined somewhat throughout the South in the 1960s; in 1960, for example, Houston ranked eleventh in residential segregation.

In 1975, the Houston City Council passed a fair housing ordinance making it unlawful to discriminate in the sale, rental, or financing of housing. It clenched a three-party agreement among the City of Houston, the Houston Board of Realtors, and HUD. During that same year, a city fair housing office was established to hear and advise on housing complaints using conciliation as a remedy first and court referral as a last resort (Houston *Post* January 30, 1975). As a result of these developments, a rash of racial discrimination suits were filed throughout the 1970s. In fact, in 1983, the Houston *Chronicle* reported that Texas led the nation in lawsuits filed under the Housing Act, and that most of them were from Houston.

Four examples of lawsuits were:

1. In 1976, the Justice Department sued the Houston Society of Real Estate Appraisers for downgrading their appraisals of property in "integrated" neighborhoods. In so doing, it was alleged that mortgage companies took for granted that loans on homes in such areas were less secure than in white communities. This confirmed the implicit assumption that property values are lowered when blacks move into an area (Houston *Chronicle* April 18, 1976).

2. In 1984, the Justice Department filed a suit against a Houston-based Harris County clerk, seeking to bar her from recording housing deeds that included racially discriminatory provisions.

3. As recently as 1986, a federal judge had to nullify a restrictive covenant, which was to exist until 1997, which barred nonwhites from owning or occupying property in a southwest neighborhood (Houston *Post* 1986).

4. As recently as 1987, a federal judge ruled in favor of a southeast Houston subdivision which was sued by the government over a racially restrictive covenant that was no longer being enforced since nearly half of the residents were nonwhite. The subdivision argued that it could not void the clause restricting it to whites without voiding all other restrictive covenants in the community.

In the 1980s, home ownership rates for blacks in the South were well over 50 percent, the highest of any region in the country, and it grew at a faster rate (Momeni 1986). The pattern is duplicated in Houston, but the concentration of black homes is in black neighborhoods.

Although Houston was among the cities that moved fastest in housing desegregation in both the inner city and suburbia, in the mid-1980s it still remained highly segregated (Houston *Chronicle* 1985). According to a comparison of two studies conducted by Taeuber (1965, 1983), some Southern cities, including Houston, decreased their housing segregation at twice the average for big cities between 1970 and 1980.

Houston declined more in segregation, but its actual level was right at the big city average (81 in a scale of 0–100, with 0 indicating no segregation). This means that Houston was more segregated in 1970 (along with Jacksonville and Richmond) and had farther to drop in order to be average; yet it remains severely segregated.

Summary

U.S. Census data indicates that since the 1940s the average black in the South experienced an increase in housing segregation, while the average white lived in a neighborhood with a slightly higher proportion of blacks. This ostensible contradiction is explained by Schnare (1978) via reference to the nature of expansion of black inner-city neighborhoods, which radiate out in all receptive directions (receptivity is facilitated by blockbusting and redlining) from the core. With more blacks moving into the inner city and displacing the few remaining whites, residential segregation increases in the core. Less segregation (or more integration) occurs on the fringes, in the suburbs, as blacks move in (until the neighborhood becomes all or predominantly black). Such a gain in integration is almost cancelled out; once it becomes a reality, more segregation occurs and the pattern is repeated.

Clearly, the net effect of the above is that Southern blacks experienced more segregation, ultimately, in both the inner city and the suburbs, where whites experience fleeting on-again off-again integration. The tendency is slight for the dispersion of black households throughout white suburbia in the South. Once a formerly white neighborhood becomes from 6–30 percent black (economic impediments notwithstanding), it falls prey to the perpetrators of white fright and flight. This pattern will probably continue unless there is some dramatic shift in the underlying causes of housing segregation: discrimination, economics, prejudicial attitudes, and information barriers.

References

Bullard, Robert D. 1984. "The Black Family: Housing Alternatives in the 80's." *Journal of Black Studies* 14:341–67.
Bureau of the Census. 1985. *Statistical Abstracts 1986.* Washington, D.C.: U.S. Government Printing Office.
Houston *Chronicle.* 1976. April 18.
———. 1983. April 12.
———. 1985. April 2.

Houston *Post*. 1973a. May 27. Section CC.

——. 1973b. June 13. Section CC.

——. 1974. "Council on Municipal Performance." October 25.

——. 1975. January 30.

——. 1986. September 5.

——. 1987. February 22.

Lake, Robert W. 1981. *The New Suburbanites: Race and Housing in the Sub-urbs*. New Brunswick: Centre for Urban Policy Research.

Matney, William C., and D. L. Johnson. 1983. *America's Black Population: 1970–1982*. Washington, D.C.: U.S. Government Printing Office.

Momeni, Jamshid A. 1986. *Race, Ethnicity, and Minority Housing in the United States*. New York: Greenwood Press.

Pennick, Edward. 1983. "Property Loss Among Blacks." *Black Collegian* 2:83–96.

Report of the City Planning Commission. 1929. Houston. 25 pp.

Schnare, Ann B. 1978. *The Persistence of Racial Segregation in Housing*. Washington, D.C.: Urban Institute.

Sorenson, Annemette, Karl A. Taeuber, and Leslie J. J. Hollingsworth. 1975. "Indexes of Racial Residential Segregation for 109 Cities in the United States, 1940 to 1970." *Sociological Focus* 8:125–42.

Taeuber, Karl A. 1983. *Racial-Residential Segregation, 28 Cities, 1970–1980*. CDE Working Paper. Madison: University of Wisconsin. March.

Taeuber, Karl A., and Alma F. Taeuber. 1965. *Negroes in Cities: Residential Segregation and Neighborhood Change*. Chicago: Aldine Publications.

U.S. Commission on Civil Rights. 1973. *Understanding Fair Housing*. Washington, D.C.: U.S. Government Printing Office.

Van Valey, Thomas L., Wade C. Roof, and Jerome E. Wilcox. 1976. "Trends in Residential Segregation 1960–1970." *American Journal of Sociology* 83:826–44.

Wintz, Cary D. 1982. *Blacks in Houston*. Houston: Houston Center for the Humanities, National Endowment for the Humanities.

Yinger, John. 1978. "The Black-White Price Differential in Housing: Some Further Evidence." *Land Economics* 54, no. 2:187–206.

16. Housing Segregation and Housing Conditions for Hispanics in Phoenix, with Comparisons with Other Southwestern Cities

There has long been interrelated research on residential segregation and the effects of such segregation on the higher cost and lower quality of housing available to Hispanics, blacks, and other minorities (Abrams 1965; Jackman and Jackman 1980; Muth 1969). While Hispanic ratio and density of city populations, relative income and educational levels, and related factors have combined to result in more marked residential segregation variations than for blacks, nationally Hispanic residential segregation has been consistently high as well. This is true in such southwestern cities as Albuquerque, Dallas, San Antonio, San Diego, and Tucson, where majorities of Hispanics are residentially segregated as well as in locales of less Hispanic density, such as Los Angeles or Sacramento where lower but still high minority ratios of Hispanics are residentially concentrated (Grebler, Moore, and Guzman 1970; Massey 1979).

Residential segregation in Phoenix falls between these limits. As reported in this chapter, somewhat less than half the Hispanic residents reside in neighborhoods which are predominantly Hispanic. However, when Hispanic residency in predominantly black neighborhoods is added, a substantial majority of Hispanics in Phoenix live in predominantly minority populated areas.

With a base Hispanic population of 15 percent (*A Demographic Guide to Arizona: 1985*, table C-1, 56–58), Phoenix has a pattern similar to other southwestern cities with a substantial Hispanic population. In past studies of Hispanics in southwestern cities, and of blacks nationally, such restricted housing in many neighborhoods resulted in significantly higher rental and home-owner costs for Hispanics and blacks compared to Anglos, who have greater access to much wider city and metropolitan housing markets (Jackman and Jackman 1980; Muth 1969; Villemez 1980; Yinger 1975).

Hispanic data for 1970 compared with 1980 is presented with the data for the city population as a whole and compared with Anglo and black population locational data. Housing segregation indices were computed for Hispanics and for blacks as a further check on emerging minority housing patterns. For Hispanics as for blacks, there was evidence of a decline in housing segregation. With respect to housing conditions, cost and quality of housing for Hispanics is compared to that of Anglos and of blacks, with stratified household income comparisons and with similar comparisons for San Antonio and San Diego, two other rapidly growing southwestern sunbelt cities.

Declining Hispanic Residential Segregation

Assessment was made of movement of the Hispanic population compared to that of the Anglo and black populations. Both U.S. census tract data and area data were correlated with birth and death records (vital events) for intercensal years. With these data sets a segregation index was constructed for intercensal years based upon the total Hispanic, as well as black and Anglo city populations. This was matched against expected distribution in five areas of the city which represent Burgess-like rings (1925) around the center of the city, insofar as these could be imposed on the Phoenix geographic patterns. An independent intercensal year test for the years 1983 and 1984 of this method of assessing housing segregation confirmed the close correlation of birth and death ratios with residential settlement patterns (Gordon and Mayer 1987).

Figure 16.1 shows the five designated areas, which are useful for residential zone assessment over time. Area 1 is the area of both Hispanic and black concentration in the past. With little variation, the vast majority of minority group members was concentrated in this older, settled, often designated "inner-city," area. Surrounding this inner-city area are four more rings, designated as Areas 2–5. Area 2 is the ring of census tracts immediately adjacent to the inner city and the area into which the Hispanic and black population would most likely spread. Area 3 represents the "middle city," and Areas 4 and 5 the newer "outer city."

Areas 4 and 5 reflect the rapid population growth of southwestern sunbelt cities in recent decades. In 1970 there were 135 census tracts in Phoenix; by 1980 the city had 185 census tracts. The highest pre-

FIGURE 16.1.   Census Tracts Combined into Five Analysis:
Phoenix, Arizona

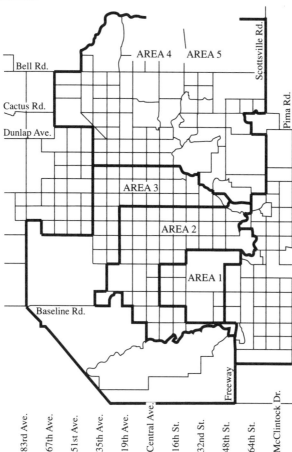

dominantly Anglo residential growth was in the northeastern part of
the city. Area 4 in 1970, subdivided into Areas 4 and 5 in 1980, represents the lowest areas of residency for Hispanics, as well as for
blacks. Consequently, it was expected that any significant shifts in
population dispersion of these groups would be reflected in their increasing numbers and proportions in Areas 2 and 3. Changes in the
predominantly Anglo Areas of 4 (in 1970) and 4 and 5 (same space
in 1980) might also occur.

As reflected in table 16.1, residential segregation of Hispanics de-

TABLE 16.1.   Percent Distribution of Population and Vital Events by
Racial and Ethnic Group and Area, Phoenix (1970–80)

	Total Population	Percent	Vital Events	Percent	Hispanic Population	Percent	Vital Events	Percent
1970								
Area 1	27,434	4.7	1,071	6.4	10,848	13.3	373	12.5
Area 2	213,349	36.7	6,729	40.5	39,945	49.1	1,609	53.9
Area 3	169,982	29.2	4,434	26.7	19,319	23.7	636	23.2
Area 4	170,434	29.3	4,388	26.4	11,283	13.9	369	12.3
Total	581,199	100.0	16,622	100.0	81,395	100.0	2,987	100.0
1980								
Area 1	25,653	4.3	981	6.2	10,737	10.5	402	11.1
Area 2	184,037	30.8	6,097	38.8	49,908	48.8	2,015	55.7
Area 3	173,285	29.0	4,402	28.0	24,377	23.8		19.9
Area 4	214,420	35.9	4,249	27.0	17,236	16.9	478	13.3
Total	597,395	100.0	15,729	100.0	102,258	100.0	3,615	100.0

clined in Phoenix between 1970 and 1980. Of particular interest is the
decline in the predominantly Anglo Area 4, farthest removed from
Hispanic population concentration. Here Hispanic vital events (births
and deaths) increased from 13.9–16.9 percent, while a stable or slight
increase in vital events continued to occur in Area 3, still removed
from the Hispanic concentrated Areas 1 and 2. There was an even
greater decline of black residential segregation in Area 4, showing an
increase in black vital events, from 3.7–10.8 percent. As Hispanic and
black residency has historically tended to be concentrated in the same
or in adjacent neighborhoods, this dual lessening of segregated residential patterns leads to the expectation of declining housing costs and
increased quality of housing for Hispanics. An examination of these
dual issues results in confirmation of the cost factor but not the quality
factor.

Assessing the Cost and Quality of Hispanic Housing

The Phoenix data to assess any changes in the historically high cost
and lower quality of Hispanic housing in Phoenix as in other cities
came from the 5 percent public use sample of the 1980 U.S. census.
For comparative purposes data is also presented on the cost and quality of housing available for blacks and for Anglos.

The cost of housing is expressed in quantitative terms. Households
are classified by whether they rent or own. For those who rent, the

Black Population	Percent	Vital Events	Percent	Anglo Population	Percent	Vital Events	Percent
9,438	32.8	385	35.5	7,148	1.5	313	2.5
17,156	59.7	641	59.2	156,248	33.2	4,479	35.7
1,091	3.8	35	3.2	149,572	31.8	3,763	30.0
1,030	3.7	22	2.1	158,121	33.5	3,997	31.8
28,715	100.0	1,083	100.0	471,089	100.0	12,552	100.0
8,590	26.1	328	26.0	6,326	1.4	251	2.3
17,573	53.3	694	55.0	116,556	25.2	3,388	31.2
3,239	9.8		11.3	145,669	31.5	3,539	32.6
3,554	10.8	96	7.7	193,630	41.9	3,675	33.9
32,956	100.0	1,261	100.0	462,181	100.0	10,853	100.0

measure of housing cost is the gross monthly rent. For home-owners, the measure used is owner cost. Rental and owner groups are each divided into three income groups (table 16.2). In addition, three household rental and owner group categories are distinguished. The analysis of the cost of housing subdivides the population into 54 groups of two rental-owner groups × 3 ethnic groups × 3 levels of income × 3 levels of housing costs. In this way the relevant variables were controlled and examined.

The quality of housing is also assessed as a further measurement of possible Hispanic effective discrimination beyond segregated housing patterns. The question addressed on the quality of housing available for Hispanics was that, even if segregated housing is in decline and owner and/or rental costs appear more equitable, "Do Hispanics receive equal quality for equal cost?" To this end a number of measures of housing quality were examined. These measures, based on available data were (a) percent without air-conditioning (a need rather than a luxury in Phoenix), (b) percent with more than one bathroom, (c) percent with complete kitchens, (d) percent with complete plumbing, (e) percent childless households, (f) percent of structures built before 1940, and (g) average persons per room. Measure (c) and (d) were eliminated after examination. There are not enough housing units, owner or rental, without these facilities in all Phoenix to make any racial or ethnic differentiations as measures of housing quality. The remaining five measures were included in the housing quality assessment.

TABLE 16.2.   Number of Households by Ethnic and Racial Group, Income Group, and Gross Rent and Owner Cost Group: Phoenix (1980)

| | Income Group | | | | | | | |
| | Under $12,000 | | $12,000–$19,999 | | $20,000 and over | | | |
	Total	Percent	Total	Percent	Total	Percent	Total	Percent
Gross rent:								
Hispanic								
Under $200	3,880	53	880	28	380	21	5,140	74
$200–$399	2,880	38	2,040	64	1,100	61	620	9
$400 and over	600	8	240	8	320	18	1,160	17
Black								
Under $200	2,240	60	240	18	60	7	2,540	43
$200–$399	1,120	30	780	57	540	60	2,440	42
$400 and over	340	10	340	25	300	37	980	15
Anglo								
Under $200	9,180	26	1,480	7	660	4	11,320	16
$200–$399	20,840	59	12,540	59	6,720	41	40,100	55
$400 and over	5,400	15	7,140	34	8,820	55	21,360	29
Total	46,480		25,680		18,900		91,060	
Owner Cost:								
Hispanic								
Under $200	2,320	50	2,140	29	520	28	4,980	35
$200–$399	1,760	38	3,780	51	1,020	29	6,560	45
$400 and over	520	12	1,560	20	780	43	2,860	20
Black								
Under $200	1,360	54	440	19	120	15	1,920	34
$200–$399	860	34	1,280	55	340	42	2,480	44
$400 and over	300	12	600	26	340	42	1,240	22
Anglo								
Under $200	15,200	47	11,120	20	4,840	12	31,160	24
$200–$399	11,360	35	24,720	45	14,420	36	50,500	40
$400 and over	5,500	17	19,440	35	20,940	52	45,880	36
Total	39,180		65,080		43,320		147,580	

Analysis of Housing Costs

Table 16.2 shows the distribution of households by gross rent, owner cost, ethnic group, and income. The Hispanic population shows a mixed pattern. Although the greatest number of households (3,880) are in the same rental and income groups as black households, a nearly equal number of households (3,780) are in the same income and owner group as Anglo households. Insofar as rent/owner and income distribution are concerned, the Hispanic population is located between the Anglo and black populations, with the black population largely composed of renters in the under $200 rental category and almost two-

TABLE 16.3.   Median and Mean Monthly Gross Rent by Racial/Ethnic Group
and Income Group: Phoenix (1980)

	Median Rent ($)	Mean Rent ($)	Median Income ($)	Mean Income ($)	Ratio Median Rent/Income	Ratio Mean Rent/Income
Under $15,000						
Hispanic	203	204	7,510	7,366	.32	.33
Black	185	198	6,235	6,664	.36	.36
Anglo	262	271	8,315	8,217	.38	.40
$15,000–$19,999						
Hispanic	260	266	17,270	17,250	.18	.19
Black	300	305	17,010	17,227	.21	.21
Anglo	325	334	17,010	17,071	.23	.23
$20,000–$24,999						
Hispanic	268	266	22,050	22,096	.15	.14
Black	306	319	22,020	22,237	.17	.17
Anglo	342	354	22,010	22,154	.19	.19
$25,000–$29,999						
Hispanic	264	273	26,112	26,599	.12	.12
Black	269	291	27,222	26,958	.12	.13
Anglo	369	382	26,848	27,124	.17	.17
Over $30,000						
Hispanic	279	309	39,302	44,546	.09	.08
Black	327	342	34,835	36,589	.11	.11
Anglo	385	408	35,650	41,008	.13	.12

thirds of renters in the under $12,000 per household income group, while the largest number of Anglo households are owners at the $12,000–$19,999 household income level.

The relationship of Hispanic housing costs was determined by dividing the households into rental groups (table 16.3) and owner groups (table 16.4) and calculating the ratio of rent to income. Both means and medians are used as a check on the possible bias each measure may introduce.

As income increases the ratio of rent to income steadily decreases (table 16.3). This is true for Hispanics as well as for blacks and Anglos, for both the mean and median ratios. For households in the under $15,000 per year income group, the rent/income ratio for Hispanics as well as blacks and Anglos is close to one-third of total income. In the over $30,000 per year income group, the rent/income ratio for Hispanics as well as for blacks and Anglos declines to about 10 percent of total household income. This finding is clear in denoting that the total pattern of income rent ratio is virtually the same for Hispanics when compared to both Anglos and blacks. The differences that do

TABLE 16.4.   Median and Mean Monthly Owner Cost by Racial/Ethnic Group and Income Group: Phoenix (1980)

	Median Own Cost ($)	Mean Own Cost ($)	Median Income ($)	Mean Income ($)	Ratio Median Own Cost/ Income	Ratio Mean Own Cost/ Income
Under $15,000						
Hispanic	199	253	8,980	8,469	.27	.36
Black	189	240	7,010	7,558	.30	.38
Anglo	208	274	9,360	9,009	.27	.36
$15,000–$19,000						
Hispanic	255	285	17,530	17,493	.17	.20
Black	289	303	16,735	17,058	.21	.21
Anglo	307	333	17,465	17,411	.21	.23
$20,000–$24,999						
Hispanic	265	295	22,858	23,780	.14	.15
Black	277	287	21,472	21,885	.15	.21
Anglo	337	360	22,238	22,289	.18	.19
$25,000–$29,999						
Hispanic	303	340	27,010	27,162	.13	.15
Black	277	372	27,010	27,006	.12	.17
Anglo	358	382	27,160	27,264	.16	.17
Over $30,000						
Hispanic	274	369	37,465	41,829	.09	.11
Black	366	372	34,700	38,338	.13	.12
Anglo	411	470	38,500	43,338	.13	.13

occur are in the proportions of Hispanic, as of black, households in the upper economic levels (table 16.1).

Table 16.4 provides the same data for owners, except owner cost is substituted for gross rental. The same basic pattern obtains. Owner cost/income ratio declines with increasing income. Again this is true for Hispanics as it is for Anglos and for blacks. The only difference between the rental and owner groups is in the under $15,000 per year income category, where owners pay a somewhat lower proportion of their income than do renters. This is true of all the groups including Hispanics.

Thus, it is clear from both the rental and owner cost data that both Hispanics and blacks do not pay a significantly greater proportion of their income for housing than do Anglos. However, discrimination in housing may enter the picture in that the higher the income, the lower the percent of income is needed for housing. Because a far greater proportion of Anglos are in the higher income groups than Hispanics or blacks, housing cost burdens fall on the latter groups disproportionately.

Analysis of Housing Quality

Whether the quality of housing available to Hispanics is equal to that available to Anglos at the same owner or rental costs is the next question. In order to assess this issue, the five indices of housing quality found in 1980 U.S. Census data and presented earlier are shown in table 16.5 for renters and in table 16.6 for home-owners.

With regard to two measures, percent without central air-conditioning and percent housing units built before 1940, the larger the percentage, the less the index of housing quality. In the remaining three measures, percent with more than one bathroom, percent childless as an index of persons in the housing unit, and persons per room, a larger percent or number means the less the index of housing quality. Looking at each of the measures in this manner in both tables 16.5 and 16.6, it is seen that within each rental and owner cost group, and in each income group, the quality of housing for Anglos is generally higher than for Hispanics or for blacks. This is particularly true for what may be the most significant and sensitive measure; that of persons per room.

A figure summarizing and weighing all five measures can be obtained by calculating a linear multiple regression equation using the five measures as independent variables. Results of this procedure are shown in table 16.7, wherein the larger the weighted quality index number, the higher quality of the housing units. By this operational index, comparative analysis can be made between quality of housing available to Hispanics compared to Anglos as well as to blacks.

Analysis of table 16.7 indicates that with a few exceptions the quality of housing units occupied by Anglos is significantly higher than housing occupied by Hispanics. Further, while the black housing quality is also less than that of Anglos with few exceptions, it is generally higher than that of Hispanics.

Among renters, the differences in quality of housing available to Hispanics are substantial. However, it is in the category of home ownership that very large differences in quality surfaced. Among home-owners, Anglo households in all income categories had much higher quality for their relatively equal costs. While the available quality of black home-owner-occupied housing was somewhat higher than for Hispanics, their quality was also much lower than that available to Anglos.

TABLE 16.5.   Selected Measures of Housing Quality by Income Group, by Monthly Gross Rent, by Racial/Ethnic Group: Phoenix (1980)

	Percent without Air Conditioning			Percent More Than One Bathroom		
	Black	Hispanic	Anglo	Black	Hispanic	Anglo
Income under $15,000						
Rent under $200	49	45	22	4	1	5
Rent $200–$349	35	44	22	10	4	5
Rent $350 and over	10	20	7	52	29	38
Income $15,000–$19,000						
Rent under $200	—	—	—	—	—	—
Rent $200–$349	17	10	22	5	27	7
Rent $350 and over	10	10	12	57	28	46
Income $20,000–$24,999						
Rent under $200	—	—	—	—	—	—
Rent $200–$349	45	65	23	18	13	15
Rent $350 and over	9	15	12	64	55	55
Income $25,000–$29,999						
Rent under $200	—	—	—	—	—	—
Rent $200–$349	—	45	23	—	9	8
Rent $350 and over	—	—	11	—	—	58
Income $30,000 and over						
Rent under $200	—	—	—	—	—	—
Rent $200–$349	—	30	13	—	0	18
Rent $350 and over	—	—	3	—	—	65

Summary and Assessment

Given a pattern of lessening Hispanic housing segregation, this chapter has addressed two questions: First, whether Hispanics pay more for housing in Phoenix, and, second, is there any difference in the quality of housing for Hispanics. For both questions comparative data was presented for Anglos and for blacks. The findings indicate that the cost of housing for Hispanics, as for blacks, is not greater than the cost of housing for Anglos at comparable household income levels. However, particularly for home-owners, the quality of housing occupied by Hispanics, as for blacks to a somewhat lesser extent, is less than that occupied by Anglos.

A further question arises, Is Phoenix unique, or are the same conditions occurring in other cities? Although no similar Public Use Sample tapes were available to us, published census tables allow a crude comparison with other selected cities. The southwestern cities of San Antonio and San Diego were selected and the results compared to

Percent Childless			Percent Built Before 1940			Persons Per Room		
Black	Hispanic	Anglo	Black	Hispanic	Anglo	Black	Hispanic	Anglo
12	16	8	16	21	6	.67	.86	.48
14	16	17	11	15	7	.71	.89	.55
15	13	21	5	2	2	.64	.68	.53
—	—	—	—	—	—	—	—	—
6	24	28	5	7	6	.84	.94	.61
21	24	21	0	7	1	.74	.68	.61
—	—	—	—	—	—	—	—	—
18	16	39	9	20	7	.60	1.07	.60
18	20	31	0	10	0	.88	.67	.57
—	—	—	—	—	—	—	—	—
—	27	35	—	18	0	—	.88	.70
—	—	33	—	—	1	—	—	.61
—	—	—	—	—	—	—	—	—
—	0	33	—	10	2	—	1.10	.70
—	—	34	—	—	1	—	—	.63

Phoenix are presented in table 16.8. The data base for table 16.8 differs in some aspects from the Public Use Sample employed for Phoenix alone. First, there is no separately distinguished Anglo population. The category "White" shown in table 16.8 includes the Hispanic population. However, Hispanics are shown separately. Thus, the only clear comparisons are between the Hispanic and black populations. Second, income categories differ from those shown in the previous tables. Third, instead of dividing the household into three rental groups and three owner groups as in tables 16.2–16.7, the median gross rent and the median owner cost were used as the base for calculating the rental/income and owner cost/income ratio.

Despite these qualifications, when comparisons are made for the data in table 16.8 with that in tables 16.3 and 16.4, an unmistakable similarity appears. Looking at Phoenix in tables 16.3 and 16.4 and table 16.8, the pattern, although not identical, is very close to that of San Antonio and San Diego. For example, among Hispanic renters in the lowest income category, the rent/income ratio is .32, whereas in

TABLE 16.6.   Selected Measures of Housing Quality by Income Group,
by Monthly Owner Cost Group, by Racial/Ethnic Group: Phoenix (1980)

	Percent without Air Conditioning			Percent More Than One Bathroom		
	Black	Hispanic	Anglo	Black	Hispanic	Anglo
Income under $15,000						
Own Cost under $200	46	53	26	27	17	47
Own Cost $200–$399	40	34	19	38	36	70
Own Cost $400 and over	47	31	11	67	76	83
Income $15,000–$19,999						
Own Cost under $200	—	51	17	—	26	66
Own Cost $200–$399	31	44	18	69	66	73
Own Cost $400 and over	—	17	10	—	83	87
Income $20,000–$24,999						
Own Cost under $200	—	57	22	—	36	70
Own Cost $200–$399	45	37	17	64	49	78
Own Cost $400 and over	57	9	3	71	97	90
Income $25,000–$29,999						
Own Cost under $200	—	52	32	—	61	67
Own Cost $200–$399	22	33	11	78	79	88
Own Cost $400 and over	—	14	6	—	95	95
Income $30,000 and over						
Own Cost under $200	—	62	18	—	27	78
Own Cost $200–$399	47	22	9	88	77	90
Own Cost $400 and over	12	8	2	76	98	98

table 16.8, it is .35. This similarity means, rough although it is, that the same patterns are being measured. Phoenix, as explored in detail in this study, does not appear to be unique. There may be broader geographic implications; Phoenix and San Diego are very much like each other with regard to the rental/owner/income ratio. San Antonio differs only in that the lower-income groups, the rent/income, and owner/income ratios are somewhat less than in the other two cities.

The findings on the comparable housing costs for Hispanics are noteworthy. Until the 1970s, the findings on cost of urban housing for Hispanics and blacks were that concentrated, segregated housing patterns resulted in relatively high-priced housing costs as a consequence of a limited competitive housing market (Harvey 1975; Muth 1969). Citing a series of studies through the 1960s in American cities in every section of the nation, Harvey observed that "low income families therefore have little option but to locate in the relatively high priced inner city. In most American cities, of course, this condition has been exacerbated by the lack of an open housing market" (62). Yet, ac-

	Percent Childless			Percent Built Before 1940			Persons Per Room	
Black	Hispanic	Anglo	Black	Hispanic	Anglo	Black	Hispanic	Anglo
51	35	49	18	17	11	.47	.67	.35
26	26	37	5	5	5	.76	.76	.44
7	35	27	7	8	4	.73	.57	.45
—	37	67	—	12	6	—	.89	.42
26	20	40	5	3	3	.62	.64	.35
—	21	24	—	4	—	—	.60	.51
—	29	65	—	6	3	—	.95	.44
41	11	35	5	3	3	.72	.78	.55
21	19	31	0	3	3	.70	.66	.50
—	30	73	—	13	2	—	.93	.47
26	16	40	0	2	2	.75	.77	.56
—	9	26	—	18	1	—	.67	.52
—	34	70	—	19	6	—	1.04	.53
35	29	52	18	2	1	.67	.81	.54
24	38	33	6	3	2	.65	.67	.51

cording to the data presented herein for Phoenix as for San Antonio and San Diego, housing costs appear comparable. While housing costs appear now comparable, at least in Phoenix, there appears continuing substantial differences in the quality of housing available for Hispanics.

The entire pattern can be summarized as follows: For total household income, independent of ethnicity the lowest income groups pay about 35 percent of their income for owning or renting, middle income groups pay about 25 percent, and the higher income groups pay about 10–15 percent. However, while there is little difference between Hispanics and Anglos in the proportion of income paid for rent or ownership, there is substantial disparity on the quality of housing. The problems of inequality of housing opportunity for Hispanics still remain to be solved. In this study Hispanics, as blacks, receive substantially less in terms of quality housing at a given income level.

An important aspect in the picture of ethnic housing patterns remains. This study has been of the city of Phoenix, not of the Phoenix

TABLE 16.7.   Weighted Index of Housing Quality by Income Group, by Racial Ethnic Group for Monthly Rental Cost, and Monthly Owner Cost: Phoenix (1980)

	Hispanic	Black	Anglo
Monthly Rent Cost*:			
Income under $12,000			
Rent under $200	22.19	35.13	35.43
Rent $200–$399	50.32	72.19	73.60
Rent $400 and over	115.43	167.86	141.72
Income $12,000–$19,999			
Rent under $200	20.52	51.04	41.08
Rent $200–$399	52.30	77.30	77.57
Rent $400 and over	122.81	139.46	151.37
Income $20,000 and over			
Rent under $200	6.71	47.64	45.26
Rent $200–$399	78.37	75.69	89.93
Rent $400 and over	189.34	168.95	169.19
Monthly Owner Cost*:			
Income under $12,000			
Owner Cost under $200	− 25.28	− 6.53	37.67
Owner Cost $200–$399	48.39	48.84	109.56
Owner Cost $400 and over	97.91	115.55	159.11
Income $12,000–$19,999			
Owner Cost under $200	− 11.52	− 1.18	71.00
Owner Cost $200–$399	72.15	81.02	120.40
Owner Cost $400 and over	141.05	102.30	179.73
Income $20,000 and over			
Owner Cost under $200	− 1.86	11.70	79.07
Owner Cost $200–$399	96.46	107.98	134.05
Owner Cost $400 and over	183.23	174.66	203.64

Number of rental households: 91,060
Number of owner households: 147,580
*Although the quality indexes for the rental and owner groups may appear to be similar, they are not directly comparable. However, within each group the indexes can be compared. The larger the weighted quality index number, the higher the quality of housing units.

standard metropolitan statistical area (SMSA). There were not enough Hispanic, with even fewer black, households in the suburban portion of the SMSA to permit the extensive cross-breaks employed in this study. Only 31 percent of the Hispanic households and 21 percent of the black households in the Phoenix SMSA (Maricopa County) lived outside the central city of Phoenix. In contrast, 49 percent of Anglo households lived in the suburbs. This says something further concerning continuing extensive racial and ethnic housing segregation.

TABLE 16.8.   Median Percent of Owner Costs and Gross Rental Costs as a Percent of Income by Income Group and Racial/Ethnic Group for Selected Central Cities: 1980*

	Income under $10,000		Income $10,000–$19,999		Income $20,000 and over	
	Rent Median (%)	Own Median (%)	Rent Median (%)	Own Median (%)	Rent Median (%)	Own Median (%)
Phoenix						
Hispanic	35.0	39.5	20.3	20.5	12.8	13.5
Black	40.2	44.2	21.2	24.0	13.4	15.8
White†	34.4	49.2	22.5	26.4	14.7	16.5
Detroit						
Hispanic	38.6	50+	18.6	19.1	11.3	11.5
Black	32.2	50+	18.0	18.7	8.5	11.3
White†	33.2	47.0	16.4	19.2	9.6	11.8
San Antonio						
Hispanic	25.1	34.4	14.6	17.4	10.0	11.4
Black	29.3	37.1	16.6	19.7	12.3	12.6
White†	24.7	38.0	15.4	21.0	11.4	13.4
San Diego						
Total	28.8	49.6	20.7	25.0	14.7	16.3
Hispanic	38.2	45.9	24.2	22.2	14.7	14.0
Black	35.9	49.2	24.4	24.1	16.5	15.1
White†	26.7	49.6	19.0	25.5	14.2	16.6

*U.S. Census does not differentiate Hispanics from whites; the Hispanic data is based on the 5 percent weighted sample as with the black data.
    Census of the Population Supplementary Reports: Persons By Race and Spanish Origin and Housing Unit Costs for Standard Metropolitan Statistical Areas (Washington, D.C.: U.S. Department of Census, 1980).

References

Abrams, Charles. 1965. "The Housing Problem and the Negro." *Daedalus* 64:86.

Burgess, Ernest. 1925. "The Growth of the City." Pp. 51–55 in *The City*, edited by R. Park and E. Burgess. Chicago: University of Chicago Press.

A Demographic Guide to Arizona: 1985. Report Number 14. Phoenix: Arizona Department of Economic Security, Population Statistics Unit.

Gordon, Leonard, and Albert J. Mayer. 1987. "A Method of Measuring Changes in Residential Segregation of Minority Groups for Inter Censal Years." Paper presented at the 1987 meetings of the Society for the Study of Social Problems. Chicago.

Grebler, Leo, Joan W. Moore, and Ralph C. Guzman. 1970. *The Mexican American People: The Nation's Second Largest Minority*. New York: Free Press.

Harvey, David. 1975. *Social Justice and the City.* Baltimore: Johns Hopkins University Press.

Jackman, Mary R., and Robert W. Jackman. 1980. "Racial Inequalities in Home Ownership." *Social Forces* 59:1221–34.

Massey, Douglas S. 1979. "Effects of Socioeconomic Factors on the Residential Segregation of Blacks and Spanish Americans in U.S. Urbanized Areas." *American Sociological Review* 44:1015–22.

Muth, Richard. 1969. *Cities and Housing: The Spatial Pattern of Urban Residential Land Use.* Chicago: University of Chicago Press.

Villemez, Wayne J. 1980. "Race Neighborhood: Differences in the Residential Return on Individual Resources." *Social Forces* 59:414–30.

Yinger, John. 1975. *The Black-White Price Differential in Housing: Some Further Evidence.* Madison: Institute for Research and Poverty, University of Wisconsin.

IV

Policies and Programs
Related to Housing Segregation
in the United States

17. Introduction to American Policies and Programs

The following chapters primarily deal with American policies in housing. The 1988 Fair Housing Amendments bill, which strengthens the Fair Housing bill of 1968, also extends antidiscrimination protection to the handicapped and to families with children. Of great importance too is the fact that the Fair Housing Amendments Act provides for administrative law judges to hear housing discrimination cases and empowers the federal government to impose fines of up to $100,000 against fair housing violators. The new law is particularly important for minority groups living in cities that do not have fair housing centers. They now have a place to which to turn if refused occupancy. The book carries to some extent a comparison with European housing policy, especially regarding attempts at dispersal, as in Sweden.

John Goering and Mobido Coulibably deal with American policies in housing, especially policies involving public housing segregation in the United States, and provide a revealing and impressive historical exposition.

A highly important development pertaining to black-white relations in the United States has been the introduction of a system of "integration maintenance" in some cities and in some suburbs. As Juliet Saltman so ably explains in her chapter, integration maintenance signifies the set of means used to help keep a neighborhood racially mixed.

However, real estate agents still constitute a problem in the obtaining of housing by members of minority groups in spite of federal legislation. As Saltman clearly states, solicitation by real estate agents plagued the three communities she studied and block-busting and racial steering still took place.

In his account of open housing in metropolitan Cleveland, W. Dennis Keating draws attention to its highly segregated pattern. Most of the efforts to encourage racial integration in housing, he points out,

303

have taken place in Cleveland's suburbs. According to the Cuyahoga Plan, the regional nonprofit agency established in 1974, racial discrimination, not economics, largely explains Cleveland's segregated housing patterns.

Keating's data reveal that, although a majority of whites, homeowners and renters, are much more tolerant of blacks than they were in the 1960s, most whites do not move in search of racially integrated neighborhoods. Deliberate local efforts will be needed to promote racially integrated living patterns. Keating points out that mere enforcement of existing fair housing laws has not made basic changes in patterns of racial segregation in housing, in spite of greater white support for integrated living. He maintains that far more comprehensive programs with pro-integrative housing incentives in an all-over pattern are necessary.

Keating points to Cleveland's mostly segregated private housing market and its largely segregated public housing. Most of Cleveland's suburbs have rejected public housing. To maintain racial integration in at least a few suburban communities, the cities of Cleveland Heights, Shaker Heights, and University Heights and their school boards joined together in 1984 to form the Eastern Suburban Council for Ohio Communities (ESCOC) and to encourage prospective black home-buyers and renters to consider the Hillcrest housing market (six communities bordering the three ESCOC cities).

However, the city of Cleveland and most of its suburbs still remain heavily segregated. Meanwhile there continue to be an alarming number of violent racial incidents, both within the city and in the suburbs. The situation is not totally bleak. The creation of ESCOC and the activities of the Cuyahoga Plan give hope that there is a constituency for open housing policies.

Elizabeth Huttman and Terry Jones deal with the overall growth of black population in the suburbs and the possibility, even the likelihood, of great growth of black population in the suburbs in the future. Huttman and Jones discuss the debate that has arisen over the policy and specific measures involved in the system known as integration maintenance, a system elaborated on by Juliet Saltman in her chapter as having favorable results for interracial housing. Huttman points out, however, that a debate has arisen over the integration maintenance system, with black insistence that it limits black opportunity. Thus a serious criticism has been made of a system that appears promising for the interracial neighborhood and warrants a thorough examination.

18. Public Housing Segregation in the United States

Public housing in America has been pilloried in the press as a gigantic monument to segregation and neglect and criticized by social scientists as putting yet another nail in the coffin of the urban underclass. For example, the historian Arnold Hirsch (1983:254–55), in his detailed study of the new or "second" ghetto in Chicago reports that "With the emergence of redevelopment, renewal, and public housing . . . government took an active hand not merely in reinforcing prevailing patterns of segregation but also in lending them a permanence never seen before. The implication of government in the second ghetto was so pervasive, so deep, that it virtually constituted a new form of de jure segregation." Government-sponsored segregation is presented as a driving force in restricting the social and residential choices of blacks in metropolitan America.

This chapter is a reconnaissance of Hirsch's assertion, exploring conceptual and empirical issues associated with segregation in federal housing throughout the urban United States. It is exploratory because only limited data are available to dissect fully the degrees, determinants, and impacts of federal housing segregation. Whatever the persuasiveness of evidence for a city, it is also important to examine national-level data for the uniformity of such patterns. To accomplish this, it is necessary to develop concepts, methods, and data to test the hypothesis that federal programs have fostered and sustained the segregation of urban housing markets. This chapter is designed to examine national-level evidence concerning the making of the "second ghetto."

Four "originating" or sensitizing issues help to focus the investigation (Merton 1982): (1) to understand the influence of legislative, budgetary, and programmatic factors in determining the racial composition of the federally mandated public housing program; (2) to appreciate how much federal housing got built, where, and for what

305

population groups (a grasp of the basic quantities and allocation of such a scarce commodity provides the basis for subsequent analysis); (3) to measure public housing segregation so that there is a common, agreed-upon yardstick for deciding on the level of "ghettoization" in federal housing; and (4) to analyze the determinants of public housing segregation given its unique legislative characteristics. To what degree, for example, has segregation in the private housing market determined subsequent patterns in public housing or, conversely, has segregation in federal housing influenced the speed and forms of the subsequent segregation of the private housing stock? The limited nature of available data and causal analyses of residential segregation will, as we shall discuss, impose a substantial constraint on this portion of the analysis.

These issues are not designed to deny the influence of locally powerful racial pressures and decisions in creating rigidly segregated federal housing. Evidence of the segregation of public housing makes it clear that such practices have been long-standing and willful. The focus of this inquiry is to search for common, nationwide patterns and influences in order to have a clearer grasp of the uniformity and degree of segregation inherent in standard operation of the federal public housing program (Semer 1976b; Kamen 1988).

Originating Questions:
Legislative and Programmatic Concerns

The first analytic issue to raise is whether, and to what extent, the legislative and political history of the federal public housing program helps to explain its current occupancy characteristics. Have such factors influenced the segregated character of the public housing inventory?

Four possible domains or fields of influence appear relevant to answering the question. The domains are interdependent and yet vary in their significance across time. Although the four domains appear relatively static, they are driven at the national and local level by a variety of management procedures and conflicts which have frequently altered the impact of the domains in specific settings. Understanding the historic and dynamic interrelationship among these four strategic fields helps to provide an answer to the basic question of how much federal housing gets built, where, for whom, and on what segregated basis.

The first domain consists of legislative and political influences. The enactment of the Housing Acts of 1937 and 1949 provided the major bases for the intervention of the federal government into the development and management of housing for the poor. Under the 1937 Act, roughly 160,000 units were built, most to provide housing for the working poor and for war workers. The public housing program was expanded by the 1949 Act with another 155,000 units built in three years with declines in production after that. Roughly 15–35,000 units a year were built up into the 1960s, with smaller numbers built thereafter. Approximately 1.3 million low-rent public housing units are in operation (Weicher 1980:34).[1]

Five political decisions, following the enactment of the Housing Acts, have had important impacts on the allocation of public housing units. the first has been the continual reduction in congressional funding for the program, which has reduced both the number of units built and their amenities so only a small fraction of the housing needy are served by federal programs (Meehan 1979; Wood 1982:32; Turner and Page 1987). Second, the decision to use the private-sector housing industry, and minimize federal involvement, has resulted in a program which is heavily driven and controlled by local influences (Bredemeier 1980:127–48; Fisher 1959:1–23).

Third, the decision to link urban renewal provisions to public housing has meant that former occupants of the sites cleared of "slum" housing had an immediate right to return to the newly built housing. Sufficient numbers of nonwhites were displaced, and then relocated to public housing, to create a fairly pronounced change in the racial occupancy of public housing (Wood 1982:67; Fisher 1959:164). These three areas of national legislative action were of such importance that, for some cities, they solidified the impact of federal housing on residential segregation. Hirsch (1983:256), for example, is convinced that "the key decisions influencing this pattern [of the second ghetto] were all taken by the early 1950s."

A fourth congressional decision that was to have important implications for what types of households were served by the public housing program was the decision in the mid-1950s to permit households of elderly persons to occupy units previously reserved for families. This decision also meant that public housing authorities could construct projects designated solely or exclusively for the elderly, many of whom were white (Wood 1982; Knapp 1986:93).

The enactment of civil rights protections for residents of federal housing in the 1960s constitutes the fifth major legislative action which affected the segregation of public housing tenants. Title VI of the Civil

Rights Act of 1964 became a tool for addressing the discriminatory character of federal housing (Luttrell 1966; Whalen and Whalen 1985; Vernarelli 1986) by prohibiting federal financial support for discriminatory practices and by establishing an enforcement mechanism to punish violators. Congress attempted to counterweight the influence of local jurisdictions on public housing, established decades earlier, with an emphasis on federal responsibilities for the civil rights of public housing tenants. The uncertain balance between federal and nonfederal responsibilities on the occupancy characteristics of public housing has been a source of public policy tension ever since (Lazin 1973).

Thus, *the second domain* of strategic influences on the public housing stock are local decision-making systems. A modest level of research has focused on local decision making in the urban renewal program, with less attention paid to the longer-term issues of public housing site selection and occupancy (Dahl 1961; Caro 1974; Hartman 1974; Henig 1982). Aiken and Alford (1969, 1970a, 1970b) explored the distinctive dynamics of the two federal programs and found evidence of "fundamental diversity and differential of cities" in their approach to federal housing programs, with suggestions of important regional and historical influences. Others, however, perceive the sharply demarcated influence of property interests in setting the ground rules for public intervention in local housing markets (Mollenkopf and Pynoos 1972; Philpott 1978:269; Marcuse 1986; Feagin 1987).

Setting aside the theoretical contest between such approaches, local jurisdictions have a number of basic rights in the provision of public housing. First, to not apply for such assistance leaving the federal government with few tools to deal with the housing and civil rights needs of the poor. The locality also plays a crucial role in selecting the sites or locale for the construction of public units. Finally, specific tenants are selected for specific units within a general scheme of preferences, tenant selection, and assignment procedures suggested by the federal housing agency (Knapp 1986:174–243). The local housing agency picks whom to house and where to house them (Weaver 1948:177; Struyk and Blake 1983; Hirsch 1983:219–45).

Demographic and social dynamics at the metropolitan level are *a third significant domain* of influences on both the demand for public housing by minorities and the increased segregation of cities. The segregation of many cities was fashioned by the rapid growth in the black population, with the postwar migration of blacks creating "a huge, new clientele for public housing" (Friedman 1968:123). At the same time, whites were moving out of public housing at a rapid rate.

The historical ecology of cities, including its ethnic composition and its economic base, has also been shown to influence the racially segregated character of public housing. Goldstein and Yancey (1986) report that in Philadelphia the location of public housing was influenced by lower property values or land costs resulting in locations in older, central city neighborhoods without access to industrial employment. Such ecological determinants surely effect the actions of the decision-making institutions identified in the second domain, but nevertheless appear to reflect an independently powerful constraint on the long-term evolution of the segregated character of public housing.

The final domain of influences are the choices and attitudes of residents living in public housing and in the surrounding private stock. The hostility toward, or acceptance of, residents of low-rent housing has always been a key factor in determining whether or not a project gets built in a certain neighborhood. Hirsch (1983), among others (Abrams 1955; McGrew 1981), describes the role of mob violence in resisting, altering, or delaying the entry of blacks and public housing units into previously all-white areas. Such hostility is often the tip of an iceberg of racial animosities and preferences that can undermine the best-laid plans of housing reformers, civil rights groups, and federal policymakers.

Latent racism, and its underbelly of fear of status and class contamination, are spontaneous forces with which both local and federal housing and planning officials must contend. Avoidance, prejudice, and class biases are interwoven in the choices of white tenants who, when asked where they prefer to live, generally elect to live in segregated public housing units (Lucas 1985; Edsall 1988; Schuman and Bobo 1988). Some minority tenants also may not wish to move out of an area where their family members, friends, and community ties are centered (Miller, De Pallo, and Rotendaro 1985). Public housing tenants do not, therefore, jettison their personal preferences when they occupy a public housing project, nor is their poverty, however temporary or permanent, an implacable bar to their access to alternative low-rent private housing.

Such preferences can undoubtedly be mobilized by interest groups with ulterior economic or political motives and will undoubtedly emerge under certain structural conditions, in certain places and not in others. They will also be shaped or reinforced by the choices of local housing authority officials who may wish to sustain the pattern of segregation which exists throughout their jurisdiction; who fear riling local officials who prefer the segregated status quo. Nevertheless, the ability of low-income white residents to "flee" desegregating projects or authorities constitutes an additional determinant of segregated public occupancy.

The interaction of the four domains of influence does not remain constant over time. For example, the major legislative decisions on the public housing program were taken decades ago, leaving courts and administrators—rather than Congress—to find ways to make the rules work either in favor of or against desegregation. Federal housing subsidies also have moved away from financing the construction of public housing units in cities to the subsidization of housing certificates and vouchers, leaving policymakers, the public, and public housing tenants with a program of only residual importance. The federal government has also become, to some, indifferent to civil rights issues, leaving local jurisdictions greater latitude to determine how segregated a housing program they can get away with (Subcommittee on Housing and Community Development 1986; Tobin 1987).

Another issue of importance in assessing how effective local authorities are in segregating or desegregating their tenants is the overall financial and management viability of the authority. Poorly managed or deteriorating public housing units, whatever the source of the deterioration, will neither attract nor hold black or white tenants, leaving growing vacancies, debts, and abandonment as likely outcomes (Bain et al. 1988).

Another issue which influences the occupancy patterns of public housing is the size and composition of waiting lists or backlogs. Waiting lists are one of the most important, yet understudied, aspects of the allocation of federal housing to households in need. Virtually every public housing authority (PHA) has long lists of families who appear eligible for housing. The largest PHAs often have several waiting lists with needs, preferences, and vacancies balanced by computer (Struyk and Blake 1982). Applicants for housing are generally screened through a complex series of federal and local requirements including income eligibility, family size, need, veteran and handicap status, residency, and racial factors tied to antidiscrimination laws.[2]

A number of factors stand out from the minimal amount of research on waiting lists and tenant assignments. First, waiting lists are long at larger PHAs, with waits of more than ten years in some cities. These waits are often longest for large families since comparatively few large rental units exist in either the public or private rental stock (Kaplan 1984, 1985). Second, most applicants on waiting lists appear to be nonwhite. In Chicago, for example, the waiting lists as of the late

1960s included 13,000 applicants, 90 percent of whom were black (Fisher 1959:259; Peel, Pickett, and Buehl 1971:82; Hirsch 1983:23). In San Francisco, while only half of the waiting list was nonwhite at this time, more than 80 percent of the families on the waiting list who were not elderly were nonwhites (Peel, Pickett, and Buehl 1971:82). Boston's waiting list was estimated to be 80 percent minority in 1983, and a survey of fifty-nine of the largest PHAs revealed that whites constituted only 14 percent of current occupants and were 11 percent of the applicants on waiting lists (Citizens Housing and Planning Association 1984).

It appears reasonable then to hypothesize that a mixture of structural, microlevel, and historical influences appear to have had a role in determining the current degree of segregation in public housing. The influence of these factors has waxed and waned as federal funding has risen and fallen, and as federal regulations have interjected requirements regarding nondiscrimination. In addition, the relatively small share of the low-income rental market controlled by public housing agencies may make it vulnerable to idiosyncratic or temporary shifts and constraints operating within local property markets.[3]

None of these strategic influences and hypotheses can be fully addressed without some attention to time-series or historical data. Knowing something about the racial composition of neighborhoods before and after the advent of public housing, as well as the connections of each neighborhood to the economic and ecological transformation of the city, is clearly a massive task. Distinguishing the role of federal housing policy before and after the enactment of civil rights statutes would be another necessary comparison.

Data Availability and Shortcomings

The following section provides a brief description of available data as well as methodological concerns tied to the conceptual issues and questions raised previously. Data on the number, allocation, and racial composition of public housing occupants are taken from a number of federal records and data files. Beginning in the 1940s, the federal housing agency collected data on the characteristics of both tenants and projects. Basic tenant-level data were gathered as part of the responsibility to certify or re-certify the incomes of tenants to determine eligibility for continued occupancy. Project-level data include information on the total units in a project, vacancies, the number of elderly households served, as well as the aggregate racial composition.

The federal housing agency also collected data on a "race relations data card" which provided project-level data on whether projects were segregated or "integrated" (Public Housing Administration 1953b).[4] The low response rate to this race relations data card, changing definitions of integrated occupancy, and the difficulty of determining how many applicants and tenants were provided an equal housing choice make these data difficult to interpret.

The decision by the president to ban discrimination in 1962 in federal housing and the passage of Title VI of the Civil Rights Act of 1964 led to new requirements covering tenant selection and assignment as well as regulations covering site selection procedures (Wood 1982:66–72; Knapp 1986). HUD's new procedures for ensuring equal opportunity in public housing were soon challenged in a series of lawsuits which have had a substantial, ongoing impact on the salience of racial issues in public housing (Luttrell 1966; Lazin 1973; Semer 1976b:150–53; Piven and Cloward 1980; Schnapper 1983; Rodrique 1985; Knapp 1986; Vernarelli 1986).

As new housing programs were established by Congress, new data collection forms were added to gather and report tenant characteristics in such programs as the Section 236 and Section 8 programs. One result has been a proliferation of parallel and duplicate racial data forms and reporting systems, each tailored to congressional requirements.

Beginning in the mid-1970s, policymakers became concerned about the quality and utility of the data being generated from these data files. Nonresponse and inattention to the management and analytic requirements for these data resulted in declines in data quality and an increased indifference on the part of PHAS and other HUD project sponsors to complete accurately all the various forms HUD had incrementally added to cover its housing and civil rights obligations.

The difficulties which HUD faced in establishing a useful system for race-related occupancy data on its programs was in the context of its other data system problems. The lack of a cohesive federal policy and priority on civil rights data collection has been important in limiting the willingness of individual federal agencies to provide the resources and support for effective civil rights data gathering systems (Office of Federal Statistical Policy and Standards 1978; Sklar 1971; GAO 1985).

As a result of these concerns, HUD and OMB began to suspend or terminate the gathering of tenant-level data until an improved data-

TABLE 18.1   Geographical Distribution of Occupied Public Housing Units by Project Date of Full Availability for Family and Elderly Households (1937–83)

	Units for Families			Units for the Elderly		
	1937–69	1970–83	Total	1937–69	1970–83	Total
Central City Locations	296,207	92,069	388,276	145,363	117,469	262,832
Percent	76.3	23.7	100	55.3	44.7	100
Non-Central City Locations	104,572	78,141	182,713	94,261	114,786	209,047
Percent	57.2	42.8	100	45.1	45.1	100

gathering and reporting system was established. In 1978, HUD established a task force to consolidate information on tenant characteristics. A multifamily tenant characteristics system (MTCS) was announced in 1981 as a proposed means for gathering and automating useful tenant characteristics data but design requirements and cost estimates were not completed until 1986, and a contract awarded in winter 1988, with report data gathered initially only from public housing agencies. It is expected that information on HUD's other subsidy programs, including census tract or zip code information, will be available to permit analyses of neighborhood characteristics or effects of federal housing.

More than ten years elapsed between the termination of automated data reporting on tenant racial characteristics and the first full year of data from the $10 million MTCS system. The result of this lengthy hiatus is an inability to provide reliable occupancy data on HUD's public housing program on a time-series basis (Burke 1984).

The last year in which reasonably comprehensive and accurate data were gathered was 1977 (Rodrique 1985; Mariano 1985; GAO 1985; Knapp 1986). These data will be used to help answer, to the extent possible, the originating questions listed previously.

The absence of racial occupancy data for specific buildings or projects over an extended period of time means that no direct test of all the foregoing hypotheses and questions is possible. There are, however, some benefits from investigating possible patterns and trends in the available data and research studies.

The first information is on the date of construction and location of housing units, in table 18.1, which provides a partial understanding of how many housing units were built, when, and where. The locational information available only permits a distinction between central city and non-central city locations, with the latter including rural PHAS as well as suburban ones.

TABLE 18.2.   Geographical Distribution of Public Housing Units for Elderly and Non-Elderly Units by Racial Occupancy of Units (1977)

	Family Units				
	Metropolitan		Non-Metro	Missing Geocodes	Total
	Central City (%)	Non-CC (%)			
Black	76	8	12	4	100
White	47	17	32	5	101*
Hispanic	82	7	8	3	101
Total	71	10	16	4	101

Source: Public Housing Occupancy System, 1977, in PD&R MULTI Data Base.
*Totals may not add to 100 percent due to rounding errors.

It is useful to note that roughly 600,000 units of public housing were built before 1960 and nearly one million before 1970, at the time when HUD's new civil rights obligations began to have effect. Since 1970, units not for the elderly have become increasingly less concentrated in central cities. While 85 percent of all such units were built in central cities during the period 1937–49, this proportion declined steadily until the period 1980–83, when only 44 percent of all units not intended for the elderly were built in central cities.

Table 18.1 indicates that the majority (76 percent) of family units were built before 1970, while almost half of central-city units for the elderly were built after that date. In non-central-city areas, 43 percent of family units and 55 percent of units for the elderly were built after 1970.[5] In the case of units with an elderly head of household, there has been a substantial decline in the proportion built in central cities from 1937 to 1983. An increasing proportion of housing for both the elderly and for families has been provided in non-metropolitan areas, increasing from 7 percent of all units not intended for the elderly in the period 1937–49 to more than a third by 1983. For housing with an elderly head of household, the increase was equally high.

Of roughly 1.3 million units of public housing, 53 percent are designated for families and 47 percent for elderly households. Units designated for families sometimes, however, contain elderly households which have aged in place (Council of Large Public Housing Authorities 1986:27). The congressional decision to permit support for the elderly has therefore promoted a substantial realignment of the allocation of units, including their increasing suburbanization.

Information on the characteristics of the occupants of family and elderly housing is, again, only available on a reliable basis for 1977 (table 18.2). As of 1977, more than three-fourths of all units built from

Units for the Elderly					All Units				
Metropolitan		Non-Metro	Missing Geocodes	Total	Metropolitan		Non-Metro	Missing Geocodes	Total
Central City (%)	Non-CC (%)				Central City (%)	Non-CC (%)			
75	8	13	4	100	76	8	12	4	100
48	18	29	6	101	48	17	30	5	100
83	5	8	4	100	82	6	8	3	99
58	14	23	5	100	65	12	19	4	100

1937 onward were in metropolitan areas, with two-thirds built in central cities and one-fifth in non-metropolitan areas. About one-fourth of family units and one-third of elderly units were built in non-central-city locations.

Table 18.2 also describes the level of racial concentration of these units, with 76 percent of black-occupied and 82 percent of Hispanic-occupied units located in central cities. Half of white-occupied units were in the central city but were primarily intended for the elderly. Whites comprised only 15 percent of the occupants of central-city family units but half of elderly units. In non-metropolitan locations, whites are 43 percent of family and 81 percent of elderly units. The data clearly suggest the concentration of nonwhite families in central city public housing authorities, with elderly households, primarily white, located outside of the central cities.

In order to get a clearer understanding whether public housing projects are located in segregated or nonsegregated portions within central cities, it is necessary to rely on research studies conducted in a handful of cities. Such studies have typically provided information on the racial composition of the census tracts within which federal housing projects are located. They have also reported this information on later HUD subsidy programs.

Table 18.3 presents a summary of evidence from four such studies; each addresses the racial concentration of public housing units for families as well as that of later programs including the Section 221(d)(3), 236 and Section 8 programs. Different thresholds of racial impaction were used in these studies, ranging from 25 to 40 percent of the tract's population. Each of the studies—with the exception of the one for Columbus, Ohio—indicates that public housing units were located in tracts that were more heavily minority than were units de-

TABLE 18.3   Percent of HUD-Subsidized Housing Units/Households Located in Minority Census Tracts, by Program, for Select Research Sites

Research Sites	Low-Rent Public Housing Units	Section 221(d)(3) Units	Section 236 Units	Section 8 New and Rehab Units	Section 8 Existing Households[4]
Patterson[1]					
(25 + % minority)	75.9	88.5	0	—	—
(n)	(1,800)	(1,430)	(206)	—	—
Fleisher[2]					
(30 + % minority)	72.0	56.0	30.0	34.3	33.6
Fischer and Orfield					
(40 + % minority)					
Denver	78.5		70.1	41.7	56.7
(n)	(3,542)	—	(3,144)	(60)	(383)
Columbus	37.3		39.4	55.4	36.1
(n)	(4,449)	—	(3,352)	(1,181)	(1,405)
Phoenix	69.3		14.8	0	31.6
(n)	(1,646)	—	(758)	(46)	(1,114)
(40 + % minority)[3]	75.0		26.5	39.0	43.0
(n)	(51,933)	—	(21,277)	(10,804)	(10,908)

1. Jacksonville, Florida, SMSA (Patterson 1979).
2. Seventeen SMSAs (Fleisher 1979).
3. Ten SMSAs (Hartford, Newark, Richmond, Atlanta, Dayton, San Antonio, Omaha, Denver, Phoenix, and Portland).
4. Family households only for Fischer and Orfield (1981) sites.

veloped under later HUD subsidy programs. Roughly 70–75 percent of the units in the various sites were located, at the time of the study, in black or transitional areas.

Considerably less racial impaction appears in the Section 236 and Section 8 programs. No information, however, is provided on the racial composition of the tracts when the projects were built. Warren (1986:496) also finds increasing dispersal of such units in Chicago, reporting that "the number of census tracts with integrated or predominantly white populations where assisted housing was located grew from 40 to 275" from 1970 to 1980.

Descriptions of the racial concentration of tracts with federal housing projects do not, however, always provide a perfect predictor of their racial occupancy. In the places a substantial minority population appears on the waiting list, units located in white areas are more likely to have nonwhite tenants. Fleisher (1979:108) makes one of the few efforts to explain such patterns but reports that "the observed differences in the percentage of minority occupied units located in predominantly white census tracts are unrelated to demographic characteristics of the metropolitan area." The location of a project in a minority area appears to result in a fully segregated project unless some form of racial quota, race-conscious tenant assignment plan, or desegregation procedure is used.

Understanding the level and degree of segregation in the public housing program is also facilitated by a brief look at earlier analyses of the race relations data gathered since the 1930s. In one of the earliest analyses of these data, Nichols (1939:70) reports that as of the late 1930s, nearly three-quarters of all units were racially segregated and only 4 percent of all units, roughly nine hundred apartments, were designed for "equal" occupancy. By the 1940s, Weaver (1948:180) reports that in 134 projects some form of state or local law authorized "controlled" or mixed racial occupancy. Beginning in 1952, the Federal Public Housing Administration released an annual report on what was termed "open" occupancy (Public Housing Administration 1953a, 1953b; McGraw 1954). The final report on open occupancy, in 1963, indicated that there were 675 "completely integrated" projects, or 36 percent of all projects with some "Negro" occupants, with 98,000 units out of the total of 500,000 subject to an antidiscrimination provision (Horne 1958; Jackson 1958; Public Housing Administration 1963; Luttrell 1966:871).

The willingness of certain states and cities to enact antidiscrimination or prointegration statutes was unevenly distributed across the United States. Southern states as well as some in the West resisted enacting any form of fair housing provision for public- or private-sector housing. This regional difference in responsiveness to the diffusion of civil rights laws takes on added importance because of the large number of public housing units located in the South. Nearly one-half of all PHAS, for example, equaling one-third of all units, are located in the thirteen Southern states. At the same time, roughly 10 percent of all units are located in New York City. The uneven allocation of such units means that public housing may be a larger or smaller share of the total rental housing stock in a given city, with a greater or lesser role in housing low-income white and nonwhite residents.

The uneven allocation of public housing units across regions, states, and metropolitan areas reflects a variety of local decisions as well as more recent civil rights constraints. Serving poor families or elderly-only households has meant that a major programmatic division often separates tenants within the same PHA. Understanding the impact of these myriad allocation decisions on racial occupancy requires the use of a standardized, readily interpretable measurement tool. The following discussion presents evidence, for the first time, on a measure of public housing segregation.

Measuring and Explaining Public Housing Segregation

Central to this exploratory analysis is the question of how much segregation exists within the public housing program. Is segregation uniformly or unevenly distributed, as likely to exist in all regions, and does its existence appear to reflect broader patterns or trends in residential segregation? Answers to these questions are of crucial significance to policy researchers and social scientists interested in constructing heuristic explanations of the determinants of overall residential segregation. As public housing looms larger or smaller in significance in such equations, analysts can help resolve issues associated with establishing public- and private-sector policy responsibilities.

Refinement of Measurements

Despite the plausibility of a locally powerful impact of public housing, only a handful of efforts have been made to measure the degree of segregation or "dispersal" of public-sector housing (Taeuber and Taeuber 1965:48–49; Wolf 1981; Warren 1986).

Measuring and explaining the role of public housing segregation has been greatly aided by refinements in both measurement and analytic procedures. Beginning with the National Academy of Sciences report on the determinants of segregation (Foley 1973), an increasingly sophisticated set of measurement techniques and causal models have been introduced aimed principally at explaining the segregation of the overall housing market (Fleisher 1979; Lieberson 1980; Taeuber 1983; Wilger 1987; Farley and Wilger 1987; Galster 1987; Massey 1987a, 1987b, 1987c; Smith 1988; Massey 1988). No comprehensive model of the determinants of black segregation, however, exists to explain the declines in dissimilarity and increased exposure since 1970, in part because no federal government or HUD policy influences have been included in these models with direct measures of housing discrimination used in only one of these assessments (Galster 1988).

As seen in the previous section, a handful of studies have related the location of public housing to the racial composition of the census tract, with comparisons also made with housing subsidy programs. Such studies provide useful descriptions of the concentration and partial dispersal of housing units, with virtually no information on the racial characteristics of the occupants of the segregated or dispersed units, nor any integration of these findings into an overall model of residential segregation.

To this point there has been no single, agreed-upon measure of the segregation of public housing on which to base comparative assessments of housing policy. Descriptive accounts, such as those by Hirsch (1983) and Bauman (1987) have demonstrated the utility of such in-depth examinations but have left unresolved the question of national or regional trends and practices.

For the purpose of this study we adopt a simple measure of the degree of segregation of tenants within a sample of the nation's larger public housing authorities using project-level occupancy data for 1977. Family and units for elderly are divided on the basis of the racial proportions of tenants living in the PHA and project, resulting in the following:

1. White-occupied project: 80 percent or more of all tenants are white households.

2. Black-occupied project: 80 percent or more of all tenants are black households.

3. Asian or Hispanic: same.

4. Racially or ethnically mixed project: the concentration of none of the racial groups exceeds 80 percent.

The separation of units into those with high levels of racial homogeneity is, of course, arbitrary.

A sample of 142 PHAS were selected from among central cities with a population in 1980 of 100,000 or more from which racial occupancy data were available. This sample was matched with additional data on the socioeconomic and demographic characteristics of cities.[6] For these PHAS, an index of racial homogeneity or segregation was constructed. The total number of units in projects with fewer than 15 percent blacks, or whites, is added to the total number of units in projects where the percentage of whites, or blacks, is between 80 and 100 percent. All other units are classified as a middle "other" or racially mixed category. Thus for each city where data on racial characteristics of tenants were available in 1977, a percentage distribution of units by race and by category of projects was established.[7] The national and regional distributions are simply the weighted averages of cities' dis-

TABLE 18.4   Distribution of Public Housing Units by Regional and Index of Segregation, by Racial Proportions (1977)

Regions	Racial Characteristics of Tenants	Percentage of Units in Projects with Less than 20 Percent	Percentage of Units in Projects with 20–79 Percent	Percentage of Units in Projects with 80–100 Percent	Index of Racial Segregation (Column (1 + 3))
Total U.S.	Whites	60	26	12	72
	Blacks	22	33	46	68
	Hispanics	80	18	2	82
Northeast	Whites	62	27	9	71
	Blacks	17	48	35	52
	Hispanics	69	30	0	69
North Central	Whites	55	26	18	73
	Blacks	21	27	53	74
	Hispanics	98	1	0	98
West	Whites	40	42	15	55
	Blacks	51	37	12	63
	Hispanics	66	29	5	71
South	Whites	72	19	7	79
	Blacks	18	16	66	84
	Hispanics	89	7	4	93

Source: Sample of 142 PHAs.

tributions, with weights based on numbers of units. This procedure makes it possible to isolate racially homogeneous projects from those which have a degree of racial mixing.

Using Measurements

Using our own measure of segregation, the data in table 18.4 report the index of segregation as well as the distribution of units by racial category for the total country and four regions as of 1977. Nationally, only 12 percent of all units are located in projects in which whites were a majority. The percentage of units in which blacks constituted a majority, more than 80 percent, was 46 percent as of 1977. There are, however, notable regional differences in the level of segregation, with blacks experiencing higher levels of segregation in the South than elsewhere. Segregation of blacks and Hispanics appears highest in the North Central area and lowest for blacks in the Northeast. It is also in this Northeast region that the percentage of units with 20 to 79 percent black occupancy is highest.

As might be expected, there are major differences in the degree of

TABLE 18.5   Proportion of Family and Elderly Public Housing Units by
Degree of Racial and Ethnic Mix of the Public Housing Authority (1977)

Degree of Racial Mix In PHA	Projects for Families		Projects for the Elderly	
	Number of Units	Percent	Number of Units	Percent
95 + percent white	63,614	7.2	121,983	49.3
95 + percent black	261,278	29.4	8,800	3.5
60–94 percent white	127,828	14.4	81,688	33.0
60–94 percent black	180,811	20.4	13,638	5.5
No group over 60 percent	154,784	17.4	18,787	7.6
60 + percent other minorities	99,625	11.2	2,542	1.1
Total	887,940	100.0	247,438	100.0

Source: Public Housing Occupancy System, 1977, in PD&R MULTI Data Base.

segregation, by region, for family compared to elderly housing. In the
North Central region, for example, where approximately one-third of
white-occupied projects are located, projects for the elderly are more
segregated than family projects. In specific locations such as Mont-
gomery, Fort Worth, Savannah, and Waterbury, all family projects
are black-occupied, while all projects for the elderly are white-occupied. The values of the index clearly reveal that a high but variable
degree of segregation in the public housing program exists in many
cities.

Classifying the number of family and elderly public housing units
by the degree of racial mixture in a PHA provides another means of
describing the segregation or separation of tenants. The data in table
18.5 describe the degree of racial mix of projects for families and the
elderly as of 1977. The data show that almost 50 percent of all public
housing tenants who lived in projects for the elderly lived in projects
in PHAs which are 95 percent or more white. Conversely, only 7 percent
of public housing tenants living in family projects were living in PHAs
which were 95 percent or more white. Roughly 14 percent of family
units and 33 percent of units for the elderly are located in PHAs whose
racial composition was between 60 and 94 percent white as of 1977.
It is not possible to draw conclusions about whether any of these
projects remain stably integrated in the absence of time-series data on
racial occupancy patterns by sites and buildings within PHAs (Ledbetter
1967; Gesmer 1977; Abt Associates 1981). The following section uses
the index of public housing segregation in an attempt to identify variables of potential importance in explaining its variations.

The Determinants of Public Housing Segregation

There are, as noted previously, a complex set of macro- and micro-level factors which may logically exert some influence on the racial occupancy patterns of public housing. This matrix of influences undoubtedly shifts over time, if for no other reason than both the cities and the public housing stock are aging. As the characteristics of the poverty population change, that too can impact on the poor in need of public shelter (Wilson 1987; Lichter 1988). Capturing this evolving network of influence is difficult. Our findings, from developing an index with social, demographic, and housing variables weighed in, showed that higher levels of segregation in family housing were associated with higher scores in this index, called an index of distress. The levels of distress were especially high in the South. Racial segregation/separation was also higher in the South for family housing.

The final originating question with which this chapter began concerned the relationship between private- and public-sector housing segregation. In its simplest form, this is a question about whether a statistically significant relationship can be found between segregation in public housing and an index of segregation, such as the index of dissimilarity. In theory, one would expect that cities which were segregated on an overall basis would have segregated public housing. However, because of the substantial concentration of black families within the public housing program one would also expect to find little variation in black family housing, with greater variation in location and degree of concentration in predominantly white-occupied housing projects.

A more refined version of this question would incorporate measures of public housing separation within an overall model seeking to explain variations in segregation scores. Does, for example, segregation in public housing help to explain a significant proportion of the variation in the index of dissimilarity in all or some metropolitan areas? Does information on the number of public housing units built on a segregated basis help to predict segregation in the total housing market? And, most important, is the placement and occupancy of public housing units a clear determinant of subsequent private-sector segregation?[8]

In an effort to address the first, simpler question, correlations were run between the index of dissimilarity and the indices of public housing separation for family and elderly housing. This is an attempt to peer into the black box of interactions between public- and private-sector

TABLE 18.6   Correlation of the Index of Dissimilarity with Indices of Public Housing Segregation for the U.S. and Regions

Region	Indices of Public Housing Segregation			
	White Family	White Elderly	Black Family	Black Elderly
Total U.S. (N = 83)	.40	−.16	.17	−.11
Northeast (N = 16)	−.002	−.09	−.20	−.04
North Central (N = 25)	.55	−.11	.39	.02
South (N = 33)	−.13	−.05	−.22	−.20
West (N = 9)	.54	−.44	−.14	−.04

practices and decisions with a relatively crude statistical tool. It involves examining the relationship between an index based on the differential spatial allocation of blacks to a measure of racial concentration within the local public housing stock in which the measure of separation is influenced by the number of income-eligible blacks and the number of units authorized for construction. It asks whether the degree of spatial concentration in the overall market resembles the degree of separation, or mixing within a subset of the same housing market.

Within many cities there is an undifferentiated, high level of racial separation in family housing, while in other places projects housing black tenants may be located in otherwise white neighborhoods. Residents of public housing projects need not be clustered or geographically segregated in the same manner as the private market, although the extent to which family housing and housing for the elderly respond to similar or different segregative tendencies is of considerable empirical interest.

There were eighty-three cities for which data were available for both the index of dissimilarity and the index of public housing separation.[9] The data in table 18.6 indicate a modest positive relationship between the index of dissimilarity and white family housing and a trivial relationship with black family housing. Housing for the elderly is negatively related to segregation scores although at only relatively low levels. The table also reveals notable regional differences in these correlations, with public housing authorities in the North Central states having the highest correlations for both black and white family separation but insignificant effects for housing for the elderly.

All public housing in the Northeast is related negatively to segregation scores, but at such insignificant levels that no importance can be given to the findings. Housing for both families and the elderly in the South is also negatively related to segregation, with slightly higher correlation coefficients for black family and elderly units.

The racial concentration of family housing units appears to be positively related to the segregation measure in the North Central region, suggesting some caution in inferring that the patterns of segregation in the "new ghetto" of Chicago will be consistently replicated throughout the rest of the United States. It also appears that housing for the elderly is generally located in a pattern which is distinct from that found in the total housing market.

This brief discussion of the correspondence between private- and public-sector housing segregation suggests, once again, that there may be powerful regional influences within the overall federal housing program. Family housing in some areas appears to have a significant relationship to, and possibly potential impact on, private-sector segregation. Housing for the elderly appears to be driven in directions slightly opposite to those impelling family housing. The lack of adequate analytic tools and time-series data prevent an extension of this assessment to the more complex questions of causality and impact.

Conclusions

Having completed this investigation of concepts, methods, and data concerning the segregation of the federal low-rent public housing program, a number of more or less robust conclusions can be drawn. These conclusions are not intended to terminate lines of inquiry, but rather to prompt others to continue examining the forms, degrees, and impacts of federal housing segregation.

The first and most apparent conclusion is that substantial inadequacies exist in federal data reporting on the location and occupancy characteristics of the public housing stock. Data systems will facilitate social science research and modeling in this relatively underexplored area.

A second equally clear conclusion is that there are relatively high levels of segregation of black residents throughout the sample of PHAS used in this study. Inferentially, the development of the current level of segregation has been affected by varying structural, political, and personal choices taken at the national and local levels. Case study information on Chicago and Philadelphia, as well as a few other cities, suggests that segregation has been a deliberate policy of local and some federal officials firmly supported by local, white residents. The absence of comparable information on a sample of PHAS, operating with varying degrees of segregation or integrated occupancy, makes it difficult to conclude that comparable levels of intent and effect exist uniformly throughout the United States. Efforts by HUD, courts, and private citizens to press for nonsegregated occupancy make the availability of post-1977 data especially relevant.

Third, the data reveal pronounced regional differences in the degree of segregation, as well as significant differences in the allocation of units between cities and suburbs.

Fourth, important differences exist in the racial concentration of occupants in family projects compared to housing projects for the elderly. This legislatively driven distinction has resulted in some jurisdictions deliberately allocating elderly white residents to certain projects or buildings, with black families concentrated in the older conventional public housing stock. An issue of considerable concern for future research efforts is to ascertain the overlap of segregated black occupancy and older deteriorating public units. It has been estimated, for example, that it will cost roughly $8 billion to repair existing public housing inventory and another $1 billion or more annually to handle ongoing repairs (Bain et al. 1988; ICF 1989). Part of these expenditures may be tied to desegregation, but all too often repairs will have to be made to units in all or predominantly black projects and PHAS.

Thus an issue which needs to be added to future research on public housing segregation and desegregation is the quality or condition of the housing stock amenable to housing any of the poor—white or black. Once having dealt with the issue of housing quality, presumably making all units equally attractive, the issue of how much choice to allow tenants and applicants would become a salient concern.

A fifth conclusion, admittedly based on only a few research studies, is that PHAS which administer subsidized housing programs other than conventional public housing may have less segregated occupancy throughout their systems than PHAS which are only administering older, conventional projects. A substantial proportion of PHAS also administer Section 8 new construction and certificates as well as housing vouchers. In addition, a growing number of states and localities are establishing their own low-rent housing programs to supplement dwindling federal assistance (Stucker 1987). Such PHAS may therefore have a more comprehensive strategy for integrating all their tenants; leaving a partial, misleading portrait of their overall record in desegregating their federally assisted public housing tenants. Other PHAS may use family public housing units solely for black families and "reserve" their locally funded or elderly units for whites. Both sets of practices are known to occur, with no information available to describe their frequency or motivation.

Finally, federal, state, and local policies aimed at the desegregation of federally funded housing may have had some impact in altering the level and forms of segregation described previously. The absence of research or evaluation studies on mandatory or voluntary desegregation makes it impossible to determine under which conditions such desegregation may occur and with what long-term impacts (Miller, DePallo, and Rotendaro 1985; Yinger 1986; Knapp 1986; Goering 1986a; Bauer 1987; Office of Fair Housing 1988). It is possible that one of the unexplained conditions which helps to foster and sustain pressures for desegregation is the level of policy commitment of the executive and judicial branches of government to housing desegregation and integration.

It is heartening that other social scientists are beginning to examine these issues.[10] This exploratory analysis may then help promote improved concepts, better measures, and more powerful assessments of historical and future trends. Comprehensive assessments of the segregation of metropolitan housing markets will likely reveal complex yet varying degrees of structural, personal, and institutional influences in which federal housing policy choices and inaction have been strategic. Such strategic actions, however, occur within a context of decisive regional influences which signal historical and continuing clumps of racism. National and regional patterns of economic and racial segregation define and reflect one of America's most visible values and powerful political conundrums. Researchers are, therefore, unlikely to discover ideal, short-term solutions for the problem of public housing segregation but can undoubtedly be a major contributor to future debate on its perpetuation.

[*Editorial note:* Public housing authorities, while pushed not to put public housing in racially impacted areas and to further integrate their housing, have faced legal problems in doing this, as in the *Starrett City* case, wherein a Brooklyn state-assisted housing complex, Starrett City, had its affirmative action plan challenged in the courts. Race was used as a criterion for accepting applicants and making the complex integrated; thus the larger number of black applicants had longer waiting periods than others. The housing administration was sued for discrimination. The two parties to the suit settled on the compromise of increased minority access by 175 units over five years, in exchange for allowance of race as a factor in consideration in applicant selection

(Blair 1984). However, the Justice Department objected to Starrett City administrators considering race a criteria in applicant selection and filed a suit calling this illegal discrimination. E.D.H.]

Notes

We would like to thank a number of colleagues who have offered useful comments on earlier drafts of this chapter, including George Galster, Peter Marcuse, Douglas Massey, Sue Neal, Robert Wilger, Rodney Green, Ray Struyk, and anonymous reviewers. Paul Burke and Harold Bunce graciously provided access to data files on public housing occupancy and urban distress. Robert K. Merton offered well-placed encouragement of this epigonous essay, stimulated by his earlier research on the sociology of public housing. A special intellectual debt is owed to Dan Fabillon. Any of the unresponsiveness, narrow-mindedness, errors, or fatuousness herein are not their doing. Also, the opinions expressed do not reflect the views of either the U.S. Department of Housing and Urban Development or the federal government.

1. A number of other low-income housing programs were created by Congress after the 1960s, adding nearly three million additional units or households to the total inventory of HUD-assisted rental housing. The low-rent public housing program, and various other subsidy programs, are administered by nearly 3,300 local public housing agencies scattered throughout the United States. Public housing units are designated for families or for elderly households and are divided into roughly 10,000 projects and many more separate sites. For background on federal housing policies and programs as they relate to minority occupancy, see Weaver 1948; Fisher 1959; Schoshinski 1969; Semer 1976a; McGrew 1981; Schnapper 1983; Marcuse 1986; and Chudacoff 1987.

2. HUD struggled from 1979 to 1988 to establish a "preference rule" clarifying all of these options and has just published regulations on the issue (U.S. Department of Housing and Urban Development 1988).

3. Of the total 29 million occupied rental units in the United States, as of 1983, approximately 12 percent were subsidized by the federal government. The housing supplied by HUD is, however, targeted at low-income households, with HUD supplying an even larger share of the housing for families whose incomes are below 50 percent of median income. In ten metropolitan areas in 1984, for example, government subsidies were provided for up to 24 percent of all such low-income households. HUD subsidies, however, covered only 5 percent of the rental stock in Los Angeles in 1984 but more than 15 percent in Boston and New York. In certain metropolitan areas such as Providence, Rhode Island, and Newport News, Virginia, HUD's share of the low-income rental stock rose to more than 30 percent. Thus, the federal government's share of low-income rental housing may be minimal or substantial in a given jurisdiction, depending on the past history of requests for such aid.

4. An integrated project was defined as one with white residents and more than one nonwhite (Negro) family. A segregated project was one in which different races were in separate buildings or sites. Projects showing "no pattern" were those where there was only one black or white family in an otherwise segregated project. More information on these forms can be found in the "Low Rent Housing Manuals" of the Housing and Home Finance Agency; Goering 1986b; Abrams 1955:308–9.

5. Table 18.1 excludes approximately five thousand units not for the elderly where the date for full availability is unknown. Of the 10,798 projects, 3,104 representing 18 percent of the units were missing computer-coded spatial identifiers. These units were allocated among the three spatial categories using proportions of units determined from a random sample of seventy-four of the projects that lacked computer-coded spatial identifiers.

6. Scattered site units managed by PHAS were excluded from the analysis. Data from the Columbus, Ohio, PHA initially selected for the sample were excluded because of data errors. This analysis is limited to fifty states and the District of Columbia; to public not Indian housing authorities; and to completed construction projects under management. The source is the HUD FORMS data system. The socioeconomic data base to which the public housing files were matched is reported in Bunce, Neal, and Gardner 1983.

7. When a particular PHA has no projects in which the concentration of one racial group exceeds 80 percent, the number of units in homogeneous projects and the index are 0. Conversely, when the concentration of one racial group always exceeds 80 percent, the number of units in homogeneous projects and the index is 100.

8. We note a criticism of the index of public housing separation; because it is constructed from the racial composition of individual housing projects, it is difficult to determine whether the score is due to the percent black in all of public housing or to actual segregation. For example, a place where 99 percent of all public housing is of one race would probably be labeled as having a high level of segregation, no matter what the distribution of the minority population was, because it would be difficult to get below the 80 percent level to be labeled integrated.

9. We are indebted to Robert Wilger of the Population Studies Center of the University of Michigan, who supplied segregation scores for central cities for 1980. The scores were for the central cities of each of the 203 SMSAS in his larger study. Scores were available for the individual central cities of select multiple central city SMSAS but not all. Each SMSA had to have a black population of at least 4 percent in order to be selected for Wilger's study. Central city segregation scores were available for 113 of the 142 cities for which some public housing segregation data were available. Segregation scores for both family and elderly housing were only available for 83 of the 113 cities.

10. Douglas Massey of the University of Chicago and Peter Marcuse of Columbia University both report their active investigations of many of the issues addressed in this chapter (Massey 1987a).

References

Abrams, Charles. 1955. *Forbidden Neighbors*. New York: Harper and Brothers.

Abt Associates. 1981. "Participation and Benefits in the Urban Section 8 Program: New Construction and Existing Housing." HUD-PDR-680. Washington, D.C.: Department of Housing and Urban Development.

Aiken, Michael, and Robert Alford. 1969. "Community Structure and Mobilization: The Case of Public Housing." Discussion Paper 36-69. Madison: Institute for Research on Poverty.

———. 1970a. "Community Structure and Innovation: The Case of Public Housing." *American Political Science Review* 64:843–64.

———. 1970b. "Community Structure and Innovation: The Case of Urban Renewal." *American Sociological Review* 35:650–65.

Bain, Dixon, et al. 1988. "Study of the Modernization Needs of the Public and Indian Housing Stock: National, Regional and Field Estimates." Cambridge, Mass.: Abt Associates.

Bauer, Esther. 1987. "Judge Warns Officials to Obey Decree on W. Dallas Projects." Dallas *Morning News* December 22.

Bauman, John F. 1987. *Public Housing, Race, and Renewal: Urban Planning in Philadelphia, 1920–1974*. Philadelphia: Temple University Press.

Blair, William. 1984. "Accord to Minority Suit Provides for More Subsidized Apartments." *New York Times* May 3.

Bredemeier, Henry. 1980. *The Federal Public Housing Movement: A Case Study of Social Change*. New York: Arno Press.

Bunce, Harold, Sue Neal, and John Gardner. 1983. *The Effects of the 1980 Census on Community Development Funding*. HUD-PDR-737. Office of Policy Development and Research. Washington, D.C.: Department of Housing and Urban Development.

Bunce, Harold, and Sue Neal. 1984. "Trends in City Conditions during the 1970's: A Survey of Demographic and Socioeconomic Change." *The Journal of Federalism* 14:7–19.

Burke, Paul. 1984. *Researcher's Guide to HUD Data: With Notes on Related Information Sources*. Office of Policy Development and Research. Washington, D.C.: Department of Housing and Urban Development.

Caro, Robert. 1974. *The Power Broker: Robert Moses and the Fall of New York*. New York: Knopf.

Chudacoff, Howard. 1987. "Absence of Public Housing Policy in U.S. Cities, 1870–1935." Unpublished paper, Department of History. Providence: Brown University.

Citizens Housing and Planning Association. 1984. *A Survey of Tenant Characteristics and Admission and Assignment Policies at the Nation's Largest Housing Authorities*. Boston: Public Housing Research Project.

Council of Large Public Housing Authorities. 1986. *Public Housing Today.* Cambridge, Mass.: Ballinger.

Dahl, Robert. 1961. *Who Governs? Democracy and Power in an American City.* New Haven: Yale University Press.

Edsall, Thomas. 1988. "Rings of White Anger." *Washington Post* November 3.

Farley, Reynolds, and Robert Wilger. 1987. "Recent Changes in the Residential Segregation of Blacks from Whites: An Analysis of 203 Metropolises." Unpublished Report No. 15. Washington, D.C.: National Academy of Sciences.

Feagin, Joe. 1987. *The Urban Real Estate Game.* Englewood Cliffs, N.J.: Prentice-Hall.

Fischer, Paul, and Gary Orfield. 1981. "Assisted Housing Programs and Racial Patterns in the Schools: An Analysis of Three Metropolitan Areas." Unpublished report, Office of Community Planning and Development. Washington, D.C.: Department of Housing and Urban Development.

Fisher, Robert. 1959. *Twenty Years of Public Housing.* New York: Harper and Brothers.

Fleisher, Richard. 1979. "Subsidized Housing and Residential Segregation in American Cities: An Evaluation of the Site Selection and Occupancy of Federally Subsidized Housing." Ph.D. diss., Department of Political Science. Urbana: University of Illinois at Urbana-Champaign.

Foley, Donald. 1973. "Institutional and Contextual Factors Affecting the Housing Choices of Minority Residents." Pp. 85–147 in *Segregation in Residential Areas,* edited by Amos Hawley and Vincent Rock. Washington, D.C.: National Academy of Sciences.

Friedman, Lawrence. 1968. *Government and Slum Housing: A Century of Frustration.* Chicago: Rand McNally.

————. 1988. "The Causes of Racial Segregation: A Critical Review and a New Methodological Direction." Urban Studies Program. Wooster, Ohio: The College of Wooster.

Galster, George. 1987. "Residential Segregation and Interracial Economic Disparities: A Simultaneous-Equations Approach." *Journal of Urban Economics* 21:22–44.

————. 1988. "The Causes of Racial Segregation: A Critical Review and a New Methodological Direction." Urban Studies Program. Wooster, Ohio: The College of Wooster.

GAO. 1985. "Fair Housing: OMB Review of HUD Requests to Collect Information From the Public." Fact Sheet GAO-HRD-86-33FS. Washington, D.C.: General Accounting Office.

Gesmer, Ellen. 1977. "Discrimination in Public Housing under the Housing and Community Development Act of 1974: A Critique of the New Haven Experience." *Urban Law Annual* 13:49–80.

Goering, John. 1986a. *Housing Desegregation and Federal Policy.* Chapel Hill: University of North Carolina Press.

————. 1986b. "HUD's Racial Occupancy Data: History and Status." Working Paper. Office of Policy Development and Research. Washington, D.C.: Department of Housing and Human Development.

Goldstein, Ira, and William Yancey. 1986. "Public Housing Projects, Blacks and Public Policy: The Historical Ecology of Housing in Philadelphia." Pp. 262–89 in *Housing Desegregation and Federal Policy*, edited by John M. Goering. Chapel Hill: University of North Carolina Press.

Hartman, Chester. 1974. *Yerba Buena: Land Grab and Community Resistance in San Francisco*. San Francisco: Glide.

Henig, Jeffrey. 1982. *Neighborhood Mobilization: Redevelopment and Response*. New Brunswick: Rutgers University Press.

Hirsch, Arnold. 1983. *Making the Second Ghetto: Race and Housing in Chicago, 1940–1960*. New York: Cambridge University Press.

Horne, Frank. 1958. "Interracial Housing in the United States." *The Phylon Quarterly* 19:13–20.

ICF. 1989. "Future Accrual of Capital Repair and Replacement Needs of Public Housing." Fairfax: ICF Inc.

Jackson, Hubert. 1958. "Public Housing and Minority Groups." *The Phylon Quarterly* 19:21–30.

Kamen, Al. 1988. "Court Lets Stand Housing Bias Ruling." Washington *Post* November 8.

Kaplan, Edward. 1984. "Managing the Demand for Public Housing." Technical Report No. 183. Operations Research Center. Cambridge: MIT Press.

————. 1985. "Tenant Assignments: How PHAS Fill Their Units." *Journal of Housing* 42:13–20.

Knapp, John. 1986. "Subsidized Housing and Race." Testimony before the House Subcommittee on Housing and Community Development. No. 99-83. Committee on Banking Finance and Urban Affairs. House of Representatives. Washington, D.C.: Government Printing Office.

Lazin, Frederick. 1973. "The Failure of Enforcement of Civil Rights Regulations in Public Housing, 1963–1971: The Co-optation of a Federal Agency by Its Local Constituency." *Policy Sciences* 4:263–73.

Ledbetter, William. 1967. "Public Housing—A Social Experiment Seeks Acceptance." *Law and Contemporary Problems* 32:490–527.

Lichter, David. 1988. "Racial Differences in Underemployment in American Cities." *American Journal of Sociology* 93:771–92.

Lieberson, Stanley. 1980. *A Piece of the Pie: Blacks and White Immigrants since 1880*. Berkeley: University of California Press.

Lucas, J. Anthony. 1985. *Common Ground*. New York: Alfred A. Knopf.

Luttrell, Jordan. 1966. "The Public Housing Administration and Discrimination in Federally Assisted Low-Rent Housing." *Michigan Law Review* 64:871–90.

McGraw, B. T. 1954. "Desegregation and Open Occupancy Trends in Housing." *Journal of Human Relations* (Fall): 57–69.

McGrew, Jane. 1981. "Resistance to Change Continues to Restrict Public Housing Choices." *Journal of Housing* (July):375–81.

Marcuse, Peter. 1986. "The Beginnings of Public Housing in New York." *Journal of Urban History* 12:353–90.

Mariano, Ann. 1985. "HUD, VA Ordered to Stop Gathering Racial, Ethnic Data on Housing." *Washington Post* March 23.

Massey, Douglas. 1987a. "Trends in the Residential Segregation of Blacks, Hispanics, and Asians: 1970–1980." *American Sociological Review* 52:802–25.

———. 1987b. "The Spatial Dimension of Segregation: Clustering, Centralization, and Concentration of Blacks and Hispanics in 1980." Unpublished paper. Chicago: Population Research Center.

———. 1987c. "The Dimensions of Residential Segregation." Unpublished paper. Chicago: Population Research Center.

———. 1988. "Residential Segregation of Blacks in American Cities." Testimony before the House Subcommittee on Housing and Community Development. Washington, D.C.: U.S. House of Representatives.

Meehan, Eugene. 1979. *The Quality of Federal Policymaking: Programmed Failure in Public Housing*. Columbia: University of Missouri Press.

Merton, Robert K. 1982. "Notes on Problem-Finding in Sociology." Pp. 17–42 in *Social Research and the Practicing Professions*. Cambridge, Mass.: Abt Associates.

Miller, Ted, M. De Pallo, and K. Rotendaro. 1985. *Feasibility Research for a Public Housing Desegregation Demonstration*. Final Report. Office of Policy Development and Research. Washington, D.C.: Department of Housing and Urban Development.

Mollenkopf, John, and Jon Pynoos. 1972. "Property, Politics and Local Housing Policy." *Politics and Society* 2:407–29.

Nichols, Franklin. 1939. "Interracial Aspects of Public Housing." *Interracial Review* (November):169–71.

Office of Fair Housing and Equal Opportunity. 1988. "Affirmative Civil Rights Compliance Actions for Public Housing Authorities." Washington, D.C.: Government Printing Office.

Office of Federal Statistical Policy and Standards. 1978. "A Framework for Planning U.S. Federal Statistics for the 1980's." Washington, D.C.: Government Printing Office.

Patterson, John. 1979. "Racial Inequality in Federal Housing Programs: A Welfare Geography Approach." *Southeastern Geographer* 19:114–26.

Peel, Norman, G. Pickett, and S. Buehl. 1971. "Racial Discrimination in Public Housing Site Selection." *Stanford Law Review* 23:63–147.

Philpott, Thomas. 1978. *The Slum and the Ghetto*. New York: Oxford University Press.

Piven, Francis Fox, and Richard Cloward. 1980. "The Case Against Urban Desegregation." Pp. 100–110 in *Housing Urban America,* edited by J. Pynoos, R. Schafer, and C. Hartman. Chicago: Aldine Publications.

Public Housing Administration. 1953a. "Open Occupancy Housing Programs of the Public Housing Administration." Race Relations Branch. Washington, D.C.: Housing and Home Finance Agency.

———. 1953b. "Open Occupancy in Public Housing." Race Relations Unit. Washington, D.C.: Housing and Home Finance Agency.

———. 1963. "Trends Toward Open Occupancy in Low-Rent Housing. Progress of the Public Housing Administration." No. 12. Intergroup Relations Branch. Washington, D.C.: Housing and Home Finance Agency.

Rodrique, George. 1985. "Racial Data on Subsidized Housing Not Compiled." Dallas *Morning News* 13:16.

Schnapper, Eric. 1983. "Perpetuation of Past Discrimination." *Harvard Law Review* 96:828–64.

Schoshinski, Robert. 1969. "Public Landlords and Tenants: A Survey of Developing Law." *Duke Law Journal* (June):399–474.

Schuman, Howard, and Lawrence Bobo. 1988. "Survey-based Experiments on White Racial Attitudes Toward Racial Integration." *American Journal of Sociology* 94:273–99.

Semer, Milton. 1976a. "A Review of Federal Subsidized Housing Programs." Pp. 82–144 in *Housing in the Seventies Working Papers.* Washington, D.C.: Department of Housing and Urban Development.

———. 1976b. "Impact of Judicial and Administrative Decisions on Legislative Policy Developments and Implementation of Housing Programs." Pp. 145–79 in *Housing in the Seventies Working Papers.* Washington, D.C.: Department of Housing and Urban Development.

Sklar, Morton. 1971. "The Racial Data Policies and Capabilities of the Federal Government." A report of the Interagency Racial Data Committee. Washington, D.C.: Interagency Committee on Uniform Civil Rights Policies and Practices.

Smith, Richard. 1988. "The Effect of Local Fair Housing Ordinances on Housing Segregation." *American Journal of Economics and Sociology* (in press).

Struyk, Raymond, and J. Blake. 1982. "Determining Who Lives in Public Housing." PR 3007-01. Washington, D.C.: The Urban Institute.

———. 1983. "Selecting Tenants: The Law, Markets, and PHA Practices." *Journal of Housing* 40:8–12.

Stucker, Jennifer. 1987. "State Funded Housing Development Programs." Unpublished report, Office of Policy Development and Research. Washington, D.C.: Department of Housing and Urban Development.

Subcommittee on Housing and Community Development, Committee on Banking, Finance, and Urban Affairs, U.S. House of Representatives. 1986. "Discrimination in Federally Assisted Housing Programs." Part 1, Serial No. 99-83. Washington, D.C.: Government Printing Office.

Taeuber, Karl. 1983. "Racial Residential Segregation: 1980." In *A Decent Home: A Report on the Continuing Failure of the Federal Government to*

Provide Housing Opportunity. Washington, D.C.: Citizens Commission on Civil Rights.

Taeuber, Karl, and Alma F. Taeuber. 1965. *Negroes in Cities: Residential Segregation and Neighborhood Change.* Chicago: Aldine Publications.

Tobin, Gary. 1987. *Divided Neighborhoods: Changing Patterns of Racial Segregation.* Beverly Hills: Sage.

Turner, Margery, and Douglas Page. 1987. "Metropolitan Housing Opportunities for Poor and Working Class Minorities." Research Paper, Project No. 3730-04. Washington, D.C.: The Urban Institute.

Vernarelli, Michael. 1986. "Where Should HUD Locate Assisted Housing? The Evolution of Fair Housing Policy." Pp. 214–34 in *Housing Desegregation and Federal Policy,* edited by John M. Goering. Chapel Hill: University of North Carolina Press.

Warren, Elizabeth. 1986. "The Dispersal of Subsidized Housing in Chicago: An Index for Comparison." *Urban Affairs Quarterly* 21:484–500.

Weaver, Robert. 1948. *The Negro Ghetto.* New York: Harcourt, Brace.

Weicher, John. 1980. *Housing: Federal Policies and Programs.* Washington, D.C.: American Enterprise Institute.

Whalen, Charles, and B. Whalen. 1985. *The Longest Debate: A Legislative History of the 1964 Civil Rights Act.* Washington, D.C.: Seven Locks Press.

Wilger, Robert. 1987. "Regional Differences in Black/White Residential Segregation: The Effects of Post-1970 Housing." Paper presented at the annual meetings of Population Association of America. Chicago.

Wilson, William J. 1987. *The Truly Disadvantaged.* Chicago: University of Chicago Press.

Wolf, Eleanor. 1981. *Trial and Error: The Detroit School Desegregation Case.* Detroit: Wayne State University Press.

Wood, Elizabeth. 1982. *The Beautiful Beginnings: The Failure to Learn: Fifty Years of Public Housing in America.* Washington, D.C.: The National Center for Housing Management.

Yinger, John. 1986. "On the Possibility of Achieving Racial Integration Through Subsidized Housing." Pp. 290–312 in *Housing Desegregation and Federal Policy,* edited by John M. Goering. Chapel Hill: University of North Carolina Press.

19. American Suburbs: Desegregation and Resegregation

Policies on integrating suburbs and keeping them so are a major issue in the United States. While suburban integration continues to be problematic, only occurring in certain areas, resegregation of these areas tends to follow and is a problem of equal concern. During the 1970s the number of blacks in the suburbs expanded three times as fast as for all persons of all races. By 1980, however, only 21 percent of blacks, compared to 40 percent of Americans of all races, lived in suburban areas (Logan and Schneider 1984).

Escape to the suburbs does not automatically equate with integration for black Americans. Although it is probable that blacks migrating to the suburbs entered communities formerly occupied by whites, this migration has not necessarily led to residential integration. What is more likely to occur with black migration is that the migrants move to neighborhoods where blacks already live or are near other concentrations of blacks.

Policy issues have been developing in relation to this resegregation of American suburbs. The practice of opening the suburbs and decreasing discrimination practices with the help of civil rights laws still exists but stands side-by-side with another issue, the appropriateness and legality of integration maintenance or racial diversity programs (also called *neighborhood stabilization programs* and *affirmative marketing*). Such programs are to keep communities racially balanced or diverse by organized interventionist activities that expand housing choices for blacks into many suburban areas, as well as retain white households and in-migration of new white households in integrated communities so resegregation of a community, after initial integration, does not occur. This is accomplished through affirmative marketing techniques that provide information and assistance to both minority and whites who are considering locating in nontraditional areas.

Government court decisions on integration maintenance and other

335

aspects of integration and desegregation are of major importance. A 1988 federal court case, *South Suburban Housing Center v. National Association of Realtors,* has sparked renewed interest in integration maintenance programs. In this case, Judge Leinenweber ruled in favor of affirmative marketing techniques to provide information, assistance, and incentives for targeted populations in order to achieve integration goals. In a related move, the Subcommittee on Constitutional and Civil Rights of the House Judiciary Committee held hearings on integration maintenance in 1988. As Galster (1989:2) concludes, "What is clear is that more congressional and public attention deservedly will be focused on this vital issue in the future."

Integration maintenance interfaces decisions made in Mount Laurel, New Jersey, where the New Jersey courts ruled that suburban communities had a responsibility to provide their share of the state's low-rent housing (in actuality, communities across the state have been paying inner-city areas to provide low-income housing).

In a related case, integration maintenance ran into trouble in Starrett city, a state-assisted housing complex in Brooklyn, New York. In Starrett City, the housing administration developed an affirmative marketing plan to ensure that groups least likely to apply, that is, whites, Hispanics, and Asians, would be targeted for special consideration. In an attempt to ensure integration of the housing units, race was openly recognized as a factor in processing housing applications. In effect, this meant that black applicants had a substantially longer wait than whites to have their applications processed (Blair 1984; Rosenberg 1982). Although such activity led to an integrated housing community, it also led to the Starrett City housing authority being sued for discrimination. Plaintiffs asserted that their Fourteenth Amendment rights were being violated, and defendants claimed that their actions were justified in view of the principle that "race based government action that burdens minorities is permissible if such steps are necessary to achieve and maintain integration" (Rosenberg 1982).

Eventually, the two sides settled their differences when Starrett City "agreed to increase its minority access by 175 units over a five year period." In exchange for this concession, Starrett City was permitted to continue recognizing race as a factor in application processing (Blair 1984). Although the parties to the suit may have been satisfied, the Civil Rights Division of the Department of Justice was not. The department objected to Starrett City considering race as a factor in the application process and filed a suit against Starrett City charging it with illegal discrimination.

Still another complexity exists in the issue of housing integration. For years it has been the accepted custom to build public housing units in inner-city areas. In more recent years the Department of Housing and Urban Development (HUD) has operated under a directive that new public housing should not be in racially impacted areas. In following through on this directive, the Justice Department under President Jimmy Carter accused the city of Yonkers, New York, and its board of education of deliberately following a policy of racial discrimination. In 1985, Judge Leonard B. Sand ruled "that officials intentionally fostered a segregated school system by consistently refusing to build low income housing in primarily white sections of town" (*Newsweek* December 2, 1985). In effect, this ruling legitimates the belief that suburbs have a responsibility to provide low-income housing. Furthermore, there is the implication that governmental action will be necessary to ensure that the suburbs live up to their responsibilities in this area.

This chapter focuses on the complexities of integration in housing, with a particular emphasis on integrated suburbs, integration maintenance, social diversity programs, affirmative marketing, and how they work.

The Suburbs and Blacks

American suburbs are increasingly the locale for residential housing, commercial and industrial activities, and community life. The majority of Americans live in the suburbs. The growth of the black population in the suburbs, both in the 1980 census and earlier, was very significant for most American metropolitan areas such as Chicago, Philadelphia, Los Angeles, Washington, D.C., St. Louis, Atlanta, Detroit, New Orleans, and Dallas. The largest increases in the black population were in Washington (17 percent in 1980, compared to 8 percent in 1970), and in Atlanta (14 percent in 1980 compared to 6 percent in 1970). In some areas more black families were in-migrants than whites, but in others the white influx was so high it dwarfed even the large black in-migration. In the United States in general, one out of five black Americans lived in the suburbs in 1980, a small proportion compared to the proportion of white Americans who lived in the suburbs.

Because of this growth of the suburbs and growth of the black population there, suburbs are where fair housing issues are being fought, such as the Mount Laurel, New Jersey, court decision (Mallach 1988) and the Yonkers decision (Kurtz 1983). The issues, including the type of institutional racism, are somewhat reshaped by the very nature of the suburbs, with their many individual, semiautonomous governments (Rabin 1987), their particular residential versus commercial configuration, their varied economic bases, and their often-limited socioeconomic groups. Opening up these suburbs relates to the characteristics of each city, including the narrowness of its boundaries, its type (for example, Chicago's industrial suburbs, Atlanta's new residential areas, or San Diego's new suburban rental enclaves), the type of tenure of housing, especially the proportion that are rentals, and the amount of its subsidized housing.

Suburbs as a Hope for a Better Life

Regardless of the type of suburb, they hold more opportunities for black citizens than do the inner-city ghettos. Because of their extraordinary growth, making them the locale of quality residential life for many Americans, it is the suburbs that offer the hope for both better housing and a better life for black families, and possibly better opportunities for integrated living. As Farley (1987:109) points out, "to the extent minority groups are absent from suburbs, they are also separated from newer and better quality housing, higher achieving public schools, and increasing suburban job opportunities." They also are denied a major source of assets. As the experts brought together by the Leadership Council state, "because most black housing demand is confined to present and future ghettos and to rental rather than ownership markets . . . these patterns [including less access to the capital for mortgages] reduce the net worth of black families because equity in a home is the only substantial source of wealth for most American families" (1987:273–74).

Lack of access to the suburbs also affects educational opportunities. As the Leadership Council points out, "The denial of home ownership in desirable neighborhoods forecloses access to better education and mainstream socialization for children. High school and college completion is a major factor in determining school achievement and completion." They add that "to the extent that different school and community environments decrease the likelihood of dropping out of school and increase the probability of entering college . . . the value of housing opportunities play a major role in determining lifetime earnings" (p. 274). And, they say, decreasing the probabilities of crime and welfare dependency.

Suburbs not only offer hope for better housing, schooling, and jobs, but also a greater hope for integration than does the central city, with its long-established ghettos. In the past, integration has seldom occurred as part of the suburban move, except maybe in the very first years after the move, because blacks moved to suburban extensions of the ghetto or black enclaves in suburbia. There seem, however, to be a few rays of hope for integrated suburban communities as more blacks move to all-white areas. Kain (1987) is the most optimistic. Of the 1980 increase in Chicago suburban black population (from a very small base), he states:

Even though the 59 black suburban communities with between 26 and 610 black households in 1980 accounted for less than 2 percent of all black households in the SMSA in 1980, the significance of the appearance of even token numbers of black households in so many widely dispersed suburban communities cannot be over-emphasized. The difference between no black households and some is enormous. In addition, each of the nearly 85,000 black households living in those communities has dozens of black relatives, friends, and co-workers. Their success in overcoming continuing discriminatory barriers is a source of information and encouragement for thousands or possibly hundreds of thousands of other black families, who even now may be considering a move to the suburbs. Further, the appearance of nontrivial numbers of black households in a large number of widely dispersed suburban communities, and even more important, of growing numbers of black children in previously all-white schools, must have begun to change the expectations of both blacks and whites about the likely impacts of black entry into formerly all-white neighborhoods. . . . As both blacks and whites cease to believe that black entry necessarily leads to the creation of an all-black slum, it will occur less often. Whites will continue to buy or rent housing in neighborhoods following black entry and blacks will no longer feel they can obtain improved housing only in a few communities and neighborhoods that have come to be recognized as acceptable for black occupancy. The resulting changes in black and white expectations could produce significant decreases in racial residential segregation with surprising speed" (p. 92).

This improved picture of integrated suburbs also comes from Obermanns' work (1980). He finds that the number of racially diverse suburbs increased from 98 in 1970 to 204 in 1978, of the 700 he studied in 23 midwestern metropolitan areas; 70 to 100 of these were internally integrated in 1978. Obermanns feels that suburbs, with their small, self-governing groups, are better equipped than cities to make integration work. Most of his racially diverse communities in 1978 (144 of 204) had less than 29 percent nonwhite births: 175 had less than 40 percent.

This optimistic picture of the future is only moderately supported by Clark, who concludes from his extensive statistic analysis that "it is possible to distill a tempered but hopeful essence. Black and Hispanic households alike have almost certainly realized progress through migration to suburban communities in the last two decades. But though the pace of minority suburbanization and the rate of suburban increase have been high, the absolute number of persons affected is small" (1987:127). Massey and Denton (1987), in their study of degree of segregation in sixty major cities, find a significant increase in housing integration for blacks in southwestern and western cities, such as Anaheim, Portland, and Austin, but little change in northern and eastern cities, and their overall estimate of the future is somewhat negative. They feel that neither social and economic status nor availability of housing had an impact on the access of blacks to integrated suburban living. For the whole standard metropolitan statistical area, they conclude that "despite the advent of fair housing legislation, more tolerant white racial attitudes and a growing black middle class with income sufficient to promote residential mobility, the segregation of blacks in large cities has hardly changed from 1970 to 1980" (p. 823). Farley (1987), a long-time researcher on racial segregation, is even more pessimistic when viewing the future. He states that "although suburbanization is probably producing modest declines in metropolitan-wide segregation levels, at present in most parts of the country there is no guarantee it will produce major declines from today's still high levels of segregation even in the West and South where decline has been most evident to date" (p. 110). He warns that although there may be increased black suburbanization, it does not mean that there will not be segregation within suburbs. Forces are at work, he adds, perpetuating segregation there; for example, realtors steer minorities to certain areas. Taeuber, from his analysis of data (1983), predicts that a continuation of the trend of slow decrease in segregation for another fifty years will leave the average central city with a dissimilarity index of 50. The suburban dissimilarity index would likely not be that much better by his calculations.

Black Household Characteristics

The black population is no longer rural (only a fifth live there), but primarily located in the central city (58 percent of households in 1980) or in the suburbs (23 percent in 1980). A large proportion still live in the South (53 percent). A portion of the black population, especially the 53 percent of the households maintained by married couples who are often both employed, has made great socioeconomic strides. Thus a noticeable part of this half of the twenty-six million blacks in America, especially the younger households with better educations, are in the American mainstream and can afford to participate in the housing market. At the same time, a black underclass exists outside this mainstream. In other words, the black population is comprised of "haves" and "have-nots," plus those older black households of two parents precariously clinging to the "haves" group. Most prominent among the underclass are the female-headed households, 44 percent of total black households (U.S. Public Health Service 1987). Almost two-thirds of these female-headed black households were below the poverty line in income in 1979 (Momeni 1986b). About 90 percent lived in urban areas by 1980, with 65 percent in central cities and about a fourth in suburbs; the latter include those in formerly rural areas, in satellite industrial suburbs, and in suburban subsidized housing. These suburban female-headed households are usually renters, although a small group own their homes. When thinking of black household expansion potential in the suburbs, one must think primarily of the half (plus) of the households not in this category. The poor group lacks not only the money to compete for quality housing, but also the household characteristics. A solo household with children is discriminated against doubly (Pearce 1988). Another group of black households at disadvantage in moving to the suburbs is the black elderly (more than 8 percent of the black population) and single men, another sizable group. These groups bring the median black income down to $15,430 in 1984 compared to $27,690 for white households. If one only looks at married-couple families, the income is much closer to that of white households.

The median income of black married-couple families was $23,420 (this excludes the black female-headed households, in which median income was only $8,650 in 1984).

Myth of Black Households' Insufficient Income for Suburban Housing

This group of married-couple households in the black community have the potential for affording housing in the suburbs. As mainstream, often two wage-earner, households, their incomes do not fit the myths of many realtors and lending institutions. With the increased education of many young black adults (even though others are drop-outs), the trend toward mainstream occupation position for some should continue. In 1984, 79 percent of black persons aged 25–34 had completed high school. More than 1.1 million blacks were in college (1983); more than 9 percent were college graduates. Blacks represented 10 percent of the college population aged 18–34 in 1983. By occupation, 38 percent were in professional, administrative, and managerial jobs in 1980.

This evidence indicates some blacks can buy or rent in the suburbs. As Kain (1986:100) reports, "The myth that black-white differences in income is a major, if not the principal, explanation of racial segregation persists in the face of large numbers of systematic analyses that show otherwise" and is a problem. Kain (1987) looks at the actual black households in Chicago suburbs in the mid-1970s and 1980s versus the predicted, by household income ability and finds from the Annual Housing Survey tapes (1975) that although 87.6 percent of Chicago SMSA black households lived in central cities, only 58 percent would have lived there (predicted group) in the absence of housing market discrimination. Looking at 1980 census data in terms of nine income categories to predict the number of black households that would reside in each of 122 suburbs of Chicago, he found that most suburbs came far below their predicted number. He found a concentration, with nearly 90 percent of all suburban black households in 1980 in 25 suburban communities, although their predicted share was only 35 percent. Hermalin and Farley (1973), looking at twenty-nine SMSAs, found the same thing. In their calculations of the actual versus expected racial mix in the suburbs based on income, they found more than 40 percent of urban blacks would be suburban; the actual figure was 16 percent of black households in suburb communities. Black ownership rates were far below those of whites in the same income bracket. Schnare's (1977) analysis of predicted black residence patterns on the basis of black household income versus actual black residential patterns for seventy-six large SMSAs with significant numbers of blacks showed that only a small percent lived in each tract and 75 percent lived in tracts with at least 50 percent black population in 1970.

Data do show more blacks buying, with homeownership considerably increased for SMSAs in 1980 compared to 1970 (including the central city)—a 40 percent change from 1970 to 1980 in Atlanta and Dallas-Fort Worth, and 72 percent in Houston (Bullard 1986). Only one-fifth of black households in 1980 lived in suburbia compared to about a half of white households, a factor in the differences in homeownership. Black homeowners are often first-time buyers, whereas whites often have equity from a house they are selling, which can be a considerable amount. With suburban house prices continuing to rise, black households' future purchases in the suburbs may be hampered. Logan and Schneider (1984) find improvement in lending institutions' willingness to make suburban housing loans to middle-class blacks. At the same time the savings and loans industry in Atlanta has been found guilty of discriminating against blacks.

Attitudes on Racial Mix

Many black households buying in the suburbs, especially higher-income normally white residential suburbs, are middle-class professionals and managers. Some are pioneers whom Clay (1979:417) views as the central suburban integrators: "These are blacks who are resourceful and have greater ability to negotiate housing and the capital market." They are also the ones most likely to take legal recourse against discrimination.

Often these middle-class blacks find that because of income, they are accepted by the white residents (although not always). Simkus (1978:83) states that "in general the higher the occupational status of whites and nonwhites compared, the greater the decrease in residential segregation." According to polls, there seems to be less prejudice against these groups. Residents are often more concerned about newcomers having the same income than being of the same race (Werthman, Mandel, and Dientsfrey 1965). Huttman (1975, 1988) found this to be true in her analysis of Reston and Columbia, Maryland, data (see Fava in Huttman 1988).

Black households' attitudes to living in racially mixed suburbs are generally good, destroying another myth of why blacks are not found in predominantly white suburbs. Farley et al. (1978) in a study of Detroit, found the ideal racial composition that blacks preferred was about half black (45 percent black neighborhoods). Whites in contrast wanted only a token black population. Of black respondents, 38 percent were willing to be the first black households to enter an all-white neighborhood; the two-thirds unwilling were afraid of not being welcome rather than disliking an integrated area. Whites were bothered by a black household population of more than 20 percent in their area; half said they would be uncomfortable or more at that point. When the neighborhood is comprised of 30 percent black residents, 41 percent of whites said they definitely would move. In another study of black attitudes, Galster (1982) again found that black preference was for neighborhoods with appropriately equal racial proportions, rather than all-black ones. In fact, one civil rights professional said that some middle-class blacks in northern California consider moving when the suburb becomes predominantly black. This would disagree with the Leigh and McGhee (1986) statement that blacks moving to the suburbs are not very interested in integration. Their overall assumption however is likely true, that "this motive [residential integration] probably is not uppermost in the minds of individuals as they [black residents] seek housing and other goods and services for their families" (p. 39). Leigh and McGhee feel that "if blacks get the housing units they want, and the characteristics include a racially integrated neighborhood, they are willing to accept integration as a useful, though not essential, outcome" (p. 34).

Suburban Segregation in Historical Context

Keeping in mind that as stated previously many more black households have the potential to live in suburban housing than actually do, and that many are willing, and in fact prefer, to live in integrated communities, the number of black households in suburbia during the last two decades—and whether or not they are in segregated areas—should be discussed.

Problems exist with the types of measurements, as they affect types of findings and explain why different researchers draw somewhat different conclusions. Some studies are of census-tract, and some of whole suburbs, and in both cases usually identify the percentage of black households of all households. A few, however, look at live births or school enrollment and yield different figures (Obermanns 1980; chapter 16). Some researchers study net increase in the black population in an area after out-migration back to the cities (and there was a considerable amount of that in the 1970s) is subtracted from in-migration for the period. Another problem is that the base for this increase may be small for many suburbs, even below 100. Another type of statistic used is the index of dissimilarity described by Saltman (chapter 1), which gives the degree of segregation. Much data is on the community level and misses the fact that a suburb can have a very segregated enclave; Obermanns (1980) locates both racially diverse communities with integrated neighborhoods and those with segregated neighborhoods.

Another problem lies in making gross generalizations. Many studies (Farley 1987; Silver 1986) break down their statistics on segregation by city and region. Because some areas have historically had extreme segregation, as Chicago, Cleveland, and other midwestern suburbs, large increases in black suburbanization must be looked at cautiously. For the South, the fact that many suburbs had left-over black rural populations affects increases (Silver 1986).

The Early Postwar Situation

The suburbs have historically had few black residents; for many decades their proportion of the suburban population has been under 5 percent. This percentage has been influenced by the high degree of white in-migration to the suburbs and in some places, especially the South where half the black population lives, by out-migration of rural black families. Location in the early period was in terms of clusters in older suburban communities and in areas on the urban fringe that were formerly rural. As Clay (1979:411) states, "These enclaves were old and established, often with an ambience more rural than urban. Many of these communities were in southern or border states." Census data show outward movement of rural blacks in the 1960s and 1970s as the areas became more suburbanized. In Houston, for example, the black population as a percent of total suburban population was 10.7 percent in 1950 but down to 5.8 percent in 1970 (chapter 15). This same type of trend was true for 1950–60 for New Orleans and Atlanta. The trend is reversing itself, but with higher-income black households moving in. According to Clay, the location situation changed fundamentally after 1965. Blacks moved to suburban communities near large central cities instead of living in fringe areas. He considers this pattern distinctly different from that of the past.

For the non-South, the total black population increased in the suburbs from 1950 to 1970, but was still low. The increase was from 3.9 percent of the total suburban population in New York in 1950 to 5.9 percent in 1970; from 2.3 percent in Washington in 1950 to 4.8 percent in 1970; and from 5.4 percent in Los Angeles in 1950 to 7.6 percent in 1970 (Hermalin and Farley 1973). Sometimes the increase occurred because city boundaries were very narrow, such as in St. Louis and Washington, D.C., and spillover was inevitable.

In general for 1970 the data showed a concentration of blacks in overspill areas (Connolly 1973); in Los Angeles in 1970, 69 percent of suburban blacks were in 12 percent of its census tracts; in Chicago, 57 percent of suburban black units were in 14 percent of the tracts. Cleveland and New Orleans were among others with large concentrations. Unlike the black middle class often moving into racially mixed suburbs, many moving into these concentrated areas were renters, with lower income and educational levels (Clay 1979). These areas had older, less attractive housing vacated by the large number of non-elderly whites leaving for the newer suburbs that opened in the 1960s. Clay states that for 1970, "only one-fifth of the black suburbanites moved into neighborhoods with significant amounts of new housing and less than one-tenth moved to neighborhoods with an owner-occupied home price of $25,000, or more" (p. 416). Thus he concludes that rather than opening up the suburbs, by 1970 an expanded accommodation of dual housing markets existed.

Segregation in the 1970s

More dispersal of black in-migrants to the suburbs occurred in the 1970s, along with dramatically increased migration to the suburbs, although most blacks still lived in the central cities. Clark (1987) reports that even with high black in-migration back to central cities, there was a rapid increase of blacks to the suburbs (net migration) between 1975 and 1980 and between 1980 and 1983—a 10.8 percent increase between 1975 and 1980 and a 14.2 percent increase between 1980 and 1983. The change in numbers in the suburbs between 1970 and 1980 was so great that the percentage of blacks living in the suburbs rose to 20.5 percent in 1980 from only 15 percent in 1960 (Farley 1987).

The increase was not the same for all regions or metropolitan areas; for some areas, the increase was primarily between 1970 and 1975 (Clark 1987). Clark found the Denver-Boulder area, Dallas-Fort Worth, Los Angeles-Long Beach, Cincinnati, Cleveland, Chicago, Atlanta, and Boston with considerable increases in blacks moving to suburbs. Newark, Philadelphia, and New York had none, a decrease, or very little increase. By region, the South varied, with areas such as Atlanta having large increases and others, with out-migration of rural blacks from suburban areas, having little or none. Silver writes of Atlanta: "between 1960 and 1980, the black population in Chicago's suburbs increased three-fold, whereas in suburban Atlanta the growth was nearly five hundred percent. The suburban share of Atlanta's metropolitan black population grew from 19 percent in 1960 to 43 percent in 1980. By contrast, the suburban proportion of Chicago's blacks grew only from 9 percent in 1960 to 16 percent in 1980" (1986:72). For Philadelphia, he finds that "in 1960, among the six SMSAS studied, Philadelphia had the largest proportion of blacks (21

percent living in the suburbs). But, the relative size of black suburbanites [population] in the Philadelphia SMSA remained constant over
the following two decades" (p. 72). In San Diego, Silver found that
rapid suburbanization for blacks came because they pushed the small
central city ghetto into the eastern fringes of the metropolis, and the
growth rate of the black population there grew from 1,632 in 1950 to
26,752 in 1980.

Dispersal and concentration seem to be occurring, although there
still seems to be more of the latter, as Massey and Denton (1987)
report for many areas. Clark (1987) finds high concentration of blacks
in the St. Louis suburbs, primarily in spillover areas. In fact, in most
of the cities he studied, there was high segregation; in only three of
the eighteen areas—Atlanta, New York, and Washington—was there
a situation of a high black percentage and low segregation. In Chicago,
Cleveland, Detroit, Los Angeles, and Miami, Clark found a low percentage of black suburban residents and high suburban segregation.
Only in Detroit did he find that suburban segregation exceeded the
city's. And Farley (1987) reports that in two national studies the metropolitan-wide segregation indices fell more than central city indices;
his St. Louis study verified this. Logan and Schneider's national analysis (1984) found a downward trend in indexes of dissimilarity for
suburban areas in the 1970s. For Kansas City, Farley found a 27-point
difference between the city and its suburbs; Hwang and Murdock
(1982) found a lower index of dissimilarity for Texas suburbs than for
cities.

Index of Dissimilarity

For cities and their suburbs indexes of dissimilarity went down considerably for blacks for a number of cities between 1970 and 1980; for
Denver, from 59 to 39; for Phoenix, from 35 to 21.

Taeuber's 1983 study found rapid black suburbanization occurred
primarily in tracts continuous to those already 50 percent or more
black. Farley's St. Louis data (1987) agree with this finding. He adds
that "suburbs with a D of 50 or lower experienced an average absolute
change of 27 points in the percentage black. Thus suburbs that appear
to be integrated in a one-time "snapshot" are more likely in transition
from predominantly white to predominantly black . . . and most suburbs that had any black population had high levels of internal segregation" (p. 107).

This does not mean that some dispersal is not occurring, although in small numbers compared to movement to segregated areas. Spain and Long (1981), using the Annual Housing Survey data, report that even for 1975, "approximately 40 percent of blacks moved to tracts which had less than 10 percent black in 1975; another 27 percent moved to tracts which were between 10 to 40 percent black." In the 23 major Midwest metropolitan areas he studied, Obermanns (1980) located an increase from 98 to 204 racially diverse suburbs (4–94 percent nonwhite) of 700 suburbs between 1970 and 1980. Of these, 174 had 5–39 percent nonwhite births. Kain (1986) also found black population growth in all-white suburbs and some leapfrogging as well as spillover.

Why Black Households Move to Segregated Suburbs

In reality, many black suburbanites live in segregated suburban areas because of a variety of factors, the primary ones being discrimination and racial steering. However, black households concentrate in certain areas for other reasons, too.

Historic circumstances may cause a concentration of black families in certain suburbs. Some suburbs are former rural areas which had large black farm populations, as in the South; some suburbs have industrial activities such as shipyards or automotive plants that employed many black workers and even provided housing for them—in some cases public housing. Chicago's black suburbs, and also some of Detroit's, are considered industrial suburbs (Silver 1986). In Cleveland, they are either industrial satellite cities or spillover areas (Rose 1976); see chapter 20 for recent changes. Some older suburbs are locales of service workers for the nearby suburbs, as is the case for New Rochelle, New York. Lake and Cutter (1980) include these historic types in their typology of six distinctive forms of black suburban settlement: black colony in industrial satellites, spillover types, metropolitan rural enclaves, subsidized housing communities, the industrial-commercial mixed community, and the outer industrial community.

Location of the suburb is also a factor in determining the degree of black concentration. Besides the formerly rural locations, there are close-in suburbs adjacent to the ghetto areas of the city. Spillover has been a primary factor in determining residential patterns of moves (Clay 1979; Clark 1987); suburbs close to an inner city absorb the outward movement of black households. In a sectorial model approach to spillover, black households move into certain sectors close to the ghetto. Evidence shows that this is the case in St. Louis (Clark 1987), San Diego (Silver 1986), Newark (Lake 1981), and Washington, D.C. (Clay 1979). For Cleveland (Kain 1986, based on Obermanns 1982), the greatest black suburban increase from 1970–80 was in the areas adjacent to the central-city black ghetto, as is also true in Chicago (Kain 1986).

Leapfrogging to all-white areas has occurred in the 1970s, but spill-over seems the major location characteristic. As Goering states, "There has been a partial cloning of racial ghettos in many parts of America" (1986:10). However, leapfrogging occurs more for black professional and managerial households that are willing to pioneer in near-white suburbs than for working-class households.

Black working-class, and even many black middle-class, people move to black suburban segregated areas because they are unsure of their welcomes elsewhere. They do not want to be the first black residents of an area. As Schermer (1979:31–32) says, "Blacks do not share precisely equivalent feelings (about the principle of fair housing opportunities as some in the public may) and it is clear that except for a courageous pioneering few, most blacks given a choice, will not be first to integrate a neighborhood. Rather they tend to search for homes where a degree of social balance has been established." Leigh and McGhee (1986) find that these black households may be more inter-ested in finding housing of better quality than their inner-city unit than in moving to integrated housing. They may fear moving into an almost all-white area because of concern over a hostile welcome and violent harassment (Valente 1983).

Another reason that black suburban in-migrants go to black areas is because they feel that an all- or nearly all-white area will have an unwelcoming school system for their children, although there will be segregated schools in black suburbs or black enclaves of suburbs.

If the new community has a liberal or pioneering orientation, such as a new town, with inhabitants known for racial tolerance, the black middle class may move in; this is also true for university communities and enclaves of writers or artists. It is the case in such new towns as Reston, Virginia, and Columbia, Maryland, which attract black mid-dle-class and working-class families and involve them in community activities, as Huttman found in her study of class and racial mix in new towns (Huttman 1975, 1988).

A major factor affecting black households that move to suburbs is the availability of housing. If an area has experienced fast economic growth, new integrated subdivisions may exist, although they may be available only if prices are within reach and mortgage interest rates low enough. If a favorable financial infrastructure—including FHA- and VA-insured mortgages or, formerly, Section 235 low-income home ownership—is available (as was true in the 1970s new towns such as Columbia, Maryland), more black households might be encouraged (Huttman 1988).

With housing expansion occurring in a particular city's suburbs, some suburbs have an out-migration of whites and many houses for sale or rent at cheaper prices than in surrounding suburbs. There will likely be an in-migration of black households attracted by such housing opportunity. This out-migration may be due to more attractive housing being available to home equity holders, to white flight from suggested "black invasion" flamed by realtors' rumors, or simply by the aged moving or dying.

Black households are more likely to take up this cheaper older housing than move to the new. Clay (1979) found that house prices did influence where blacks moved; only one-fourth of black households moved to suburbs that had a significant amount of *new* housing, and only one-tenth to areas with a median or higher housing prices. This may be even truer today, as suburban housing prices for new units rise to the point that it is primarily those with home equity who can buy in, a situation unfavorable to black first-time buyers (Clark 1987). Thus, a dual housing market exists.

The reasons for a dual housing market lie in discriminatory activities, especially racial steering, that is, sending black households to particular suburbs. Although steering is outlawed by Sec. 804 Title VIII and by court decisions (*Zach v. Hussey,* 394 F. Supp. at 1047; *Havens Realty Corporation v. Coleman,* 455 U.S. 363, 366 n. I. [1982]), it still occurs (Wienk et al. 1979). Helper (1986) and Pearce (1979, 1988) describe the powerful role of real estate brokers in concentrating black households by steering black buyers to mixed or black residential areas and white buyers to white areas. Schermer (1979) points out that some real estate firms appear to be "transition specialists," who seek out and become especially active in racially changing neighborhoods and are likely to be involved in racial steering.

Discriminatory Treatment by Realtors, Landlords, and Sellers

Racial steering is not the only form of discrimination that both keeps blacks in certain suburbs and keeps them out of others. Other discriminatory activities are differential treatment of black prospective buyers or renters interested in white suburbs in terms of information provided, courtesy, terms of leases or sale, price, and general knowledge of availability of units (chapters 1 and 14). At a later stage in the housing attainment process it may be discrimination in terms of credit checks, insurance arrangements, or mortgage approval (Feins and Bratt 1983). Discrimination in lending has been documented for Atlanta-area savings and loans banks (*International Herald Tribune* 1989).

These practices are described in detail elsewhere, as are the audit mechanisms for locating them (chapter 1). In the HUD Housing Market Practice survey of forty major metropolitan areas (Wienk et al. 1979), of 3,264 sales and rental audits, blacks on average were likely to confront some sort of discrimination in 27 percent of their attempts to find rental units and 15 percent of their attempts to find units for sale. James, McCummings, and Tynan (1984), in studying the sunbelt, found that realtors were less aggressive for Hispanics and blacks than for Anglos (see also Lieberman and Carter [1982] and Spain and Long [1981]). The HUD Housing Market Practice survey (Wienk et al. 1979) found whites favored more in information on housing availability, especially in the North Central region, where in 55 percent of the cases whites were favored more than blacks; in the South, whites were favored more than blacks in only 33 percent of the cases and in almost half there was no difference in treatment.

Levels of discrimination can also vary by characteristics of the black household. Black professional or managerial household heads may be forceful in demanding their rights and in circumventing and challenging discrimination, even through lawsuits. The degree to which realtors respond to antidiscrimination laws and to association guidelines on client treatment may vary with the class of black clients. However, audit studies (Newburger 1984) in a wide variety of communities indicate that black middle-income groups are still discriminated against. When testers are matched by income, the black group is not treated as well as the white middle-class—in other words, they are discriminated against. In the working class, the group most likely to suffer discrimination are the female-headed households, who represent unstable families to potential landlords (Momeni 1986b; Pearce 1988).

All these factors have caused blacks to be concentrated in certain suburbs when they move from central cities or nonmetropolitan areas. Their movement to a limited number of suburbs has caused a process of resegregation of what were white communities first. Resegregation is a major concern, and programs—called integration maintenance or racial diversity or neighborhood stabilization programs—to avoid it are debated widely. Over twenty years after the Fair Housing Act of 1968, this joins the integration of the suburbs as a major issue. Because blacks have funneled into a limited number of suburbs due to racial steering and similar reasons, there is usually a process of racial transition. First comes minimal integration, often by black middle-class "pioneer" families. They are followed by others until a community becomes resegregated, with a large proportion of the population black. This can happen to one neighborhood of a suburb rather than the whole suburb. It is a discouraging development for fair housing activists who have worked hard to open up the suburbs and find their efforts futile as the suburbs become increasingly black. As Goering states: "The price of success [of some integration] is the introduction of unanticipatic consequences, such as selective integration and resegregation, requiring new policy responses" (1986:9). And resegregation is hard to deal with as Saltman (1989) points out: "My long and tedious research has convinced me that it is easier to integrate than to maintain it. The natural desegregation technique, lawsuits under Title VIII of the Fair Housing Act, may not easily work to stop resegregation." As Polikoff (1986:69) states, "Assume a community in which all vestiges of past discrimination has been eradicated, in which a truly open, 'unitary' housing market existed, and in which integration characterized all residential neighborhoods. Assume also that a racial concentration began to develop in one neighborhood. By hypothesis, the developing concentration is *not* the result of discrimination. In such a situation, would HUD be free under Title VIII to utilize its techniques of site selection criteria and affirmative marketing [for public housing] to forestall resegregation?"

The process of resegregation can be a self-fulfilling prophecy of blacks' entrance into a community, signaling its turning black as far as whites are concerned. If a suburb is directly in the path of spillover from the ghetto it is more difficult to avoid resegregation. For example, Markham, Illinois, which in the late 1960s was praised for stable integration, saw its black population, only 2.5 percent in 1950, move to 21 percent in 1960, to more than 50 percent in 1970, to 70 percent in 1980, and to nearly 75 percent in 1984 (Polikoff 1986).

This process of resegregation is outlined by Schelling (1972), who states that what happens is that white fears of declining property values, deteriorating schools, and rising crime rates (when blacks start to move in) lead to a self-fulfilling prophecy. He adds that if whites flee the neighborhood when the first blacks (middle class) move in, the middle-class blacks are followed by low-income blacks, who because of racial segregation have nowhere else to go. Because of the high prices of houses, these pioneer black middle-class owners pay to move in; in reality, property values often go up and seldom go down (Yinger 1979, 1987; Schafer 1979). Schelling's model of low-income blacks following the black middle class lead into a community is not always likely unless cheap rental housing is available.

When the process of resegregation occurs, reversal is difficult, as the *Harvard Law Review* report "Benign Steering" (1980:953) points out: "Every time a community resegregates the pattern of racial separation and hostility is reinforced, thereby increasing barriers to black entry in the remaining white communities and making stable integration more difficult once black entry has begun. . . . the movement toward racial equality will continue to languish until some communities break out of the cycle of resegregation by creating a stable interracial environment which demonstrates that racial harmony is not merely desirable but also attainable."

To keep an area integrated is indeed difficult, for it means not only that most white households stay, but also that new white ones move in. Even if white families are encouraged to stay in a community that has "opened up" to include at least 7 percent black families—the very low "tipping point" Farley et al. (1978) found in the Detroit study, or a higher one more likely in many areas—there is always turnover in housing. Some white households leave for nondiscriminatory reasons such as change in job. There must be a white family willing to move in to replace each one that moves out in order to avoid a trend toward resegregation. If it is not a spillover area, the newly integrated community may be an island of integration in a suburban sea of whites-only housing.

Intervention activities, some qualifying as integration maintenance or racial diversity programs, are important here. Many experts, such as Yinger (1986), believe that without such intervention, continued stable integration is unlikely in the same location over an extended period. Intervention activities to keep any integration are supported by many civic groups convinced of its necessity. The Leadership Council for Metropolitan Open Communities has said that "we will not end the dual housing market if deliberate efforts to open up communities result in resegregation" (Goering 1986:274). Yinger (1986:296) concludes that "the prospects for stable integration through market forces are not encouraging." Yinger thus considers intervention necessary

(p. 297): "Every case of a stable integrated community with a substantial black population, such as Oak Park, or Shaker Heights, involves intervention by a well-financed housing center and by local government" (see also Goodwin 1979). Orfield (1986:26) agrees that "these experiences [in increasing urban integration] indicate that successful housing integration required concerted intervention in the housing market."

Characteristics of Integration Maintenance and Affirmative Action Marketing Programs

Integration maintenance and affirmative action programs are the most prevalent strategies for suburban housing integration; however, such policies are not without controversy.

The intent of integration maintenance programs, as well as affirmative marketing efforts, is to maintain stable integration after initial minority families enter into a community or neighborhood. Traditionally, there has only been transitional integration followed by white flight and then resegregation. Integration maintenance programs, sometimes referred to as *racial diversity programs,* wish to encourage dispersal of blacks and other minority newcomers throughout the community rather than allowing them to concentrate in one or two areas. In addition, integration maintenance efforts attempt to stem white flight by encouraging white households to stay when black families move in, and by enticing new white households to move into integrated areas.

To meet a variety of objections by different types of opponents to integration maintenance programs, proponents have tried to clarify terminology and specify their actions. Regarding terminology, Saltman (1989) uses the term *neighborhood stabilization,* as well as *integration maintenance,* and says neighborhood stabilization means to her the organized effort to maintain neighborhoods as racially integrated. Polikoff in the congressional hearings on integration maintenance argues that *racial diversity,* not integration maintenance, should be the appropriate nomenclature for the hearing because the latter may connote a precise numerical goal. Rather, integration should be thought of as a "process of healthy competition in the residential marketplace" in which home-seekers and apartment-seekers from various racial groups are involved (Galster 1989).

Another term Galster uses (1989) is *stable integrative process* (SIP), which he suggests should be a federal policy, just as residential integration should be. Polikoff argues such residential integration is indeed a federal goal (some argue it is not), a goal stated in a 1988 HUD notice as a goal of Title VIII of the Civil Rights Act and also by former Secretary of HUD Samuel Pierce (Galster 1989). Galster defines SIP as "a dynamic in which home seekers representing two or more races actively seek to occupy the same vacancies in a substantial proportion of a metropolitan area's neighborhoods over an extended period" (p. 2). Galster argues that SIP is unlikely without aggressive coordinated policies and can be achieved in ways that expand housing choices. Like Polikoff in the congressional hearings, he takes pains to distinguish choice-expanding techniques from quotas and makes a case for pro-integrative financial incentive plans (Galster 1989).

Integration maintenance (IM) programs rely heavily upon the organizational interaction of such groups as real estate agents, nonprofit fair housing organizations, municipal housing authorities, and potential buyers or renters. When such groups come together to promote integrated housing, it is generally referred to as *affirmative marketing*. The overall intent is to promote integrated housing by insuring that realtors do not limit client opportunities in purchasing or rental of property. In the HUD-approved Affirmative Marketing Plan, groups least likely to apply for housing opportunities, such as blacks, Hispanics, and Asians, are targeted for special outreach efforts. For affirmative marketing plans to be successful, there must be aggressive intervention by both the private and the public sector. With an overall goal of maintaining neighborhood diversity and neighborhood stabilization, the various interest groups have a vested interest in expanding the opportunities available to potential buyers or renters. Their purpose is to see that realtors, sellers, and buyers do not give preference to certain racial groups or steer clients to particular racial areas. The idea is to inform diverse groups about available housing in nontraditional areas (for blacks, integrated or all-white areas; for whites, the nontraditional choice of integrated areas). Affirmative marketing provides information and encouragement to buyers and expands their areas of house hunting in an effort to widen their choices.

Affirmative action strategies and integration maintenance programs are based on the belief that inaction will only lead to resegregation of neighborhoods. In recognizing that affirmative action must be taken to prevent resegregation once integration has begun, Polikoff points to the efforts of several integrated communities across the country that have adapted such plans (1986:44). Polikoff outlines the following actions that these metropolitan areas have taken to maintain integration:

1. Race-conscious housing counseling: a counseling service that encourages home-seekers to consider housing options that persons of their race are unlikely to consider.

2. Affirmative marketing: attempts to induce or require real estate agents to inform racial groups about available housing in neighborhoods to which members of such groups are not likely to be attracted without special efforts.

3. Racial record-keeping: maintaining records on the racial composition and home-buying and apartment-seeking "traffic" of subdivisions, blocks, or other areas.

4. Notification of intent to sell: attempts to require or induce owners to provide advance notice of housing to be placed on the market.

5. Solicitation bans: prohibitions of real estate solicitation if property-owners give notice that they do not wish to be solicited (or if other requirements are not complied with).

6. Sign bans: prohibitions against the display of "for sale" or "sold" signs on residential real estate to avoid panic selling by whites—a controversial prohibition.

7. Housing quality/public service standards: rigid enforcement of housing quality standards and improvement of public services in neighborhoods threatened with resegregation.

8. Litigation: suits against real estate brokers for racial steering, usually based on "testing" by teams of blacks and whites who visit real estate offices and pretend to be looking for homes.

Integration management programs may give buyers incentive to buy in nontraditional areas. Such affirmative marketing, as Richie of the East Suburban Council for Open Metropolitan Communities says of his group's efforts, is to use information and persuasion, not legal compulsion and coercion, to motivate people to make integration housing choices that favor integration (Galster 1989).

An example of an integration maintenance program is that of Park Forest, Illinois, which, Helper (1986) reports, involves educational programs, real estate activities, legal problems, public relations, and above all, counseling on available housing for sale and rent. The program is also concerned with planning, commercial development, revitalization, and school desegregation; most of its thirty activities are funded by the municipality.

As Polikoff mentions, the IM organization may originate litigation (lawsuits) or may simply bring pressure against landlords or realtors for their discriminatory activity banned by Title VIII, including racial steering. Under the 1988 Fair Housing Amendments Act this may be more difficult, as "intent," as well as "actions" are needed to prove discrimination. These regulations are being protested by many civil rights groups. IM organizations will usually test housing discrimination with equally matched auditors before taking action on litigations.

Another important activity, one Weaver (1960) considered paramount to holding white residents in racially mixed developments, is promotion of an above-ordinary level of amenities and the environment. This might include recreational areas, well-lighted streets, clean areas, special schools, community activities, housing, and code enforcement. Park Hill Association, in an integrated area of Denver, included upkeep of property and crime control through Neighborhood Watch and a community police commission, as Helper (1986) details. Another IM program works for successful school integration, which both Yinger (1986) and Helper (1986) feel are essential for an integrated community. Some communities promote magnet schools to help assure newcomers that quality education exists and to encourage white entry into the community, as well as halt withdrawal (Wegmann 1977). As Helper states (1986), when single black people move into rental units, whites can hardly raise their exaggerated fears about changes in the educational quality. In suburbs with many aged whites, as is increasingly true of older suburbs, there is also less concern over the quality of the education. There may be hostility, however, to newcomers with large families because of fear that school taxes may go up.

Debate over Integration Maintenance and Affirmative Marketing

Not everyone agrees that integration maintenance programs are the way to proceed. Some argue that an element of paternalism, even racism, is associated with such efforts. For example, in Chicago, chapters of the NAACP and the Southern Christian Leadership Conference in the early 1980s have gone on record to oppose integration maintenance efforts, which the NAACP felt placed unnecessary restriction on black mobility and infringed on individual rights (Chicago *Tribune* 1984; Polikoff 1986:45). The Southern Christian Leadership Conference more bluntly stated that "integration maintenance reinforces the myth of 'White Supremacy and Black Inferiority'" (Position Paper,

Chicago Suburban Chapter, sclc, n.d., p. 5, quoted in Polikoff, 1986, p. 45). The National Association of Realtors, however, argues that integration maintenance programs are intended to scatter minorities, thereby reducing their threat to any one community. Some have criticized racial steering of blacks away from already highly integrated communities, or even ones with a fairly low concentration when the percentage of black households exceeds what is considered a tipping point (a debatable percent often found to be between 7 and 14 percent). This proportion of black households is the ratio or concentration of blacks beyond which many whites find the situation unacceptable; when the ratio is higher, they begin to move (Farley et al. 1978). Characteristics of the white population may determine the tipping point, with a more liberal, educated group more likely to accept a larger proportion of black households.

Saltman (1989:7) maintains that affirmative marketing (including racial counseling) differs from racial steering as "affirmative marketing encourages people of the race *least* likely to consider moving to an area to do so. This would mean blacks moving to white areas and whites to integrated ones. Steering on the other hand encourages those *most* likely to move to an area to do so. This would mean whites to white areas and blacks to black or integrated areas." She adds that affirmative marketing is supported by law and expands choice, whereas racial steering is illegal and restricts choice. The National Association of Realtors, both in the 1988 congressional hearings and the federal court case (sshc v. nah), argue that Title VIII forbids taking race into account in dealings with clients, for then they will be subject to charges of steering. They argue that freedom of choice in housing should not be constrained and that most im programs constrain black households because they are concerned with overrepresentation of black households in the relevant housing market.

Some black organizations have complained that because the focus in racial counseling in im programs may be on keeping the white population from moving after integration has occurred, the programs bow to white wishes of what is an acceptable composition of an integrated community. In racially conscious counseling the burden may fall on black families as it encourages them to purchase in mixed rather than in areas of concentrated black households. However, Polikoff (1986) argues that im programs are pursued not because a black majority community is undesirable, but because a racially diverse one is desirable. He further argues that hud agrees and has produced guidelines for preserving racially diverse neighborhoods. In 1988 Polikoff also argued that affirmative marketing, housing counseling, pro-integrative publicity, and equity assurance (guaranteeing a certain housing equity in integrated areas) expands choice. He further argues that racial diversity programs do not stigmatize blacks by "catering to white prejudice." Polikoff (Galster 1989:2) says "just as some black families understandably fear hostility when pioneering in all white communities, so many white families understandably fear the resegregation syndrome. Racial diversity programs are designed to allay fears and avoid self-fulfilling prophesies of a dynamic that no families want, thus they cannot be accused of pandering to bigotry." Blacks who want integrated living may support them; Ritchie, director of one IM program, said their main support came from blacks (Galster 1989). Black households, especially those middle-class ones not wanting the resegregation process, may move to another suburb when too high a concentration of blacks occurs, according to one Bay Area civil rights leader. Yet some civil rights organizations feel that IM limits black choice, making it harder for blacks to get their first priority, decent housing (Leigh and McGhee 1986). Civil rights organizations also oppose IM groups' support for the view that whites should only feel safe and comfortable when they are the majority (Goering 1986).

In general the responses of these groups are mixed. Although the Chicago NAACP in 1984 and the NAACP national office in 1985 (Goering 1986:15) were against IM programs, the NAACP national research director was quoted in 1984 as lauding the fact that some communities, already integrated, had taken steps "to reverse the illegal practice of steering blacks only to black and integrated areas" (Polikoff 1986:60). Former Secretary of HUD Samuel Pierce's statement favoring integration maintenance is cited, and the NAACP executive states that "the NAACP, which stalworthy supports integration, has counseled that affirmative marketing techniques *that do not use hard and fast exclusionary quotas* to prevent resegregation are valid" (Chicago *Tribune* February 4, 1984).

The National Urban League has also had serious reservations about IM programs. In 1984 they opposed any policy that would "limit for any reason access of minority group members to any housing they could afford." It opposed "any policy of so-called 'spatial deconcentration.'" It did not object to the movement of blacks to suburbs by personal choice, even if this movement eventually resulted in the neighborhoods no longer being racially integrated. The league then opposed any action that would maintain housing integration by denying free access to housing for minorities (Goering 1986:13).

Whether choice and integration maintenance are in conflict is a question. Saltman (1989:7) argues that they are not: "The implication is that in order to preserve integration blacks have to be restricted. My research shows that this is a false assumption. Every successful example I found in this movement [neighborhood stabilization] used no quotas and no denial of choice to anyone. What they did use was affirmative marketing, which is an expansion of housing choices for all—whites and blacks alike." Yinger (1986) also feels that the issue need not be choice versus integration. However, Lake (1986) does see the goals of integration as very much in conflict with the goals of choice, which he considers important. Certainly these IM groups use as their goal choice expansion, as true in the Oak Park strategy. By giving information about all housing opportunities, not just in non-concentration suburbs, they are not limiting access. Their counseling is of all choices and involves black families. One group that has done this is the South Suburban Housing Center (SSHC), which has participated in the landmark federal decision. In this report they state that "in practice very few clients—none in recent years—have been unwilling to consider such locations [integrated housing areas]. SSHC's current policy is . . . all clients are to receive available SSHC information as they may request. From January through December 31, 1977, SSHC counseled a total of 477 clients, 160 of whom were majority and 317 of whom were minority families. Of 129 clients with whom SSHC maintained contact beyond the first interview, 70 chose to move to non-traditional locations, the remaining 59 clients (22 majority and 37 minority families) moved to traditional locations" (Polikoff 1986:62).

While counseling is the most important part of IM efforts, as Polikoff says, it is the most controversial and if done poorly the most dangerous. Some IM efforts focus on stopping realtors from steering black families to concentrated areas and on provision of better amenities to keep whites. In the West Mt. Airy, Pennsylvania, neighborhood organization effort, Helper (1986:184) finds that "the organization did not try to hold onto white people or to prevent black entry . . . it tried to heighten demand for West Mt. Airy as a place to live by lowering the turnover rate and raising the level of house prices." Above all, it tried to establish a sense of community through its large mixed group organization (one-third of all community households in 1973). It worked to avoid having realtors showing homes on a racially selective basis and got information on forthcoming sales. The community, at the time of the Heumann study (1973) had 58 percent white and 43 percent black residents.

These characteristics of IM indicate why the debate over it may be exaggerated. IM efforts should be considered legitimate due to the existence of a federal court decision legitimizing affirmative marketing, and in the major attitude change of whites toward black neighbors which increases blacks' welcome in many suburban communities and changes attitudes of realtors. With the majority of the American population in the suburbs, they are no longer homogeneous. Hispanics, Asians, and other groups live in the suburbs, as do young single people and the aged. It is only natural that black households, especially two-parent households, will reside in the suburbs, too. Only the underclass, including most black female-headed households (Momeni 1987) will be left in decaying, inner-city, low-cost rentals—and even some of these households are in suburbia.

The need is to see that when blacks are in suburbs, they are not isolated in segregated ones—and thus the need for affirmative marketing. In a federal court decision "the promotion of integrated housing and neighborhoods" was declared one of the primary goals of the Fair Housing Act by Judge Leinenweber (*South Suburban Housing Center v. National Association of Realtors*). The judge stated that "special outreach efforts which further promote racial integration and diversity are not now and never have been a discriminatory housing practice." The court found the SSHC's efforts were to expand the information about the availability of housing to all home-seekers, to promote racially diverse living, and prevent resegregation, and such efforts had a beneficial effect. The judge rejected the National Association of Realtors' contention that SSHC affirmative marketing efforts in the nine southern suburban municipalities of the Chicago area were unlawful.

Historically, IM or affirmative marketing programs have not only survived, but also have grown and received praise. Saltman (1989:7) states that "the neighborhood stabilization/integration maintenance issue appeared when National Neighbors first began 20 years ago, surfacing periodically throughout their existence (I found it in Indianapolis much earlier, later in Hartford and Milwaukee, and in Akron both early and later). I found it elsewhere across the country. And it has touched us all in the two recent legal decisions involving Starrett City and South Suburban fair housing agencies of Chicago. I am referring in the simplest terms to the meaning and intent of 'stabilization' and 'integration maintenance.' There has not been a time in this movement when the issue has not been present."

This policy issue will not disappear, but it is unlikely that we will avoid resegregation of the suburbs if we do not address the issue.

References

Blair, William. 1984. "Accord to Minority Suit Provides for More Subsidized Apartments." *New York Times* May 3.

Bullard, Robert. 1986. "Blacks and the American Dream of Housing." Pp. 53–68 in *Race, Ethnicity and Minority Housing in the United States,* edited by Jamshid Momeni. Westport, Conn.: Greenwood Press.

Chicago *Tribune.* 1984. "Resolution Pertaining to the Attempted Control of the Mobility of the Black Population in a Free Market." Statement of the Far South Suburban Chapter, Chicago area, NAACP. February 4.

Clark, Thomas. 1987. "The Suburbanization Process and Residential Segregation." Pp. 115–37 in *Divided Neighborhoods,* edited by Gary Tobin. Beverly Hills: Sage.

Clay, Phillip. 1979. "The Process of Black Suburbanization." *Urban Affairs Quarterly* 14:405–23.

Connolly, H. X. 1973. "Black Movement to the Suburbs." *Urban Affairs Quarterly* 9:91–111.

Farley, John. 1987. "Segregation in 1980: How Segregated Are America's Metropolitan Areas." Pp. 95–114 in *Divided Neighborhoods,* edited by Gary Tobin. Beverly Hills: Sage.

Farley, Reynolds, Harold Schuman, Suzanne Bianchi, Diane Colosanto, and Shirley Hatchett. 1978. "Chocolate City, Vanilla Suburbs: Will the Trend toward Racially Separate Communities Continue?" *Social Science Research* 7:319–44.

Feins, Judith, and Rachael Bratt. 1983. "Barred to Boston: Racial Discrimination in Housing." *American Planning Association Journal* 49:344–55.

Galster, George. 1982. "Black and White Preferences for Neighborhood Racial Composition." *American Real Estate and Urban Economics Association Journal* 10:39–66.

———. 1989. "Congressional Hearings on Integration Maintenance." *Trends in Housing* 27(4):2.

Goering, John. 1986. "Introduction." Pp. 9–17 in *Housing Desegregation and Federal Policy,* edited by John Goering. Chapel Hill: University of North Carolina Press.

Goodwin, Carol. 1979. *Oak Park Strategy: Community Control of Racial Change.* Chicago: University of Chicago Press.

Harvard Law Review. 1980. "Benign Steering and Benign Quotas: The Validity of Race-Conscious Government Policies to Promote Residential Integration." 93:938–65.

Helper, Rose. 1986. "Success and Resistance Factors in the Maintenance of Racially Mixed Neighborhoods." Pp. 170–96 in *Housing Desegregation and Federal Policy*. Chapel Hill: University of North Carolina Press.

Hermalin, Albert, and Reynolds Farley. 1973. "The Potential for Racial Integration in Cities and Suburbs." *American Sociological Review* 38:595–610.

Heumann, Leonard. 1973. "The Definition and Analysis of Racial Integration: The Case of West Mt. Airy." Ph.D. Dissertation, University of Pennsylvania.

Huttman, Elizabeth. 1975. *Class Mix in a New Town: The Case of Jonathan New Town*. Hayward: California State University Press.

———. 1988. "New Communities in the United States." Pp. 345–67 in *Handbook on Housing and the Built Environment*, edited by Elizabeth Huttman and Willem Van Vliet. Westport, Conn.: Greenwood Press.

Hwang, S. S., and S. H. Murdock. 1982. "Residential Segregation in Texas in 1980. *Social Science Quarterly* 63:737–48.

International Herald Tribune. 1989. "Report Finds s&l's Rejecting Blacks for Loans." February 16:7.

James, P. J., B. McCummings, and E. A. Tynan. 1984. *Minorities in the Sunbelt: Segregation, Discrimination, and Housing Conditions of Hispanics and Blacks*. New Brunswick: Rutgers University Center for Urban Policy Research.

Kain, John. 1986. "The Influence of Race and Income on Racial Segregation and Housing Policy." Pp. 99–118 in *Housing Desegregation and Federal Policy*, edited by John Goering. Chapel Hill: University of North Carolina Press.

———. 1987. "Housing Market Discrimination and Black Suburbanization in the 1980s." Pp. 68–94 in *Divided Neighborhoods*, edited by Gary Tobin. Beverly Hills: Sage.

Kurtz, Howard. 1983. "Lawsuit in Yonkers Challenges a Suburban Tradition of Bias." *Washington Post* May 2.

Lake, Robert. 1981. *The New Suburbanites: Race and Housing in the Suburbs*. New Brunswick: Center for Urban Policy Research.

———. 1986. "Postscript: Unresolved Themes in the Evolution of Fair Housing." Pp. 313–26 in *Housing Desegregation and Federal Policy*, edited by John Goering. Chapel Hill: University of North Carolina Press.

Lake, Robert, and Susan Cutter. 1980. "A Typology of Black Suburbanization since 1970." *The Geographical Review* 70:167–81.

Leadership Council for Metropolitan Open Communities. 1987. "The Cost of Housing Discrimination and Segregation." Pp. 268–80 in *Divided Neighborhoods*, edited by Gary Tobin. Beverly Hills: Sage.

Leigh, Wilhelmina, and James McGhee. 1986. "A Minority Perspective on Residential Racial Integration." Pp. 31–42 in *Housing Desegregation and Federal Policy*, edited by John Goering. Chapel Hill: University of North Carolina Press.

Lieberman, Stanley, and Donna Carter. 1982. "Temporal Changes and Urban Differences in Residential Segregation. A Reconsideration." *American Journal of Sociology* 88:296–310.

Logan, John, and Mark Schneider. 1984. "Racial Segregation and Racial Change in American Suburbs, 1970–1980." *American Journal of Sociology* 89:874–88.

Mallach, Alan. 1988. "Opening the Suburbs: New Jersey's Mt. Laurel Experience." *Shelter Force* 11:12–13.

Massey, Douglas, and Nancy Denton. 1987. "Trends in the Residential Segregation of Blacks, Hispanics, and Asians: 1970–1980." *American Sociological Review* 52:802–25.

Momeni, Jamshid. 1986a. "Introduction." Pp. 21–25 in *Race, Ethnicity, and Minority Housing in the United States,* edited by Jamshid Momeni. Westport, Conn.: Greenwood Press.

———. 1986a. "The Housing Conditions of Black Female-Headed Households: A Comparative Analysis." Pp. 89–108 in *Race, Ethnicity and Minority Housing in the United States,* edited by Jamshid Momeni. Westport, Conn.: Greenwood Press.

Newburger, Harriet. 1984. *Recent Evidence on Discrimination in Housing.* Washington, D.C.: Office of Policy Development and Research, Department of Housing and Urban Development.

New York Times. 1987. "Jersey Lagging in Suburban Housing for the Poor." June 1.

Obermanns, Richard. 1980. *Stability and Change in Racially Diverse Suburbs: 1970–78: Summary.* Cleveland Heights: Heights Community Congress.

———. 1982. "Racial School Enrollment Patterns in Metropolitan Cleveland: 1978–80." *The Cuyahoga Plan's Open Housing Report.* March.

Orfield, Gary. 1986. "The Movement for Housing Integration: Rationale and the Nature of the Challenge." Pp. 18–30 in *Housing Desegregation and Federal Policy,* edited by John Goering. Chapel Hill: University of North Carolina Press.

Pearce, Diana. 1979. "Gatekeepers and Homeseekers: Institutional Patterns in Racial Steering." *Social Problems* 26:325–42.

———. 1988. "Minorities and Housing Discrimination." Pp. 301–12 in *Handbook on Housing and the Built Environment,* edited by Elizabeth Huttman and Willem Van Vliet. Westport, Conn.: Greenwood Press.

Polikoff, Alexander. 1986. "Sustainable Integration or Inevitable Resegregation: The Troubling Question." Pp. 43–74 in *Housing Desegregation and Federal Policy,* edited by John Goering. Chapel Hill: University of North Carolina Press.

Rabin, Yale. 1987. "The Roots of Segregation in the Eighties: The Role of Local Government Action." Pp. 208–26 in *Divided Neighborhoods,* edited by Gary Tobin. Beverly Hills: Sage.

Rose, Harold. 1976. *Black Suburbanization: Access to Improved Quality of Life or Maintenance of Status Quo?* Cambridge, Mass.: Ballinger.

Rosenberg, Robert. 1982. "Starrett City Created a Model Integrated Community." *Real Estate Review* 12:63–68.

Saltman, Juliet. 1989. "Racism and Integration Maintenance." *Trends in Housing* 27:7.

Schafer, R. 1979. "Racial Discrimination in the Boston Housing Market." *Journal of Urban Economics* 6:176–96.

Schelling, Thomas. 1972. "A Process of Residential Segregation: Neighborhood Tipping." In *Racial Discrimination in Economic Life,* edited by Anthony Pascal. Lexington, Mass.: D. C. Heath.

Schermer, George. 1979. *Realtors as Gatekeepers.* Ann Arbor: Michigan Advisory Committee to U.S. Commission on Civil Rights. July 9:31.

Schnare, Ann. 1977. "Residential Segregation by Race in U.S. Metropolitan Areas: An Analysis Across Cities and Over Time." Working Paper 246-2. Washington, D.C.: Urban Institute.

Silver, Christopher. 1986. "Housing Policy and Suburbanization: An Analysis of the Changing Quality and Quantity of Black Housing in Suburbia Since 1950." Pp. 69–88 in *Race, Ethnicity and Minority Housing in the United States,* edited by Jamshid Momeni. Westport, Conn.: Greenwood Press.

Simkus, Albert. 1978. "Resident Segregation by Occupation and Race in Ten Urbanized Areas, 1950–1970." *American Sociological Review* 43:81–93.

Spain, Daphne, and Larry Long. 1981. "Black Movers to the Suburbs: Are They Moving to Predominantly White Neighborhoods?" Special Demographic Analysis CDS 80-4. December. Washington, D.C.: Bureau of the Census.

Taeuber, Karl. 1983. "Racial Residential Segregation, 28 Cities, 1970–1980." CDE Working Paper. March. Madison: University of Wisconsin.

Trends in Housing. 1989. "Federal Court Judge Approves Affirmative Marketing Programs in Chicago." 27(4):12.

———. 1989. "Report Finds S&L's Rejecting Blacks for Loans." 27(4):12.

U.S. Bureau of the Census. 1981, 1983, 1984. *Current Population Reports.*

U.S. Public Health Service. 1987. *The Facts: The Black Population.* Washington, D.C.: Government Printing Office.

Valente, Judith. 1983. "Cross Burning, Vandalism Reported in Maryland Suburbs." *Washington Post* 30:C2.

Weaver, Robert. 1960. "Class, Race and Urban Renewal." *Land Economics* 36:235–51.

Wegmann, Robert. 1977. "Desegregation and Resegregation: A Review of the Research on White Flight from Urban Areas." Pp. 11–54 in *The Future of Big City Schools: Desegregation Policies and Magnet Alternatives,* edited by Daniel Levine and Robert Havighurst. Berkeley: McCutchan Publishers.

Werthman, Carl, Jerry Mandel, and Ted Dienstfrey. 1965. *Planning and the Purchase Decision: Why People Buy in Planned Communities.* Berkeley: Institute for Urban and Regional Development, University of California.

White, Michael. 1988. *The Segregation and Residential Assimilation of Immigrants.* Washington, D.C.: Urban Institute.

Wienk, Ronald, Clifford Reid, John Simonson, and Frederick Eggers. 1979. *Measuring Racial Discrimination in American Housing Markets: The Housing Market Survey.* Washington, D.C.: Office of Policy Development. Department of Housing and Urban Development.

Yinger, John. 1979. "Prejudice and Discrimination in the Urban Housing Markets." Pp. 430–68 in *Current Issues in Urban Economics,* edited by P. Mieszkowski and M. Straszheim. Baltimore: Johns Hopkins University Press.

———. 1986. "On the Possibility of Achieving Racial Integration through Subsidized Housing." Pp. 290–312 in *Housing Desegregation and Federal Policy,* edited by John Goering. Chapel Hill: University of North Carolina Press.

———. 1987. "The Racial Dimension of Urban Housing Markets in the 1980s." Pp. 43–67 in *Divided Neighborhoods,* edited by Gary Tobin. Beverly Hills: Sage.

20. Open Housing in Metropolitan Cleveland

Decades after the Kerner Commission warned of two societies—one black and one white—and after the passage of the federal fair housing law, Cleveland, Ohio, continues to have one of the most segregated housing markets in the United States. Based upon 1980 census data, Cleveland and its suburbs is among the nation's worst segregated central cities and metropolitan regions. In 1980, 44 percent of the city's population and 23 percent of Cuyahoga County's population was black. On a scale of housing segregation in which a score of 100 represents total segregation, Cleveland rated 87.5 in 1980, compared to 90.8 in 1970. Chicago remains the worst-segregated large city, with scores of 91.9 in 1970 and 87.8 in 1980. Among midwestern cities generally, the segregation index average score dropped from 87 in 1970 to 78 in 1980.

In Cleveland, 22 of 35 neighborhoods were racially "isolated" in 1986, as they were in 1968. While Cleveland was one of the first cities to establish a Community Relations Board to deal with racial problems, it was a decade later until the city council enacted a controversial fair housing ordinance in 1988. In testimony before Congress in 1987, the civil rights activist Jordan Band recounted examples of increasing racially motivated confrontations and violence in Cleveland. In addition to a primarily segregated private housing market, most of the city's public housing is segregated and most of Cleveland's suburbs have rejected public housing.

Most of the hope and efforts to encourage racial integration in housing have taken place in Cleveland's suburbs. In 1980 less than 10 percent of the population in the suburban communities of Cuyahoga County was black, and most suburbs had a black population of less than 2 percent. This was still a significant increase over 1970. The leading agency promoting racial diversity in housing is the Cuyahoga Plan, a regional nonprofit fair housing agency established in 1974 and funded by Cuyahoga County, several suburban cities, and local foundations. According to the Cuyahoga Plan, if black families lived in

367

suburbs they could afford and were randomly dispersed, no Cuyahoga County suburb would have had a black population of less than 11 percent in 1980. Its conclusion is that racial discrimination, not economics, largely explains Cleveland's segregated housing patterns (Cuyahoga Plan 1983).

The metropolitan housing market, like that of Cleveland, is split between east and west. Most of the urban and suburban black population lives to the east of the Cuyahoga River, which divides the area. Most black suburbanization has been in the eastern suburbs. Two suburbs—East Cleveland and Warrensville Heights—went through a rapid racial transition in the late 1960s and early 1970s and have both largely resegregated according to the 1980 census. In contrast, two other older eastern suburbs have integrated and maintained their racial diversity.

Shaker Heights, renowned as one of America's first planned suburbs, originally excluded blacks and other minorities through restrictive covenants, as did most American suburbs. As blacks began to move to Shaker Heights in the 1950s and 1960s after restrictive covenants were ruled illegal, there was white resistance. However, neighborhood and civic leaders encouraged peaceful integration, which led to several city ordinances designed to outlaw discriminatory housing practices and to promote stable racial diversity. Shaker Heights established its own municipal housing office in 1967 to work with prospective home-buyers and renters and cooperative realtors and to market Shaker Heights as an integrated community (Alfred and Marcoux 1970). The black population of Shaker Heights is approximately 27 percent. While Shaker Heights is considered an affluent suburb with expensive housing stock, there is access for those with moderate incomes. To expand this access, Shaker Heights in 1986 created a Fund for the Future of Shaker Heights supported by local foundations and designed to encourage residential integration by providing below-market mortgage loans to homebuyers, black and white, willing to make pro-integrative moves within the city. During its first two years the fund made forty-five loans.

Neighboring Cleveland Heights has a similar history. Racial transition began in the early 1970s. When problems arose, concerned residents, civic groups, and churches formed the Heights Community Congress in 1972. The congress became the catalyst in persuading the city in 1976 to adopt comprehensive fair housing policies similar to those of Shaker Heights to promote and maintain stable racial diversity. The black population of Cleveland Heights is approximately 25 percent.

In the remainder of the eastern part of Cuyahoga County, only three cities have a black population of more than 10 percent. The western communities in the county are much more racially segregated; in 1980, most had less than 5 percent black population.

The best-known example of segregated housing on Cleveland's west side is the city of Parma, Cleveland's largest suburb with a 1980 population of 92,000, fewer than 1 percent of which was nonwhite. Parma was sued in 1973 by the U.S. Department of Justice and found guilty in 1980 of violating federal fair housing laws in several respects. It has since been subject to a remedial court order (Cooper 1988). In the absence of racial litigation, other segregated western Cleveland suburbs have not voluntarily initiated fair housing programs.

The same is generally true of the eastern suburbs. Fearing that it would be increasingly difficult to maintain integration in only a few suburban communities, the cities of Cleveland Heights, Shaker Heights, and University Heights and their school boards joined together in 1984 to form the Eastern Suburban Council for Open Communities (ESCOC). Its purpose is to encourage prospective black homebuyers and renters to consider the predominantly white housing market of Hillcrest. Hillcrest consists of six eastern suburban communities which immediately border the three ESCOC cities to the north. ESCOC has received financial support from local foundations and has worked with sympathetic neighborhood groups and realtors. Its unique voluntary regional approach has induced many blacks to look for housing in Hillcrest, and many have bought houses or rented apartments. ESCOC has had to overcome such obstacles as the 1983 firebombing of a black family's house in Lyndhurst and the refusal of city officials in such cities as South Euclid to join ESCOC and publicly support its activities.

In the past there have been efforts to institute metropolitan government in Cleveland, but they have failed. Efforts to persuade the suburbs to enter into cooperative agreements with the Cuyahoga Metropolitan Housing Authority (CMHA) to decentralize public housing within Cuyahoga County have also generally failed. The regional planning agency (NOACA) has no viable regional fair-share plan for subsidized housing.

In this vacuum, the Metropolitan Strategy Group (MSG) has emerged as a major lobbying force for fair housing in Cleveland's suburbs. It consists of all those agencies and organizations involved in promoting open, fair housing. Its chair, Charles Bromley, also serves as president of National Neighbors, a major national organization promoting interracial neighborhoods. The MSG has lobbied municipal, county, state, and federal governments to promote neighborhood integration and fair housing and serves as a clearinghouse for both types of activists. Perhaps its most notable success was the creation in 1986 by the Ohio Housing Finance Agency (OHFA) of a Pro-Integrative Bonus Program. This $6 million set-aside allowed fair housing and other agencies to offer below-market mortgages to eligible first-time homebuyers willing to make integration moves into racially imbalanced neighborhoods. This experimental program was created in the wake of protests by MSG that the state's mortgage revenue bond program was reinforcing rather than changing segregated residential patterns in metropolitan Cleveland. After an interval of two years and MSG intervention, OHFA reviewed the program in 1988. Ohio's state government has not taken an active role in addressing such controversial issues, leaving responsibility at the local level. While MSG's members have supported the strengthening of the federal Fair Housing Act enacted in 1988, there was little hope of federal leadership for open housing during the 1980s.

What has been accomplished in Cleveland's suburbs these past two decades? If the sole criterion of change is the segregation index, there has been little progress. Cleveland and most of its suburbs remain heavily segregated. While some residential racial patterns have changed, and many suburbs now have either a very small minority population (still generally under 5 percent), only two of Cleveland's fifty-nine suburbs have a minority population proportionally about the same as that of the county—Cleveland Heights and Shaker Heights. While there has been no resegregation recently as occurred much earlier in East Cleveland and Warrensville Heights, those eastern suburbs with a growing minority population have usually not initiated voluntary pro-integration policies. Meanwhile, there continue to be an alarming number of violent incidents involving race, both within the city and the suburbs. In the absence of concerted, intensive, and protracted efforts by public officials and community leaders at all levels of government, it is difficult to be optimistic about dramatic changes that will alter Cleveland's basic patterns of residential racial segregation, both within the central city and the surrounding suburbs.

However, the situation is not totally bleak. Cleveland Heights and Shaker Heights have maintained their status as voluntarily pro-integration maintenance communities for one to two decades with citizen support and that of the municipal governments. The creation of ESCOC and its innovative approach is a promising step to expanding the housing choices of blacks seeking suburban housing and possibly inducing other suburban governments to consider initiating pro-integration policies before a crisis necessitates their action. The existence of the MSG and its advocacy for regional pro-integration programs like OHFA's Pro-Integrative Mortgage Bonus program and the activities of the Cuyahoga Plan in both investigating and documenting racial discrimination in housing and working with suburban communities to promote open housing give hope that there is a constituency for open housing policies.

In Parma, there has been progress, although the pace has been slow. The city successfully appealed the appointment of a special overseer to audit implementation of the federal court order. Therefore, a local fair housing committee and an oversight committee did not begin their work until 1983. Since then, the city has applied for and received Community Development Block Grant (CDBG) funding from HUD, part of which has paid for programs mandated by the court order. Parma established its own housing agency and has attracted minority tenants with Section 8 vouchers. In 1987, Parma's first subsidized housing project, a sixty-unit Section 8 project, was completed. In 1988, a long delayed advertising program was launched—with the involvement of the Cuyahoga Plan—to attract minority homebuyers. The Parma city administration has been supportive in its efforts to promote fair housing, as evidenced by the passage in June 1988 of a municipal fair housing ordinance, passed before any of Parma's neighboring suburbs adopted similar fair housing policies.

The Cuyahoga Plan's audits have confirmed that racial discrimination still affects the choices of blacks seeking to purchase homes and rent apartments in Cleveland's suburbs. A comparative study was conducted of housing search patterns and attitudes on housing integration in Cleveland's suburbs (Keating, Palmer, and Smith 1987, 1988). A sample of more than four hundred home-buyers in twelve Cleveland suburbs who purchased houses in 1985 was surveyed in 1986, and almost half responded to a follow-up survey in 1987.

This study revealed that these homebuyers primarily chose their houses and neighborhoods for conventional reasons (e.g., renters who wanted to own). Racial patterns were not the primary reason for their moves or their selection of a house. Attitudes on racial integration in housing varied considerably; most respondents already lived in Greater Cleveland, and about 40 percent purchased a house in a suburb where they already lived. Those who preferred to live in a racially integrated neighborhood were more likely to choose to live in Cleveland Heights and Shaker Heights and were more likely to use these housing offices to locate their home. In contrast, the highest rate of preference for living in all-white or predominantly white neighborhoods was found among Parma homebuyers, all of whom were white in this sample from 1985. Attitudes in the Hillcrest communities were less polar. Almost all black homebuyers favored racially integrated neighborhoods.

When asked if they favored government intervention to promote racially mixed neighborhoods and open housing, the most support came from homebuyers in the communities with voluntary integration management programs—Cleveland Heights and Shaker Heights. The lowest levels of support came from Parma, where only 23 percent favored such government intervention. The range of white support for open housing went from 50 percent in Parma to 85 percent in Cleveland Heights. These attitudinal results suggest that those suburbs with overt and well-known pro-integration management housing policies will attract those whites who generally favor such policies. In fact, Cleveland Heights and Shaker Heights aggressively seek to attract these prospective homebuyers, however, the communities without fair housing policies do not attract as many. The case of Parma suggests that court-ordered mandatory fair housing policies do not necessarily change the opinions of many residents on open housing.

National opinion surveys since the 1960s have shown that gradually a majority of Americans have come to favor open and fair housing legislation and policies (Schuman, Steeh, and Bobo 1985). This study shows that Cleveland, despite its still heavily segregated housing market, is no exception. A survey released in June 1988 by the Citizens League of Greater Cleveland confirmed this conclusion. Seven hundred and fifty residents of Cuyahoga County were interviewed in February and March 1988; when asked if they would like their neighborhood to be racially integrated, 66 percent overall agreed, while only 28 percent disagreed. Support for racially integrated neighborhoods was strongest among renters (77 percent versus 61 percent among homeowners) and blacks (74 percent versus 60 percent for whites). However, when asked why they chose to live where they did currently, only 2 percent volunteered racial balance as an answer. This survey did not define racial integration. My study defined racially integrated neighborhoods as those with a white population ranging from 50 to 80 percent. Fifty-nine percent of the overall sample of homebuyers preferred to live in such neighborhoods, whereas 25 percent preferred predominantly white (80 percent or more) and 15 percent preferred all-white neighborhoods.

What these data reveal is that although a majority of whites, homeowners and renters alike, are much more tolerant of blacks than was true two decades ago, most whites do not move in search of racially integrated neighborhoods. Local efforts to promote the racially integrated living patterns, which are our stated national goal, must actively seek to educate and attract prospective homeowners and renters. Because so few suburbs have undertaken such activities voluntarily, it is essential that regional organizations like ESCOC, the Cuyahoga Plan, and the MSG exist and receive public and private financial support and, just as importantly, the cooperation of all cities within metropolitan areas. Mere enforcement of existing fair housing laws has not significantly changed basic patterns of racial segregation in housing, even while white support for integrated housing has risen. Much more comprehensive programs, including pro-integrative housing incentives, are essential. If they only exist in a few suburbs, then Cleveland's pattern of most suburbs being segregated seems very likely to continue.

References

Alfred, Stephen J., and Charles R. Marcoux. 1970. "Impact of a Community Association on Integrated Suburban Housing Patterns." *Cleveland State University Law Review* 19:90–99.

Cuyahoga Plan. 1983. "A Report on Population and Race." Cleveland: Cuyahoga Plan of Ohio.

Cooper, Phillip J. 1988. *Hard Judicial Choices: Federal District Court Judges and State and Local Officials.* New York: Oxford University Press.

Massey, Douglas S., and Nancy A. Denton. 1987. "Trends in the Residential Segregation of Blacks, Hispanics, and Asians: 1970–1980." *American Sociological Review* 52:802–25.

Keating, W. Dennis, William J. Palmer, and Linda S. Smith. 1987. "A Comparative Study of Three Models of Racial Integration in Housing in Cleveland." Cleveland: College of Urban Affairs, Cleveland State University.

————. 1988. "An Analysis of 1985 Homebuyers' Attitudes in 1987." Cleveland: College of Urban Affairs, Cleveland State University.

Schuman, Howard, Charlotte Steeh, and Lawrence Bobo. 1985. *Racial Attitudes in America: Trends and Interpretations.* Washington, D.C.: Howard University Press.

21. U.S. Neighborhood Stabilization Efforts

One outgrowth of the U.S. Civil Rights movement of the 1960s was the neighborhood stabilization movement—the organized effort to maintain racial pluralism in urban neighborhoods. This chapter is part of a larger study designed to portray the national neighborhood stabilization movement (Saltman 1990). I will present a comparative analysis of the movement as it developed and succeeded in three urban neighborhoods in three different cities from 1956 to 1986.

A persisting topic of urban research in the United States has been neighborhood change or succession. Three differing perspectives have emerged, offering divergent views of the future of racially changing neighborhoods. The first and most traditional approach I term *degenerative* because it suggests an inevitability of neighborhood decline after racial change has occurred (Molotch 1972; Wilson 1983). The second approach, *interactionist,* focuses on the relationship between social support networks and neighborhood preservation. This perspective does not accept the inevitability of decline and suggests the possibility of neighborhood stability through social support networks (Ahlbrandt and Cunningham 1978; Fischer 1976; Hunter 1975). Consistent with this approach is the theory that organizations can create a sense of community when none exists in racially changing neighborhoods (Hunter 1974, 1975).

A third approach—one supported herein—suggests that racially integrated neighborhoods can stabilize if sufficient resources and institutional networks are mobilized early for collective action (Saltman 1984; Taub, Taylor, and Dunham 1984). This is an interventionist perspective, linked to policy implications. My conclusion offers a model strategy for neighborhood stabilization—the maintenance of viable pluralist neighborhoods.

Methodology

The urban neighborhoods and their organizations were selected according to six criteria: comparability of age, continuity, size of community, type of community, region, and purpose. Thus they all represent long-standing neighborhood stabilization groups in medium-sized cities in northern or midwestern industrial areas, whose original purpose was stabilization as here defined. They were from fourteen to twenty-eight years old, and all were founding members in 1970 of National Neighbors—the only national organization devoted solely to neighborhood stabilization.

During the spring and summer of 1984, I made field visits to the neighborhood study sites in Indianapolis, Rochester, and Milwaukee. During each field visit, taped interviews were held with organizational and community leaders, past and current. Primary historical materials were collected including newsletters, correspondence, minutes of meetings, annual reports, brochures, and other printed material.

In addition, visits were made to local governmental planning departments to secure census data, school data, and other pertinent information concerning the city and its neighborhoods. Finally, many hours were spent in the library of local newspapers securing copies of newspaper articles about the neighborhoods, its organizations, and each city's development over the past two decades. Photographs were taken of the study neighborhoods, showing the condition of streets, housing, business district, and facilities in each area.

In the larger research covering the whole movement across the country, I found various types of neighborhood-organization combinations. From these I developed three analytical models: (1) Model A (Success): the live movement-organization (MO) and the successfully maintained pluralist neighborhood; (2) Model B (Conditional): the live MO and the neighborhood which became predominantly black, and (3) Model C (Failure): the dead MO and the predominantly black neighborhood. Only Model A (Success) and the study neighborhoods of Indianapolis, Rochester, and Milwaukee will be discussed herein. Figure 21.1 shows each of the study neighborhoods of Model A, and the changes in their racial composition over time.

Model A (Success): Live MO/Pluralist Neighborhood

Sociohistorical Context. All three neighborhoods had pervasive, long-standing racism in their cities, manifested in housing and school segregation. All three had massive urban renewal projects in their inner cities which dislocated blacks, forced their migration to new neighborhoods, and led to the formation of the movement organization (MO) in each neighborhood studied.

FIGURE 21.1.   Racial Composition of Subareas of Neighborhoods (1970, 1980)

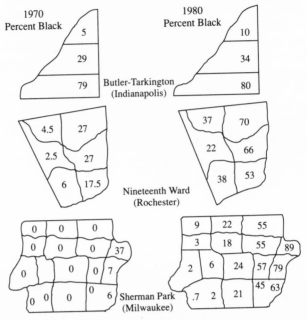

Racism in Indianapolis was seen in segregated churches, housing, schools, employment, and recreation. In housing, for example, segregation was reinforced by an ordinance prohibiting blacks from moving into white neighborhoods without the written consent of a majority of the neighborhood residents (Madison 1982). When from 1950 to 1960, urban renewal began to clear hundreds of acres of land occupied by blacks, they pushed northward to the bottom section of the study neighborhood, Butler-Tarkington.

In Rochester, waves of black migration from the South after World War II ended in two major black enclaves in the center of the city, the areas selected for massive land clearance for urban renewal projects. By 1964, when three days and nights of riots rocked the city, blacks had been displaced by urban renewal six and seven times and shunted into ever-shrinking ghetto areas. Some spilled into the 19th Ward, the study neighborhood (*Times-Union* February 12, 1952; *Democrat-Chronicle* July 22, 1984).

Early racism in Milwaukee—city of beer, bratwurst, and gemütlichkeit—is shown in a brief newspaper article. Responding to the presence of blacks who were then half of 1 percent of the city's population, the article noted that the real estate board wanted to restrict the black population to "a certain area of the west side . . . because they are growing so rapidly that something will have to be done" (Milwaukee *Journal* September 16, 1924). Containment of blacks succeeded; the black living area was four blocks long and three blocks wide, with a population density twice the average for the city. By 1967, when the black population had risen to 12 percent of the total, they were still confined to the inner core of the city. Approximately 1 percent, however, lived outside the inner core, mostly on the northwest side of the city in an area that came to be known as Sherman Park, the study neighborhood (Still 1948; Aukofer 1968). Extensive urban renewal in the 1960s had brought them there. City riots in the 1960s in Milwaukee left 100 persons injured and 1,740 arrested, President Kennedy and Martin Luther King had been shot, and a federal open housing law had been passed. Racial discrimination in housing was not halted in any of the three cities, however, as later national and local audits revealed (HUD 1979).

Inception/Goals. Four families in Indianapolis in 1956, and seven in Milwaukee in 1970, founded the MOS in the study neighborhoods (BTNA History 1968; Johanneson 1980). In Rochester, however, the clergy of eleven neighborhood churches were the catalysts for the group's formation in the Nineteenth Ward in 1965.

In all three communities, the goal of integration maintenance remained consistent throughout the existence of the MOS. Although the words differed over time, the intent was the same. Butler-Tarkington Neighborhood Association (BTNA) in Indianapolis had a stated goal of achieving "an ideal racially integrated beautiful neighborhood" by promoting cooperative efforts among residents, churches, and civic groups, and preventing intergroup conflict (BTNA Newsletter December 1961).

The stated goal of Rochester's Nineteenth Ward Community Association (WCA) was to provide a model "for the possibility of a racially integrated community within a stable residential area . . . open to all who could afford to maintain a home" (Nineteenth WCA Newsletter March 15, 1966). Five years later, they modified this to "create a conscious multiracial community where individual and cultural differences are not only tolerated but celebrated, and where people share a sense of community" (Bush and Weiss 1979).

Milwaukee's Sherman Park Community Association (SPCA) stated its goal as "to serve and promote the interests of the neighborhood as well as the uniqueness and diversity that exists in Sherman Park. Members . . . believe that our future lies in encouraging people of all races, religions, and national origins to come together to meet our common goals of good quality education, beautiful homes and streets, and preserving the most attractive, convenient and interesting place to live in Milwaukee" (spca Proposal to Ford Foundation 1976).

Structure. Indianapolis's BTNA was the only group in the model that remained essentially unfunded and totally voluntary throughout its existence. Rochester's WCA and Milwaukee's spca were eventually well funded for housing rehabilitation projects and other special programs requiring offices and staffing (spca Annual Report October 4, 1977; Milwaukee *Journal* September 12, 1978; Nineteenth WCA Minutes; sp Plan; sp Redevelopment Corp. October 23, 1980).

All three organizations had elected boards of directors consisting of officers, committee chairs, and area representatives. In all three communities, however, the real power and control lay in the executive committee and the president. Standing committees conducted much of the work of the organization in all three study areas. Leadership in all three was primarily white and middle class, although intensive efforts were made to recruit black leadership—with minimal success. All three groups had great difficulty in securing representation from lower socioeconomic level portions of their neighborhoods, which were predominantly black.

Funding amounts seemed to reflect size of neighborhood. BTNA was essentially unfunded except for short special programs having modest grants. Rochester's budget for its organizational activities rose from $1,000 a year when it began to $24,000 twenty years later. Its special projects, however, were funded for $250,000, and had separate staff and offices. Milwaukee's spca went from no funding in its first seven years to more than a quarter of a million dollars in its seventh year and half a million soon after. Staff rose from one to twenty-three, with deep tensions and conflicts soon revealed. By 1984, eight executive directors had come and gone (Hagedorn 1983; spca Minutes 1970–84; Milwaukee *Journal* April 16, 1977).

From figure 21.1 it is evident that all three study neighborhoods had three areas within them, racially defined. One area was predominantly black, one was racially integrated, and one was predominantly white. Most leadership and membership came from the racially integrated area in all three communities. However, program boundaries in all three neighborhoods consciously included black areas from the outset. In fact, most of the MO's housing rehabilitation funds in each neighborhood were spent in the predominantly black areas.

Programs. Common concerns in the three MOS were housing, schools, and zoning. Common enemies were real estate agents who practiced blockbusting and racial steering, owners who did not maintain their properties, and special interest groups who attempted to alter the zoning of the neighborhood from residential to other uses.

Housing strategies in all three organizations included correcting real estate practices, promoting affirmative marketing of their areas, and securing funds for rehabilitation of deteriorated properties. One real estate practice that plagued all three communities was solicitation by real estate agents, which promoted panic and flight among residents. As a result, all three MOS successfully obtained bans on for sale signs and solicitation through their city councils or state legislatures. These strategies required extensive contacts with local and state governmental representatives and agencies, private corporate executives such as lenders, businesses, and industries, and all the media.

Indianapolis's BTNA used a seven-year study of a land-use plan for their area as a basis for much of their action program. Developed in cooperation with the City Planning Department, this plan provided a set of goals and standards for use throughout the BTNA's existence. Every time zoning changes were proposed for their area, the association successfully blocked them by citing the land-use plan and showing how the proposed change would be inconsistent with it. The BTNA Housing Committee, through its Housing Information Service, tried to achieve racial stabilization with a conscious effort to attract white home-seekers to the integrated neighborhood. In addition to affirmatively marketing their own area, they worked for fair and open housing throughout the county, to increase freedom of choice in housing for minorities. The association successfully had one of its main thoroughfares declared a Historic Preservation Area (BTNA History 1968; Annual Report 1971; BTNA Newsletter 1963–70; Minutes 1963–70; Indianapolis *Star* 1963–84).

Rochester's 19th WCA formed a Real Estate Service staffed by volunteers; the service consistently sold homes in the area for higher prices than professional agents were obtaining. The amounts of money that these sales would have produced in agents' commissions were noted carefully and referred to as bargaining points to persuade agents and brokers to modify blockbusting and steering practices. The Housing Committee worked with appraisers and lenders to modify their policies and practices. They obtained a cease and desist order from the state attorney general that blocked real estate solicitation in the Nineteenth Ward (Nineteenth WCA Real Estate Committee Report 1973; Bush and Weiss 1979; *Democrat-Chronicle* May 11, 1968; *Times-Union* November 19, 1971).

Milwaukee's SPCA conducted a real estate audit in 1976 to test for racial steering. One year later SPCA filed a formal complaint with HUD against four major real estate companies, charging violation of the federal fair housing law. Ultimately, this led to the formation of a metropolitan fair housing center as a separate agency, which became one of the most vigorous such groups in the country (SPCA Proposal to Ford Foundation June 10, 1976; Transcripts).

All three MOS obtained rehabilitation grants for their areas; BTNA in Indianapolis through the Neighborhood Housing Services, Rochester's Nineteenth WCA through its city and the state, and Milwaukee's SPCA through the city and state. The grants involved extensive lobbying on the part of all three groups and constant proposal writing by Rochester and Milwaukee's groups.

All three MOS were consistently involved in efforts to desegregate their cities' schools and neighborhoods. In Indianapolis, a lawsuit filed by the NAACP in 1965 resulted in a countywide plan for racial balance in all schools, extensive busing, and the end of neighborhood schools. BTNA was supportive of all desegregation efforts, and participated actively in other actions to bring and maintain quality education. They prevented an elementary school in their area from being a feeder school to an all-black high school and instead obtained an open enrollment policy for it before the countywide plan was in effect. They succeeded in having the only "naturally integrated" elementary school in Indianapolis, which exempted it from any busing when the court orders were implemented (BTNA Education Committee Policy Statement 1964; Newsletters 1964–73; Transcripts).

In Rochester, the schools were part of a voluntary citywide open enrollment policy to achieve racial balance, supported by state mandates since 1960. The Schools Committee of the Nineteenth WCA was active in all phases of school reorganization planning and participated in extensive curriculum revision to improve the quality of instruction in their neighborhood schools. A Ford Foundation grant in 1975 aided their efforts to improve the image of the public schools in their area (Bush and Weiss 1979; Nineteenth WCA Remarks to Board of Education by WCA President September 4, 1969; *Democrat-Chronicle* October 23, 1975).

Milwaukee's MO also was intensively involved in the maintenance of racial balance in the public schools, as well as the provision of high-quality education. SPCA supported the efforts of others who had filed a lawsuit against the schools in 1968 before the organization formed. Court orders mandated some changes in the city school system, including urban-suburban transfers and attendance zone shifts. SPCA's Schools Committee monitored school policies and practices throughout its existence (SPCA Annual Report 1977; Transcripts).

Additional program activities common to all three MOs were membership drives, community social events, newsletter preparation and distribution, other special projects such as youth recreation in Indianapolis and Rochester, and senior outreach in Milwaukee. Crime prevention programs were conducted in Rochester and Milwaukee's study neighborhoods. Block organization was not prominent in Indianapolis or Rochester, but became a major program in Milwaukee (SPCA Annual Report 1977; Newsletters 1977–82).

Impact

The influence of each MO was considerable. In each of their major program areas, the three MOs sought to influence institutional policies and practices with substantial degrees of success. All three associations, throughout their existence, presented unified, strong, stubborn images and succeeded in influencing key decision makers on local and state levels.

Indianapolis's BTNA, recognized as the oldest neighborhood group in the city, influenced the real estate industry, the school administration, and the city government in providing recreational facilities for area youths and in saving their park and numerous other establishments from conversion to other usage. BTNA also influenced their state government in having one of their major streets declared a historic preservation area and influenced the national Neighborhood Housing Services in providing housing rehabilitation for selected areas of their neighborhood (BTNA History 1968; Indianapolis *Star* 1962–84; BTNA Newsletters 1960–84).

Rochester's Nineteenth WCA influenced the real estate industry, the appraisers, the lenders, the police, the schools, the local city council, and regional housing agencies of the federal government. They were known as the strongest community organization in the city and received a national citation for their efforts from the National Commission on Neighborhoods (Bush and Weiss 1979; *Democrat-Chronicle* 1968–84).

Milwaukee's SPCA received local awards for their work, statewide recognition for their reduction of housing deterioration, and national acclaim for filing one of the largest suits of racial steering in the country. Their success in obtaining almost half a million dollars in city and state funding is also a measure of their impact. Some of their funding came from the Ford Foundation for several years, another indicator of their widespread recognition (SPCA Newsletters 1970–84; Milwaukee *Journal* 1970–84; Transcripts). In all three study neighborhoods some community and MO leaders went on to elected or appointed offices in city and state government, a positive factor for each MO and its neighborhood.

Factors of Success

The factors of success can be divided into those that relate to the organization and its participants (internal) and those that relate to the larger social environment (external). The external factors would include the physical amenities of the neighborhood, the role of the city toward neighborhood groups, the economic base of the city, the extent of school desegregation in the city at large, public housing location, financial support by outside agencies, and the role of the state.

Internal. Organizational structure in the three study neighborhoods does not appear to be a significant factor in accounting for the successful stabilization of the three areas. The Indianapolis MO had no staff or sustained funding, the Rochester group had part-time staff from its inception and separate staff and offices for other funded projects, and the Milwaukee MO had extensive staffing for funded projects but no separate staffing for the operation of the organization itself. Of the two funded groups, the Rochester structure was more successful in maintaining harmony within the group. The Milwaukee structure was much less conducive to internal peace; Indianapolis, unfunded, remained internally congenial.

One internal factor—the participants in the MO—is intertwined with an external factor. Both Indianapolis and Rochester study neighborhoods had significant amenities which attracted people to the area. In Indianapolis's Butler-Tarkington neighborhood, for example, the presence of a major private university in its central tract was a major stabilizing force. Indianapolis's MO was aided by having an active adjacent neighborhood organization which shared some common boundaries. This provided double strength and energy in mutual efforts which benefited both neighborhoods. Similarly, Rochester's 19th Ward was very close to two major universities, which attracted professional people to the neighborhood, providing abundant human resources for the neighborhood association. Milwaukee's Sherman Park did not possess such amenities, and its human resources were waning in its third phase of development. All three study areas showed some deterioration of their business areas, but Indianapolis and Rochester also showed some revitalization in at least one commercial strip of their area. Milwaukee did not.

External. Turning to external factors, those outside of the organization and its participants, we note the role of the city toward neighborhood organizations. One specific example of the city's helpful role in both Indianapolis and Rochester was its participation in the Neighborhood Statistics Program offered by the U.S. Census Bureau. In Indianapolis, the city assigned specific city program planners to work with each neighborhood organization for constant liaison. In Rochester, the city had an outright grant program for housing rehabilitation anywhere in the city. In addition, the Rochester MO received a special grant from the city for affirmative marketing and promotional efforts. In Milwaukee, the city government began a vigorous neighborhood development program in 1977, which was beneficial for the study neighborhood.

The economic base of Indianapolis was banking and manufacturing, and as a state capital it was not as adversely affected by economic decline in the late 1970s and early 1980s as was Milwaukee. Rochester, too, was fortunate in maintaining employment during those periods of recession because of its high technology focus. These were positive factors for the two study neighborhoods and their associations. Major economic recessions would have threatened the success of many of the MO's programs. In Milwaukee, however, the study neighborhood and the MO did feel the pinch of economic decline, as did their more run-down business areas. This was partially offset in Milwaukee by the secure source of funding by United Way for the operation of the organization (Transcripts). State funding of special rehabilitation projects also seemed secure and offered hope for the maintenance of the group's programs despite the city's and the neighborhood's economic problems.

All three communities had citywide school desegregation programs, which were beneficial to the study neighborhoods in their struggle for racial pluralism maintenance. Citywide busing in Indianapolis began in 1971, and later expanded to countywide busing, so the "neighborhood school" was no longer a meaningful concept. Residents in any neighborhood of the city could expect two things—racially integrated schools everywhere, and neighborhood schools nowhere. This effectively removed one stigma from racially integrated neighborhoods since their schools were no more racially identifiable than those of any other neighborhood. Thus, families could be encouraged to move to the pluralistic Butler-Tarkington neighborhood, for example, without worrying about their children attending racially isolated schools there. This enabled BTNA's Housing Information Service and Affirmative Marketing programs to succeed.

In Rochester, although not as effective a school desegregation program as in Indianapolis, 19th Ward residents had numerous options for choices for their children's schooling. One resident remarked, "I never took a bus to school, and Emily [daughter] has never *not* taken a bus to school" (Transcript). Rochester's citywide open enrollment policy, with special elementary and junior high magnet programs, was supported by state mandates for school racial balance for more than twenty years.

In Milwaukee, with the least effective school desegregation program of the three cities, court-ordered school desegregation removed from the study neighborhood the burden of having racially identifiable schools, although they did exist elsewhere in the city. Thus, affirmative marketing programs for the study neighborhood had some chance of success. In Milwaukee, too, the presence of an active and effective metropolitan Fair Housing Center was a significant positive force for the maintenance of racial pluralism in Sherman Park.

One more external factor was important in the successful maintenance of pluralism in the three study neighborhoods—the absence of public housing concentration in the neighborhood. This absence was true for Indianapolis and Rochester, somewhat less so for Milwaukee. In Milwaukee, some scattered site subsidized housing was beginning to have an impact on one of the sectors of the study area—that with the most low-income and minority households. However, a city plan for regional mobility of public housing residents—developed through SPCA's influence—was being actively considered to reduce the subsidized housing concentration in the city. City planners came to recognize the vulnerability of racially integrated neighborhoods, with the presence of public housing there making it more difficult to affirmatively market the neighborhood.

All three MOS played a critical role in preserving their neighborhoods as desirable, stable, pluralistic communities. They each performed a holding action while stabilization was sought through a vigorous combination of programs and strategies. But other forces—external to the organizations—were essential to the success of their efforts. The amenities of neighborhoods, the city's supportive role, the absence of public housing concentration in the study neighborhood, and the school desegregation program for each city were the four major external forces in the neighborhoods' success and the organizations' survival. Without these, it is not likely that either the neighborhoods or the organizations would have successfully survived as pluralistic communities.

Conclusions

From the comparative analysis it is evident that racially transitional urban neighborhoods do not inevitably become resegregated. Whether they do or do not depends on a number of critical factors, some related to internal organized efforts, some external to those efforts. Racism in each of the study neighborhoods accounted for the initial black concentration in each city. When urban renewal in each city displaced these black enclaves, their movement to new neighborhoods was the precipitating factor leading to movement formation in each neighborhood studied. These "defended" neighborhoods (Suttles 1972) then became "conscious communities" (Hunter 1975) committed to the goal of neighborhood stabilization, or the maintenance of racial pluralism. They were movement organizations rather than mere interest groups because their goal was a change-oriented, nontraditional one. They were swimming upstream against the usual pattern of white flight and integration avoidance (Saltman 1977).

The mobilization of resources in each community involved tangible and intangible sources of support (Freeman 1983). The intangible resources were found in people's skills, time, and commitment; the tangible resources were spatial, financial, and political assistance. Of the three possible strategies of persuasion, bargaining, and coercion (Wilson 1973) all used the first two, and Milwaukee used the third—coercion—in lawsuits.

Although independently formed, each with no knowledge of the other, their specific strategies were similar since they confronted common problems that threatened their shared goal. These common problems were rooted in a legacy of racism that prevailed in each community. All the MOs had a constant struggle with proposed zoning changes that threatened the nature of their existent land use. These proposed zoning changes were not trivial. In Indianapolis, one proposed change would have converted the only neighborhood park in Butler-Tarkington into a parking lot; in Milwaukee, a giant freeway would have cut through the heart of the Sherman Park neighborhood.

Besides zoning changes, all three MOS confronted real estate practices that included racial steering, blockbusting, and panic selling. They all faced lending institutions reluctant to grant conventional mortgages in their racially heterogeneous neighborhoods. As a consequence they all became inundated with vacant houses and fast foreclosures. They all saw their commercial areas change from prosperous, well kept, diverse, interesting, pleasant business districts to shabby, declining ones. They all watched their schools become increasingly racially isolated. And they all experienced continuing turnover of neighbors with the resulting loss of friends and MO supporters.

In response to these shared situations, it is not surprising that they developed some common strategies for dealing with them. All MOS firmly and successfully resisted zoning changes, promoted their neighborhoods through affirmative marketing techniques, sought rehabilitation funds for deteriorating properties, organized varied community and recreational events, established newspapers with mass distributions, promoted fair and open housing in their metropolitan regions, sought bans on for sale signs and real estate solicitation, and intensively worked for racial balance and quality education in their public schools.

Yet, despite these intensive efforts and their successes, the movement is a fragile one. In other cities MOS did not survive, and their neighborhoods did not remain integrated. Each of the successful MOS and their neighborhoods are also vulnerable. People in all of them were apprehensive about the future, and not at all certain that their gains would last.

The special fragility of this particular movement of neighborhood stabilization stems from the sociohistorical legacy of racism. Drawing on theoretical perspectives from the field of race relations, I suggest that just as the offspring of black-white matings are socially defined as black in this country (Lieberson 1980:32) so too when neighborhoods become racially integrated they initially assume the same status that the incoming minority group has in the society at large. Thus, the neighborhoods are subject to the same levels of domination, discrimination, and segregation in the local community as the minority group experiences in the larger society.

This is especially manifested through institutional racism, which operates impersonally to foster and maintain segregation in housing, schools, and businesses. These three vital aspects of any neighborhood are interlinked in a circular pattern so that racial change in any one of them leads to further change in the other two, and eventually to total resegregation of the neighborhood.

This is an additive model of neighborhood change. Its cycle can be broken only with organized efforts to intercede in any one of the three interacting links. Such intervention is the substance of the neighborhood stabilization movement, but organized efforts—although necessary—are sometimes insufficient for achieving successful neighborhood stabilization.

From the comparative analysis, it was apparent that two particularly critical external factors affect a movement organization's effectiveness in achieving neighborhood stabilization. The first factor is the existence of a systemwide school desegregation plan. The second factor is the absence of public housing concentration in the transitional neighborhood. To the extent that these occur, the transitional area can be successfully marketed, promoted, and maintained as a pluralistic, viable neighborhood. Without these, the best MO's efforts will fail. But even with these, there is reason to be uneasy about the future. Racially transitional neighborhoods are fragile entities, subject to immense institutional forces which could topple them outright or slowly and systematically destroy them, along with the organizations struggling within them.

Policy Implications

An interventionist policy approach is necessary, and timing is critical. Affirmative massive intervention must occur before the neighborhood is racially identifiable, or the chance of success will be minimal. Such intervention would be designed to focus on the three links of the additive process and to strengthen the MO.

Especially critical in any policy implementation would be the coordination of school and housing strategies. As has been noted (Orfield 1981), school and housing policies interact at many levels, and potential policy changes involve many agencies and interests. A comprehensive approach such as is being conducted for the first time in the Cleveland area would link municipal governments and public school administrators in a joint program to achieve racial integration in neighborhoods and schools (E. Suburban Council 1986). Another supportive strategy would offer financial incentives for pro-integrative moves (Los Angeles City Council, Farrell-Ferraro Resolution 1982), as is being conducted in Ohio (Ohio Housing Finance Agency 1985).

The maintenance of an integrated urban neighborhood is not likely with only a neighborhood organization at work, no matter how dedicated, creative, and effective it may be. A neighborhood organization is a necessary but insufficient condition for success. It is clear that external forces and institutional processes affect all neighborhoods and must be included in any strategies for neighborhood stabilization. Specific policies to achieve stabilization of urban integrated neighborhoods depend on eight conditions.

1. Maintenance of a flow of both whites and blacks into the area through extensive affirmative marketing campaigns.

2. Technical assistance and moderate funding to neighborhood organizations to enable them to function more securely and effectively.

3. Reduction of the mobility potential of residents by improving the neighborhood schools and business areas in quality, racial balance, and security.

4. Maintenance of quality housing and streets to insure pride in the area as a desirable integrated neighborhood.

5. Reduction of residents' anxiety about the neighborhood by alleviating fears of loss of money, status, security, and neighborliness.

6. Provision of an adequate supply of housing for people of all income levels throughout the metropolitan area.

7. Funding of a metropolitan fair housing agency, with well-designed regional mobility programs and incentive payments for pro-integrative moves.

8. Public commitment by city, county, state, and federal officials for social impact statements citing effects of governmental expenditures on housing and school integration maintenance.

These conditions are essential to counteract all the previous years of stereotyping and misconception about racially integrated neighborhoods. But who can implement these efforts? Logically, it would seem that since government was one of the first institutional forces responsible for both racial concentration and then racial displacement through urban renewal, government—at all levels—should be the major force responsible for undoing its past effects. This could be done in cooperation with adequately funded MOS on the local level.

Together, they could mount a vigilant, ongoing effort to contact the major institutional networks affecting housing, schools, and businesses. Their understanding and cooperation must be secured to achieve constructive changes in policies and practices affecting the death and life of integrated neighborhoods. Such integration is maintained with enormous difficulty; special and extraordinary efforts are required to sustain it. Whether such efforts will receive the necessary commitment and support will determine the future of urban neighborhoods.

References

Ahlbrandt, Roger, and James Cunningham. 1978. *A New Public Policy for Neighborhood Preservation*. New York: Praeger.

Aukofer, Frank. 1968. *City with a Change*. Milwaukee: Bruce Publishing.

Butler-Tarkington Neighborhood Association (Indianapolis). 1971. *Annual Report*.

———. 1960–84. *Newsletter*.

———. 1963–70. *Minutes*.

———. 1964. *Education Committee Policy Statement*.

———. 1968. *History*.

Bush, Mim, and Margaret Weiss. 1979. *19th Ward Community Association: A History*. Rochester.

Democrat-Chronicle (Rochester). 1968–84.

Eastern Suburban Council for Open Communities, Cleveland. 1986.

Fischer, Claude. 1976. *The Urban Experience*. New York: Harcourt, Brace.

Freeman, Jo. 1983. *Social Movements of the Sixties and Seventies*. New York: Longmans.

Hagedorn, John. 1983. *Dreams of the Seventies, Facts of the Eighties*. Milwaukee: Bruce Publishing.

HUD (U.S. Department of Housing and Urban Development). 1979. *Measuring Racial Discrimination in American Housing Markets*. Washington, D.C.: Office of Policy Development and Research.

Hunter, Albert. 1975. "Loss of Community." *American Sociological Review* 40:537–52.

———. 1974. *Symbolic Communities*. Chicago: University of Chicago Press.

Indianapolis Star. 1958–84.

Johanneson, M. 1980. *A Brief History of Sherman Park Community Association*. Milwaukee: Bruce Publishing.

Lieberson, Stanley. 1980. *A Piece of the Pie*. Berkeley: University of California Press.

Los Angeles City Council 1982. *Farrell-Ferraro Resolution*.

Madison, James. 1982. *Indiana through Tradition and Change*. Indianapolis: Indiana Historical Society.

Milwaukee *Journal*. 1970–84.

Molotch, Harvey. 1972. *Managed Integration*. Berkeley: University of California Press.

Nineteenth Ward Community Association (Rochester). 1966–84. *Newsletter.*
——. 1967–84. *Minutes.*
——. 1969. *Remarks to Board of Education.* September 4.
——. 1973. *Real Estate Committee Report.*
Ohio Housing Finance Agency. 1985. *Report on Mortgage Revenue Bonds.* Columbus.
Orfield, Gary. 1981. *Toward a Strategy for Urban Integration.* New York: Ford Foundation.
Saltman, Juliet. 1977. *Integrated Neighborhoods in Action.* Washington, D.C.: National Neighbors.
——. 1984. "Neighborhood Stabilization Strategies as Social Inventions." *Journal of Voluntary Action Research* 13:37–45.
——. 1990. *A Fragile Movement: The Struggle for Neighborhood Stabilization.* Westport: Greenwood Press.
Sherman Park Community Association (Milwaukee). 1970–84. *Newsletters.*
——. 1970–84. *Minutes.*
——. 1976. *Proposal to Ford Foundation.*
——. 1977. *Funding Application to OPEN.*
——. 1977. *Annual Report.*
——. n.d. *Brochure.*
Still, Bayrd. 1948. *Milwaukee, the History of a City.* Madison: State Historical Society of Wisconsin.
Suttles, Gerald. 1972. *The Social Construction of Communities.* Chicago: University of Chicago Press.
Taub, Richard, D. Garth Taylor, and Jan Dunham. 1984. *Paths of Neighborhood Change.* Chicago: University of Chicago Press.
Times-Union (Rochester). 1968–84.
Wilson, John. 1983. *Introduction to Social Movements.* New York: Basic Books.
Wilson, Thomas. 1973. "White Response to Neighborhood Racial Change." *Sociological Focus* 16:305–18.

22. Conclusion

Segregation: A Social Problem?

The wide variety of situations and insights described herein might confuse the reader. It is not immediately clear what the segregation of Hispanics in Phoenix has in common with the segregation of Turks in Berlin. Each social reality is unique, particularly as it is experienced in the social relations of everyday life by the individuals concerned. Yet one nevertheless can generalize from these individual situations, exploring the common underlying social processes.

Segregation can objectively be defined as an unequal distribution of people with common characteristics at a certain place and time (Friedrichs 1977). In this book we focus on the dimension of place and describe housing segregation as "the spatial separation of different population groups" (chapter 1). In fact, a certain amount of segregation is normal. The probability of an equal distribution of people over certain areas is about 0. On the other hand, the probability of any degree of segregation is nearly 1.00. In itself, segregation—as it is generally measured, for example by means of an index of dissimilarity—is not always felt to be a problem by the segregated inhabitants and thus cannot always be considered a social problem. Segregation should be considered as one of several factors that cause a social problem; the degree to which segregation contributes to a problem cannot be determined precisely. For example, at a certain point (the so-called tipping point), an increasing out-migration of the established population from the segregated area can be observed. However, it is not known at what percent the tipping point comes into effect.

If segregation is considered a social problem, the question is, For whom is it a problem? It might be that a local government advocates the dispersal of minority groups, whereas the people concerned do not worry about their residential segregation and object to plans for dispersal. Whether segregation is problematic or not also depends on the social class of the segregated inhabitants of a given area. Gener-

391

ally, it is not considered to be a problem by many if privileged people live in segregated areas (Blauw 1980; see also chapter 8). Yet good reasons may exist to promote a social mix and thereby facilitate social contacts between different social classes (Berndt 1969).

Segregation of people with a cultural background different from that dominant in the country need not be considered a problem. Some would say, however, if segregation is accompanied by social inequality and discrimination—for example, unequal access to attractive segments of the housing market—then it may be assumed that segregation has disadvantages. These should be ameliorated by appropriate housing policies. For realistic policymaking, it is instructive to explore the underlying processes of urban housing segregation, and the studies presented herein provide a good basis for doing so. In this book we describe the possible causes of segregation and examine the possible functions of segregation as Durkheim (1950, orig. 1895) proposed, both for the minorities themselves and the society in which they live. Some conclusions will be drawn with regard to appropriate housing policies.

Reasons for Minorities' Housing Position

Minorities who live segregated in the cities of Western Europe immigrated because of the political or economic situations in their countries of origin. Most refugees had a political motive, and guest workers an economic one. American immigrants had the same reasons, but the most prominent American minority—the black population—came involuntarily as slaves.

The stream of migrants from one country to another, however, cannot simply be explained by the political and economic differences between the country of origin and the country of destination. As Portes (1989) assumes, a particular relationship often exists between both countries. Thus, France, Great Britain, and the Netherlands received immigrants from their former colonies: Algerians emigrated to France, Pakistani and Indians to Great Britain, and Surinamese to the Netherlands. West Germany, having no colonies, recruited a relatively large proportion of its migrants in Turkey (chapter 2). The United States received a disproportionately high number of immigrants from countries that had particular economic or political ties, for example, Mexico, Puerto Rico, and Vietnam. Most immigrants started in a subordinate position in society. Over time some groups have become fully integrated into the receiving society, whereas others have remained in a weak social and economic position. Four factors influence the capacity of an immigrant group to acquire a position on the housing and labor markets more equivalent to that held by the established population. First, it takes time (sometimes generations) to adjust to, or at least to integrate into, the new society. Thus the second and third generation of migrants—of Chinese, Italian, Polish, or whatever origin—generally hold higher positions in the new society than their parents. The assumption is less easy to test in Western Europe because the immigration of the minorities in question is a much more recent phenomenon. Labor migrants from Mediterranean countries migrated to Western Europe in the 1960s and the first half of the 1970s. The second factor is that immigrant groups with a relatively close cultural affinity to the receiving society seem to have a better chance of acquiring a stronger position, both on the labor and the housing markets. Italians and Spaniards, if they have not already repatriated, are more integrated in the other Western European societies than Turks and Moroccans, especially if controlling for their length of residence. Particularly significant is the immigrants' fluency in the host country's language. Immigrants from the former colonies have an advantage in this respect. A third factor is the orientation toward the country of origin, both in terms of the intent to return and the financial obligations toward family members there. As long as the guest workers believed they would eventually return to the country of origin, they had to save their money. Income could not be spent on improving their housing situations. A fourth factor regarding minorities' position on the housing market is the degree to which minorities are visible and thus more vulnerable to discrimination. Whether minorities are actually discriminated against or not will be discussed later.

Comparing Segregation

The term *segregation* refers to certain people with common characteristics and to a certain place. This book discusses the segregation of ethnic minorities in cities. Although their position in the various countries is not completely comparable, contributors to this volume reveal a certain amount of segregation of minorities, whatever their specific characteristics, in Western European and U.S. cities. It would be interesting to compare the segregation in the different West European countries with that found in the United States. This presupposes comparable data on segregation; however, if data are available, it is seldom comparable. In some cases concentration of minorities has been described instead of segregation. Concentration is measured by comparing the percentage of a certain minority in the city's total population. For example, most minorities in the Netherlands are concentrated in the four largest cities (chapters 3 and 10); 25 percent of Stockholm's minority population live in the district of Spånga, whereas only 6.5 percent of the total Stockholm population live there (chapter 5). As far as segregation has been measured in the United States, it has been done at a census tract level; in Europe, at a city's district level. This shows a relatively low index of dissimilarity (ID) for minorities in Zurich (27 for Turks in 1980) (chapter 8), in Hamburg (about 30 for six minority groups) (chapter 6), and a relatively high ID of 70 for minority groups in a few areas in some major cities in Great Britain although there are differences in the degree of segregation by region.

Comparison of the Western European figures with those for the United States supports the general assumption of a relatively high degree of segregation in U.S. cities: the mean ID for blacks in U.S. cities is 70–85 (chapter 14). However, the index of dissimilarity used (Taeuber and Taeuber's) concerns the block level. As a high correlation has been found between the index of dissimilarity at block and census tract level, these figures indicate a significant difference between segregation of blacks in the United States and segregation of minorities in Western Europe.

Instead of broad generalizations on statistical data, the chapters in this book explore the processes underlying minorities' residential segregation and their housing situations. Some are case studies, which provide insights in the ways minorities have been hindered in obtaining more appropriate housing. The following discussion tries to integrate the outcomes of the studies into a model that might provide insight into the complex of variables involved in the phenomenon of segregation.

A Model of Segregation

Segregation is generally considered to be a result of migration and/or residential mobility (for example, white flight or chain migration). The initial assumption in developing this model is that segregation is the result of demographic events like birth, death, and migration. Segregation may be reinforced by a high birth rate among minorities or a high death rate among the established population (chapter 16).

The decision to relocate depends on a household's potential to adjust to its current housing situation or to modify its dwelling to meet current needs. If these options are not available, the household may prefer to move to a more suitable dwelling. Whether the move actually occurs depends on the fit between the household's demand and the available housing supply. However, even if good fit is feasible, an actual move might be blocked by such obstacles as discriminatory practices or regulations. On the demand side, certain variables have to be taken into account. Demand is not only determined by a household's preferences, but also by its means to obtain a better and probably more expensive dwelling. Both preferences and means are determined by household characteristics such as number of persons and income of the wage earners.

As discussed previously (chapters 3, 6, and 7), the move of minorities to the urban periphery in European countries cannot simply be attributed to their preference for living elsewhere. Affordable housing has been made available due to the established population's dislike of some types of social housing built on the urban periphery. The native population has either moved out or been unwilling to occupy this housing. Thus the existence of a large stock of good-quality housing—subsidized housing—that is vacant can cause segregation. A large proportion of social housing in the housing stock is crucial if a government wants to keep residential segregation low, but to do this the government also has to control who goes into vacancies. The unpopularity of urban periphery estates has made such control difficult. Thus, it is important to differentiate between the public and private housing sectors as generally it is more possible for the government to control the public housing sector than to control private sector housing.

A second assumption in developing the model is that the societal context actually influences the interplay of supply and demand in the housing market, and thereby the resulting segregation. Societal context consists of the remaining institutions in society, such as education, political parties, and characteristic cultural beliefs. This societal context influences the outcome of the segregation process. Society's prejudices, which might result in discrimination toward an ethnic minority by those who have the power to allocate dwellings, certainly play a role (figure 22.1).

This model allows integration of different explanations of segregation. As Saltman showed in chapter 1, segregation theories can be classified according to the variables they put forward as the most

FIGURE 22.1.   A Model of Segregation

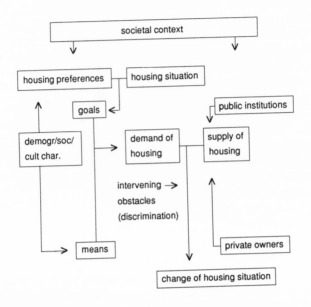

Source: Blauw (1985).

important determinants of segregation. Thus we can distinguish ecological, economic, intergroup, sociopsychological, and institutional
theories.

In the ecological perspective, the societal context (a large concentration of a heterogeneous population) and the demographic and social-cultural characteristics are associated. It is assumed that people
will cluster in their "natural" areas in an "organic" way. This may
result from voluntary actions (the sociopsychological theory); housing
preferences are then considered as the independent variable. As Saltman remarks, the economic explanation of segregation, taking income
level as the independent variable, is clearly an incomplete one: "only
a small portion of housing segregation can be accounted for by income
alone." Both the ecological and the economic explanations may be
integrated in our model by confronting the goals, which result from
housing preferences and the existing housing situation, with the variable of means, whether material (income) or immaterial (market
knowledge).

The institutional explanation focuses on the involuntary aspects of
residential location. The key variables are found in the interaction

between the households who demand housing and the institution (real estate agents, housing associations, individual owners and so on) that supply housing. In our model the frictions, or "intervening obstacles," include discriminatory practices.

The intergroup relations between minorities and the dominant group are rather difficult to grasp. The attitude toward the other group is expressed in people's behavior and can determine the decision to move to another neighborhood (as in white flight) or to discriminate against minority households looking for better housing.

The Application of the Model: Introductory Remarks

The model does not explain segregation in any given situation, but it might help to focus systematically on relevant variables. These variables are not to be considered separately; the model concerns their relationships. For example, the model suggests that the sociopsychological theory (regarding voluntary clustering) does not fully explain the phenomenon of segregation. A move to appropriate new, nonsegregated housing is only feasible if a household's means are sufficient, if the supply fits the demand, and if there are no intervening obstacles. Another example is that according to the theory the lower quality of the ethnic minorities' housing situation cannot be attributed to discriminatory housing practices alone (the variable "intervening obstacles"). In the early period after their arrival, it might be impossible to house a large number of immigrants, and yet the households' means might be insufficient to gain access to housing that meets a certain standard in the receiving country. This applies, for example, to Moroccan and Turkish immigrants in Western Europe, who initially wanted to save money to meet family obligations or to invest in business after returning to their native country. However, the authors herein emphasize that discrimination is a major reason for their continued segregated housing situations in many cases.

The model can be applied to a comparison of segregation in the United States and Western Europe. Although the figures on segregation might be difficult to compare, it is clear that the amount of segregation in the United States, notably of blacks, exceeds the amount of segregation of minorities in Western European countries. To compare segregation in the United States and Western Europe it would have been better if the new American ethnic groups, such as Vietnamese, had been included, instead of just blacks and Hispanics. The degree of segregation of blacks and Hispanics cannot be attributed to their preference for segregation. As Johnston, McDaniel, and Gordon and Mayer demonstrate, the segregation of blacks or Hispanics cannot be explained by limited financial means. It is supposed that they have been, and still are, discriminated against on the housing market. If so, has discrimination had a lesser or greater impact in the United States than in Western Europe? And what is the role of the other relevant variables, for example, the societal context and the type of housing supplied? The studies in this volume imply that the United States differs from Western Europe in these respects. In the United States, society is less structured by governmental intervention than in Western Europe. Also, housing stock differs with regard to the degree of public and private ownership. In Western Europe, a large proportion of the housing stock consists of social housing owned by local governments or state-controlled housing associations (chapter 12). It may be argued that in a situation with more control by the state over both production and distribution of housing, it is easier to open segments of the housing market to minorities. Explicit discrimination can also be prevented more effectively.

The U.S. government does provide some housing for minorities. However, the government's overall ability to change minorities' housing situations, and consequently alleviate segregation, is less effective in the United States. Even when the U.S. government has intervened by invoking Kennedy's Executive Order and civil rights legislation, it has had less impact than European authorities (see chapter 14).

As a counterpoint to the rather detailed studies herein, it is possible to generalize on the European situation. Despite the euphoria about a growing unity of Europe after 1992, it would be misleading to reduce the Western European countries to a common denominator. These countries differ even with respect to the role of the state. Consequently the amount of segregation and concentration of minorities differ as is apparent from the chapters on Britain and on Sweden, West Germany, and the Netherlands.

The same argument may be applied to a comparison of discrimination, assumed to be relatively strong in Great Britain compared with other Western European countries. The Thatcher government has retreated from housing activities more than have other European governments. Consequently, British housing stock comprises a relatively smaller proportion of newly built public housing and thus the government has somewhat less ability to control discrimination, although a fourth of the stock is still council housing. Other variables besides the societal context (here the political situation in the country) might account for this difference; in chapter 4 Phillips and Karn observe a racist attitude in this country.

Negative prejudices and discriminatory practices are sometimes but not always blatant. They can also be latent or lie under the surface, as Friedrichs and Alpheis suggest with regard to West Germany. Racism and related discriminatory behavior, although present, could be difficult to document. To determine discrimination on both the labor market (Veenman 1988) and the housing market, a succession of methods may be applied. First, statistics can demonstrate that segregation of an ethnic minority is present with regard to residential area or type of dwelling. If this inequality cannot be attributed to the minorities' lower incomes, discrimination may have taken place. Legislation itself might have a discriminatory effect (chapter 11). However, if the intent of legislation is to prevent discrimination, it does not guarantee that discrimination will not take place in practice. It is difficult to determine whether or not rules are obeyed or are interpreted in such a way that they retain their discriminatory effects.

A second method to determine discrimination is to interview those who supposedly discriminate, for example, administrators who allocate dwellings. However, the discriminatory action might be the result of a misinterpretation by the respondent, and careful examination of the situation is called for. A third method is to interview those who may have been discriminated against. They could be confronted with the results of the statistical analysis and asked for their comments. The anonymity of those respondents must be maintained in order to gather reliable information. Often discrimination is presumed to have taken place on the basis of the first method, sometimes judged to exist from this data combined with data from the second method, and seldom on the basis of the third one. In the United States, the most used method is the audit described by Saltman and others. An audit involves testers, one black and one white, applying for the same advertised available apartment; landlord reactions to each is recorded and compared.

Functions

The model concerns the possible causes of segregation. This represents one approach to understanding the phenomenon. Another approach is to examine the functions of segregation for society as a whole and for the minorities themselves. In other words, Why does segregation persist? One explanation is that ethnic minorities themselves prefer

residential segregation and that living together is functional and facil-
itates mutual help and social interaction because there are no language
barriers. Living together promotes the maintenance of an ethnic culture, and minorities can benefit from specialized facilities in their
neighborhood (chapter 4; Blauw 1980). This argument might be particularly relevant for immigrants who have recently arrived. But over
the course of time it loses relevance, for example with regard to blacks
in the United States.

Sometimes local governments attempt to legitimize their policy with
this argument. In fact, a local government might acquiesce to the
desire of an established population to keep their neighborhood white
for economic reasons. It proves that even if the housing demanded by
minorities is available, actual moves are prevented by "intervening
obstacles." Analogous to their situation on the labor market, their
function is "to stand by," to fill in the dwellings that would otherwise
remain vacant because they are not considered desirable by the established population. Two strongly related hierarchies can be distinguished: a hierarchy of population groups and one of housing types.
Thus, the underprivileged are not expected to move into the more
attractive houses. That would undermine their function in the economy. Minorities "choose" to live in areas where the dwellings are
considered inferior by the established population. This explains why
in Sweden the minority households do not live in the city centers but
on the outskirts (chapter 5). It also explains why ethnic minorities in
countries like France and West Germany move to the urban periphery;
there the established population have left apartments in low-standard
fringe area social housing. Even if minority households acquire a
"ticket" (for example a higher income) to entry into a more attractive
segment of the housing market, this does not guarantee that they are
able to obtain a better dwelling. As Boudon (1979) shows via a sim-
ulation, lower-class people may acquire a better starting position on
the labor market as a consequence of higher qualifications; however,
they may still be the last in line. The same argument can be applied
to the minorities' position on the housing market.

Policies

Policymakers have two options with regard to segregation policy. They
may legitimize a laissez-faire attitude and the retention of old policies
by referring to the lack of data and the complex nature of the segregation process. Or they may legitimize this attitude by referring to the

researchers' "degenerative" perspective, suggesting the inevitability of neighborhood decline after racial change has occurred (chapter 21). A second option is to reassess their policies in light of recent insights and to be prepared to change these policies accordingly. Policymakers who take the second option may find the results of the studies presented in this book useful.

Dispersal of immigrant concentration is a debated policy in Western European countries. Because, according to some scholars, segregation in itself in some countries does not prevent ethnic minorities from interacting in society, policies aiming at their dispersal have been viewed critically. However, most scholars view integration as advantageous, giving minorities equal opportunities to jobs and evaluation. In the United States, segregation is seen as establishing "two nations," each isolated from the other, one underprivileged. Those European scholars arguing enforced dispersal is not needed say restrictions on the access to certain residential districts (as the Berlin Zuzugssperre) have a negative effect on the migrant laborers' housing situation (chapter 11). These scholars would conclude that spatial measures do not necessarily resolve social problems, which are also attributed to the cultures peculiar to the ethnic minorities. Some policymakers, especially in the Netherlands, regard the minority's main problems (employment and housing) as similar to those of low-income groups in the established population, although they also consider the minority's situation as a consequence of discriminatory practices.

In general, American scholars give more evidence to support the assumption that segregation is due to discrimination (Tobin 1987). Through audits, income analysis, studies of the institutional actors in the housing market, and studies of minority and white attitudes to integrated living, they have tried to locate the type and degree of discrimination against minorities in the housing market. Housing activists in the United States have tried to locate means to halt segregation through fair housing actions, including affirmative marketing (chapter 19).

Future research in Western Europe must concentrate more on determining the type and degree of discrimination against minorities in the housing market, as suggested, through audits and other means of studying the actions of institutional actors, including housing authorities, private landlords, sellers, the real estate industry, and lending institutions. Segregation is still at a low level in most European cities, and there is still a chance of avoiding the American situation of "two nations."

A policy focusing on the social problems of these groups and discrimination against them should at least provide them with basic political rights and should remove any obstacles to efforts to improve their housing situation, as a democratic society purports to do.

References

Berndt, Heide. 1969. "Ist der Funktionalismus eine funktionelle Architektur? Soziologische Betrachtungen einer architektonischen Kategorie (Is functionalism functional architecture? A sociological essay on an architectural category)." Pp. 9–50 in *Architektur als Ideologie*, edited by Heide Berndt, Alfred Lorenzer, and Klaus Horn. Frankfurt am Main: Suhrkamp.

Blauw, P. W. 1980. "Segregatie: een overzicht (Segregation: An overview)." Pp. 9–24 in *Soort bij soort*, edited by P. W. Blauw and C. Pastor. Deventer: Van Loghum Slaterus.

———. 1985. "Segregatie en migratie in het stadsgewest (Segregation and migration in urban areas)." Pp. 75–89 in *Het stedelijk woonerf*, edited by J. P. Burgers and P. A. Stoppelenburg. Tilburg: I.V.A.

Boudon, Raymond. 1979. *La logique du social: Introduction à l'analyse sociologique* (The logic of the social: Introduction to sociological analysis). Paris: Hachette.

Durkheim, Emile. 1950 (originally 1895). *Les règles de la méthode sociologique* (The rules of the sociological method). Paris: Presses Universitaires de France.

Friedrichs, J. 1977. *Stadtanalyse Soziale und räumliche Organization der Gesellschaft* (Social and spatial organization of society). Reinbek bei Hamburg: Rowohlt.

Portes, Alejandro. 1989. "International Migration: Theoretical Perspectives on Its Determinants and Modes of Incorporation." Paper presented to the conference "Current Trends in Migration and Social Mobility of Migrants," Utrecht, March 30–April 1.

———. "The Costs of Housing Discrimination and Segregation: An Interdisciplinary Social Science Statement." Pp. 268–80 in *Divided Neighborhoods*, edited by Gary Tobin. Beverly Hills: Sage.

Veenman, J. 1988. *Discriminatie op de arbeidsmarkt* (Discrimination on the labor market). Rotterdam: Erasmus University, Institute of Sociological-Economic Research (ISEO).

23. Summary and Future Trends

In chapter 22, Blauw provides general theories and analysis derived from this book's studies and related data; he discusses the reasons for segregation: the process of segregation, the functions of segregation, government policies, and officials and scholars' underlying assumptions that play into their policymaking decisions.

Here I will be more specific, focusing on and summarizing findings from each chapter. The focus in this book has been to describe the degree and type of segregation of minorities in Western Europe, especially in six countries, in order to correct the image many American urbanologists have of characteristics of European cities and to inform them and race relations experts about the dynamics of ethnic segregation in Western Europe. Our belief is that these dynamics of ethnic concentration and group invasion-succession are not only reshaping Western European cities, but also creating tensions within the local population that spill over to the political arena and influence regional and national elections. In West Berlin, for example, a rightist government has moved into power, in Hesse, West Germany, the migrant issue influenced both party slogans and election outcome, and in France, LePen's antiminority position, including opposition to the use of subsidized housing, gave his party many votes in 1988 (chapter 7). As affordable housing units become more scarce, with demand far outrunning supply due to decreased government construction of subsidized units or provision of such subsidies to nongovernment sources, and as some subsidized housing estates become even more stigmatized, this competition for housing and the tension over it will worsen. With the late 1989 movement of many East Germans as well as Poles and other German-origin groups to West Germany, a total of over 750,000 in 1989, tensions and competition for housing increased greatly in West Germany over the previous year.

The authors of the chapters on Western Europe provide ample evidence that ethnic concentration or segregation does exist to varying degrees in these cities, although it is always far below the concentration of black households in the United States. The European writers, in their main purpose of describing the location of ethnic concentrations, present somewhat different pictures for different countries. The pattern does not always follow the invasion-succession theories put forth by American researchers, principally because government policy in Europe influences where immigrants live much more than it does in the United States. This has been especially true since the 1970s when minorities, to some degree, were given access to subsidized housing. A number move to the particular peripheral locations where there is social housing, especially the more unpopular social housing. As the private rental housing supply decreases in these European countries—in some cases due to conversion to home ownership, particularly in Great Britain, the Netherlands, and West Germany, and in others due to urban renewal—many immigrants push to get into social housing. Home ownership is beyond the reach of many and is made less so by discriminatory practices of lending institutions, for example, those in Britain. If social housing is unavailable, as it is to many, they overcrowd existing private rentals. Of course, if the local population moves to better-quality housing, as Blauw and Mik say is the case in the Netherlands, this helps the immigrants' situation.

Thus preferences of natives influence immigrants' location and concentration. If, as Lindén and Lindberg report for Stockholm, locals desire to stay in the central city's well-maintained units rather than buy in outer areas, this trend affects immigrants' location. Arend reports locals do not like to move out and thus there is a mixture of locals and immigrants in the central city of Zurich rather than a concentration of the latter. In America, most households, if they can afford to do so, hope to move out of the central city; substantial numbers buy in the suburbs while others rent there. Swiss are unlikely to own suburban housing; to a lesser degree this is also true in France, Sweden, the Netherlands, and West Germany. For the middle class, however, the trend is in that direction, although sometimes to old villages or new towns rather than to American-type private suburbs. In Britain there has been a suburban movement and a greater tendency to own homes under Thatcher's government encouragement.

The housing segregation picture that Blauw describes for the Netherlands has a number of similarities to that of other Northern European countries, but also differs in some significant ways. Both ex-colonials and guest workers are found in the Netherlands. In contrast Sweden has only guest workers and refugees; West Germany, guest workers, refugees, and those of German-origin; Switzerland, only guest workers and a very few refugees; and France and Britain, primarily ex-colonials. Because status influences rights, treatment, and ability to stay, this status is important in relating to access to housing and desire for better housing. Blauw centers on the Surinamese-Antillian groups and Turks and Moroccan guest workers, although he does mention the early postwar influx of immigrants from Indonesia who had rights as Dutch citizens, a group that the government worked hard to assimilate into Dutch society by provision of resources and even some dispersal policies, and did so with a fair degree of success. Blauw describes the Dutch housing evolution pattern for the Turks and Moroccans; they settle first in employee housing, immigrant guest houses, and occasionally slum-area units of cities. As families arrive, more move into the latter. Surinamese and Antillians first live in government housing and then move to inner-city, often private, units. This pattern is also true for West Germany. In France, it was first employee housing, hotels run by ex-colonials, and inner-city private units, as well as industrial suburban area shantytowns, then government-built industrial suburban hostels just for immigrants. In Switzerland, immigrants first live in employee barracks and inner-area low-standard housing, sometimes also the basements of buildings.

In most of these countries, but seldom in Swiss cities, the housing evolution was to social housing for some immigrant families. It has seldom been to home ownership, except for the South Indians who pushed to purchase substandard units in Britain. Home ownership has occurred in the Netherlands, Blauw reports, where 15 percent of Turks and 14 percent of Surinamese own; it is possible that half of the Turks and Moroccans, many in urban renewal areas, are in government-subsidized housing, which includes local authority housing, and non-profit subsidized housing association units. Sometimes the buildings are high-rent units that locals reject, a situation also true in West Germany.

Blauw reports that the segregation level is low; 15 percent of the population in large cities normally consists of ethnic minorities. However, he found few ghettos; the areas of highest concentration for minorities have only 40 percent minority population. The high-concentration area of Bijlmermeer outside of Amsterdam, often cited, is unusual, and the concentration is decreasing as renovation and other revitalization efforts proceed. As for other countries, the degree of concentration varies by ethnic group. In the Netherlands it varies in relation to the Dutch culture, with the Surinamese in Rotterdam having a low index of dissimilarity (D) of 34 (although Italians are lowest, with a D of 29), Turks 54, and Moroccans 53. Surinamese, often single, are scattered throughout Amsterdam and other cities. They are more willing, Blauw finds, to pay higher rents and to take government rent subsidies than Turkish and Moroccan households. Another influence on concentration is size of households, with Turks and Moroccans needing larger units and thus pushing for low-standard, subsidized, local-authority units. Location is also limited by prejudice; Blauw feels that housing authorities do worry about residents' opinions and their possible protests against living near Turks. As far as immigrants' housing preference is concerned, Blauw finds increased immigrant satisfaction with housing over time, as do Friedrichs and Alpheis for Germany.

Blauw also describes government policy changes. At one time, government made provision for ex-colonials and now requires that new projects have a certain percent of minorities. Blauw believes that the government will watch over the ethnic composition of estates to see that they do not develop a concentration of minorities. He does see the immigrants' worsening position in the job market affecting their housing situation.

Lindén and Lindberg take a narrower and more specific focus on housing segregation in Sweden, centering on the degree of ethnic concentration among the 10 percent of the population that are new immigrants (usually excluding Finns from their coverage). They examine the degree to which minorities are centered in particular tenure types, which they term housing segmentation versus segregation. Their unique contribution to this volume centers in this type of outlook: their interest is in degree of home ownership, although they do not discuss discriminatory barriers to home ownership as do Phillips and Karn for Britain and Johnston and Saltman for the United States.

Lindén and Lindberg raise the issue of housing equality, or freedom of choice. They question whether it is acceptable to have a part of the Swedish population with lower housing standards, a distinct culture, and limited access to home ownership (including apartments) than for the rest of the population, or whether all households should be integrated into the community, and have the same high housing standards and home ownership tenure.

Lindén and Lindberg also discuss the concept that, over time, immigrants will require Swedish housing standards; they will have better knowledge of the housing market and desire a better standard of housing. In this context they examine housing standards of immigrants by how long the groups have been in Sweden. They find that housing conditions for these groups are gradually improving and coming closer to Swedish residents' standards. Lower housing standards, they assume, are a stage in assimilation into the Swedish society; however, they do admit that the income of immigrants can influence their ability to become apartment owners.

Lindén and Lindberg find the degree of segregation low in Stockholm, with a limited concentration of minorities as well as a mixture of different minorities in only a few districts. They do not believe this is due to segregation, although some involuntary segregation exists due to discrimination of landlords and selective housing authority allocation of units, as well as to voluntary segregation in terms of cultural desires.

Phillips and Karn, in examining the picture of housing segregation of South Asians and West Indians in Britain, first discuss the history of immigrants' arrival in Britain after the war as ex-colonials needed in the labor force and with rights of residence guaranteed. From the 1970s on, further immigration was limited and family migration narrowed by legislation; increased unemployment and even homelessness, as well as substandard, overcrowded accommodations, occurred. Phillips and Karn describe ethnic settlement, with concentrations in ethnic enclaves in industrial cities and London. They point out that although in overall areas the D may not be high, for some streets or some council housing concentration may be high indeed. White flight has opened up some low-standard private rentals or even owned houses to immigrants, and also some unpopular council housing. The situations are different for South Asians, who often become owners of substandard large houses that they sublet (often in slum areas), and for West Indians, who are usually renters. West Indians are more likely to live in council housing, which opened up to them in the 1970s, with half of them in such housing now.

Phillips and Karn emphasize factors in the process of segregation, for example, the two groups' low economic standing, their status as ex-colonials, and the host population's often racist attitudes. They find reasons for considerable ethnic clustering, including the benefit of self-help and satisfaction of cultural needs for ethnic institutions, as well as a safe haven from racial harassment, something not mentioned in the other European studies.

Phillips and Karn view segregation as related to the deprivation of these groups in the housing market and their inability to get decent housing because of their economic situation and discrimination. Although many immigrants prefer integrated areas, including outer-city areas, council housing administrators who allocate units do not realize this desire or respond to it and instead allot them to older, inner-city council housing units. Such housing allocation is even more common for housing associations, and more discriminatory treatment is likely if these organizations take over management of council housing. Phillips and Karn also describe discriminatory treatment existing in the private market, including actions of building societies (i.e., lending institutions) and realtors; immigrants must pay high prices to borrow money at unfavorable terms.

Chapter 4 concludes with a discussion of changes and improvements in policies against discrimination, although the authors warn that racism has been increasing in Britain. However, council housing officials are made aware of discriminatory housing allocation practices, and today more equality goals are pursued. Pressure exists for the use of legislation against discrimination, including agitation by newly elected black parliament members. More attention is given to preferences of minorities, again a trend beginning in other European countries, although slowly. A second generation of immigrants exists and is also found in other European countries. Phillips and Karn see this second generation as having attitudes oriented more to an open society and away from clustering to meet cultural needs or to provide a safe haven.

They detail the government's plan in Birmingham to disperse immigrants and limit the number housed in any area. The plan did not work, in part because of white fear of blacks moving into their area. Current emphasis is on policies to end poor housing conditions of blacks and to meet their housing area preferences. The discussion relates to Mik's on the dispersal of immigrants policy in the Netherlands, a policy that was abandoned by the cities involved, which then moved to a housing area improvement and individual help policy.

Phillips and Karn discuss a wider variety of issues for Britain than do most of the other authors in this volume, indicating their broad interests in the subject, including Britain's institutional aspects, degree of segregation, housing authority allocation policies, immigrant preferences, and legislative role. This broader orientation may be due not just to greater familiarity with American research approaches but to the greater degree of racism and discriminatory treatment in Britain compared to other European countries (although hostility to Turks seems fairly widespread in other countries).

The many aspects of the complex and dynamic West German minority housing are described by Friedrichs and Alpheis. West Germany is becoming a multi-ethnic nation, as are Sweden and the

Netherlands. The governments have not yet fully reacted to this change, however. By 1986, 7.4 percent of the West German population was foreign born, certainly a much smaller number than in the United States. The three groups in Germany are guest workers, such as Italians, Yugoslavians, and Turks; German-origin expatriates, whose number has dramatically increased since events of the fall of 1989; and the newer refugees, some of whom are from Asia. The ban on guest-worker recruitment, a long-time labor policy, came in 1973 as economic conditions in West Germany worsened; however, families kept coming. The birth rate of these groups is higher than for native-born Germans, as is true in Sweden, the Netherlands, and elsewhere. Thus it is not surprising that some schools, such as those in the Hamburg inner-city areas, have an 80 percent minority school population, again a phenomenon true in some districts in Britain, France, and elsewhere. By 1986, two-thirds of the guest workers had lived in West Germany for more than eight years, again a situation true in other European countries, such as France with its North African population. A second-generation population was established.

The postwar policy in West Germany was to have worker contracts with other countries, mainly of single persons housed in employee housing, although more and more in inner-city apartments. Then in the 1970s came two developments, the restrictions on immigration of foreign workers and an increase in arriving families, also true in France, Britain, and the Netherlands. Family housing had to be found. Although West Germany, like France, tried policies of repatriation and gave workers monetary incentives, including return of social security payments, only about 300,000 returned home, leaving many behind, some of whom received unemployment benefits. This policy is no longer actively pursued, but neither is a citizen-integration strategy, although there has been some movement to allow those who have lived in West Germany a long time to vote in local elections. Their rights, as Arin also points out, are limited. In order to get welfare rights, one must claim inability to support one's family, which could be a reason for expulsion. Friedrichs and Alpheis claim that this may be the reason that few guest workers apply for welfare benefits. They also point out that these integration policies, as well as other responsibilities for labor, are usually at the local level.

As far as residential segregation nationally and for the Hamburg case study, they find ethnic minorities overrepresented in the inner areas adjacent to the central business district, often areas designated for urban renewal—a situation true in Britain and the Netherlands, as well as France, although in France and West Germany many minorities live in peripheral social housing. In Sweden, immigrants may live on the periphery of cities such as Stockholm more than in the well-maintained central city. An outward movement of foreigners occurs in Hamburg. The main reason they still are so highly represented proportionately in the inner areas is that more Germans have moved than immigrants, although the foreign born are also moving out as Hamburg loses population. Friedrichs and Alpheis query whether Germans are moving for better housing or because of the concentrations of foreign born. Drawing on Loll's data, they believe it is to get better housing and not because of discrimination. They feel there are no ghettos in Hamburg; foreign born compete with low-income Germans for cheaper housing. In Hamburg Alpheis found a D in 1986 of 29.8 for all 180 tracts, yet no area had a D nearly as high as parts of United States cities. The concentration in some inner-city areas was somewhat high, and most school attendance was comprised of minorities (60 to 80 percent).

Friedrichs and Alpheis also examine housing quality and individual assimilation for Turkish and Yugoslavian immigrants, both of the first and second generation. Cognitive assimilation, not length of stay, generally affects housing quality, that is, the ability to use the language related to whether immigrants lived in buildings and units lacking hot water, central heating, or toilet. This was especially true for the Turks, who are not well housed in general, although a few of the first generation are better housed than the second generation. Second-generation Turks had worse housing than Yugoslavians of the same age and skill, and more first-generation Yugoslavians were better off. For Yugoslavians, cognitive assimilation in terms of years of schooling influenced quality of building and language, which affected quality of unit. Years of schooling did not have this effect for Turks. From this analysis of degree of assimilation and housing quality, Friedrichs and Alpheis draw hope that more assimilation will mean better housing quality, as do Lindén and Lindberg for Sweden. Although they are generally optimistic about the future, they worry about the effect of decreased employment opportunities for immigrants. With a change in skills needed during a period of technological change, and with fewer manufacturing activities, immigrants, who have less schooling and fewer skills than their German counterparts, encounter difficulties in the job market. There is much competition with the less-skilled sector of the German population, which will grow with the heavy immigration of East Germans and others of German origin since the opening of the Eastern bloc. This will also increase housing competition and negative stereotyping of Turks and other groups such as Asian and Iranian refugees.

In France the political arena has become involved and antiminority spokesman LePen has gained votes from his statements that social housing should be for the native French—forgetting that Algerians *are* French nationals. France differs from Germany in that most immigrants there are ex-colonials.

Blanc traces the history of immigrants in France after World War II. Most North Africans, especially Algerians, Moroccans, and Tunisians, have been long-time residents of France, with second and third generations growing up there. The large group of Algerian workers, plus those in the French army, are in every part of France, although more often in industrial centers and Paris. Other immigrants include Portuguese and now large groups of black Africans. Single people came first and were the dominant group up to 1974, when immigration was cut off except for family members, who came in large numbers, as in other countries. As in other countries, immigrants were first housed in employee barracks, but also in immigrant-run hotels in inner cities and shantytowns around Paris industrial suburban activities. Then the government, eager to recover run-down, inner-city areas from immigrants, built transient cities of guest hostels for single immigrants in industrial suburbs. Often several nationalities were mixed without concern for cultural identity. The hostels became unpopular for many reasons, including high rents, paternalistic-authoritarian management attitudes, and the fact that many immigrants imported family members in the 1970s and became long-term residents. They needed "decent housing" to obtain a residency permit for their families. After the end of worker immigration in 1974, they no longer traveled back to North Africa and thus had no need to save on housing in order to send money home, as was also the case in West Germany.

The French government, favoring those immigrants already in the country, pushed for housing improvements, Blanc says. One special immigrant housing policy was to encourage employers to help immigrants by using 20 percent of their employee funds for housing for immigrant workers. The National Commission for Immigrants' Housing, Blanc states, was concerned that this would provoke new urban segregation through funding specific housing for immigrants. Some suggested it was better to fund public and private housing organizations and encourage them to accept ethnic minorities, an orientation that has prevailed. Because of high vacancies in low-standard 1960s-built social housing, since the mid-1970s housing authorities have taken in immigrants as native French moved out, often to buy private housing with the help of government mortgages (a situation similar to that of other countries in Northern Europe). By the late 1970s in Lyons, most immigrants lived in outer-city and suburban-area subsidized housing; in Marseilles, they were in large public housing estates in the northern suburbs, as well as in the port area. By 1982 a third of all Algerians and even more Moroccans were in social housing, but only 13 percent of French households were.

Thus the location of housing of immigrants in France changed to more peripheral locations, as it did in West Germany, Sweden, and, to a much lesser degree, the Netherlands. From 1977, the government tried to rehabilitate or modernize both inner-city and suburban public housing, giving help to low-income tenants. They increased the rent slowly for nine years, but also provided rent subsidies to poorer tenants who applied. Blanc states that most low-income people in inner-city areas did not trust the plan and moved, whereas the programs for the suburban modernized apartments were used. Families with incomes slightly above the poverty level did not receive rent subsidies and, with higher rents, they were forced to move. In the Netherlands, rent subsidies to help poor families pay the high rents of new social housing have helped poorer immigrants with large families. Those families are eligible for a large subsidy. In the United States, the income limitations of public housing cut out any who are upwardly mobile, including whites.

Blanc argues that French inner-city urban renewal and rehabilitation policies were conceived to thin out the immigrant population and move it to the suburbs, something akin to American urban renewal, often known as "Negro removal" of the 1960s. Yet official government policy is to help the poor—all poor.

Another aspect of Blanc's discussion concerns the establishment of immigrant urban villages and cultural institutions. Barou, quoted in chapter 2, provides even more details on this phenomenon.

Blanc feels any government attack on discrimination is weak, although there is a 1972 law on direct, but not indirect, discrimination. Compared to policy in Britain, he finds it timid, with agencies not wanting to announce publicly that they are doing anything to help immigrants, although their previous policy had been to provide specific immigrant programs. This reluctance may be due to LePen's campaign against immigrants and their use of social housing. The policy in

France is to treat all poor alike, although in the suburban social housing modernization program, social development of communities (DSG)
aid includes measures that favor North Africans. There are indications
the new arrivals from black Africa may not be treated as well as their
immigrant forerunners.

The housing situation for minorities in Switzerland is noticeably
different from other European countries. There is far less government
involvement in terms of providing housing, regulating dispersal, or
monitoring discrimination. There is strict government regulation of
work and residency permits for foreign workers and more privileged
foreigners.

In Switzerland, foreigners are dispersed and comprise the underprivileged, that is foreign workers often on short-term work permits,
half of whom are Italian; privileged foreigners, which include non-
workers and those employed by international agencies and firms; and
refugees, who included Hungarian and Czech freedom fighters, and
now include Asians and Africans. Numbers of foreigners from Austria
and Germany have declined, but those from Yugoslavia and Turkey
have increased. In general the government, concerned with "overforeignization," has decreased the number of foreign workers and, in
many areas, foreign purchases of residences. However, although only
15 percent of the total population, the large remaining group (up to
a third of the Swiss labor force) is not concentrated to any major
degree. Some Swiss have moved to suburbs, increasing the proportion
of foreigners in major cities, but Arend sees the Swiss in general as
rooted to their city dwellings, often well-maintained units in their still
clean and pleasant medium-sized cities (a situation similar to Stockholm's). In older housing areas he sees aged Swiss holding on and
thus causing a mix of population. In Geneva a large foreign population
is created by the many international agencies. In Zurich Ds are low;
the highest are for Spanish (32), Italians (28), and Turks (27). For
1970–80, all Ds increased slightly between the underprivileged nationalities and the Swiss.

In older housing, the fact that it has been occupied by underprivileged and refugees has allowed landlords to keep filling these units
and in fact, Arend states, hold off renovation. Thus the newcomers
filled a function in the Swiss housing market. Some refugees, including
Hungarians and Czechs, also filled vacant private housing estate units
in the suburbs in an era of overbuilding.

More immigrants live in the inner-city rings of Swiss cities. Arend
found slightly more underprivileged (guest-worker) foreigners in older

dwellings, compared to Swiss of the same family type. He also found more overcrowding; a third of the guest workers had more than one person to a room. One-fourth of the one-person guest-worker households lacked their own bath or kitchen.

Arend presents three possible causes for segregation in Switzerland: rents, degrees of accessibility to area, and attractiveness of area. Nearly half of the variance of the percentage of foreigners in different city districts can be explained by lack of accessibility to housing, such as Zurich's fair amount of social housing and building cooperatives, along with rent levels. The lack of access to state housing differs from the situation in other European countries, as does the lack of representation to any degree in peripheral areas, which in other countries, are often social housing estates. The Swiss ability to decrease foreign-worker population differs from that of other countries.

Arend finds the population of Zurich reacting relatively "mildly" to the intrusion of the foreign population, although they may resent surrendering residential space to further immigration. He feels that this low prejudice may be because immigrants are the more familiar Italians and Spaniards, rather than more culturally different groups such as Moroccans and Turks which are characteristic of other countries. Yet Arend worries that the increased rents may change the situation. The recent renovation of buildings, helped by the willingness of investors who believe they can make a profit by doing so, will raise rents still higher. Such investment is different from that in many countries; certainly in the United States there has been a disinvestment in inner-city areas except for some gentrification. In some countries government investment has been used, as in the Netherlands, France, West Germany, and Britain, a situation also true in the United States in the 1960s and early 1970s, when funds were more available.

An important discussion of government policy on housing segregation is provided by Mik, a leading Dutch researcher on this issue. Devoting chapter 10 primarily to the issue of dispersal policy, he details the Dutch policy debates that have occurred, ones also found in West Berlin over similar policy and in Birmingham. In addition, Mik provides an analysis of changes in policy in the Netherlands from the 1960s onward and stresses differences between national policy and local government or housing authority policy.

Mik also provides 1976 and 1984 data from surveys of immigrants on factors that cause assimilation-integration. He uses these results, which show some integration, as an argument against dispersal. The data are close to that in chapter 6, and both find language of importance in determining degree of assimilation.

The dispersal policy was implemented in major Dutch cities but then stopped, as was the case in Birmingham. The idea was to limit migration to any area through housing after a certain degree of ethnic concentration occurred. This could be called a decrease in concentration of minorities in the central city, something the French also tried through urban renewal-rehabilitation and provision of special housing. The Dutch opened new subsidized housing (local authority and housing association units) to minorities, saying a certain percentage of units should be for them, again a similar effort to France's. At the same time, government watched to limit overconcentration.

Critics of dispersal policy feel that it limits choice and free access to areas. There was a move in the Dutch cities, which never had as strict a dispersal policy as Arin says West Berlin has had, to encourage voluntary dispersal. With the end of that policy, a move was made to establish a policy to help everyone in a low-income area, Dutch poor as well as immigrant poor. Such a policy was also introduced in France and existed in the United States during the 1960s and to varying degrees since. The Dutch justified the turn in policy by saying minorities were fairly integrated into Dutch society. The dispersal policy is somewhat akin to U.S. government efforts to desegregate public housing and to nonprofit agency efforts in some cities to achieve integration maintenance and encourage black households to move to less-segregated suburbs. Neither effort has had the power behind it that either Dutch or West Berlin housing allocation authorities enjoyed.

In reality, from Mik's data, only a small proportion of Rotterdam minorities in 1984 had actually moved to peripheral areas, although for one such area the percent minority moved up to about 10 percent. For Turks and Moroccans, Mik finds more concentration in 1984 than in 1976; for Surinamese slightly less. The highest concentration in Rotterdam areas was a D of 39, far below the United States. Minorities were now in the second ring because the Dutch had moved.

Mik found mixed results for causes of concentration. While the highest degree was for the unemployed, it was otherwise about the same for all occupational groups. The data also showed that the lower the income, the more segregated the area of residence. Concentration was high in areas of poor-quality housing, including older, poor-quality, local-authority housing. The fact that housing was acquired through friends, as was true of the Turks, increased this concentration. Important factors in 1976 in influencing the degree of segregation were

the proportion of poor and young, as well as the age of buildings in
the area and degree of outward movement of the Dutch. By 1984, the
percentage of unemployed and aged in the area replaced other factors,
but outward movement of Dutch residents was still important. This
was, Mik feels, due more to their improving housing conditions than
to other factors, as Friedrichs and Alpheis found. Mik found spatial
location of subsidized housing unimportant in relation to increased
segregation.

Mik feels Dutch prejudice is not responsible for out-migration;
however, he does find that some prejudice exists and is higher in
medium-segregation areas, especially toward Surinamese. In conclusion, he feels that education on prejudice is needed as well as concentration on the unemployment problems of immigrants, and not the
dispersal policy, with a change in emphasis from worker policy to a
policy for unemployed immigrants.

Arin provides another chapter on European policy, a case study of
local policies for immigrants in West Berlin. He details the complex
role of the state in housing segregation, a role very different from that
of local or national government in the United States, in that it is much
more powerful in dictating actions. The West Berlin Senate has influence over half of the housing supply in the city, not only over rents
(private-sector rent control until it ended and social housing rents; 86
percent of the units are rentals), but also over ability to inhabit private
rentals because it checks housing standards and can deem units "uninhabitable." Through its housing department and its work with social
housing providers, the Senate has power over the regulation of allocation of social housing units to immigrants and can demand that a
certain proportion of units be for minorities. Arin feels, however, that
the government does not have strong anti-discrimination laws like
those of Britain.

It also has the power to increase the supply of housing, which Arin
feels is not used enough, although in 1988 the government decided to
build many new units to house the increasing influx of German-origin
immigrants. With the 1989 opening of access from East to West, many
more Eastern Europeans have increased housing needs, competition,
and tensions in West Germany.

A major power that the government does use is the ability to disperse heavy concentrations of immigrants. The West Berlin government through 1988 banned the movement of immigrants into three
districts of heavy concentration, including Kreuzberg. Arin details

how this policy, like others such as inspection of private immigrant units to classify them as habitable, hurts immigrants even though it was enacted with good intentions. He sees the Berlin Senate as having a goal of integration, and considering segregation a negative condition. There is a much stronger resolve than found in most other countries, and a belief in the dispersal policy and opening a proportion of social housing as being the right courses. But Arin feels that there are contradictions created by implementation that cause such policies not to work and actually help create a housing situation that has effects opposite to those anticipated. The housing situation was complex and thus affected the goals. Large families of Turks and other guest workers wanted cheap units and turned to old units that in most cases were small, which comprise half the housing stock in West Berlin. They were faced with the possibility that authorities would say the Turks were overcrowding these units, and thus the units were uninhabitable. New units of social housing were large, but the rents high. The guest workers and refugees found a better chance of housing in areas designated for urban renewal, such as parts of Kreuzberg; however, when these sections were rehabilitated, the new units were rented to more privileged foreigners, although a number of Turks also benefited.

Arin complains that the government ban on more minorities in areas of heavy immigrant concentration is not right since it is in these areas that immigrants have the best chance of finding an apartment. Arin feels this policy is "short-sighted, overlooking the social problems that cannot be mastered through spatial measures." He says "restrictive political methods are the worst way to mitigate social problems" and adds that the spatial dispersal goal is propaganda. In the meantime, migrants carry the brunt of responsibility for bad housing conditions, including overcrowded, old units. Arin says that the nonprofit housing groups considered the order for a specific proportion of social housing for minorities in terms of a proportion of all their units, not the new ones. Thus they did nothing, as they said that minorities were already represented in the older units to the proportion specified.

Arin asks whether the dispersal policy leads to integration as assumed, and what is integration. While negative on dispersal, his arguments differ from those in the Netherlands. They are based on details of problems of implementation in West Berlin. As the situation worsens, with the influx of Eastern Europeans in 1989 and after, concentrations may become greater, the housing situations of Turks, Yugoslavians, and Asian immigrants worse, and tensions higher.

In my chapter on segregation in social housing, data are brought together for many countries and compared to the United States. The conclusion is that governments are letting segregation increase.

In comparison with the European studies and their focus on spatial locale of minorities and change over time, as well as on government policy regarding dispersal and housing allocation of subsidized units, the American chapters herein have a different focus, one close to the different methodological approaches mentioned in chapter 13. Gordon and Mayer's chapter is somewhat closer to the European researchers' interests, as it covers areas in Phoenix where minorities live, quality of minorities' housing, and, unlike European studies, housing cost by income level. McDaniel provides the same type of data as some European researchers, but he is discussing blacks in the post-Civil War period rather than an incoming-post World War II immigrant group— long-term residents, not new arrivals. In his Houston case study he discusses, as do the Europeans and Johnston for Gary, Indiana, the development of segregation and the changes over time. Then McDaniel moves to institutional factors, which are given much more prominence in all the American chapters than in the European accounts.

Johnston centers first on discrimination against blacks in the South, then in the United States as a whole, and then the Midwest, particularly Gary, Indiana. He provides a variety of statistics and material, some of it different from that of the European researchers. He begins with a historical account, finding spatial integration in the antebellum South, which was made possible by strict caste norms of social interaction. Then by the 1900s Johnston notes the development of strict state and local segregation laws, soon replaced by racial zoning and covenants that continued into the 1950s. From the mid-1960s, he notes federal government directives and laws forbidding discriminatory housing practices. In the case of Gary, Johnston traces the creation of prejudice due to strong local segregation attitudes among incoming Eastern European immigrants.

Johnston places major emphasis on the institutional actors, realtor, and lending institutions that he sees enforcing housing segregation of blacks, especially before 1970. He illustrates the realtors' postwar code of ethics and practices, later rewritten, and gives data on community demands that realtors segregate home buyers by area in relation to their ethnic or racial background. In a complex research exercise he shows how lending institutions are unlikely to provide conventional mortgages in areas where black households are likely to apply, forcing them to use VA and FHA mortgages. He further shows how such action will help a city such as Gary deteriorate.

At the same time, Johnston shows increasingly positive white attitudes to black integration, as well as willingness of blacks to live in mixed areas. In a complex income evaluation, he shows how many black households can afford to buy in Gary—many more than live in many areas, especially suburban ones. Jones and I discuss the same issue, but the European authors do not because home ownership is so low among minorities in Europe.

Johnston also covers another aspect not covered in European research, the degree to which housing discrimination laws are effective in the Gary area. He stresses the lack of mechanisms for filing complaints in many communities, and thus the low number of complaints—rather than low degree of discrimination as authorities say. When cases are filed, Johnston shows that most are won.

In the chapter on the South by McDaniel, the antebellum movement of blacks to urban areas, partly due to loss of land through foreclosure and lack of wills, is examined. McDaniel then discusses housing integration of servants in backyard areas and then development of strict residential segregation. He cites changes in the FHA "homogeneous community" (no blacks) policy in the 1950s and 1960s, as well as the presidential Executive Order, civil rights legislation of the 1960s, and Supreme Court cases. He considers segregation still high in the South, with only minor changes from 1970 to 1980 (Jones and I find more). Black movement to the suburbs is seen in terms of areas adjacent to already existing ghettos, which Jones and I also find. The myth still exists of housing values decreasing as blacks move in, although studies show otherwise, and this causes white flight.

McDaniel describes how in Houston enclaves in wards were first areas of black concentration and then eventually the whole ward became black. He found several such areas, as well as suburban enclaves segregated later. Realtors established special middle-class black subdivisions close to already black areas, and city authorities prescribed segregated public housing in the early days.

Gordon and Mayer provide a glimpse of housing segregation of Hispanics, especially those in Phoenix. They focus on degree of segregation, housing costs, and quality housing for minorities. Housing segregation of Hispanics and blacks decreased 1970–80 in Phoenix, but concentration was still in the inner city, although more of both groups moved to the middle rings of the city. They did not include the suburbs in their discussion, where half the Anglos live.

The detailed breakdown by income level and renter and owner category provides reliable data on whether Hispanics and blacks paid more for housing. Little difference existed for each income category between groups, but many more Anglos were in the high-income category and so paid less for housing in relation to their income. Again this type of study is seldom done in Europe. Gordon and Mayer's analysis of data from other cities show similar income-rent or owner cost ratios, which they see as proof that segregation does not naturally create high housing costs. For all ethnic groups the lowest income group spent about a third of their income for housing; the high-income group spent only 10 to 15 percent. Major differences between Anglos, Hispanics, and blacks in the same income category exist in housing quality. Overcrowding was especially likely for Hispanics; living in older units was likely for both, especially low-income blacks and Hispanics.

Goering discusses the variables that cause segregation in public housing, such as more blacks on the waiting list or siting of units. His material indicates how hard it will be to end segregation and the importance of statistics to define the problem, although they are difficult to obtain. His material is useful to European housing authorities who find greater minority concentration in their housing. Jones and I discuss housing segregation or integration and then resegregation in the suburbs. The reasons blacks go to segregated areas are complex. Financially blacks could afford to live in many more suburbs. The degree of black movement to the suburbs has greatly increased in the last decades but most is still to black enclaves or areas moving in that direction; integration is a short-lived phenomenon. Yet data also show some true integration occurring in recent years and a hope for more. IM is also discussed. The follow-up chapters cover this income maintenance activity in specific communities. Such efforts by nonprofit groups are difficult to maintain, and the controversy over attempts to encourage blacks into a broader spectrum of white suburban areas will continually run into trouble. At the same time, it is the only hope to avoid resegregation.

Thus future hope exists for more integration, especially of middle-class blacks and Hispanics, but it can easily falter, especially for those with low incomes and certainly for female-headed households. In Europe governments still have the chance to take the right steps to keep segregation low, including that in social housing. Yet the Mik and Arin chapters, as well as the country overview chapters, warn of problems. Even allowing schools to become 60 to 80 percent minority, as in a few areas of Hamburg, can be a turning point. Certainly some immigrant groups will assimilate more than others, but some who are culturally different from their host populations may have difficulties, such as South Indians, West Indians, and Turks. If it increases, competition for jobs and housing will cause more segregation. If new immigration is high, as it is to the western part of the FRG or to parts of the United States, this may increase competition.

Contributors

HANNES ALPHEIS is a professor at the Institute of Comparative Urban Studies, University of Hamburg.

MICHAL AREND is a sociologist and planner for a private consultant firm and the author of various publications on housing and minority problems in Switzerland.

CIHAN ARIN is currently co-owner of UrbanPlan, a planning and research office for architecture and urban planning in Berlin. From 1984 to 1989 he was assistant professor at the Institute for Urban and Regional Planning, Technical University of Berlin. He is the coauthor and coeditor of *Urban Renewal in West Berlin: Strategies for a Reactivation of Existing Urban Structures* and the coauthor and coeditor of a special issue of *Bauwelt* (no. 40, 1988), which dealt with the urban development process in Istanbul. His research interests include city and neighborhood development planning, segregation and ethnic processes in European cities, and urban renewal and the housing market in West Germany.

MAURICE BLANC is a senior lecturer at the University of Nancy II, where he teaches in the Institute of Sociology and the Adult Education Department. His research interests include citizens' participation in urban planning and ethnic minority housing. He is currently working on a comparative study of France, Great Britain, and West Germany.

WIM BLAUW is associate professor of sociology at Erasmus University, Rotterdam. His research areas are housing, segregation, migration, and public spaces. He has written books on the social effects of suburbanization and on international migration, and has edited books on urban segregation and public life and public spaces.

MODIBO COULIBABLY is a doctoral candidate in the Department of Economics at Howard University. In 1986–87 he served as a research associate at the Department of Housing and Urban Development.

JÜRGEN FRIEDRICHS is a professor at the Institute of Comparative Urban Studies, University of Hamburg. He has published widely on various aspects of urban development and spatial segregation.

JOHN GOERING is Deputy Division Director, Office of Policy Development and Research, Department of Housing and Urban Development, where he is program manager for fair housing research activities. He has taught sociology at Leicester, England, Washington University in St. Louis, the Graduate Center in New York, and the University of North Carolina at Chapel Hill. He has published over two dozen articles and written two books on housing, race, and federal policies, including *Housing Desegregation and Federal Policy* and *The Best Eight Blocks in Harlem.*

LEONARD GORDON is a professor and chair of the Department of Sociology at Arizona State University, with a particular research interest in patterns of urban racial and ethnic relations.

ROSE HELPER is professor of sociology at the University of Toledo. She is the author of *Racial Policies and Practices of Real Estate Brokers* and many articles on race relations and housing.

ELIZABETH D. HUTTMAN is professor of sociology at California State University. She has edited or written six books, including *Housing Needs and Policy Approaches: Trends in Thirteen Countries* (coeditor), *Handbook on Housing and the Built Environment* (coeditor), *Housing and Social Services for the Elderly, Introduction to Social Policy,* and *Social Services for the Elderly,* and has published chapters in books on homelessness, limited growth, and new towns. Dr. Huttman is founder and co-organizer of the International Sociological Association Working Group on Housing and the Built Environment; she has organized sessions for the last three world congresses and coedits the group's research notes. For many years she has served as an officer in the Society for the Study of Social Problems. She has been an active member in the community section of the American Sociological Association and the social ecology section of the International Sociological Association; she also particpiates in several urban and regional development groups.

BARRY V. JOHNSTON is a professor of sociology at Indiana University Northwest. He has published many journal articles on housing and the history of American sociology and is the author of a forthcoming book on Pitirim Sorokin.

TERRY JONES is chair of the Department of Sociology and Social Services, California State University at Hayward.

VALERIE KARN is professor of environmental health and housing at the University of Salford and a leading researcher on race relations. She has written widely on housing issues in Britain and is a member of a number of British housing bodies, including the Duke of Edinburgh Inquiry into British Housing. She has recently published a comparison of approaches to homelessness in the United States and Britain and is currently working on a book on housing performance in these two countries.

W. DENNIS KEATING is a professor in the Colleges of Law and Urban Affairs at Cleveland State University and director of the Urban Planning, Design, and Development Program. He is coauthor of *Housing and Community Development Law* and is a contributor to several books on housing, development, and neighborhood policy and urban planning. He is currently writing a book on racial transition and housing integration policies in Cleveland from 1960 to 1990.

ANNA-LISA LINDÉN is associate professor of sociology at Lund University. Her major research interests include housing policy, housing patterns, demographic processes, and environmental conflicts. She has headed several research projects and published several books; in 1989, with Göran Lindberg, she wrote a book on housing segmentation and changing patterns in the Swedish housing market.

GÖRAN LINDBERG is associate professor of sociology at Lund University. In the eighties he headed research projects on housing problems in Sweden. His books have focused on segregation in cities and the management of public housing; in 1989 he coauthored, with Anna-Lisa Lindén, a book on housing segmentation and changing patterns in the Swedish housing market.

CLYDE O. MCDANIEL, JR., is professor of sociology at Houston Community College and Prairie View A&M University. He has published fifty articles and four books.

ALBERT J. MAYER is a professor of sociology at Arizona State University, with research interests in urban demography and the nature of the modern city.

GER MIK is a professor at the Economic Geography Institute, Erasmus University, Rotterdam and author of a major segregation study.

ALAN MURIE is professor of planning and housing at Edinburgh College of Art/Heriot-Watt University, Edinburgh. He previously taught urban studies at the University of Bristol. His principal research interests are housing and housing policy. He is editor of *Housing Studies*; recent books include *Housing Inequality and Deprivation, Selling the Welfare State* (with R. Forrest), *Housing Policy and Practice* (with P. Malpass), and *Home Ownership: Differentiation and Fragmentation* (with R. Forrest and P. Williams).

DEBORAH PHILLIPS is a lecturer in the School of Geography at the University of Leeds and was previously a research fellow at the University of Salford. Her major research interests are race and housing in Britain. Recent publications include *Ethnic Minority Housing: Explanations and Policies* (with P. Sarre and R. Skellington).

JULIET SALTMAN is professor emerita of sociology at Kent State University. Her specialties include race relations, social movements, and urban communities and she is the author of six books and numerous articles; her most recent book is *A Fragile Movement: The Struggle for Neighborhood Stabilization*. She has been a consultant to federal and local agencies on urban affairs and has served on the board of directors for National Neighbors, OPEN, and the National Committee Against Discrimination in Housing. She was a founder of two community groups for fair housing and neighborhood stabilization in Akron, Ohio. Among the many awards she has received for her work is the Doublass Society Award from Rutgers University for distinguished career and community service.

Index

Affirmative marketing. *See* Integration maintenance

Afro-Caribbean immigrants. *See* West Indian immigrants (U.K.)

Algerians, xi, xii, 21, 23, 25, 28–29, 31–32, 38, 145–54, 392, 411–12

Amsterdam, 30, 180, 183–84; Bijlmermeer, 21, 50–51, 215, 229–301

Assimilation and integration, 22–23, 33, 97, 108, 126, 134–40, 164–65, 182, 190–91, 194, 211, 232, 355, 377, 393, 410, 414, 417; black attitudes toward, 257–58, 260, 343–44, 371, 419; white attitudes toward, 249, 257–59, 309, 343, 371–72, 376, 406, 419

Auditing techniques, 12, 36, 351, 371, 380, 399, 401

Bangladesh immigrants. *See* South Asian immigrants

Barou, Paul, 28–29, 31–33

Berlin, West: dispersal policy of, 205–13, 416–17; government policy of, 199–214, 416–17; housing concentration in, 210–12; housing conditions in, 203–5, 402, 413; housing segregation in, xii, 21, 36, 199–214; housing stock of, 26, 202–4, 403, 416–17; rents in, 34, 37, 202–3; urban renewal in, 218, 416–17

Birmingham, U.K., dispersal policy, 38, 82–85, 414

Black American population, 7–8, 239–300, 305–90, 418–20; and degree of segregation, 35, 37, 243–67, 272–83, 286–88, 337–38, 367–68, 394, 397–98, 418–20; discrimination against, 7–8, 245–67, 272–83, 375–76, 403; history of, 7–8, 22, 243–49, 254–59, 272–308, 337–38, 344–48, 418–20; northward/westward migration of, 243–47, 254, 308–9; and segregation and discrimination in the South, 8, 243–44, 247–50, 272–83, 337–38, 340, 345, 368–69, 376; and segregation in housing, 239–300, 305–90, 404, 418–20

Chinese immigrants, 22, 25, 32

Civil rights court decisions, 11, 13, 274–75, 310, 326, 336–37, 350, 361; *South Suburban Housing Center* v. *NAR* (Chicago), 13, 336, 361; Starrett City, 326, 336; Yonkers, 337

Civil rights legislation (Europe), 11, 39, 67–68, 81–87, 153, 226; compared to U.S., 13–14, 39, 87, 153, 268, 315

Civil rights legislation (U.S.), 7, 11–12, 39, 252–53, 261, 350, 352, 355, 357–58, 371, 399, 412, 416–17

Cleveland, fair housing efforts, 367–73

Colonial relationships, immigrants, 21–22, 143–44, 172

Czechoslovakian immigrants, 25, 28, 156, 413

Discrimination and prejudice in housing practices (Europe), 24, 34, 58–60, 63, 67, 76–78, 102, 113, 141, 153, 174, 177, 190, 194–95, 207–8, 398

Discrimination and prejudice in housing practices (U.S.), 245–46, 259, 281, 292, 309

Discrimination, laws against. *See* Civil rights legislation

427

LIBRARY OF CONGRESS CATALOGING-IN-PUBLICATION DATA

Urban housing segregation of minorities in Western Europe and
the United States / Elizabeth Huttman, editor. Juliet Saltman and Wim
Blauw, co-editors.
   p. cm.
  Includes bibliographical references.
  ISBN 0-8223-1060-0
  1. Discrimination in housing—United States. 2. Discrimination in
housing—Government policy—United States. 3. Discrimination in
housing—Europe. 4. Discrimination in housing—Government policy—
Europe. I. Huttman, Elizabeth D., 1929- . II. Saltman, Juliet.
III. Blauw, Wim.
HD7288.76.U5U83 1991
363.5'1—dc20   90-3221
                                                       CIP